THE URBAN SETTING THESAURUS:

A Writer's Guide to City Spaces

ANGELA ACKERMAN
BECCA PUGLISI

MORE WRITERS HELPING WRITERS® BOOKS

The Emotion Thesaurus: A Writer's Guide to Character Expression
The Positive Trait Thesaurus: A Writer's Guide to Character Attributes
The Negative Trait Thesaurus: A Writer's Guide to Character Flaws
The Rural Setting Thesaurus: A Writer's Guide to Personal and Natural Places

First print edition, June 2016
ISBN-13: 978-0-9897725-6-3
ISBN-10: 0-9897725-6-X

Edited by: C. S. Lakin (www.livewritethrive.com) and Michael Dunne (www.michael-dunne.com/)

Book cover and interior design by: Scarlett Rugers Design 2016
www.scarlettrugers.com

EBook formatting by: Polgarus Studio
www.polgarusstudio.com

ABOUT THE AUTHORS

Angela Ackerman and Becca Puglisi are bestselling authors, writing coaches, and international speakers. Their books are available in five languages, are sourced by US universities, and are used by novelists, screenwriters, editors, and psychologists around the world. Angela and Becca also co-founded the popular Writers Helping Writers site, a hub for writers to hone their craft, as well as One Stop for Writers, an innovative online library built to help writers elevate their storytelling.

DEDICATIONS

To every writer who ever dreamed, and then had the courage to follow that dream wherever it led. And especially to Lee, for not using the ants.

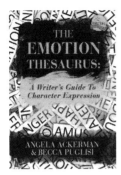
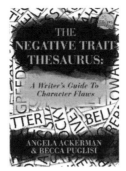

PRAISE FOR THE EMOTION THESAURUS

"One of the challenges a fiction writer faces, especially when prolific, is coming up with fresh ways to describe emotions. This handy compendium fills that need. It is both a reference and a brainstorming tool, and one of the resources I'll be turning to most often as I write my own books."

~ **James Scott Bell, best-selling author of** *Deceived* **and** *Plot & Structure*

PRAISE FOR THE POSITIVE AND
NEGATIVE TRAIT THESAURUS BOOKS

"In these brilliantly conceived, superbly organized and astonishingly thorough volumes, Angela Ackerman and Becca Puglisi have created an invaluable resource for writers and storytellers. Whether you are searching for new and unique ways to add and define characters, or brainstorming methods for revealing those characters without resorting to clichés, it is hard to imagine two more powerful tools for adding depth and dimension to your screenplays, novels or plays."

~ **Michael Hauge, Hollywood script consultant and story expert**,
author of *Writing Screenplays That Sell*

ONE STOP
F O R
WRITERS

Wish you had a powerhouse writing resource at your fingertips that could save you valuable time while elevating your storytelling? One Stop for Writers™ might just be the answer. Brought to you by Becca and Angela, the authors of this and other bestselling writing books, along with Lee Powell, the creator of Scrivener for Windows, the One Stop online library is the resource you've been searching for.

Our unique thesaurus collection covers emotions, settings, weather, characterization, symbolism, and other elements of description, and will help set your book apart by bringing the fresh imagery and deeper meaning that your readers crave. Along with an array of unique tools, tutorials, structure maps, timelines, and generators, you can also plan and organize your writing like never before.

Find us online at www.onestopforwriters.com, where registration is always free.

TABLE OF CONTENTS

THE GIANT MISCONCEPTION: WHO CARES ABOUT THE SETTING?

When discussing the bones of structure for strong storytelling, certain elements always get top billing. Characters, for example, usually crest the food chain, and rightfully so—as they and their emotions are the beating heart of any story. The hero in particular is what draws a reader in, as his inner world is a complex landscape of needs, desire, fears, and the hope that some greater fulfillment might be his. Readers empathize with the protagonist's journey of self-discovery as he conquers obstacles on the road to his goal. They also cheer at each achievement that gets the main character closer to that place where he feels satisfied and complete.

The red carpet is also rolled out for plot, because without outer events to shape the hero's path (providing opposition and opportunity as he chases his goal), readers are left with a character who wanders aimlessly and without purpose.

Plot and characterization are the two titans of storytelling—there is no doubt. Other important elements often taught by editors and story coaches tie into these heavyweights: voice, pacing, conflict, theme, description, and dialogue.

But what about the setting? Where does it fit in on the importance scale?

That's a good question. Newer writers sometimes make the mistake of assuming that the setting is no more than a backdrop for a story's events; it's a necessary part, but it's not important enough to waste too many words describing, and it's definitely not worth stressing over when it comes to choosing the right one for a scene.

Of course, this type of thinking is the downfall of many writers because, while it's often overlooked, the setting is, in fact, a powerhouse of storytelling description that deepens every scene. Not only does it anchor the reader in events as they unfold, but, chosen carefully, the right setting can help characterize the story's cast, deliver backstory in a way that enriches, convey emotion, supply tension, and accomplish a host of other things to give readers a one-of-a-kind experience. In fact, out of all the ingredients that make a compelling story, setting is one of the most versatile yet often underutilized.

Why is this? Simple: it's due to a misconception that readers aren't interested in the setting and will skip right over descriptive passages. Because of this, writers often don't look beneath the surface to see what a setting can truly do; they miss out on all the ways it can shine a light on a character's mind-set and add depth to the bigger story. Instead, they focus on giving only enough setting detail to provide context for the reader. And while context is important to provide a sense of place, it's only a sliver of what the setting brings to the storytelling table.

Describing a setting does come with challenges. Finding the perfect balance of showing and telling that won't slow the pace can be tricky. An avalanche of description may cause readers to skip ahead, but we also don't want to provide so little that they have to work hard to visualize the scene. If mounting frustration over being unable to imagine the character's world reaches a critical point, the book cover may close and never reopen.

There are no two ways about it—setting description is important. Perfecting the balancing act of "how much" is a skill all writers should master. This is why understanding the many functions of the setting and learning how to do more with less is key to keeping readers immersed in the fictional world.

There's more to it than just plucking out a few details and slapping them together; it's about selecting ones that create a sensory experience, since description that offers real texture often triggers memories for readers, making them feel emotionally part of the scene. In this book and its sister volume, *The Rural Setting Thesaurus: A Writer's Guide to Personal and Natural Places*, writers will learn exactly how to use settings to draw readers into the story and pave a pathway for empathy to form between them and the characters.

THE SETTING AS A VEHICLE FOR CHARACTERIZATION

I n storytelling, our number one job is to make readers care. We want to ensure that our fiction captivates them on many levels and that our characters seem like living, breathing people who continue to exist in readers' minds long after the book closes. To create this level of realism, we must delve deep into our world and our characters so we can show who they are at every opportunity, drawing the reader in closer.

When it comes to characters, showing rather than telling is the most powerful means of providing insight into the personality of each member of a story's cast, including the protagonist. Simply put, letting readers see for themselves who our characters are through their behavior is much more riveting than us explaining it through bloated chunks of information. A writer can use narrative to introduce a vengeful character, but it would be much more spellbinding to describe her actions as she traps a former abuser on his fishing boat, douses the decks in gasoline, and tosses on a flare. It is what a character does, thinks, and feels that readers find most compelling. The setting can play a vital role in drawing out new layers of our characters for readers to discover.

GETTING PERSONAL WITH SETTINGS

In real life we see a lot of generic—food brands, medicine, cleaning supplies, bottled water, batteries, and other bits and bobs. There are even certain locations we spend time at that are fairly universal across the map, having the same look or feel. A place such as a lake, the stands at a sporting event, a movie theater, or the hallways of a high school will have similar features regardless of whether it is located in California or British Columbia. In fact, because of this commonality, authors often use these types of settings in novels, knowing readers will acclimate quickly and begin filling in the details on their own, leaving more word count flexibility for other things, such as describing the action.

While we do want to encourage readers to participate in the story by imagining the world to some degree, there is no room for "generic" in fiction beyond the occasional transitional scene. Using commonality as a crutch to avoid creating meaningful description shortchanges the reader and causes the writer to miss out on valuable opportunities to deepen bonds of empathy.

Transitional settings aside, if a location is important enough to be part of a scene, then it should also have a specific identity. How do we bring this about? Through personalizing the setting to our protagonist, sculpting it to reveal characterizing details about who he or she is.

Some settings are simpler to personalize than others. A character's home or workspace is easy to fill with details that indicate her personality type, interests, and hobbies, as well as her values and beliefs. A work cubicle that comes with the standard office supplies but also has a calendar with vacation days exuberantly circled surrounded by a photo tornado of past trips tells us plenty about the character who works there. For starters, she likely isn't in love with this job. She also has a strong sense of work-life balance and prizes travel. A closer look at the photos might reveal even more insight: that she loves to ski, that she has a young family, or maybe even that she drinks too much. This would be a much different character than someone whose workspace is antiseptic neat and bereft of decoration except for a single motivational poster to the tune of *Fortune Favors the Bold*. In this case, readers would see that the character works hard, is highly organized and opportunistic, and she sees this job as a stepping-stone to something greater.

Amazing, isn't it? All that characterization through the simple placement of personal setting details, and without a whole lot of work.

When the setting isn't a place that the character is particularly intimate with, we can still bring out personalization details that reveal the layers of who she is. What a character notices, feels, and interacts with in each location will show readers more about what is important to her.

Imagine a woman waiting for a cab outside a row of shops along a main street. It's closing in on Christmas, so holiday music drifts from speakers outside the shops, colorful tinsel and glittery bows flutter as doors open and close, and a dusting of snow gives everything that clean feel. It's the first time she's been out in a week after a recent miscarriage and has just come from an appointment with her doctor. How could the author personalize this setting to show who she is and what she believes in while hinting at this sensitive situation?

> Linda waited at the curb, scanning the oncoming traffic for the telltale yellow paint indicating a cab. Behind her, boots crunched through snow and shopping bags crinkled with cold as the bustling midafternoon shoppers hurried to finish off their Christmas lists. Cheerful holiday music floated out of store speakers and an unbearable tightness filled her throat. Christmas. One more bit of normalcy shoved in her face, one more thing rolling forward like a locomotive, ignoring her need to hide away and grieve.
>
> The doctor's visit had sapped her energy and she just wanted to get home, but each cab that passed seemed to already have a fare. Linda gave up and was heading for a nearby bus stop when she noticed a child standing alone in front of a toy store. Her breath caught at the perfection of the toddler, his cheeks lit with the glow of the winking lights on display, standing on tiptoe, his fragile breath fogging the glass. Shoppers walked past, paying him no mind, and something heavy settled in her gut. No one stopped; no one reached for his hand. Who was watching out for him? Where were his parents? Someone could come along and scoop him up, and only the ghost prints of his mittens on the snowy ledge would show that he'd been there at all.
>
> She jolted toward the boy, heat flashing through her body. Just as she reached him, a woman's voice called out in Spanish. The child spun and ran toward a parked car at the curb, where a mother was loading two other children into the vehicle. The boy jumped and wobbled, pointing back at the display, and his mother laughed as she lifted him into his car seat.
>
> Linda trembled, watching the car drive off. She touched her forehead, running the scene through her mind, wondering how she'd missed the obvious,

how she'd completely misread the situation. Thankfully, a cab pulled into the slot that the mother's car had vacated, and she rushed to nab it before someone else could. She needed to get home now more than ever.

In this scene, we plant characterizing details within the setting. What is revealed about Linda? She's still very much caught in the current of grief and is resentful of Christmas upstaging her loss. She's also practical—looking for a bus stop when catching a cab becomes difficult. And then there's the toddler, who becomes a focal point for her deeply embedded maternal instincts, and the interaction between mother and child shows readers what Linda wants most and yet cannot have. Through specific detail, this setting becomes personalized to the character; readers are carried along as she interacts with it, experiencing her churning emotions just as she does.

When it comes to painting a setting for readers, think beyond "window dressing" detail. Get personal, get inside your protagonist's head, and show the world in a way that allows your audience to discover the deeper side of your hero or heroine.

THE EMOTIONAL POWER OF POINT OF VIEW (POV) FILTERING

Chances are, you've heard of deep point of view. Imagine a camera lens that zooms in for a close-up; deep POV is when the description filters directly through the point-of-view character (usually the protagonist) on a deep, emotional level. Readers see what he or she sees and feel what he or she feels. It allows for intimate characterization and creates a shared experience in which the story comes alive through the character's senses, thoughts, beliefs, emotional focus, and judgments. Done well, lines between reality and fiction blur temporarily as readers are caught up in what the POV character experiences as events happen.

Not every story uses deep POV, but all writers work to create a level of closeness between the character and reader, which requires a deft hand to bring about. The setting is the story element that facilitates this, since conveying the hero's emotion-driven viewpoint makes a scene come alive. Experiencing details from the setting through the protagonist's emotions and senses makes the reader feel truly part of the story. This means that choosing the right setting for each scene is important to not only help events unfold but increase reader-character connection.

Taking advantage of a deeper POV means really understanding how crucial sensory description is to the story (which will be covered more in a later section) and how settings should include an **emotional value**. This is where the setting has a specific emotional tie to the protagonist and possibly other characters. It holds meaning in some way, or acts as a symbol, charging up the scene.

For example, it may be that the setting is symbolic of some past life event and serves as a reminder of what happened and the feelings associated with it. Imagine a character being asked to an important business lunch in the same restaurant where his girlfriend turned down his marriage proposal. Even though time has passed, maybe years, an echo of that hurt and rejection will affect him while he's there and, in turn, will influence his behavior.

If the setting is someplace neutral to the protagonist and there is no emotional value based on past knowledge or experience, we can still bring one to the forefront by creating mood. This is done by choosing sensory descriptions that reinforce a specific emotion (fear, peacefulness, unease, pride, etc.) that we want the character (and the reader) to feel. Mood can also be created through the use of light and shadow, universal symbolism, weather, and other techniques, which are all covered in depth in *The Rural Setting Thesaurus*. Regardless of whether emotional values are intrinsic or are added via mood, choosing a setting that evokes an emotional response is important, since a character's feelings about his environment add realism to the scene while drawing readers in.

So how do we go about creating this emotional value? The first step is to brainstorm the best setting match for a particular scene. This is achieved by looking at what will happen in the scene and which emotions are at play. First, identify your hero's scene goal—what must he do, learn, or achieve? And what do you want him and the other characters involved to feel? Once you know the answers to these questions, imagine different types of settings where this scene might take place, ones that fit the story and are logical locations for your character to visit. Make a list if you like. Often the settings that pop immediately to mind are the most obvious, but with a bit of digging, some more creative and interesting choices can be unearthed too.

Once you have a few options, look at each potential setting in turn and think of how you can describe the location to evoke a specific mood that will make your character's emotional reactions more potent. Tension can be a factor too. Depending on what is about to happen in the scene, you might want your character to feel off-balance. Or maybe you wish to lull him into a false sense of security so he doesn't see what's coming. Either way, the details you pick to describe the setting will help steer his emotions.

Finally, think about what the character will learn, decide, or do as a result of what happens in the scene. The setting can act as an amplifier for this end result simply by surrounding the character with **emotional triggers** that will lead him toward that decision or action.

Imagine a man who, at the urging of his business magnate parents, has worked his way up at a capital investment firm. Offered a powerful new position that will finally please his success-driven parents, he discovers that he will need to travel almost constantly, meaning he will have to sacrifice having a family. Maybe he is in a committed relationship, and he and his partner have been talking about adoption. This career move would end that dream.

As he wrestles with this choice, we want to place him in a location that we can stock with emotional triggers to help direct his thoughts. In this case, we could choose a park where his parents used to bring him as a child (supplying an emotional value), or place an urban playground right across the street from the high-rise where he works (symbolizing his two worlds in conflict).

Each location will provide excellent opportunities to place emotional triggers. Imagine our character noticing children climbing on a slide or kicking around a soccer ball in a field, or a young couple pushing a baby stroller along a concrete path. These triggers represent a future he might have if he rejects the offer and stays to build a family. Or perhaps we choose a different trigger in the setting, such as a father ruffling his son's hair as he successfully flies a kite in the park, representing the yearning our character has for his own father's approval. A third option might be to show an older man in a power suit going for a lunchtime walk, dominating a conversation via his cell phone. This trigger acts as a glimpse of who our hero could become if he sticks to the career path: rich, powerful, respected . . . and potentially alone.

Choosing a strong setting for the scene and then seeding it with these triggers creates a push-pull effect, one that amplifies a character's internal struggle. Through the hero's interaction with the setting, we can home in on the needs, desires, moral beliefs, fears, and personal biases that drive his behavior. How the protagonist reacts to these triggers will not only allow characterization to naturally seep through, it also alludes to past experiences that may still have power over him in the form of emotional wounds.

For a practical guide to evaluating a setting's emotional value and possible triggers, see the Emotional Value Tool in Appendix A.

USING THE SETTING TO CHARACTERIZE THE REST OF THE STORY'S CAST

Not only does the setting let us characterize the protagonist, it can also reveal the traits, attitudes, beliefs, and emotions of non-POV characters—something that is often difficult to do unless one is writing in omniscient POV.

Have you ever attended a reception or wake in a deceased person's home? Few situations can bring together an eclectic mix of personalities like a funeral, and the aftermath in which family and friends socialize and pay their respects can become a painful bed of hot, bright coals. Gathering together people who may have chosen to remain apart is the perfect recipe for opening deep wounds. Stress and grief, not to mention alcohol, can fuel words that are better left unsaid. Conversations can also turn into confessionals in which secrets are let out of their boxes and arguments can resurrect old feuds or give birth to new ones.

Take the following estranged family coming together to mourn the passing of their mother— brothers and sisters, in-laws and cousins, who are close and distant, some of whom don't always get along. As they gather to halfheartedly pick at a meal and catch up during the wake, each person will have a different viewpoint as events unfold. While it can be a challenge to show all of this through the POV character's perspective, the setting is once again the vehicle that gives us a way to do so:

> To Laura, the parlor was always the coldest room. The pale-green paint and sheer lace curtains reinforced the chill, framing her mother's pristine couch and the Oriental rug no one was allowed to step on. Someone had lit the fireplace, likely in hopes it might brighten the cheerless room, but the crackling heat didn't seem to get far. This probably had less to do with the January snowfall spiralling outside the window and more with the people in the room with her.
>
> Tammy and Rick had claimed the two suede wingbacks in the corner, regally waiting for the procession to arrive. Their hushed voices and sharp glances at Laura made it clear she featured in their conversation. Clearly her siblings were put out over Mother leaving the house to her, something they likely believed she had orchestrated while caring for her this last year. The truth was, Laura was as surprised as anyone. If anything, she expected the house to go to Charlie, the baby of the family and, she suspected, Mother's secret favorite.
>
> Laura took a sip of hot tea from a china cup, her gaze going to where Charlie stood at the bookcase pretending to browse. But the stoop of his shoulders told her that he'd spotted the framed picture she'd recently put there. It was one of Allan, his twin, who'd died of meningitis at age four. Laura had rescued the tipped-over picture from the back of the mantel, where it had been hidden by a cluster of Tammy's family photos that she'd obviously moved to the

center. Laura had dusted often enough to know that their mother had given everyone's pictures equal billing, but equality was something Tammy never quite understood.

Laura crossed to Charlie, taking careful steps over the wooden floor to avoid clacking, as Tammy had done when she'd made her entrance in high heels and a too-short skirt.

"You okay?" She placed her hand on Charlie's back.

"Remember when this was taken?" Her brother brushed his thumb over the smooth gold frame.

In the faded photo, Allan dangled by his arms from a low branch on the maple tree out back. Barely a sapling then, it now towered over the house. Laura gave a soft laugh. "How could I forget? Five minutes after Allan did something, you had to do it too."

"Only, he didn't manage to break his arm like I did." Charlie smiled, his eyes wet, and replaced the picture on the shelf. She could only imagine what Mother's death had dragged up for him; he'd hardly been old enough to really know what it was to be a twin before the specialness of it was stolen away.

The doorbell chimed, but Laura didn't move to answer it. Marissa would get it. Charlie's wife loved people and was a born hostess and child wrangler, and when she'd offered to take on those duties, Laura had been more than happy to let her.

Voices drifted from the hall as mourners stamped off the snow and shucked off coats. Odors of garlic and sage wafted from the foil-covered casserole dishes they carried. Laura's chest tightened at the small talk and niceties that would have to take place before she'd be allowed to privately grieve. How long did these things go on for?

Her cup rattled ever so slightly against the saucer, and Charlie pulled something from his jacket. He tipped a pewter flask over the gold china rim, first hers, then his. The burn of scotch drifted up between them, and they shared a grin, youngest to oldest.

In this small scene, not only do setting details anchor the reader in this moment, they become a conduit for characterization and emotional showing. As each separate character interacts with the setting, we gain a sense of who they are and what they feel, despite remaining steadfastly in Laura's point of view. Symbols are incorporated, helping to form an image of what's being felt. The décor chosen for the room—pale mint, lace curtains, the rug everyone was forced to walk around and not on, even the weather outside—these all help show the mood in this scene and reinforce the idea that distance exists between family members. By the placement of photos on the mantel we see that Mother was fair, yet her choices for this room suggest she was fussy and perhaps a bit unfeeling herself, which may have factored into the current family dynamic. The picture of Allan, in particular, becomes a symbol of loss and allows a tiny snippet of the past to shine through.

The interaction over the picture, and then later the flask, shows readers that Laura and Charlie are close. The gossipy nature between Tammy and Rick and their choice of seats implies that they hold a view of self-importance. Tammy's altering the arrangement of family photos to place hers at the center speaks volumes. And even if we did not know that Laura cared for her mother this past year, her rescuing Allan's picture conveys her role as caretaker in this family.

As you can see, done well, descriptive choices and the setting itself can actively convey so much to readers, especially when it comes to characterization and mood building.

SETTING MATTERS: THE IMPORTANCE OF *WHERE*

The choice of where to set one's story can affect the tone of the entire book, and often genre will help dictate the scope of locations to be used throughout the story. Let's say you've written a contemporary young-adult novel. Most likely, high school is the obvious overall setting choice for your YA story.

But the whole thing can't take place at school. Important events in the life of your main character will happen elsewhere: at home, at work, hanging out with friends, on dates, and while getting from one place to another. Settings need to be chosen for each individual scene, and the key to making these choices is knowing the important events in your story. The right setting is like a musical score, giving each scene a deeper emotional intensity through mood, symbolism, and personalization.

Your protagonist will also help narrow down the choices. Is she popular? An epiphany might occur at a house party or on a school trip. Is she shy or introverted? A confrontation could likely happen on the way home from school, at the family ice cream parlor where she's forced to work, or in her backyard.

When it comes to finding a location for a scene, some writers might feel limited by the range of typical settings within their genre, but this doesn't have to be the case. Creativity is one place where all writers shine, and we owe it to our readers to find the perfect locales for each scene, ones that can enhance events so they have the biggest impact. This doesn't always mean choosing a big, splashy location that readers might not often see in novels. Sometimes settings with the greatest traction can be rather mundane.

In Laurie Halse Anderson's *Speak*, the main character, Melinda, spends most of her time at school, but due to a recent traumatic event, she is utterly disconnected to everything. So Anderson creates an unexpected haven for Melinda: the custodian's closet. Suffering from PTSD, she goes there repeatedly when she needs to regroup. This unlikely location provides a welcome respite not only for Melinda but for the reader too.

When a setting has an emotional tie to the protagonist, even if at first glance it seems boring or one-note, it can be reinvented, surprising readers and offering them something new to experience. If you are struggling with a choice, try a bit of exploration; test out various places in your mind to see which provides the best opportunities for emotional values and triggers.

GETTING THE BIGGEST EMOTIONAL BANG FOR YOUR SETTING BUCK

As you can see, choosing the right setting for each scene greatly affects a writer's ability to characterize the story's cast and make readers feel part of the action. However, in the throes of plotting, it can be tempting to use a convenient setting that fits with where the characters happen to be—especially when the main action is low-key, like a conversation that needs to take place. Don't be fooled—to pack the biggest storytelling punch, the setting should earn the right to be chosen, even if the interaction between your characters is nothing more than a simple dialogue exchange.

To illustrate this, let's look at another example. Say our main character Mary has returned to her childhood home on the advice of her therapist, with plans to confront her aging father about the physical abuse she suffered at his hand as a child. Her goal is to face him and make him know how much it hurt her so she can achieve closure and move past this emotional wound. The nature of this dialogue scene is such that it will contain powerful emotional turmoil regardless of where it takes place, but that's no excuse for us not to squeeze out even more raw tension by getting specific with the setting choice.

This scene could take place in myriad locations, such as in the car as Mary's father picks her up at the airport, in his workshop as he sands down his latest hand-built canoe, or at the kitchen table over a meal.

Of all these places, which will hold the most emotional triggers for Mary? For example, if the family zealously followed spare-the-rod-spoil-the-child beliefs due to a skewed view of religious tenets, and this was the excuse for the beatings Mary endured, could this religious symbolism be shown through a cross displayed over the kitchen door? Or perhaps a cross-stitched verse could sit prominently above the family's kitchen table—a place where Mary was punished if she spoke before finishing her food, even if it was just to ask for water. This might make for a strong setting because the kitchen is drenched with negative memories.

But let's explore our other options. The scene could also take place in her father's workshop, where Mary was often dragged to be violently punished, weeping and begging for mercy. This location would certainly put Mary on edge, which would result in amplifying tension for the reader too. The events that took place in this room chain her to the abuse, yet her standing up to her father in this setting would be a strong declaration that she will move into a future that is untainted by past violence.

The third option, a discussion in a car, means Mary has a captive audience. Her father cannot get away from her accusations; he cannot escape responsibility for destroying her childhood. In the car, he must face what he's done. However, unlike the other two settings, there's no emotional connection to Mary, which is a missed opportunity to bring a deeper intensity to the confrontation through triggers. But choose the kitchen where she feels the yoke of religion bearing down on her—this is powerful, and will force her to fight feelings of unworthiness caused by her past emotional abuse. Likewise, taking her to the workshop will challenge her resolve as memories from the past bombard her. Both settings are stronger options than the two being conveniently trapped during a vehicle commute.

Choosing a setting that has specific meaning to the characters and provides strong context for the events taking place allows the author to charge the scene with emotion, creating opportunities for the characters to reveal more of themselves in an active and natural way.

THE SETTING AS A VEHICLE FOR DELIVERING BACKSTORY

To achieve a deeper level of characterization and provide insight into the hero's motivation, writers occasionally need to introduce backstory. Backstory, which is a character's defining experiences and interactions that occurred before the novel begins, is a difficult element to wield, simply because this necessary information also provides a minefield of problems if not handled correctly. There are two types of backstory: **visible backstory** for readers and **hidden backstory** for authors.

Hidden backstory is the information authors need to know about a character: likes and dislikes, how hobbies and pastimes developed, the bases for his greatest fears, the sources of his deepest wounds. It will also contain information about who and what influenced the character in the past (both good and bad) and how different events helped to shape his personality. This type of backstory is usually done in the brainstorming phase of a novel, and its purpose is to allow writers to know their characters on an intimate level so they can seat themselves inside the characters' heads and write each of their actions and behaviors authentically.

Depending on the writer's zeal, the planning of this backstory can almost be a novel in itself. For more information on character building, we recommend *The Positive Trait Thesaurus: A Writer's Guide to Character Attributes* and *The Negative Trait Thesaurus: A Writer's Guide to Character Flaws*.

Visible backstory is what readers will need to know to better understand the character's motives—why he does what he does. Certain behaviors only make sense when the reader can peek behind the curtain. A glimpse at the past will help lend shape to what the character desires and why, and what he fears, hopes for, and is obsessed with.

When it comes to visible and hidden backstory and how much of each should be revealed, imagine a cold tankard of beer. Hidden backstory is the gold liquid that takes up most of the real estate, yet it is not exposed. The foamy top of visible backstory is the creamy froth rising to be tasted first. Make this your formula when choosing how much backstory to introduce. Only a small amount of what the author knows about the character's history should make it into the novel, so what does go in really needs to count.

Visible backstory gives a reader **context** when it's important. For example, you could read about a character who avoids everything red: tomatoes, pomegranates, holiday sweaters—he even grows ill at the sight of blood. If the author shows him refusing to buy a couch because it is red or even throwing away a gift basket of beautiful red apples, it stands out as odd, unreasonable, and may even put readers off because they don't get it. However, with a subtly added touch of backstory, suddenly there is context for this behavior.

Lucas traded his paint roller for a blue-smudged cloth, wiped his hands, and then pressed his knuckles into his hips to stretch. His back resisted the move to straighten, but stiffness couldn't steal his grin. This was the third coat and hopefully the last, but it was worth doing. To give both himself and the house a fresh start, he needed to do this with his own hands. And now, midday light streamed through the window and glimmered off the blue paint, an expansive wall stretching across the room like his own private sky.

His gaze found a thin slash of old crimson paint at the top of the wall, and his lips flat-lined. Why the previous owners would choose such a hue, he couldn't fathom, but he wouldn't live in this house until all of it was covered. Twenty years had gone by, but the sight of that shade never failed to put him back in Gramma Jean's pantry, with the damp rot and moldering fruit and rats scrabbling behind red-lacquered walls. Lucas could not look at the color without remembering the screams wrenching from his throat and the pain of his tiny fingers clawing at the door until they bled. Gramma Jean might have been long dead, but the memory of what she'd done, over and over, remained.

The doorbell chimed, and Lucas jolted his gaze from the red strip. Some time on a ladder with a small brush and it would be as if the red never was. If only the past could be so easily erased. He swallowed down the bitterness coating his mouth and threw on his best "friendly new neighbor" smile on his way to the door.

Now, with the addition of backstory, we see Lucas' behavior for what it is: echoes of fear from a past trauma. Not only does this give readers clarity regarding his actions, it pulls them in through this personal doorway to an old wound that still pains him.

The problem with backstory is that it easily slows or stops the pace. We writers get so caught up in showing this past moment that we drop a giant chunk of unnecessary information on the reader. The trick to writing backstory well is to weave it into the current scene in a meaningful way and only give what readers need to understand the action. The fact that Lucas is painting the wall has real meaning, rather than it being just a chore to complete in a new house. Using the red paint as a trigger effectively allows us to dip into the past for context, provide a deeply disturbing sensory image of abuse, and then return to the present as someone rings the doorbell. In this case of meaningful backstory delivery, the setting comes to the rescue.

Backstory and setting also partner up well when authors need to show how someone in the story has grown or changed. Having a character revisit a location after an internal shift has taken place allows us to show him making a mental comparison with what he knew before to what he thinks and feels now.

Imagine the memories that might be churned up for a protagonist when he stands in the alley where he was cornered and beaten as a teen for being a different ethnicity than his attackers. The sights, smells, and sounds become a portal to the past as he relives the moment. However, now as an adult and a police officer, these past phantoms do not hold the power they once did; rather than feel fear, the burning light of determination fuels him. His mission is to protect the people in his world so they won't suffer as he did, something the author will be able to show authentically because the protagonist was exposed to this particular setting.

Settings can also facilitate backstory revelations on a larger scale, such as when the world itself has undergone a change. One example might be a protagonist who revisits the prosperous village where he raised his family—only, now it is war-ravaged and bearing the mark of poverty. This scene will reveal a lot about the events that took place in his absence.

This also works in situations in which readers need to imagine a past that belonged to someone other than the POV character. Consider a protagonist searching for his birth father; he finally tracks him down, only to learn that he died in a car accident just a week earlier. As the next of kin, our character is let into his father's apartment, and the well-chosen description provides clues of his father's lonely, solitary life: cluttered rooms with drapes sealed in dust, "Dear Occupant" junk mail piling up on the table, a lack of family photos and keepsakes. Not only will these setting details provide insight into how this man lived, they will also organically create an opportunity for the protagonist to share his thoughts about discovering his father too late, and the pain of being so close to filling a void, only to discover it can now never be filled.

WITH BACKSTORY, CHARACTER INTERACTION IS KEY

As the author, your decisions on what to describe will have direct bearing on how backstory is delivered. The most important aspect is ensuring that the character is interacting with the setting, either on a **micro** or **macro level**. For example, a micro interaction might include you having the character single out something within the setting and use it as a backstory focal point, such as Charlie holding the photo of his dead twin, in the earlier example. A macro-level interaction might include showing your character returning to the dairy farm where he grew up and allowing some backstory to seep in as he completes farm chores or tours the property.

Another creative option is to use character interaction with a setting to only *imply* backstory. Withholding information—the right information—creates tension by delaying gratification, priming readers for a bigger reveal later in the story.

Consider a female character who was mugged after seeing her mother off at the train station for an early departure. Placed in the similar setting at a later date, her behavior will reflect discomfort, especially if many of the same factors are in place: the sun brightening the sky, chasing off the last oranges and pinks of sunrise; a lack of people around the station, and wind pushing at dead leaves and litter along the track, causing them to tick and scrape against the cement.

In this setting, the character will naturally be on high alert, and we can show her edginess through actions, such as her constantly glancing about for sketchy people, slipping a canister of pepper spray into her pocket, being sensitive to noise, and consciously trying to control her breathing. A mix of these behaviors will alert the reader that she's expecting something negative, or at least trying to be prepared if something bad does happen. Without a drop of backstory, naturally inquisitive readers will immediately start asking questions. *Why is the character nervous? Why do certain sounds or smells seem to grate at her nerves? Did something bad happen to her long ago?*

Sometimes it's better to not share backstory and instead keep readers asking questions. Their desire to get answers will keep them turning pages, and the setting is a great vehicle for alluding to a past event without giving everything away. Just be sure that your backstory is compelling enough so that when you do finally reveal it, readers are left feeling satisfied, not disappointed.

THE CROWN JEWEL OF SETTINGS: SENSORY DETAILS

To draw readers fully into a scene, we want to create a sensory feast for their imagination. This means using different senses to keep the description fresh and vivid so each location we describe comes alive. We want to help them forget that they're reading about fictional events, instead making them feel as if they're right in the scene sampling the same sights, smells, tastes, textures, and sounds as the POV character or narrator.

Have you ever read a book so well drawn you wished you could visit? One that stuck with you long after the story was over, and your mind kept imagining that place, dreaming up ideas of what might be happening now and what the people there might be doing? I'm sure you have; settings that have real texture tend to send the imagination into a synaptic-firing frenzy. One that stands out to many is Hobbiton from *The Lord of the Rings*. The fields of lush grass, the dome-shaped homes filled with the promise of cozy comforts and lavish meals, the drifting smoke trails of Gandalf's pipe—these things place readers in a world they long to visit, where one can almost smell the sharp cheeses waiting on a platter and feel that silky grass beneath one's bare feet.

Drawing on multiple senses as we describe the setting creates a layered landscape, one that feels incredibly real. The deeper we can connect readers to each setting we draw, the more we create that longing to be part of the world we have built. Each detail should be chosen not only to bring readers into the scene but to send a message, one that evokes an emotional response. That message is entirely up to the author, but at the heart of it should be the intent to make the reader feel something powerful.

SIGHTS THAT GIVE LIFE TO FICTION

It's no surprise that out of all the senses, sight is the one writers rely on the most, since describing what the character sees helps readers visualize it too. But to create truly compelling description using sight, we want to filter everything described through the POV character or narrator's emotions first.

Perhaps you've heard this popular saying: "There are two sides to every story—what you saw and what actually happened." It contains a truth that can carry forward into fiction, because characters interpret what they see depending on how they are feeling. Consider this small example in which a father returns home after a weekend business trip:

> Leroy closed the door to the apartment, squinting in the midday murk. His eyes adjusted and the handle of his suitcase slipped from his grasp. In the kitchen, the shadows pooling across the counter became tangible shapes—an apocalypse of broken eggshells and omelette fixings alongside two frying pans rimmed with dry scrapings. Stacks of plates and cutlery filled the sink, and the

refrigerator door stood ajar. His pulse shot up. All this after two frigging days on the road? *Old enough to be left on their own, my ass.* He'd wring their necks when they got home from school.

But look at how the same scene appears to change when it's viewed from a different emotional perspective:

> Leroy closed the door and fell against it, a pent-up breath sawing out of his lips. His legs trembled, barely holding him. *That logging truck . . . if I hadn't changed lanes when I did . . .* Numb, he stared into the dark apartment, gathering his wits, waiting for the heaviness of his near-death experience to lift. His vision adjusted to the gloom, and a kitchen wreck greeted him: cartons of juice on the counter, a pan of scorched eggs on the stove, a mountain of dishes ringing the sink. Good God, even the fridge door hung open a crack. A short laugh burst out of him. Those two, so sure they were ready to be on their own. He grinned, shaking his head. *At least they managed to cook something while I was away.*

The same scene, yet two totally different descriptions, both filtered through Leroy's emotions. In the first, anger causes him to notice every minute detail. In the second, relief allows him see the humorous side of the messy kitchen and feel gratitude that he's even there to see it.

As you can see, filtering a description through the POV character's emotions will alter how the reader experiences the setting, so take the time to think about what your character or the narrator is feeling in each scene and how certain details might be highlighted to reinforce it. For more help with showing your characters' emotions, consider checking out *The Emotion Thesaurus: A Writer's Guide to Character Expression*.

SMELLS THAT TRIGGER EMOTIONAL MEMORY

Have you ever smelled something that immediately brought back a moment from your past? It's likely you have, since the part of the brain responsible for smell lies in close proximity to receptors that help store memories. This means that, of all the senses, smell is the one most likely to evoke emotional memories from readers' pasts, which brings about that all-important sense of "shared experience" that will draw them deeper into the story.

Ironically, smells are often forgotten in fiction, which is why turning a critical eye to your description and adding a few odors is important. The beauty of this sense is that the smells we choose to include can become symbols for something deeper, helping to reinforce mood and elicit emotion. If your character's car has just broken down in a parking lot and she's waiting for a tow truck, the smell of yeasty bread and savory spices wafting from the bakery next door might pull her out of a foul mood (and likely cause a spike in hunger). But change that to the queasy scent of sun-baked asphalt and the reek of sour beer from the nearby bottle return depot, and the character's mood will likely only get worse.

Specific scents tied to locations also add realism. In fact, if smells are left out in these cases, the reader might sense a void in your description. Consider the briny scent of algae down at the harbor or fresh popcorn and salt at a theater. These iconic smells help place the reader in the scene. If your setting contains a smell that is hard to forget in real life, make sure you don't forget it in your fiction.

SOUNDS THAT INFUSE THE WORLD WITH REALISM

Another sense that adds rich dimension to a setting is sound. None of us lives in a noiseless vacuum, and our characters should not either. Layering the character's world with sounds also helps readers ease into a setting; like important puzzle pieces, they aid readers in forming a mental picture. Sounds are much more than realistic stage dressing, however. Like the other senses, they can be used in a variety of ways.

Because of our instinctual human need to protect ourselves and the automatic response of fight or flight, we tend to be hyperaware of sound, especially any that shift suddenly or do not seem to belong to the environment. If we mirror this premise in the story world, sounds become an excellent technique to alert the reader that something is afoot, foreshadowing change to come, either good or bad. Not all sounds have to be loud to evoke a response either. A door hinge slowly creaking at the wrong time can have the exact same effect as a rapid barrage of gunshots.

If you are purposefully reinforcing a specific mood in your setting, think about the circumstances of the scene and what emotions are at play. Then use sounds to either heighten these emotions, adding tension, or diminish them. For example, if your character is walking home after a late night babysitting and has felt watched each step of the way, heading into her driveway and hearing the pinging of her brother's truck engine as it cools will likely put her at ease. That sound represents safety, the knowledge that someone is close by if she needs help. Likewise, the crunch of footsteps on the gravel behind her or a lightbulb smashing on the porch ahead will only heighten her fear.

To do more with less when it comes to sensory description, try to include sounds that have a greater purpose than just adding realism. The more you get into the habit of making deliberate choices with your setting descriptions, the tighter your writing will become, ensuring that your storytelling skills will provide the audience with an unforgettable reading experience.

TASTES THAT BRING READERS INTO THE STORY WORLD

Of all the senses, taste is the least used, mostly because food and drink rarely have direct bearing on a scene. After all, watching a character eat isn't exactly the most riveting action unless his taste experience ties in with the plot line (usually through high stakes), such as trying to detect poison in his drink, judging entries at a high-profile culinary event, or knowing that if he doesn't nail the meal, his own head may end up on the plate.

Eating is often a necessary physical function or a social activity, so to use this sense properly in our description, we should make sure it adds meaning beyond the actual taste experience. This sense can be a challenge, but it's also an inventive way to help readers experience a scene. The three elements to help steer writers when using this sense are **context**, **comparison**, and **contrast**.

Context is all about helping to tie together the who, where, when, and why. Is the character eating in someone's home, in a restaurant, around the campfire, or standing at a food vendor's cart? Why is the meal happening in this space? What does the quality of the food and location say about the people in this scene? Context that involves taste is a unique way to provide answers to unasked yet pertinent questions. Then to add to the mental picture, comparison and contrast between the character and what she's sampling can hint at personality, show relationships, and even help to infuse emotion and mood. For example, does your volatile, outspoken character prefer spicy, sweat-inducing foods *(comparison)*? Or is your character at a charity gala sipping some of the most exquisite champagne she's ever tasted at the very moment she discovers her husband is having an affair *(contrast)*? Both these techniques use taste to show character details in a way that is both unexpected and memorable.

Taste also allows writers a way of bringing the everyday into the fictional world. In real life, people need sustenance, so why should it be different in a story? In fact, characters who never seem to eat or drink will likely be noticed, and the reader's trust in the author's storytelling skills may waiver. Even if taste isn't helping to characterize and has no direct bearing on the plot, it should still be included once in a while to add realism and build reader trust.

TEXTURES THAT ENCOURAGE SETTING INTERACTION

Of all the senses, textures allow the most interaction with the setting, not only supplying movement and helping the pacing flow smoothly but also creating an inner path to the character's mind-set. Texture is all about exploration, both for the character and, through him, the reader. Because textures are universal, they can help the setting seem more real, and describing how something feels will remind the reader of his own past experiences with that same texture.

Imagine a character who is at the vet clinic to have her beloved pet put down. With each stroke of the soft fur, the character struggles to let go. As they live this moment, readers will likely be taken to a point in their pasts where they too experienced a strong connection with an animal; either they will remember the horrible turmoil they felt at a similar incident, or it will open a door to imagining what it is like to be in the character's shoes. Either way, done well, the silky texture of the dog's fur will cause empathy to bloom, tightening the reader's connection to the character.

An important thing to remember when it comes to textures is to make each one count. After all, a character must act to come in contact with something, and all actions should further the story. Having a character touch or pick up something without reason is a waste of words. But if the texture is included to reinforce a mood, reveal an emotion, or show readers something deeper about the character, then it is pulling its storytelling weight.

Another way the sense of touch elevates description is when it is used to foreshadow or symbolize. For example, a stinging cut incurred while running past a rusted dumpster may foreshadow danger to come. Or if the character is already in danger, perhaps fleeing from a pursuer, the pain becomes a symbol of the cost of being caught and a reminder that some risks are worth taking.

FINDING BALANCE WHEN USING THE SENSES

While a large portion of sensory description tends to focus on what is seen, nonvisual sensory details add the layering that can take descriptive writing from good to great. Don't feel pressured to use all the senses all the time; by mixing just a few, the image created is so much more interesting than if a single sense is used. Sometimes, experimenting is a good way to create a multisensory effect. For example, while metaphors and similes often tend to be visual, using other senses instead can lead to fresh writing. Consider these descriptions from the classics:

The bells ceased as they had begun: together. They were succeeded by a clanking noise, deep down below; as if some person were dragging a heavy chain over the casks in the wine-merchant's cellar. (Sound, from *A Christmas Carol*)

Never in his life had he seen a river before—this sleek, sinuous, full-bodied animal, chasing and chuckling, gripping things with a gurgle and leaving them with a laugh, to fling itself on fresh playmates that shook themselves free, and were caught and held again. (Sound and Texture, from *The Wind in the Willows*)

There was a smell of saddle soap, mixed with the unmistakeable, personal smell of armor—as individual a smell as that which you get in the professional's shop on a golf course . . . (Smell, from *The Once and Future King*)

Each snippet above supplies readers with a concrete visual, but it does so through a sense other than sight, resulting in an evocative image. A well-placed smell, taste, sound, or texture can deepen the impact of any setting and help readers feel more involved in what's happening. This also reinforces deep POV, since description filtered through the point-of-view character's senses is more tangible and puts readers in tune with the character's emotions.

URBAN WORLD BUILDING: THE PROS AND CONS OF CHOOSING A REAL-LIFE LOCATION

With a great deal of fiction taking place in the contemporary world, it's only natural that many settings choices are located in urban areas. After all, in our modern world, most of our time is spent in the nerve centers of society, either for work, education, or play. It makes sense that our fiction should mirror real life.

Using an urban setting comes with its own special challenge—the decision whether to go with a real-life location or to build one from the imagination. Choosing a real-life location can help the writer center herself in the character's world more firmly, especially if the place she has chosen is one she knows intimately.

Naming a specific city or mentioning a well-known landmark also gives readers an immediate sense of place and allows authors to infuse their descriptions with a level of realism that may otherwise be difficult to achieve. Being able to draw on one's memories to re-create the sights, smells, sounds, tastes, and textures will lead to effective showing, and authenticity will shine through as personalization and fiction collide. Readers familiar with the area will also be drawn in as that feeling of shared experience with the character kicks in more fully, making it easier to identify with the protagonist and care about his or her desires.

Some genres, such as political thrillers, often feature real locations both to convey immediacy and reinforce the idea that the story events could potentially happen in the real world, grabbing readers on a gut level. But there are some drawbacks to choosing a real place. Readers may love to read about somewhere they have visited or even lived, but in order for this to work, the writer must know that location down to its bones. If an author gets some of the details wrong, readers will notice and be pulled out of the story. Some may even grow upset at the author's lack of research.

Another drawback of using a real setting concerns something authors have no control over: locations change over time. Businesses come and go, and buildings are leased, redesigned, or torn down. Neighborhoods can be revamped or even wiped off the map to make room for an overpass or freeway. So even if one does make sure the descriptions of a particular setting are current at the time of the story's writing, those locations may not stay that way. As well, readers won't always know about such changes themselves. People who lived in the area ten years ago may still picture it as it used to be and can become disoriented when the description doesn't align with their memories. Readers can also bring their own biases into a story. If your character frequents a favorite real-world deli where a reader happened to once get terrible service, the differing opinions can drive an emotional wedge between himself and the character.

Because of the potential potholes that can develop when describing a real-world setting, some choose to fashion an entirely fictional urban location instead. Building a world from scratch means readers will have no personal attachments to it, there will be no biases to contend with, and you can build the setting exactly as you picture it. The downside is that fictional worlds require more elbow grease to successfully render the author's mental picture into a tangible place that readers can easily visualize. Locations (including cities or countries that are not part of the real world) will prompt readers to wonder what else may be different—the way governments are run, how society functions, gender roles that come into play, and a host of other details. Writers choosing this route need to plan their worlds down to the smallest detail to make them feel as rich and believable as the real one.

When it comes to contemporary settings, often the easiest solution is to meet in the middle by choosing a mixture of both real and imaginary. Selecting a real country or well-known city lays the foundation for how everything works and what readers can expect. Then, by creating a fictional space within the larger setting (a neighborhood, a town, a street, etc.), authors can weave in whatever urban elements best fit the story rather than being hemmed in by actual landmarks and possible reader bias.

Regardless of whether your setting is real or imagined, it is important to include some constants from the everyday so readers can relate to the characters and what they face in their fictional worlds. Even if a setting is something completely new and special, details rooted in the familiar will help orient readers. Small things, such as a man with a cart hawking unheard-of but fragrant kabobs, are still reminiscent of a real-world Polish-sausage street vendor who salts the air with drool-worthy aromas. Likewise, the routines of children heading off to school, of parents meeting up to socialize, and of authority figures patrolling the streets all mirror a reader's everyday experiences, no matter how fantastical the setting you're introducing them to. Adding known elements to a new place can lead to a reader's trust in the author when it becomes clear that the necessary details for even the most unfamiliar of urban locations will be shared.

COMMON SETTING SNAGS

The setting is a true chameleon when it comes to accommodating whatever the writer needs it to do: characterize, reinforce mood, reveal backstory, add symbolism, or provide conflict. As you can imagine, any storytelling element that so greatly influences events comes with a few common snags to watch out for.

With any type of description, pacing is important, and this goes double for any detail involving the setting. Too little description, and the reader is flung into a scene without being properly grounded; too much description will steamroll the action flat. Understanding which setting location is the perfect match for each scene is really the key step, as it helps us circumvent so many problems, including the three biggies: **boring**, **flat,** and **confusing** settings.

PUTTING READERS TO SLEEP: AVOIDING BORING SETTINGS

We've all heard the saying, "This is about as much fun as watching paint dry." Well the literary equivalent when it comes to settings is going overboard by describing each detail to the point that readers cannot wait for something—anything—to happen. Here are some of the biggest contributors to a setting that begs to be skipped.

Overdescribing:

Priming readers for the action in a scene requires some evocative setting details to set the stage, add or release tension, reinforce mood, or symbolize something significant. However, it's a slippery slope that develops when a writer moves from combining a few carefully selected details to bloating up pages with a rainstorm of description. It's easy for writers to get caught up in the current of detailing the world they've built, but readers should fill in some blanks for themselves too—otherwise the story will never be finished.

To avoid overdescribing, we need to be selective with our details. To help with this, imagine the setting as a character. Describing her height, weight, eye color, and hairstyle as she waits for her name to be called in an interview is not compelling because it doesn't tell us anything beyond her physical appearance. Instead, a writer should choose details that help to characterize and show emotion, such as her constant tugging at ill-fitting dress clothes, the tightness in her body posture, and the way she rubs at her chest as if massaging out a deep pain. These details give readers a glimpse inside the character's anxiety as well providing a brief outline of her outer image.

With the setting, we need to apply these same principles, doing more with less. To make sure your setting adds something beyond priming the stage, try using a setting checklist (Appendix B). This can help you plan each scene's location in light of what it can accomplish to further your story.

Purple Prose:

Similar to overdescribing is purple prose, which results when we get so caught up in making our description stand out that our writing becomes overrun with sensory images, metaphors, and flowery phrases. If we find ourselves describing the petal of a forget-me-not as winter-ice azure instead of light blue, or we compare a sunrise cresting a mountain range to the glorious fire-crown of a queen on her throne, we've gone to the purple side.

Language is our bread and butter, and commanding a strong vocabulary while understanding how to utilize figures of speech is important. But if we overdo it, readers only see the words and not the fiction. We never want to break the storytelling spell, so sometimes this means killing our darlings. If a turn of phrase sounds achingly beautiful but doesn't further the story, it needs to go to the description graveyard.

Getting Too Technical:

Some locations have a lot going on, and they require a bit more time to show, such as alien planets, tech-heavy or virtual environments, or a mazelike battleground where enemies meet. For these types of areas, the success or failure of the scene will depend on our ability to show the unusual setting well enough to anchor readers in the unfamiliar place.

Sometimes our attempt to help readers fully picture a foreign setting results in us getting bogged down in the technical details, breaking things down piece by piece, which stalls the pace. As with a gun, readers don't need to know every bolt and pin to understand what it does. With difficult settings, think about how to bring out the bigger details by drawing on comparisons readers are familiar with. Then add refining details that evoke a certain mood, facilitate backstory, or utilize a different aspect of multifaceted description. By giving readers enough rope, they will be able to pull themselves along and see the scene without sacrificing story movement.

Backstory Whirlpools:

Earlier we looked at just how effective the setting can be as a vehicle for introducing natural backstory as it applies to the events of a scene. While the setting is a true goldmine for helping to reveal deeper story meaning through characterization and backstory, we have to take care not to get caught in the past either. To avoid being dragged into a backstory whirlpool, adopt a "get in and get out" mentality when it comes to showing the past through description or flashbacks. The setting is a trigger; as such, it should do its job quickly and effectively. Only show backstory that is critical to a particular scene, giving readers context for a character's behavior and thoughts or to better understand the stakes involved. Often it can be helpful to choose a sensory detail that acts as a gateway to the present: a sound that ties in to what's happening in the current scene, a smell that draws the character back to the now, or even a texture that snaps the connection to a past moment.

Setting as an Island:

The anatomy of a scene is like the workings of a cuckoo clock; it takes many cogs, pins, and weights to keep everything moving and functioning as it should. Anything that stops this process greatly damages the effectiveness of the writing, and often what freezes the machinery of a scene is singling out the setting description.

Stopping the story to specifically point out setting details will create a disruption in the flow that feels out of place, especially if it goes on too long. Instead we should treat the setting as a casing that holds everything together—the outer wrapping that cocoons all the storytelling elements into an organized, cohesive unit. Then, with this in mind, we can lace together our setting description so seamlessly, it's hard to tell where it begins or ends.

> The car slowed, its headlights splashing across the dewy grass and the pale siding of the neighbor's house. Donovan's breath froze as he crouched, the manicured hedge scratching his skin and plucking at his clothes. The deep rumble of Eric's Charger thrummed in Donovan's chest. He cringed, waiting for the motor to cut, for the door to squeal open. His brother's best friend must have seen him crossing the pedestrian bridge, but Donovan was sure he'd lost him in the maze of houses and yards. Yet, here he was. Eric and his odd smile had always left Donovan uneasy, not to mention how he kept showing up at the strangest of times.
>
> Seconds dragged by, cold seeping through the knees of his jeans where they pressed into the damp soil. He prayed that his pursuer would go away, but Eric never forgot a debt. It didn't matter that the debt belonged to Donovan's dead brother, or that he was nothing like his twin. At best, Eric would hound him until he agreed to settle accounts. At worst, he'd end up in the reservoir like his brother.

Were you able to imagine what was happening in the scene above, including the "why" behind the character's actions and emotions as he interacted with the setting? I hope so. Describing the setting as the action unfolds is so much more involving than sidestepping the events taking place to focus on setting details alone. Just as they do in this scene, the cogs of sensory detail, emotion, contextual backstory, and tension should work together, enhancing the plot rather than taking away from it.

AS FAR AS THE EYE CAN SEE: AVOIDING FLAT SETTINGS

On the other side of this problematic coin is flat settings, caused by overly lean or lackluster descriptions. This particular issue is one that is caused by a multitude of reasons.

Ho-hum Settings:

Not to flog a dead horse, but with the huge selection of incredible books out there, there's no room for standard-issue. This goes for plot, characters, and, yes, even settings. Whichever location we choose for our scene to take place, we want to make sure our stamp, our unique vision, is working to make the world vivid and believable.

Even if we choose a setting that seems to be in almost every novel known to man, we can still show how this particular space fits our POV character like the proverbial glove. If our location is a boarding school, specific elements will influence what it is like. Large or small, urban or rural, public or private—all these factors will say something about where the character lives or what her financial situation is, and will allude to her attitude about boarding school as she relays sensory details through her point of view. Is the school well tended or run down? Are the teachers enthusiastic or lackadaisical? Is there an emphasis on sports programming, on the arts, or on extracurricular activities and clubs? The answers will help your boarding school break the generic mold.

As mentioned earlier, whether a location is known to the character or not, settings can be personalized and seeded with emotional triggers if they don't come with emotional values built right in. A park should never just be a park. A hotel room should never be just a hotel room. The choices you make about sensory details, lighting, people, and the symbols tied to each location will characterize the story's cast and influence how readers connect to each scene.

Sensory Starvation:

No one enjoys eating only one thing, even if that one thing is bacon or chocolate. Likewise, readers can grow bored by settings that are conveyed through only one of the senses. Sight is our primary go-to since we rely on it so heavily in real life, so it's easy to only draw on visuals to describe. To combat this we need to think about how the character is experiencing the scene in other ways—through smell, taste, touch, and sound—and how these sensory inclusions make the character's world more dimensional and real.

Sometimes it can be helpful to imagine yourself as the character and place yourself in the moment. Think about the emotions he's feeling: what does your character expect to happen in this location? Depending on his mind-set, he will be tuned in to different things. If your character is uncertain or worried, his fight-or-flight instincts may be dialed up, putting his senses on alert for threats. As such, he would be more likely to notice odd movements or a noise that doesn't fit rather than something benign, such as a child drawing with chalk on the sidewalk.

If you struggle with remembering to describe the lesser-used senses, don't worry. Thinking "sensory" is something that gets easier with practice, and of course the entries in this book and its sister volume will help prompt you to build new description habits.

Crutches Rearing Up:

When it comes to describing, all authors play favorites. As you're crafting a scene, perhaps you include a rusted-out yellow pickup truck parked at the curb. Nothing wrong there, unless you also find your character chaining up his banana-yellow bike to a rack outside a bakery that happens to have yellow-lacquered doors. Then there's a problem, because unintentional repetitions will flatten the description of those scenes.

Crutches can be sensory as well. Perhaps you love the sound of the wind sliding through a bounty of leaves. Independently, this sensory detail can really help readers experience the setting, but if you find yourself mentioning the sound of the wind in many different scenes, readers will notice. And the golden rule is to never let readers see the writing. It's one thing if the repetitions are deliberate, such as the wind's moaning being used as a motif throughout a story. But if the sensory details are cropping up by accident, it's time to break out the editing knife.

A great way to combat crutches, be it a color, a sensory detail, a turn of phrase, or a figurative language choice, is to write down your favorite details and go-to techniques. Take your list and randomly check several scenes during your editing passes. Do you spot any descriptive patterns? Do you use way too many similes? If so, weed a few of those out and replace them with something fresh.

The good news is, if you can't seem to see your repetitions, critique partners usually will. Fresh eyes can typically spot the things we're blind to. Make a note asking a beta reader or critique partner to keep a list of any words, phrases, or descriptions that come up time and again. Then once you're back in editing mode, you can replace these repeats with fresher imagery while also keeping an eye out for ones your early readers may have missed.

Weaker Writing:

Tied to ho-hum settings are those that are watered down by weak word choices, adjective and adverb abuse, and a general lack of variation when it comes to descriptive techniques. Ideally, we want to utilize different sentence structures and draw from an array of figurative language so the writing not only leads to emotion-centric imagery but is also a pleasure to read. For more specific lessons on writing techniques that can be used to amp up your descriptions, please refer to *The Rural Setting Thesaurus*.

Growing one's command of language happens through practice (write, write, write!) as well as observing while we read. Remember: everything about writing is a work in progress. Mastery, by nature, is impossible, but we continually improve when we keep ourselves open to learning. Wherever you are on the path, there's always another step to take, which is one of the true joys of evolving as a writer.

WHERE IN THE WORLD? SETTINGS THAT CONFUSE

The third snag we want to avoid is reader confusion, which often happens when our setting description lacks the clarity to ground readers in the scene. As writers, we find it easy to focus so much on an amazing plot twist or tense romantic clash that we neglect the setting, assuming that readers are following along just fine. But without a strong sense of place, readers may find themselves confused. Here are two areas to watch out for as you write.

Movement Hiccups:

Sometimes, during revision, description edits can mess with movement sequences, creating confusion. This happens because when we tighten scenes, description is often the first thing to go. The result? One minute, a character is sitting on a stool at a pool hall waiting for his turn to drop the 8-ball; the next, he's standing at the bar swiping shots off an absent server's tray. These hiccups are jarring and can snap readers out of the story. The good news is that they're fairly easy to fix. Simply give each edited scene a final pass read, specifically looking for smooth movement transitions as a character goes from A to B while interacting with C.

Fast-Action Sequences:

While setting descriptions should take a backseat when high action is underway, they still need to be present so readers can fully imagine what's happening. Fight scenes, in particular, can create a quagmire of confusion because so much of the focus rests on the conflict between characters. It's easy to forget about the setting altogether while the battle royal becomes a bloody sequence of punches, face kicks, and the occasional knee to the groin, but if readers can't "see" the scene, you'll lose their attention.

Whether your scene is all about the clash, the car chase, or the habañero-hot tryst, think about how elements of the setting can come into play. During the fistfight, are holes punched in the drywall, or is Mother's treasured collection of glass owls wiped out in a single shove? In the tire-squealing car chase, does your character almost take out a mailman, sideswipe a school bus, or mow down a high-end restaurant's patio topiary? As frantic lovers rush for the bedroom, are pictures bumped askew, does the mattress slide halfway off the platform, is an embarrassing teddy bear keepsake swept aside so it doesn't spoil the mood? No matter what type of action you have, choosing setting details that fit naturally with the events will help readers better imagine (and enjoy) the scene.

OTHER URBAN SETTING CONSIDERATIONS

One of the biggest advantages of choosing an urban setting is how adaptable it is. The setting should work hard for the story, pushing ahead the plot and reinforcing the messages the author wishes to convey. Here are a few final considerations to keep in mind as you build your urban world scene by scene.

BE SPECIFIC AND UNIQUE

No matter how common the setting, your urban location should be tailored to become one-of-a-kind to your readers. A thousand decisions rest on your shoulders, each an opportunity to make the setting feel like it's been plucked right out of the real world. Imagine your character walking down a street. You decide how crowded or empty the sidewalk is, what sort of buskers are entertaining passersby, how much traffic clogs the streets, whether the buildings in the neighborhood indicate poverty or prosperity, and everything in between. You direct the reader's sensory experience by weaving in the starchy scent of boiling noodles from a nearby Pho restaurant or by describing a gritty whirl of dust, courtesy of the debris-laden wind from a construction site across the street.

Urban locations can also mirror real-world familiarity through the cadence of store openings and closings, rush-hour traffic patterns, couriers making deliveries, and buses or subways arriving at each stop on a route. These details ring as authentic, allowing you the freedom to play with other setting choices that will work best for your story.

GET OFF THE SETTING HAMSTER WHEEL

When coming up with the right setting is hard, we often pull ideas from movies or books that are similar to ours. However, recycling common settings too often can steal the uniqueness from our stories. Readers love a fresh experience, so before going with a tried-and-true setting, think outside the box. A party place for teens doesn't always have to be at the beach or in someone's house while the parents are away. Why not have them sneak into a shutdown construction site or an empty warehouse that's up for sale? Add some beer, a few spray cans, and the unexpected appearance of a security guard with a stun gun, and you've got a unique setting primed for a storm of conflict.

When there's a lot going on inside the character, it can also be tempting to purposefully stick with common locations to keep the focus more firmly on the inner turmoil. However, centering too much on what's happening inside the character often leads to pacing problems. The right setting supplies opportunities for symbolism, active backstory delivery, and emotional showing through interaction, so stretch yourself to find settings that provide the best inner landscape connection while keeping the pace and plot rolling forward.

FINAL THOUGHTS FROM THE AUTHORS

While each setting in this book has been extensively researched, our entries serve as a baseline only. The reality is that any real-world setting will have infinite—but different—cousins. A forest in Alaska will not have the same animals, plants, and trees as one in Southern California, not to mention those in other countries like Borneo or New Zealand. If your novel takes place in a specific location of the real world, take the time to investigate what might be different from what's listed in the entries.

You will also find that we included many different possible details for each setting that may or may not be found in every version of a particular location; for example, not all pawnshops will have landscaping equipment and tools, but we included this detail so you can decide if your pawnshop should. Not all bakeries have a sit-down area to eat—but maybe yours needs one. These seeming discrepancies are deliberate, offering you a broad variety to select from, so instead of taking an all-inclusive approach, be sure to choose details from our entries that work for your setting.

When it comes to choosing a real location, remember the climate. The time of year, proximity to the equator, and season will alter your setting in subtle yet important ways. In parts of Canada, darkness begins to fall around four pm in December, yet during the long days of summer, the sun may not fully set until ten o'clock at night. Proximity to a mountain range or coastline can have a big effect on temperatures and the type of weather as well. Is your location prone to tornadoes or earthquakes? Is the air dry or moist? As a result, do people more often wear flip-flops or hiking boots? To ensure you have the facts, make Google your friend—or better yet, try to visit the location yourself.

While we have tried to include a strong representation of the most common fictional settings between the urban and rural volumes, by no means is this setting thesaurus complete. Some settings are very much alike; in this case, we often chose to profile one that could act as a starting point for a range of similar locations. If you can't find the exact setting you're looking for, think of other places that are similar, since they may have the descriptive detail you need.

Please also note that in these entries we chose details from a variety of character viewpoints. In the police car entry, for example, details from both the front and back seats are included. So if your character is a police officer, he will have access to the controls in the front cab of his cruiser, but description coming from his viewpoint would not include the finer points of being trussed up in the backseat. As you're describing your setting, think about what your character would logically be able to see, hear, taste, smell, and touch so you never break out of point of view.

When it comes to your settings, never forget emotion. Filtering descriptions through your narrator or POV character's feelings will influence what she notices about where she is and how she feels about it. Emotions can create bias, tainting how a person feels about her location. This bias is passed on to readers, helping them to feel more connected to the character as they see the world through the same lens.

Finally, we recommend using this book in tandem with *The Rural Setting Thesaurus*, since the lessons there will give you an even greater command of setting elements, allowing you to bring readers more deeply into each scene. If you would like to see a list of the settings explored in the rural companion, there is one included at the end of this book.

THE
URBAN SETTING
THESAURUS

In the City

ALLEY

SIGHTS

Stacks of water-stained crates, litter (crushed takeout cups, crumpled wrappers, cigarette butts, empty liquor bottles, broken glass), a rust-pitted dumpster leaking unidentifiable fluid, puddles of dried vomit, greasy-looking puddles, dirt and grime, ratty blankets or fabric scraps (if a homeless person is using this space for sleeping), flattened cardboard boxes and broken wood pallets, rats, cockroaches, spiders, ants, birds that eat garbage (magpies, pigeons, crows), a metal fire escape attached to a building, street cats or dogs, employees ducking out the back door for a smoke break, broken or discarded furniture, graffiti and mildew stains on the brick walls of nearby buildings, newspapers and leaflets blown into piles in corners, grimy barred windows and doorways, a chain link fence at one end, streetlamps that don't fully penetrate the darkness, a wash of light as a car passes on the street, metal doors that have small plates etched with the name of the business on them, signs that say *No Loitering* or *Loading Area*, criminal activity (muggings, drunken brawls, murders, break-ins, drug use)

SOUNDS

Wind scraping trash into the corners, dogs rooting through garbage, cats meowing, people coughing or talking in low voices, music from a club's back entrance, the clink of bottles, a trash bin lid slamming down, the crinkle of a trash bag as it's tossed into a bin, garbage lids being knocked to the ground by hungry animals, the patter of rodent feet, the jingle of keys as a door is locked or unlocked, glass shattering, the clatter of a chain link fence as someone climbs over it, the sputter of a car engine turning over nearby, sounds from the street (horns honking, tires squealing, shoes clapping against the sidewalk), the far-off wail of a siren, arguments drifting through the open windows of residential buildings, the splatter of stomach contents and groaning as someone gets sick, shuffling footsteps through alley debris, a rattling wheel from a homeless person's shopping cart, swearing as bouncers throw someone out of a club or bar, the sudden click of a switchblade opening

SMELLS

Rotting garbage, body odor, animal and human waste, motor oil, cooking smells drifting from open windows and restaurants, wet cardboard, mildew, vomit, a beer smell from broken bottles, cigarette smoke, musty fabric, mold, car exhaust

TASTES

Alcohol, food from trash bins or brought out of shelters, warm beer, cigarettes

TEXTURES AND SENSATIONS

Rough bricks beneath a palm as one uses the wall for support when inebriated, the squishy, wet give of stepping on trash that is unseen in the darkness, the suction of sticky grime pulling at one's shoes, slipping in grease leaking from a dumpster, the shuffle of paper litter and leaves underfoot, the cold metal of a garbage bin lid, metal edges catching at one's clothing or skin, hoisting the heavy lid of a dumpster to toss trash in, the smooth familiarity of a beer bottle, the prod of a gun in one's side or the hot pinch from a blade during a mugging, pain from being beaten, tripping over debris left in the alley, sifting through garbage for something usable, the cold wetness of water seeping into one's shoe after stepping in a puddle, metal wire digging into fingers as one climbs a chain link fence, shattering a window with an elbow, using a shoulder against a door to break-in, gripping a pull handle or doorknob, sleeping on a musty couch or strip of dirty cardboard

POSSIBLE SOURCES OF CONFLICT

Getting mugged
Dropping one's purse or phone in the dark and trying to find it
Discovering a feral or stray animal in the alley scavenging for food
Finding a dead end when one needs a shortcut
Being followed
Coming across a crime in progress (a break-in, a mugging, a drug deal)
Having a business owner call the cops, forcing one to find another place to rest
Trying to get some sleep but being woken up by a shelter worker

PEOPLE COMMONLY FOUND HERE

Building residents, business owners, criminals, homeless people, police officers, shelter care workers

RELATED SETTINGS THAT MAY TIE IN WITH THIS ONE

Ambulance (254), big city street(38), cheap motel (46), condemned apartment building (50), homeless shelter (74), run-down apartment (116), underpass (128)

SETTING NOTES AND TIPS

Make sure your alley description fits the environment and the conflict that will unfold there. An alley between two apartment buildings will have smells and sights much different than one that sits outside a bar or deli. Consider the city's size, time of year, type of businesses nearby, and the frequency of human or animal traffic in this area. Think about the debris likely to collect in this location, and the amount of lighting that might shine out of barred windows and from streetlights, and use these to create the mood you're going for.

SETTING DESCRIPTION EXAMPLE

The alley between Buck's Oil & Lube and The Bread Bowl was Alfred's favorite Saturday stop. Sure, the November wind howled like wolves trailing an injured deer, but hunkered under his newspaper-and-scraps blanket, he barely felt it. The bricks at his back were warm from the bakery ovens on the other side and yeast lay thick in the air, masking the usual stench of motor oil from the dumpster. Pulling his rough cap down over his eyes, he burrowed into his warm corner and imagined butter-glistening loaves fresh off the rack. Maybe he'd get lucky and Margaret would be working, and she'd bring him a bag of day-old buns with packets of raspberry jam.

Techniques and Devices Used: Contrast, multisensory descriptions, simile, weather
Resulting Effects: Characterization, establishing mood

BANK

SIGHTS
Glass entryway doors, mats on the glossy floors, security guards spaced out around the area, video cameras, a line of cashier wickets along one wall with a roped area to guide customers to the front of the line, a table with pens on a chain where deposit slips and forms are filled out, tellers (accessing counting machines and computers, drawers of cash and traveler's checks, filing cabinets, printers and fax machines, stamps and stamp pads, a paper shredder station, locked drawers, a debit machine), a pair of cash machines by the door or outside the entrance, signs on the wall displaying mortgage rates, a rate-of-exchange currency board, posters reminding clients to invest their money safely, a waiting area (with a coffee machine, magazines and plastic chairs), a floor manager behind a desk, offices for loans and investments, a hallway leading to a bank vault and safety deposit box room, tile flooring, large glass windows, trash bins, a long line (customers shifting foot-to-foot, people with wallets out, purses or cash deposit bags)

SOUNDS
The ruffle of paper as bills are counted by hand, the sound of the teller's voice as she rattles off amounts, the thunk of a stamp on paperwork, a teller calling out to the next customer in line, soft music in the background, coughing, people speaking in low voices, the gurgle and hiss of the coffee machine, feet shuffling in the lineup, doors and drawers opening and closing, the tap of keys on the keyboard, the scratch of a pen, a purse or deposit bag unzipping, a bank card being slapped on the counter, a receipt spitting out of a machine, the whir of the fax machine, heels clicking across the floor, the air conditioning or heat rumbling on

SMELLS
Cleaners (pine, lemon, ammonia), paper, warm electronics (a dusty, ozone-type scent), perfume or cologne mingling in the air, coffee, bad breath, food warmed up in an unseen break room, hair products

TASTES
Cheap candies from the bowl, mints, gum, water, coffee, tea, purchased sandwiches or food from home being eaten on a lunch break

TEXTURES AND SENSATIONS
Pushing open a heavy or sticky door, shifting one's weight while waiting, absently shuffling one's checks and deposit slips, the hard edge of a service counter pressing into one's ribs or forearms, struggling to use a pen that's secured to the counter with a too-short cord, crisp and stiff bills, bills that stick together and make it difficult to count them, a smooth receipt, angling one's body at the ATM machine to block the sun or shield the screen from others, the slice of a paper cut

POSSIBLE SOURCES OF CONFLICT
Money going missing due to a bank error
A bank machine eating a customer's card

Impatient, line-cutting customers

A holdup

A medical emergency (such as a customer who faints or has a seizure)

A security guard on a power trip

A teller's drawer being short of money at the end of the day

An aggressive bank employee pushing credit cards, loans, or other incentives on a customer

Forgetting one's PIN code or account number

A power outage that makes it impossible for a customer to withdraw money at a crucial time

Opening a safety deposit box to discover one's contents are missing

PEOPLE COMMONLY FOUND HERE

Bank robbers, bank workers, customers, delivery people, security personnel, security specialists making bank deposits or refilling bank machines with cash

SETTING NOTES AND TIPS

Banks will appear different based on size and the clientele being serviced. Big banks may have more security measures than a regular bank because they have greater amounts of money on hand. Some banks may also feature a drive-up service, by which customers can deposit checks or withdraw money.

SETTING DESCRIPTION EXAMPLE

My hat pulled low, I grabbed a white envelope from the table and gave my jacket a leisurely pat down as if searching for a pen. I clocked seven, no . . . eight cameras. Four tellers, but six wickets, so two might be on break. The bank manager was in his glassed-in office, and a loan officer sat next door, sorting paperwork that wheezed out of his asthmatic printer. Angled away from the nearest camera, I made a show of bending over the envelope, as if to write. After the hit, the cops would be sure to scroll through old footage, but they wouldn't give me a second thought if I appeared to be a customer like everyone else. While scribbling nonsense on the paper, I noticed a security guard near the entrance who rubbed at his chest as if it hurt. *Interesting.* He kept glancing down the left hall that, according to the schematics, led to the restroom. Classic afternoon heartburn. I smiled. My bet was he'd head down there for a drink, unknowingly creating the perfect opportunity for someone like me. Not that I'd act on it; this wasn't my first rodeo. Patience meant freedom. Today was about two things—making sure the lay of the land matched my blueprints, and getting an accurate headcount.

Techniques and Devices Used: Multisensory descriptions, personification

Resulting Effects: Foreshadowing, hinting at backstory

BIG CITY STREET

SIGHTS
Multi-lane traffic, stoplights, sidewalks packed with pedestrians (business professionals heading to meetings, shoppers weighed down by bags, older women dragging a dolly for their groceries, dog walkers, students with backpacks, friends heading out for coffee), dented trash cans, vehicles (honking cars, taxi cabs, delivery vans, police cars, buses), panhandlers, storefronts with security shutters or window alarms, graffiti, trash and cigarette butts gathering in gutters, cars parked along the curb, bus stops, uniformed doormen assisting patrons in and out of residential buildings or high-end hotels, fire hydrants, cab stands, light poles, store awnings, large chain stores, colorful food trucks and street vendors, upscale businesses and specialty stores, narrow alleyways, tall brick buildings with fire escapes, large signs on buses and buildings advertising businesses and products, entertainment flyers for special events papering light poles and electricity boxes, construction (scaffolding taking over sidewalks, security fencing, wood panels and tarps blocking access, cranes moving heavy materials, wooden walkways detouring around a site), street sweepers late at night, planted trees in the sidewalk, decorative lights strung up, buskers playing music and entertaining those passing by, menu stands and restaurant employees trying to entice people to come try the food

SOUNDS
Sirens, horns honking, people talking on their cell phones, the ping of crosswalk lights, delivery trucks beeping as they back up, brakes squealing, people swearing or yelling, heels clacking on the sidewalk, construction noise (jackhammers, air tools jittering and whining, heavy loads of lumber or pipe being dropped), the whoosh of a city bus speeding past

SMELLS
Pollution (car exhaust, motor oil, etc.), cooking oil from fast food fryer vats, coffee being brewed, sweat and body odor, perfume, wet concrete during a rainstorm

TASTES
Food and drink bought from street vendors, restaurants, cafés, and wine bars

TEXTURES AND SENSATIONS
Tired feet after a long day at work, being bumped and jarred by other people on the sidewalk, one's heel catching in a sidewalk crack or grate, being splashed by cold water from a car driving through a puddle, squeezing oneself through a busy coffeehouse doorway, the smooth handle of a cab door, the give of springs as one sits on a cab's seat, gripping tight to a purse strap to dissuade theft, mashing one's head against the shoulder to hold a phone in place and keep one's hands free, the cold drizzle of rain sliding down one's collar when one has forgotten an umbrella, the gritty pelt of dirt against one's face when a gust of wind carries dust from construction sites, exhaust burning one's throat and causing a coughing fit, the cold wind barreling between buildings

POSSIBLE SOURCES OF CONFLICT
One's purse being snatched
Getting lost in a big city
Being dropped off by a cab in the wrong location
Pickpockets
Food poisoning from poorly prepared street food
Being bumped and dropping one's phone or keys down a grate
Witnessing a crime or random act of violence
Losing a child in the rush of a busy street
Being double-parked
Getting a parking ticket
One's car getting trapped when other drivers parallel park too closely

PEOPLE COMMONLY FOUND HERE
Business owners, employees, homeless people, locals, police officers, taxi drivers, tourists

RELATED SETTINGS THAT MAY TIE IN WITH THIS ONE
Alley (34), art gallery (190), bank (36), bookstore (160), casual dining restaurant (140), city bus (256), coffeehouse (142), construction site (52), deli (144), fast food restaurant (148), parade (222), parking garage (100), police car (270), pub (152), taxi (280)

SETTING NOTES AND TIPS
The location of a street, as well as the time of year, will change the way it looks and feels. Some urban streets are walled by high-rises filled with Fortune 500 companies or expensive apartments; doormen can often be found on the sidewalks, waiting under fancy awnings to assist clients or apartment owners in and out of buildings. Other areas of a city may not be in a business district or prime real-estate area. They may even be located in an area where the buildings are older and crime is more prevalent. Also, some big cities have neighborhoods that are dominated by a specific ethnicity. Specialty stores and restaurants in this area will often cater to this specific group of people, adopting the colors, styles, and advertising that is common for that culture.

SETTING DESCRIPTION EXAMPLE
After a brutal three-hour meeting going over specs, I needed a break. I headed toward a latte stall near the start of Ratton Avenue's popular shopping district. Sunlight gleamed against the office windows, but the sidewalk was damp from an earlier storm, forcing me into a child's game of leapfrog over the pools of water. When the kids were little we'd had so much fun after the rain, jumping in puddles and scattering water with our matching red boots. I smiled. Those days were long past, but I drew in a deep, clean breath and for a moment, they were somehow here with me too.

   Techniques and Devices Used: Contrast, multisensory descriptions, weather
   Resulting Effects: Hinting at backstory, reinforcing emotion

BOARDROOM

SIGHTS
Plain colored walls (decorated with pictures of company leaders, logos, awards, plaques, and other markers of company pride and prosperity), a TV or media screen for presentations and virtual meetings, laptops, hookups for electronic equipment, an intercom and teleconferencing phone, comfortable chairs around an oblong or rectangular table, glasses and pitchers of ice water, pens and notepads with the company logo or a business motto, information portfolios or meeting materials in folders, a whiteboard or glass board for brainstorming and planning, bright overhead lighting, windows with a view of the landscape, microphones (if it's a large room), board members and support staff seated and ready to contribute, a few stylish personalization touches that work with the company's brand (a bamboo planter that represents prosperity, a feature painting that is a special landscape or modern art image, etc.)

SOUNDS
A loud voice on speakerphone, the whir of a fan inside a laptop or piece of media equipment, the steady drone of air conditioning, chairs creaking, people with heads close together speaking in low voices to discuss a side point, an open discussion between participants, papers rustling, the squeak and dab of a marker against a whiteboard, a cell phone that is quickly muted, the gurgle of water as it is poured into glasses, raised voices and a hand thumping against the table during heated discussions, pacing footsteps, team members standing up to stretch, a tap on the door as lunch or requested materials are delivered, the whoosh of chair's height being adjusted

SMELLS
Cologne, perfume, air freshener and cleaning supplies, hot food being brought in (during a lunchtime meeting), coffee

TASTES
Water, breath mints, gum, coffee, tea, food brought in for longer meetings (sandwiches, pizza, pastas, salads, cheese and fruit platters)

TEXTURES AND SENSATIONS
Sorting through meeting materials, fingers sliding over the smooth sheets of paper, leaning back in a plush chair, air from the air conditioner or heating moving over one's skin, the cold condensation on a glass or water bottle, a pen gliding over paper as one signs a contract, swiping a phone screen or tablet to set a reminder or to access one's calendar, sound-muffling carpet underfoot, kinks in the neck or shoulders from sitting too long, rolling back and forth in a chair, the glare of the afternoon sun shining through the window and into one's eyes, sweating from sitting in direct sunlight

POSSIBLE SOURCES OF CONFLICT
Financial troubles
Insider trading being revealed

Firing a board member

Disagreements about the company's direction

Personal conflicts entering the workplace

An office romance gone bad

Employees jockeying for position

Being pressured to agree to things that one morally opposes

Struggling with maintaining a healthy work-home balance

Having to deliver an important presentation and feeling unprepared

Being undermined by rivals

PEOPLE COMMONLY FOUND HERE

Accountants, business owners and shareholders, company management, interns and support staff, people making reports or advising (department heads, lawyers, management consultants hired by the company)

RELATED SETTINGS THAT MAY TIE IN WITH THIS ONE

Elevator (56), office cubicle (96)

SETTING NOTES AND TIPS

Boardrooms will often fit the style of the business. A creative-focused company would probably have a decorative or relaxed atmosphere whereas a more serious firm, such as a law office, might be more traditional in style. One thing to consider is whether clients use the boardroom space or if it is just for company employees. If it's the former, the space will likely reflect a vibe of professionalism and success in order to reinforce client confidence.

SETTING DESCRIPTION EXAMPLE

A blue folder, a pen, and a glass sat in front of each chair, perfectly square and spaced—a sure sign that Glen with his OCD-like tendencies had been the one to set up the room. Besides, the cloying weight of his cologne in the air was unmissable. Someone really ought to have a word with him about less being more—someone other than Andrea herself, since she had no patience for people with zero common sense. Like her manager, and these stupid mandatory safety meetings of his. Why did a property management firm need to talk about Christmas light safety, or hear statistics about speed-related auto accidents? Good grief, that's what Google was for. Each one of these meetings made her want to throw herself out the window.

    Techniques and Devices Used: Hyperbole, multisensory descriptions

    Resulting Effects: Characterization, reinforcing emotion

CAR ACCIDENT

SIGHTS

During: a car in one's lane or a barrier approaching, the frightened faces of the people in the oncoming vehicle right before impact, hoods crumpling, glass fracturing, passengers being thrown forward in their seats, airbags deploying in white clouds, each moment in time cut into small flashes rather than a conscious stream

Aftermath: broken glass, the cars involved parked at odd angles, vehicles that are smashed and crumpled, the strobe of police lights, smoke and steam, chunks of twisted metal or plastic, shattered windshields, emergency vehicles (police cars, a fire truck, an ambulance, a tow truck), paramedics and firefighters kneeling beside trapped people in cars or stabilizing victims for transport, policemen with bright flak jackets (securing the scene with yellow tape, creating barricades, redirecting traffic, interviewing witnesses and taking statements), a crowd of onlookers, a rubbernecker holding up a phone to record the scene, smears of blood and bandages, pooling liquid (coolant, gas, oil), medical bags and gurneys, cars parked along the highway, deployed airbags, removed car doors lying on the pavement, air paramedics in a helicopter, fires being put out with the blast of foam extinguishers, jerky flashlight beams and car headlights lighting the scene and backlighting smoke at night, broken guardrails or snapped trees, branches scattered on the ground

SOUNDS

During: tires screeching, horns blasting, brakes grinding, gasps and screams, seat belts snapping taut, the crunch of metal, glass shattering, thumps as people and objects are tossed about, the snap of trees or signs, the screech of metal sliding along a barricade

Aftermath: the hiss of liquid spilling across a hot engine, other cars skidding to avoid a collision or braking to a stop so they can help, the engine pinging as it cools, shattered glass falling to the ground as victims begin to stir, people banging on the glass and calling out to see if the victim is all right, ringing in the victim's ears, panicked fast breaths, crying, moaning, screaming, a crackle as flames blossom, blistering paint and heating metal, coughing as toxic smoke rushes into the cab, broken glass and bits of metal being ground into the asphalt as a victim slithers out of an upside-down car through a broken window

SMELLS

Spilled gasoline, burned rubber, oil and other motor fluids, smoke, blood

TASTES

Blood, tears

TEXTURES AND SENSATIONS

During: stiffening one's arms against the steering wheel and pressing back into the seat, the jerk of the seat belt strap against one's chest or hips, being tossed side to side, bashing one's head and side against the door, the snap of a head whipping back and forth, bruising pain as one is pelted with objects inside the car (purses, bags, pets, and anything else which is loose), going stiff all over to brace for impact, a spray of chemical dust in the face as the airbag deploys, being thrust back by the force of an airbag

Aftermath: growing slowly aware of where one is and feeling numb with shock, the sensation of time running slow and thoughts fogging, disorientation, growing conscious of pain from a million cuts and bruises or a major injury point (a concussion, a pinned or broken limb, a piece of the car penetrating flesh), intense fear and worry over others who are in the car, trying to move and being unable to do so, building frustration and panic, blood dripping along one's skin or gushing from an arterial wound, the uncontrolled shivering that accompanies shock

POSSIBLE SOURCES OF CONFLICT
A fire starting in one of the cars
Toxic smoke filling the cab of a vehicle
Broken bones that leave a survivor immobile
Having an injured loved one (especially a child) in the backseat and being unable to reach or see them
Waking in a vehicle with dead passengers

PEOPLE COMMONLY FOUND HERE
Bystanders, fire and rescue teams, media crews, paramedics, police officers, victims

RELATED SETTINGS THAT MAY TIE IN WITH THIS ONE
Rural Volume: Country road (156)
Urban Volume: Ambulance (254), big city street (38), emergency room (58), hospital room (76), police car (270), police station (106), small town street (120)

SETTING NOTES AND TIPS
Minor car accidents may not involve the police or paramedics; these responders usually only are brought in if a person is hurt or the damage reaches a certain threshold. Keep in mind that the sensory detail should be tailored to the viewpoint of the narrator or point-of-view character. Also, characters will notice different things depending on who they are in the scene. A bystander will notice details about a car accident that the victim will not, and vice versa. Police officers also tend to be observant by nature and will pick up on things that others will miss.

SETTING DESCRIPTION EXAMPLE
Mary woke in the darkness, ears ringing and thoughts dull. *Where…?* Smoke rolled in through a hole in the windshield and she gagged at its oily stench. She twisted, trying to get away from it, but something pinned her in place. Pain flared in her shoulder and hip, bringing with it a flash: a truck skidding, its trailer fishtailing into her lane, the map of terror on the driver's face as his rig slid close. Her foot punching the brake, a scream ripping at her ears. *A car accident.* She tried to call for help, but all that came out was a sob.

Techniques and Devices Used: Light and shadow, metaphor, multisensory descriptions, tension and conflict

Resulting Effects: Establishing mood, hinting at backstory, reinforcing emotion

CAR WASH

SIGHTS

Drive-up bays, corrugated metal walls or plastic splash curtains between the bays, wet concrete, flashing green and red lights, a ticket booth with an attendant or an automated pay portal for transactions, high ceilings and florescent lighting, pools of suds, spraying wands and brushes dispensing soap and water, iridescent-water that shimmers as chemicals are carried toward floor drains and grates, wall clips for spraying floor mats, mist-laden air, dirt and clumps of mud sloughing off vehicles, dull chrome and hazy headlights becoming bright once more, light that glimmers off clean paint, garbage bins, small bits of paper debris and gravel littering the floor or being caught in the drain, waxing tools, water pooling in low spots on the concrete, a flash of brake lights coming on as a person prepares to drive out, vehicles exiting and parking outside so they can be wiped down or vacuumed

SOUNDS

The blast of a sprayer, automatic doors rising and lowering, the ding of a timer going off on the soap dispenser, echoing voices as parents yell at their kids to close the window or door, the splat and plop of suds and dirt sliding down the car and landing on the concrete, dripping water, the gurgle of the drainage system, cars shutting off and then firing up again, receipt tape chattering out of an automatic pay portal, a glass window sliding open as people drive through to pay an attendant, doors and tailgates clicking open and shut, the splash of water as one steps or drives through a puddle, the clank of a floor grate as a car drives over it

SMELLS

Moist air, water, soapy chemicals and hot wax, mildew, wet concrete, exhaust fumes

TASTES

No tastes are associated with this setting. But since many car washes are attached to gas stations, occupants of the vehicle may stop to pick up a drink or snack on the way in or out.

TEXTURES AND SENSATIONS

Water spraying the skin, wet cuffs, water and soap sliding down a forearm, twisting the timer for a soap or wax dispenser, the weight of the spraying wand, the side to side motion of waving it to rinse, scrubbing at the windows with a brush, wet feet (if wearing flip-flops), re-gripping a slippery handle, soap suds that drip on one's feet if standing too close to the car, a blob of suds sliding off the vehicle onto one's hand, digging into one's pocket for keys or money, pulling on a wet car handle, a neighbor's careless sprayer handling resulting in a shot of water to the face or back

POSSIBLE SOURCES OF CONFLICT

Chemicals or poor equipment maintenance that damages or scratches one's paint job
A car that refuses to start after the washing is complete
Something disturbing falling out of the front grill as one hoses it off (a bloody dog collar, a clot of hair)

Running into a rival while using the car wash
Locking oneself out of the car

PEOPLE COMMONLY FOUND HERE
Employees (attendants and maintenance personnel), the car wash manager, vehicle owners and their passengers

RELATED SETTINGS THAT MAY TIE IN WITH THIS ONE
Convenience store (162), gas station (70), old pick-up truck (268), parking lot (102)

SETTING NOTES AND TIPS
Manual car washes may look different depending on how old they are, and whether they are a standalone business or belong with a gas station. Some may have a drive-in lane system where one pays and then waits for a single roll-up door to open as a bay inside empties. Others will have bays that stretch out in a row, and a vehicle simply chooses an empty stall and drives in, or waits for the current vehicle using it to vacate. Some car washes will have attendants washing the cars and others will not. Still more may run on a coin-operated system and have change machines nearby. As the author, you are in control, so design your setting in a way that will further the plot events or provide conflict opportunities for your scene.

For example, if two rivals are to meet up inside and conflict ensues, a car wash with many bays and hard plastic spray curtains between stalls will provide better access and therefore more opportunity for clashing. One character could block another's vehicle from exiting to anger them, key their car when their attention is elsewhere or even plant something incriminating inside the victim's car.

SETTING DESCRIPTION EXAMPLE
Trevor pulled up in his Z-28, but the bay was occupied so he shifted into neutral and cranked up the tunes. Ahead, some old guy was hosing down his hummer, throwing up gouts of spray. The dirt sloughed off, giving way to bright red paint. Globs of mud and gravel fell from the bumper in giant clumps and Trevor nodded, impressed. He had to give Grandpa here props; wherever he'd gone off-roading in between his old people routine of dropping kids at daycare and working a 9-to-5er, he'd managed to bring half the mountain back with him.
　　Techniques and Devices Used: Contrast, hyperbole
　　Resulting Effects: Characterization

CHEAP MOTEL

SIGHTS

External: a vacancy sign that only partly lights up, a marquee advertising rooms for rent by the hour, a single- or double-story building, peeling paint on the exterior, windows with cloudy corners, lights that don't work, external staircases, overgrown hedges and withered plants, uneven sidewalks with grass growing through the cracks, trash blown against the curb and littering the parking lot, seedy-looking characters coming and going at all hours, people sitting outside the rooms in plastic chairs

Internal: low ceilings, threadbare and stained carpets, doors that don't open smoothly, multiple locks on the inside of the door, mismatched furniture, tables with water stains and cigarette burns, thin coverlets and lumpy pillows, walls with bubbling or peeling wallpaper, dim lighting, ash trays, air conditioning units that don't work properly, a TV that's secured to the wall, outdated lighting fixtures and décor, dripping faucets, discolored ceiling tiles from a past leak, a sink with rust stains in the basin, a warped or foggy mirror, exposed plumbing in the bathroom, cracked tiles with dirty grout lines, skimpy towels, a grungy shower curtain, a room lacking the usual hotel compliments (shampoo, lotion, a hair dryer, an iron, a remote control), a line of ants traveling up a wall, rat or mouse droppings

SOUNDS

The creak of a door as it opens, sounds coming through the thin walls (a neighbor's television, voices, traffic), the ring of a telephone, people having sex, neighbors fighting, crying babies, barking dogs, traffic from the nearby highway or interstate, people knocking on doors, a squeaky bed, the constant drip of a leaky faucet, clanking pipes, a toilet that runs loudly, footsteps passing by outside, a rattling radiator or air conditioning unit, the hum of overhanging power lines, the intermittent buzz of a neon light that's on the fritz, the whine of mosquitoes

SMELLS

Must, mold and mildew, dust, stale cigarette smoke, old carpet, takeout or delivery food smells (pizza, burgers and fries), animal fur

TASTES

Greasy takeout or delivery food, old musty air that tastes foul, junk food and snacks from a vending machine

TEXTURES AND SENSATIONS

A lukewarm or cold shower, a lumpy or hard mattress, scratchy bed linens, tossing and turning due to an inability to get comfortable or fall asleep, itchy bedbug bites, sweat dampening the hair due to a broken air conditioner, huddling or curling up to keep warm when the radiator stops working, rough towels, the bite of a mosquito, drafts blowing in through poorly sealed doors or windows, a carpet that feels greasy under one's bare feet, knocking one's head on a low-hanging light

POSSIBLE SOURCES OF CONFLICT

Being assaulted or spied on

Being a germaphobe

Discovering that one has no money after checking in

Being solicited by a prostitute

A door that won't lock

Having to sneak one's pet into a motel where animals aren't allowed

Having loud neighbors

A room that's uncomfortably hot or cold

Having to take cold showers

Difficulty falling asleep due to all the noises

Working at a motel where illegal activities are going on

Needing to protect one's children from the seedy characters who frequent the motel

PEOPLE COMMONLY FOUND HERE

Cleaning staff, desk clerks, drug dealers, loiterers, motel guests, pizza delivery people, prostitutes

RELATED SETTINGS THAT MAY TIE IN WITH THIS ONE

Convenience store (162), fast food restaurant (148), old pick-up truck (268), truck stop (284)

SETTING NOTES AND TIPS

Motels differ from hotels in that motels were initially created to provide lodging to motorists, so they're often found along highways and near tourist attractions. Hotels tend to be larger and offer more amenities and services, such as room service and a pool.

SETTING DESCRIPTION EXAMPLE

John woke, skinned in sweat. The room was musty and warm—much warmer than the humid spring day outside. He clambered out of bed, wincing as the springs shrieked. The ancient dragon of an air conditioner squatted silently in the semi-dark. John approached it and punched a button. He turned knobs. Finally he kicked the side of it and while it didn't turn on, an impressive plume of dust blasted out. He sneezed, loud enough to send a roach skittering up the wall and behind a loose heating vent. Clearly, he'd picked the Taj Mahal of motels.

Techniques and Devices Used: Contrast, metaphor, multisensory descriptions

Resulting Effects: Establishing mood

COMMUNITY CENTER

SIGHTS
A parking lot filled with cars, a large field (for playing soccer, flying kites, and games of tag), a double-door entranceway, parents dropping kids off for programs (scout meetings, robotics club, a babysitting course, youth group events), large rooms with skylights and windows, kitchen facilities, a large meeting room (with folding tables and stackable chairs, a sound system, tile floors) that can be decorated for various events (wedding receptions, community meetings, youth dances, Christmas parties, family reunions, swap meets), a management office where organizers work (running the center on a day-to-day basis, renting out hall space, setting up meetings), a cloak room, a bulletin board where community news is posted, flyers advertising upcoming events and fundraisers (such as a community garage sale, a bottle drive, a pancake breakfast, movie night in the park), restrooms, a youth lounge (with old couches and armchairs, a pool table or foosball table, TV, and board games stacked on a shelf), moms and toddlers showing up for a playgroup, a yoga class setting out mats and running through warm-up stretches, storage rooms (to hold folding tables and chairs, custodial items, artificial plants, sound equipment)

SOUNDS
A heated discussion in a meeting room, sounds of hammering and wood pieces dropping as a scout troop builds wooden derby cars, children talking and laughing during an afterschool program, people calling out directions to helpers as they set up the center for a dance, a Master of Ceremonies giving a speech to the bride and groom at a wedding reception, the sound of a hanger scraping a rod in the cloak room, phones ringing in the office, toilets flushing, the trickle of water at a drinking fountain, shoes squeaking on the floor, the flutter of papers on the community board when the door is opened and a breeze gusts in, muffled outdoor noises (cars pulling in and out of the parking lot, parents yelling to kids, a basketball bouncing on an outdoor court)

SMELLS
Coffee brewing, food smells (if an event has been catered or the group is using the kitchen to prepare food), the musty smell of an older building

TASTES
Water from the drinking fountain, refreshments served by groups renting the hall, coffee, tea, heated meals from home in the employee and volunteer breakroom

TEXTURES AND SENSATIONS
Holding a phone to one's ear while checking the community calendar for room availability, wind fluttering one's clothes when a draft sneaks through an open door, the rhythmic sweep of a broom as one cleans up after a fiftieth wedding anniversary dinner, wadding up tablecloths to take them to the cleaners, manhandling tables onto their side to collapse the legs for storage, shoes slipping on a wet tile floor on a rainy day, lounging on an old sofa in the youth room, hefting decorations out of a storage closet for an upcoming event, dust from old décor making one sneeze

POSSIBLE SOURCES OF CONFLICT

Groups that rent a room and then don't show up or refuse to pay

Vandalism (broken windows, graffiti-sprayed walls, ruined landscaping) that will cost valuable community funds to fix

Financial issues that limit the center's capabilities

Having a huge demand for programming yet few people willing to volunteer their time

The center being used as an emergency shelter with not enough space to service the population

A hall space being double-booked

PEOPLE COMMONLY FOUND HERE

Building employees, community members, kids, maintenance and janitorial staff, organizers and members of special groups using the space to host events and hold meetings, teens

RELATED SETTINGS THAT MAY TIE IN WITH THIS ONE

Rural Volume: Church (154), gymnasium (114), wedding reception (192)

Urban Volume: Outdoor pool (218), outdoor skating rink (220), parking lot (102), rec center (230)

SETTING NOTES AND TIPS

The size and condition of a community hall will depend a lot on the affluent nature of its residents. A poorer community will have a smaller space and fewer amenities than a trendy community filled with multi-million dollar homes. However, big or small, community centers are hotspots for all sorts of local activity where people in the community can run into one another—even if they'd rather not. An ex-husband with a new girlfriend, a group of bullies from school, even that creepy neighbor down the block are all drawn in by local meetings and events, which can lead to glorious friction, fireworks, and explosions. When choosing this setting, ask yourself how you can use a space owned by everyone to either bring people together or set them at one another's throats.

SETTING DESCRIPTION EXAMPLE

When Leroy had gone with his toolbox, Carla got up from her desk and walked to Evanwood, the smallest of the three halls up for rent. The room was quiet, the lights off, the floors neatly swept. This was the favorite space of the Orchid Group, a yoga studio that held classes here once a week. They'd been long-time renters, but lately they'd taken to turning up the heat until it was a blistering fire pit so the gals could enjoy a hot yoga session. Carla didn't know what was worse—the heating bill or the dead body smell that took days to air out. She smiled at Leroy's handiwork: a clear plastic box covering the thermostat. That was the end of that little problem. If only balancing the books had such an easy fix.

Techniques and Devices Used: Metaphor, multisensory descriptions

Resulting Effects: Characterization, hinting at backstory, tension and conflict

CONDEMNED APARTMENT BUILDING

SIGHTS
Crusty paint peels and rippled wallpaper, colorful graffiti (tags, pictures, racial slurs, random numbers and messages), floors strewn with litter (broken drywall and glass, empty beer cans, alcohol bottles, trash, rags, old dirty mattresses, cigarette butts, used needles), ragged holes in the walls bleeding mouse-chewed insulation, broken plaster, doors hanging from broken hinges, rats or mice skittering through debris, squatters using the space to sleep or party, trash-covered stairwells, rusty or dented mailboxes near the entrance, spiderwebs hanging off old light fixtures, a broken elevator, exposed pipes and loops of loose wiring hanging through holes in the ceiling, torn-up flooring, old chewed rugs or carpet, dirty windows (missing panes, with rusted grates, or with boards over them), condom wrappers, crumbled brick and other rubble, yellowed newspaper and smashed mirrors, dirty toilets, refuse-filled bathtubs, dirt smudges and footprints on the walls from a previous occupant's kicking, broken furniture, abandoned personal items (such as broken vacuums, smashed TV sets, mugs, appliances, ugly paintings hanging askew or lying on the floor, magazines, an old couch or chair missing its cushions), wall vents furry with dust, cupboard doors hanging open, shelves covered in rat feces and dead flies, holes in the walls that provide a view into the next room, dirt-streaked stairwells, exposed rebar, missing light switches and doorknobs, drawers open or missing, cockroaches, smashed bookcases and counters, dead animal skeletons, abandoned nests, rot and black mildew splotches on the walls, weeds growing on window ledges and balconies

SOUNDS
Doors that creak when they're pushed open, the wind whistling through broken window panes, flies buzzing, rats or mice chewing insulation and skittering behind the walls, the crunch of glass and debris underfoot, voices from people within, groans and creaks from the building, footsteps crossing the floor above, someone nearby smashing the walls or dragging furniture, water dripping during a storm, traffic noises from outside

SMELLS
Rotten carpet, mildew, musty cushions and fabric, dirt, pot being smoked, urine and feces, body odor, dead things, wet dog fur, a rancid smell from the fridge

TASTES
The burn of cheap alcohol, the pull of smoke into one's lungs, the acrid and bitter taste of chemicals or drugs being huffed to get high, cheap fast food, food dug out of dumpsters, dusty air

TEXTURES AND SENSATIONS
Taking careful steps through a room scattered with broken furniture and pieces of plaster, glass crunching underfoot, dust from a countertop coating one's fingers and streaking one's clothing, slamming a length of wood or pipe into an old couch to see if anything is nesting inside, sleeping on a threadbare bed of rags and old cushions, shoving a door open with one's shoulder, the slight

give of a soft spot in the floor as one steps on it, the squish of soaked carpet that has been exposed to the elements, a rusty fire escape railing, a fire escape that shifts and sways under one's weight, a cold draft sliding in through a broken window and chilling one's skin

POSSIBLE SOURCES OF CONFLICT

The state of the building becoming dangerous (floors that give way, stairwells that are crumbling and rickety)

Discovering something disturbing inside (blood, a dead body, signs of a blood ritual)

The building being in disputed gang territory, putting those who use it in jeopardy

Being attacked by someone while inside

Hearing a baby crying

Injuring oneself in a fall and not being able to get help

Experiencing something paranormal while inside

Police officers showing up frequently to toss squatters out of the building

PEOPLE COMMONLY FOUND HERE

Building inspectors, drug users, firefighters, gangs, paramedics, police, squatters

RELATED SETTINGS THAT MAY TIE IN WITH THIS ONE

Alley (34), ambulance (254), homeless shelter (74), police car (270), run-down apartment (116)

SETTING NOTES AND TIPS

The level of decay will depend on how long the building has been abandoned and whether it was closed up properly before it became condemned (boarded up windows, doors that were chained shut, water pipes emptied, etc.). Anything of value will likely have been looted and removed, but it's always possible that an unusual item might be found squirrelled away in one of the rooms. Condemned buildings often become crack houses, where strangers will come to buy, sell, and share drugs, and then get high together; this gathering of desperate people with little to lose can create a volatile environment for your characters.

SETTING DESCRIPTION EXAMPLE

Weak, tea-stained light lit the stairwell and debris clouded the steps. I picked a path through the litter and rat feces, avoiding the wires spilling from the broken wall like a corpse's innards. Every few steps I would stop and listen, praying to hear nothing but building creaks and loose paper shifting in the drafts. Empty, these old buildings made a good place to get some rest, but rarely were they vacant. And all too often others would come, not to sleep, but to use the rooms and anyone in them as a destructive release.

Techniques and Devices Used: Light and shadow, multisensory descriptions, simile

Resulting Effects: Establishing mood, tension and conflict

CONSTRUCTION SITE

SIGHTS
Support columns and rebar sticking out of cement, stacks of lumber, steel-framed walls, sheets of plastic and tarps covering supplies or walling off dangerous areas, rented dumpsters, workers (in flak jackets and steel-toed boots, wearing safety glasses, ear protection and hardhats), a portable office trailer (for bigger construction sites), sheets of plasterboard, tables, bags of cement, sawhorses, stacks of PVC pipe, coils of hose and electrical wire, spools of rubber or plastic tubing, paint-splattered scaffolding that climbs up the structure's side, an expandable garbage chute dropping into a dumpster, wood pallets (loaded with cinderblock, pipe, and roofing materials), dollies, small forklifts, new windows with stickers attached, duct and venting systems, ladders, railings, tar paper, a cement mixer, sanders, table saws, air compressors, wheelbarrows, large equipment (cranes, dump trucks, flatbed trucks delivering supplies, bulldozers), chemical toilets, gravel piles, buckets, tool chests, diagnostic and mechanical equipment, debris (nails, tags, stickers, ripped plastic sheeting, roofing paper, flattened cardboard boxes, water bottles, lumber ends, sawdust), a fence surrounding the site, safety signs, inspectors touring the site and making sure workers follow protocol

SOUNDS
The chug of heavy equipment engines, a back-up sensor beeping, the whine of air compressors and drills, hammers banging, a nail gun methodically thudding, boots clanking up metal staircases and clomping across wooden scaffold platforms, music drifting from a worker's radio inside the structure, the high-pitched grinding of a saw cutting wood, a measuring tape retracting, blueprint plans being furled or unfurled, wind causing plastic sheeting and tarps to flap, construction workers yelling, the clang of metal on metal, lumber or piping being dropped, the hiss of gas from a lit torch, jack hammers busting up concrete, the creak of wood and wire as support beams are lifted into the air, ringing in the ears, the wet plop of concrete being poured, backhoes scraping through the dirt

SMELLS
Fresh-cut lumber, dirt and dust, burning plastic, smoke, vehicle exhaust, sawdust, the chalky scent of cut plasterboard and spackle, chemicals, glues and paint, body odor, cigarette smoke, overheating motors from electrical tools and equipment, metal, cement

TASTES
Some settings have no specific tastes associated with them beyond what the character might bring into the scene (chewing gum, coffee, cigarettes, etc.). For scenes like these, where specific tastes are sparse, it would be best to stick to descriptors from the other four senses.

TEXTURES AND SENSATIONS
Ear protectors mashing against one's safety glasses, squinting to see through smudged glasses, sweat and dirt on the skin, the heat of a hardhat on a hot day, thick gloves rubbing against calluses and blisters, accidentally bashing a finger with one's hammer, a jackhammer sending a

quaking vibration throughout one's body, slivers, cuts and scrapes, wiping sweat from a brow or the back of the neck, the vibration or jerk of air-powered tools or motorized equipment (cranes, forklifts, flatbed trucks, dump trucks, haulers), the weight of carrying an awkward or heavy load, sawdust covering a fresh cut of lumber, a measuring tape sliding through one's fingers, maneuvering a level into place, the give of a shovel as it digs into mud or gravel, aches and pain that come with demanding physical labor, the balanced feel of a full tool belt slung around one's hips

POSSIBLE SOURCES OF CONFLICT

Theft at the construction site
An injury or death onsite
Poor planning leading to a partial collapse
Rainfall flooding the site and ruining the foundation or equipment
An employer being caught altering the financial records
Digging the foundation and discovering human bones
Mistakes that affect one's deadline

PEOPLE COMMONLY FOUND HERE

Construction workers, developers, engineers, food truck vendors, safety and building inspectors, truck and heavy equipment operators

RELATED SETTINGS THAT MAY TIE IN WITH THIS ONE

Rural Volume: Landfill (168)
Urban Volume: Old pick-up truck (268)

SETTING NOTES AND TIPS

Construction sites are highly specific to the type of project. The construction site of a new bridge will have different equipment and supplies than the site of a house being built, or even a hospital. There also might be a lot of "sprawl" onsite if the area is large, but operations tend to be more space-conscious within the city.

SETTING DESCRIPTION EXAMPLE

Randy arrived early, his coffee steaming in the morning air. With the electrical crew rushing to make deadline the night before, he expected a mess of wire and plastic sheaths onsite. Instead he found crushed beer cans, red paintball marks all over the plasterboard, two chunky puddles of vomit, and an exploded chemical toilet. His coffee dropped at the sight of the Big Blue Turd on its side with a giant hole blasted out the bottom. Its lifeblood, sewage and chemicals, seeped into the gravel and chunks of blue plastic and feces covered a stack of windows awaiting install. Randy's hands twitched with the desire to choke something. Not only was this going to be an expensive clean up, but the BBT had serviced too many jobs to deserve such a violent end.

Techniques and Devices Used: Multisensory descriptions, personification
Resulting Effects: Establishing mood, passage of time, reinforcing emotion, tension and conflict

COURTROOM

SIGHTS
Gleaming polished wood (paneled walls, the bench and witness stand, chairs, tables, doors, lectern), a small desk for the court reporter and court clerk, the bar (a wooden railing or barrier separating the proceedings from the gallery benches), a jury box off to the side filled with jurors, a black-robed judge wielding a gavel, a bailiff standing at attention to keep order, desk microphones, reporters, camera crews (in high-profile cases, unless the proceedings are closed), a witness box, federal and state flags, a clock on the wall, tagged bags of evidence, posters or slideshows that detail aspects of the scene, crime scene photos, closed circuit television, desks for the plaintiff and the defendant, a door leading to the judge's chamber, a wide central corridor in the gallery seating area for the witnesses to be brought down, highly secure windows (or none at all), files and paperwork, laptops, a projector and screen, video courtroom testimony, an easel for presenting evidence, remotes for audio equipment, well-dressed lawyers pleading their cases, family members and friends in the gallery (clutching hands tightly, holding onto purses, covering their mouths, crying, nervously fingering jewelry, listening intently), members of the public and law students observing the proceedings and taking notes

SOUNDS
Fans, the whooshing sound of air conditioning or heaters, gurgling pipes in the walls, traffic or sirens outside, people shifting in seats, wooden chairs and benches creaking, the rustle of papers, testimony being given, footsteps across the polished floor as the prosecutor or defense attorney addresses the court and questions witnesses, throat clearing, coughing, sniffing and quiet sobbing, the clink of chains if the defendant is secured by ankle cuffs, feedback from the microphones, a creaky gate in the bar, the rustle of fabric, audio evidence (taped phone calls, a security video, a 911 call), whispering, the judge's pounding gavel, the gentle tapping of keys from the court reporter's box, reactive gasps at evidence or testimony, doors opening and closing

SMELLS
Treated wood (lacquer, polishes, varnish), pine or lemon cleaner, stale air and closed room smells (sweat, perfume, hair products and cologne all mingling in the air), a neighbor's coffee breath, overheating electronics

TASTES
Water, tears, mints, a dry mouth, cough drops

TEXTURES AND SENSATIONS
A hard wooden seat, arms brushing against spectators seated to either side, a crumpled tissue held in a tight fist, nervous gestures (fiddling with a key fob, zipper tab, watch, a piece of jewelry), tells that indicate one's emotional state (clenching one's hands, fingernails biting into one's palms, rubbing at one's face, pinching the bridge of the nose, wiping at tears, biting a lip, shaking extremities, rigid posture that leads to tight muscles and a sore neck), a hard wooden floor underfoot as one walks to the witness stand, metal cuffs that irritate one's wrists, a flush creeping

up one's skin at the realization that an entire courtroom is watching, sorting through papers and files, the tight cling of plastic gloves when handling evidence, rolling a pen between one's fingers, a cold glass in one's palm, sweat dripping down one's back and sides in an airless courtroom, crossing and uncrossing one's legs, fingering a cherished item in one's pocket, squeezing a loved one's hands as the verdict is read, the shoulders dropping and a heaviness in the stomach as a guilty verdict is read, a lightening sensation in the chest as a loved one is exonerated

POSSIBLE SOURCES OF CONFLICT
A hung jury
Antagonistic witnesses
A biased judge
Escape attempts
A victim responding angrily or violently when justice is not served
Witnesses who commit perjury
A bomb or chemical threat
Power outages

PEOPLE COMMONLY FOUND HERE
Court recorders, criminals, judges, jury members, law students and other members of the public, lawyers, police officers, psychologists or field experts called in to give testimony, reporters, security personnel, victims and their family members, witnesses

RELATED SETTINGS THAT MAY TIE IN WITH THIS ONE
Juvenile detention center (80), police car (270), police station (106), prison cell (108)

SETTING NOTES AND TIPS
The size of a courthouse and the type of proceedings the room typically handles will influence the setting. For example, a courthouse used to hearing high-profile cases for capital offences may actually have bulletproof boxes for the accused, as well as enhanced security. This would differ from a small town courthouse that typically deals with smaller, misdemeanor offences.

SETTING DESCRIPTION EXAMPLE
In the gallery, watchers grew quiet, their fans going still in the humid air as Ellis Laruso entered the prisoner's box. He flashed a smile as bright as his orange jumpsuit and around the room, heads shook and hands covered mouths to catch sobs. This young man, the governor's son from Kentucky who poisoned an elementary school's drinking water, was a monster.
    Techniques and Devices Used: Contrast, simile
    Resulting Effects: Characterization, tension and conflict

ELEVATOR

SIGHTS
Metal doors, poster ads or special event notices behind glass, an occupancy notice, the latest inspection report, bright overhead lights with plastic panel covers, smudges and fingerprints on the walls, small bits of debris on the floor (crumpled gum wrappers, dirt, pea gravel), a sanitizer dispenser right outside the entrance, an operation panel with buttons that light up when pushed, a red emergency stop button, a slot for a key, a handrail, speakers in the ceiling or side walls, an emergency intercom button, a false grate or metal slot roof, an emergency escape panel, passengers pretending to ignore one another (checking watches or cell phones, staring up at the digital readout, moving toward the front as the elevator gets close to their floor), mothers with baby strollers or travelers with suitcases that take up most of the space, a sign that states the maximum weight load

SOUNDS
Metal rubbing against metal, squeals and squeaks, hydraulics pressing the doors shut, the crackle of the intercom, music from speakers, squeaky brakes squeezing the elevator's wires, the car shuddering and jerking as it slows, a metallic hum of machinery, people coughing, rustling clothing and jackets, people requesting that a certain floor number be pushed, small talk, a *bing* sound as the floor is reached, people apologizing as they make their way out of the elevator, the shriek of an alarm as the emergency button is pushed, feet shuffling as people step back to make room for more passengers

SMELLS
Wet or dirty mats on the floor, a collage of hygiene products (perfume, body spray, hairspray, aftershave) trapped in a tiny room, stale cigarette smoke clinging to a smoker's clothing, dirty diaper smells from babies in strollers, cough drops or mints, bad breath or beer breath, the astringent scent of hand sanitizer as someone rubs some on their hands, sweat or body odor, cleaning products, savory or greasy smells coming from takeout food containers being delivered, coffee in someone's to-go cup

TASTES
Gum, candies, cough drops, pop, coffee, iced drinks, juice or water brought into the elevator, snacks being munched

TEXTURES AND SENSATIONS
Smooth buttons, leaning into the wall to make room for others, holding one's breath or pressing one's arms close to the sides in order to take up less space on a crowded elevator, a metal handrail, shying away from the grimy walls, tipping one's head back to watch the floor numbers change, being jolted off-balance by a shuddering elevator, being hyper-aware of the distance between oneself and others, someone's breath stirring one's hair or landing on the back of one's neck, arms that grow tired from holding one's items during a long elevator ride, rolling a stroller back and forth to soothe a fussy baby, the rubber bumpers gently closing on one's hand as someone tries to stop them from closing

POSSIBLE SOURCES OF CONFLICT

A power outage that stops the elevator between floors

An elevator malfunction

A fire in the building

Being in the elevator with someone who makes one feel unsafe (by ranting, growing violent, staring or getting too close, asking inappropriate questions, arguing with himself)

People making out in the elevator

A screaming child

Kids being rowdy

Other passengers being disrespectful of one's personal space

Entering an elevator and coming face-to-face with someone one has been avoiding

PEOPLE COMMONLY FOUND HERE

Building security, business men and women, cleaning staff, customers, delivery people, people who live or are staying in the building

RELATED SETTINGS THAT MAY TIE IN WITH THIS ONE

Boardroom (40), office cubicle (96), hospital room (76), run-down apartment (116)

SETTING NOTES AND TIPS

Some elevators may be monitored by camera, especially in high-profile or security-enforced buildings. Some of these cameras may be actually recording, while others are just for show. Elevators may also have glass walls and can differ in size depending on how they are being used. Some are larger and have a bigger weight allowance, while others may be small and only permit a few people on at a time. Consider size when it comes to your character's comfort level, since many people can feel claustrophobic in elevators. The condition of the elevator can also heighten anxiety if that's the mood you're trying to build.

SETTING DESCRIPTION EXAMPLE

Emma clutched at the sticky metal handrail as the elevator lurched to a stop. The door opened and a smiling woman pushed a stroller in. As the lift continued its jerky, shuddering descent toward the lobby, Emma shook her head. How could this woman coo and laugh with her baby, so at ease at being placed in a filthy, airless coffin that was probably maintained by a drunk repairman? Didn't she see this death trap for what it was?

Techniques and Devices Used: Contrast, metaphor

Resulting Effects: Reinforcing emotion, tension and conflict

EMERGENCY ROOM

SIGHTS

Automatic sliding doors that lead to a waiting room full of beat-up chairs, patients with varying degrees of injury or illness (with broken bones and bloody noses, cuts, scrapes, bruising, holding garbage bins to catch vomit, pressing ice packs to injuries, wearing surgical masks, crying, holding onto the person next to them for support), loved ones waiting to hear a report on a patient (reading magazines or books, using a device to surf the internet, clutching at purses or holding tight to jackets slung over an arm, sleeping in a chair, pacing), garbage bins, half-finished coffee containers left on tables, chaotic piles of newspapers and magazines, employees (nurses, orderlies, janitorial staff) in color-coded scrubs, a dividing curtain or glass to separate people who may have a contagious disease from the rest of the patients, a glassed-in admitting and reception area, clerks taking information, restrooms, hand sanitizer stations, vending machines, signs pointing to other hospital areas, stretchers zooming past with paramedics attending to victims, doctors in scrubs and white coats passing through the area, people in wheelchairs, intoxicated people loudly complaining about the wait, worried parents and friends crammed together, small children huddled in parents' arms, cab drivers coming in for pickups, bandage carts, stethoscopes hung around necks, people whispering, security personnel patrolling the facility, a triage area, a room for casting broken bones, X-ray and CAT scan rooms, sliding doors to the individual rooms where patients are waiting (lying in treatment beds, hooked up to IV poles, wearing blood pressure cuffs as a nurse takes measurements, wearing heart monitors)

SOUNDS

Murmuring, crying, labored breathing, someone gagging and throwing up, moaning and whimpering, a loved one whispering a prayer, newspapers rattling, people arguing, magazine pages being turned, glass doors sliding open and shut, patients being called to the admitting station, someone being paged over the intercom, police or security radios, the calming voice of a nurse, the rustle of paperwork, a pen scratching as someone fills out a form, swearing, drunken slurring, coins clinking in the vending machine, a candy bar or pop hitting the tray, sirens outside as ambulances pull up, the squeaky wheel on a crash cart or stretcher, a defibrillator charging, bleeps from heart rate monitors, supplies being yanked from protective packaging (dressings, needles, tubes), curtains being jerked closed, paramedics concisely relaying vital signs to a nurse, doctors barking orders, drawers on medicine carts sliding open and banging shut, screams

SMELLS

Antiseptic, cleaning products, hand sanitizer, vomit, body odor, booze breath, air-conditioned or filtered air, blood

TASTES

Some settings have no specific tastes associated with them beyond what the character might bring into the scene (chewing gum, mints, lipstick, cigarettes, etc.). For scenes like these, where specific tastes are sparse, it would be best to stick to descriptors from the other four senses.

TEXTURES AND SENSATIONS
Plastic or thinly-padded seats offering little comfort or room, metal arm rails digging into one's forearms, a plastic admittance band sliding along one's wrist, the prick of an IV needle, anxiety and worry, one's bed being raised or pushed, nurses or paramedics manipulating one's body to gain access to a wound, a painful area being probed by a doctor, pain increasing as one is moved from bed to bed, the blissful release as pain killers kick in, feeling increasingly cold or burning up as one's temperature reaches critical levels, the uncontrollable shivering that accompanies shock, pain associated with specific injuries, various illness symptoms

POSSIBLE SOURCES OF CONFLICT
A person who is paranoid or violent from drug use
A large accident that overtasks the ER staff (such as an accident involving a city bus, an apartment fire, or a terrorist attack)
Needing care but not having the correct documentation or insurance
An airborne illness that spreads quickly, infecting others
Being treated by a doctor who is sleep-deprived
Having an allergic reaction to medication
Trying to treat patients who aren't honest about their histories
Discovering a serious problem with a patient who was admitted for a minor issue
Losing a patient (especially a child)

PEOPLE COMMONLY FOUND HERE
Custodial staff, doctors, family and friends for support, nurses, orderlies, paramedics, police officers, sick or injured people

RELATED SETTINGS THAT MAY TIE IN WITH THIS ONE
Ambulance (254), car accident (42), hospital room (76), waiting room (132)

SETTING NOTES AND TIPS
Hospital ERs will differ slightly due to funding, the size of the area they service, and the typical type of emergency cases they see. Ones that are in high crime locations will likely have tighter security measures and more security officers on staff. They will also be well-versed in treating stabbing and gunshot victims, whereas a small town hospital may have lighter security as their cases mostly deal with children who grow too sick to wait for a doctor appointment, bone breaks, heart attacks, car accidents, and strokes.

SETTING DESCRIPTION EXAMPLE
After the symphony of coughing, hacking and wheezing that greeted Becky in the ER waiting room, she found the closest antibacterial hand dispenser and starting working it like a gambling addict hitting up a slot machine.
> **Techniques and Devices Used:** Simile
> **Resulting Effects:** Establishing mood

EMPTY LOT

SIGHTS

Cracked pavement with weeds and grass growing through it, tufts of dead grass choked with litter (chocolate bar wrappers, takeout containers, straws, balled-up napkins, cigarette butts), a bag of trash half-hidden in the weeds, broken glass, a scattering of bricks or broken curb pieces, flattened cardboard and discarded plywood strewn about, a sun-faded realty sign, graffiti sprayed on the walls of nearby buildings, gravel and dirt, hardy dandelions adding dabs of yellow beauty, an old rubber bike tire twisted into a figure eight, sagging or broken fencing, stunted trees or bushes, discarded hair ties, pen lids and gum wrappers near a sewer grate, potholes filled with water after a rainstorm, an old shirt plastered to the ground in a dirty heap, a turned-over shopping cart, discarded condoms, drug needles and homemade pipes, kids using the lot as a play area (playing hopscotch and tag, jumping rope, kicking old cans and soccer balls), someone taking a shortcut and racing across the lot, a dog peeing on a tuft of grass

SOUNDS

The wind fluttering a plastic bag caught in a bush, a scrap of newspaper sliding across the pavement, street sounds (traffic moving past, pedestrians walking on the sidewalk, horns honking, sirens, squealing brakes, an airplane flying overhead), leaves rustling in the breeze, the patter and drip of rain in a storm, rats and mice skittering around the perimeter, birds cawing, the sounds of voices coming through open apartment windows, sounds associated with children playing (chatting, laughing, talking trash, balls bouncing, cans being kicked, a jump rope thwacking against the concrete, hand games, feet stomping during a hopscotch game)

SMELLS

Hot pavement, rotting garbage, mildewing cardboard, urine or feces, dust, grass

TASTES

Some settings have no specific tastes associated with them beyond what the character might bring into the scene (chewing gum, snacks, cigarettes, etc.). For scenes like these where specific tastes are sparse, it would be best to stick to descriptors from the other four senses.

TEXTURES AND SENSATIONS

Uneven ground that interrupts one's stride, long grass poking at one's bare ankles, something sharp piercing one's shoe, sleeping on the hard-packed earth or pavement with only a thin slice of cardboard for a bed, a concrete step that one sits on while waiting for a friend, the burning sun beating down on one's head, heat rising off the concrete slab, stepping in a puddle and being splashed with tepid water, hair rising on the back of the neck as one senses danger, the heavy thump of footfalls as one runs across the lot, being pulled along by a dog one is walking, bare feet slapping the concrete as one jumps rope, chalk bumping over uneven asphalt as one draws a hopscotch square, kicking debris aside to make room to play

POSSIBLE SOURCES OF CONFLICT

Being jumped or mugged in a dark lot at night when no one is around

Owning property adjoining the lot and having land value decrease because of homelessness or crime

Saving one's money to buy the lot only to have a big corporation snatch it up for another purpose

Being lured into an isolated lot and being victimized

Having criminals use a lot next to one's residential home for illegal activities

Getting busted buying drugs

Using the lot as one's home and being kicked out by the cops

Encountering unsavory people in the lot

PEOPLE COMMONLY FOUND HERE

Criminals, homeless people, kids playing or hanging out, locals taking a shortcut, nearby property owners walking their dogs

RELATED SETTINGS THAT MAY TIE IN WITH THIS ONE

Condemned apartment building (50), big city street (38), construction site (52), parking lot (102), small town street (120)

SETTING NOTES AND TIPS

Empty lots hold untold potential for conflict and interesting plot twists because they are often in areas where people seldom go and are rarely patrolled by police. Because they are poorly lit, they can make the perfect place for clandestine meetings or exchanges. Imagine what a character might see or overhear as he attempts to use the area as a shortcut or what he might witness after waking up from a drunken binge.

SETTING DESCRIPTION EXAMPLE

Dennis hated meeting up in No-Man's Land, the strip of crumbling, heaving asphalt split apart by weeds and time. Once a parking lot, now it was a sometimes-dangerous island where the lights from the street didn't quite reach, ignored by the cops. With a field of wild grass on one side, swampy woods on another, and the crumbling wall of a demolished grammar school on the third, there were plenty of shadowy places to hide and ample ways for a person meeting a friend in the dark to go missing.

    Techniques and Devices Used: Light and shadow, metaphor, passage of time

    Resulting Effects: Establishing mood, foreshadowing

FACTORY

SIGHTS

A massive corrugated metal building with giant delivery bays in the back, smoke stacks pumping out white smoke, a large emblem or logo of the company on the exterior, a sales and administrations office or wing (desks, phones, computers, office staff), an office engineering department where equipment is researched and designed for production (mechanical and electrical engineers using computers with 3-D technology design simulation capabilities, drafting stations, etc.), a manufacturing center (an open and well-lit warehouse with technicians and specialists, tools and machinery, robotic machining cells, cement floors with painted lines to delineate walking paths, industrial shelving, an automated painting booth, pallets, raw materials, hoses, valves, molds, chains, tools, inspecting stations in a temperature-controlled environment, safety signs, buttons that activate flashing lights attached to poles in case of an injury or emergency shut down situation, eye wash stations, first aid centers with accessible kits), janitorial staff sweeping debris off floors or changing out trash bins, multiple stations with air hoses and industrial drills and wet or dry saws, a metal walkway over the assembly room floor for observation, an assembly and production center (on an assembly line, hardhat-wearing technicians making all connections and double-checking with diagnostic equipment, production managers, safety personnel), a packaging center (pallets, plastic wrap, cardboard boxes, forklifts, stickers and labels, delivery trucks)

SOUNDS

The whir and buzz of machinery, air compressors, metal clinking or the whine of metal grinding against metal, the clack of interlocking rollers or chains on assembly lines, the hiss of an industrial press, sounds echoing in the large space, backup warning beeps for heavy equipment or small manual lifts, the whisper of a push broom against the floor, heavy tools being dropped onto a workbench, the clank of heavy boots on a metal set of stairs

SMELLS

Smells will largely depend on what product is being produced. Motor oil, grease, metal, rubber, hot machinery, chemicals, wood, paint, and resin are common smells that might be present in more commercial, non-organic product factories.

TASTES

Coffee or bottled drinks are possible, but food and drink are usually not allowed on factory floors. If the factory produces food for consumers (such as a beer bottling plant, cookie or candy factory, a frozen pizza production line) there will be a quality control tasting center that does random tasting on products.

TEXTURES AND SENSATIONS

Sweaty fingers inside thick gloves, the pinch of a hardhat or hairnet on one's scalp, running fingers along metal or plastic grooves to clear debris left over from the machining process, the grittiness of sandpaper, greasy fingers from fixing or lubricating moving parts, cold metal on the skin, being pinched or poked while assembling small components with one's bare hands, wiping away greasy sweat from one's forehead with the back of the hand, plastic or wood shavings coating one's fingers, the squishiness of an ergonomic floor pad under one's station, hot feet inside heavy work boots, tired feet after a long day of standing, sorting through a box of clips or fasteners to apply to a product piece

POSSIBLE SOURCES OF CONFLICT
An onsite injury
Sabotage from a disgruntled employee
Union worker strikes
Bad PR (Public Relations)
Unsafe or unsanitary processes
Nighttime vandalism or theft
Financial troubles
The plant shutting down and workers losing their jobs
Another employee wielding authority in order to intimidate or abuse others
New technology or mechanization that threatens factory workers' jobs

PEOPLE COMMONLY FOUND HERE
Business administrators, factory workers, health and safety inspectors, investors, janitorial staff, management, truck drivers and delivery personnel

SETTING NOTES AND TIPS
Factories may look, sound, and smell different depending on where they are located, how much technology they use, and what they manufacture.

SETTING DESCRIPTION EXAMPLE
Madeline moved in the rhythm she had established over the last five years—select a steel plate, slide it into the press, jam her thumb against the hanging button and watch the press drop down on the thin sheet of VG 10, stamping out the shape of thirty identical knife blades. Then she opened the press, removed the used sheet, and inserted another as the thirty cutouts rattled down a funnel and into a box for shaping and sharpening. Oh, the glamour of working in a knife factory. Still, after Ian had left her with a son to raise, she was grateful for a job. Callouses on her hands and black grime that never quite washed off was worth being able to put food on the table. Besides, the finished product was quite beautiful when you understood the work that went into it, and in a small way she found joy in being part of the process.

    Techniques and Devices Used: Multisensory descriptions, passage of time
    Resulting Effects: Characterization, hinting at backstory

FIRE STATION

SIGHTS
A large, multi-truck bay (for fire trucks, paramedic trucks, rescue boats, a ladder truck and ambulance), painted marks on the cement floor to designate staging areas or to organize specific equipment, firefighter gear at the ready (boots, bunker pants, helmets, an oxygen tank, gloves, a jacket, a hood and mask, a spanner belt for holding an axe and other tools), hoses that pull exhaust from running trucks waiting in the bay, a fire investigation truck, florescent lighting, giant roll-up garage doors, ladders, an intercom, fire extinguishers, dormitory bedrooms for firefighters (a bed and small table, some gear nearby to start the dressing process), several firefighter poles, a large bathroom, a locker room with lockers and showers, a workout room (free weights, resistance training, cardio equipment), a full kitchen (with multiple fridges, a stove and microwave, a pantry, counters, coffee pots, pots and pans, an eating hall with long tables), a watch room and administration area (dispatch officers, computers, printers, maps, emergency radios, a phone switchboard), a training room (with comfortable chairs, a television, a whiteboard, manuals)

SOUNDS
A dispatcher alerting the crew regarding emergency calls, sirens, heavy boots running over the floor, rumbling engines starting up, echoes off the high truck bay walls, shutter doors opening and closing, the clang of air tanks being set down on the concrete floor or stored in cabinets, the drag of hoses being laid out for inspection, the metal doors of storage compartments being opened and shut, the clink of tools and couplings being joined and secured to hoses, tool box lids slamming closed

SMELLS
Exhaust, meals being cooked, cleaning supplies, smoky uniforms and equipment, rubber from one's mask, the metallic tang of air from an oxygen canister, creosote, sweat

TASTES
Hearty and healthy meals that one might cook at home yet are portioned to serve a crowd (pot roast and potatoes, spaghetti or lasagna, hamburgers and potato salad)

TEXTURES AND SENSATIONS
Shoving feet into fire-proofed steel-toed boots, the snap of a suspender against the shoulder when pulling on fire retardant pants, the heaviness of a full tool belt dragging on the hip, the press of an air canister on one's back, the give of a mattress when one's shift is over at last, the bounce of a seat as one climbs into a fire truck, the heaviness of a hose on the shoulder while carting it to the truck, the cold metal handle of a toolbox, thick gloves sliding over calloused hands, being jounced and bounced in the cab of the fire truck, collapsing into a bunk after a midnight call, the satisfaction of showering away the sweat and ash from fighting a fire

POSSIBLE SOURCES OF CONFLICT

Equipment malfunctioning or vehicles breaking down

Fires or emergencies that occur simultaneously and strain resources

An illness sweeping through the fire hall (like a flu or food poisoning)

A firefighter falling in the line of duty

A crew member being investigated for a breach of protocol that resulted in injury or death

Post-traumatic stress disorder

A fire at the fire hall itself

Personal issues between firefighters that cause problems on the job

PEOPLE COMMONLY FOUND HERE

A fire prevention chief and chief of training, a safety chief, administration staff and dispatchers, civilians requiring assistance in emergencies, firefighters, paramedics, police officers, school tour groups, the fire marshal

RELATED SETTINGS THAT MAY TIE IN WITH THIS ONE

Rural Volume: House fire (62)

Urban Volume: Ambulance (254), police station (106)

SETTING NOTES AND TIPS

Many fire halls have several companies or units that run in 24-hour shifts. Smaller stations may not have the full array of emergency vehicles, but most will have two fire truck units and a paramedic ambulance. They might also be staffed by volunteer firefighters. When not actively fighting fires, the company maintains equipment, cooks and cleans the firehouse, sleeps in shifts, works out, or trains in new equipment usage, technology, and firefighting techniques.

SETTING DESCRIPTION EXAMPLE

A blaring sound pulsed through the bunkhouse floor. There was no in-between—one moment the sleeping firefighters were shrouded in the dark, and the next, they were awake and leaping out of bed, snapping on lights, shoving glasses on their faces and racing for the door. Like a wave smashing the shore, the seven-man crew poured out into the narrow hall where a pole waited at the end, fast-tracking the way to their gear and rig that stood ready below.

Techniques and Devices Used: Light and shadow, multisensory descriptions, simile

Resulting Effects: Foreshadowing, tension and conflict

FITNESS CENTER

SIGHTS
Glass walls, a locker room, product display cases (holding exercise bands, workout gloves, fitness equipment, supplements endorsed by athletes and famous bodybuilders, fitness DVDs), television sets affixed to the walls in front of cardio equipment (treadmills, stationary bikes, stair climbers, elliptical machines), a rowing machine, a squat machine, resistance bands, black safety mats, personal trainers spotting clients and helping them use equipment efficiently, a lat pull-down machine, an abduction machine, medicine and stability balls, a rack of kettle bells and a weight tower for dumbbells, leg curl and leg press machines, free weights at a power lifting station, barbells and plates, a curl bar and triceps bar, jump ropes, a chin-up bar, a room for group aerobics, yoga and dance classes, a pro shop area selling nutritional supplements and equipment (wraps, gloves, chalk, weightlifting belts, active wear, water bottles), towels and antibacterial spray or antibacterial wipes for cleaning machines, mirror panels along the wall, incline and decline benches, flat benches, hyperextension benches, weight scales, restrooms, a community board filled with special event notices and inspirational messages, clients dripping sweat with towels draped around their necks

SOUNDS
Music, heavy breathing, grunts and groans, sudden blasting exhales, swearing, trainers shouting encouragement, the clank of metal (bar bells bouncing against the floor after a dead lift, plates sliding home, free weights being returned to the rack), resistance-powered machines wheezing out air, the pattern of footfalls on a treadmill, beeping as one sets the incline on a running machine, the hiss of air conditioning, TV noises, clients chatting between workouts, the distant voice of a class instructor calling out directions, music from the spin or dance class

SMELLS
Sweat, deodorant, antibacterial cleaner

TASTES
Water, protein smoothies, hydration drinks, energy drinks, caffeine pills tossed back with water, energy bars or chews

TEXTURES AND SENSATIONS
The powdery dust of weightlifting chalk, the cold metal of a plate or barbell, the cinching tightness of a weight belt, the soft give of a workout mat underfoot, sweat sliding down one's neck, face, sides, and back, swiping at sweat with a cottony soft towel or T-shirt, taking a swig of cold water and rejoicing in its coolness, accidentally bashing a knee against a bench, one's feet relentlessly pounding the treadmill, fatigued muscles that quiver during a workout, a painful tearing sensation as a muscle or tendon is injured, a padded bench under one's back, stretching between reps, the pleasant burn of muscles being worked out, muscles twitching as they reach the end of their endurance

POSSIBLE SOURCES OF CONFLICT

Arguments over who was next to use a machine

Anger over people who don't put equipment back where it belongs

Someone tripping over a bar bell

Having something stolen from one's locker

Being ogled by another gym member

Chatty members who don't let others work out in peace

Injuries resulting from improper use of equipment or not knowing one's limits

Steroid rages

A rude or abusive trainer

Being sexually harassed by a trainer or other member

Body issues keeping one from visiting the gym as much as one would like to

PEOPLE COMMONLY FOUND HERE

Bodybuilders, equipment technicians, gym employees, people desperate to lose weight, people interested in physical fitness, the gym owner and manager, trainers

RELATED SETTINGS THAT MAY TIE IN WITH THIS ONE

Outdoor pool (218), outdoor skating rink (220), rec center (230)

SETTING NOTES AND TIPS

Bigger gym chains may have extensive exercise facilities, such as a pool, sauna, hot tub, and squash and basketball courts, along with separate rooms for hot yoga or spin classes. Gyms that are smaller may have older machines or a smaller variety of them, resulting in a person struggling to get a complete workout when the gym is busy. If any of the equipment is broken or if someone is hogging a machine, this will increase possible tension and conflict between gym users.

SETTING DESCRIPTION EXAMPLE

Amanda hopped on an empty treadmill next to a paunchy guy wearing a gray T-shirt ringed in sweat. He looked done in, yet the gym had only opened, so he must be a newbie. Typical. Every January a tidal wave joined up, determined to get in shape. Most quit before month's end. She gave him a nod in greeting, pretending to not notice his creepy up-and-down stare, and then programmed her machine to a light run. *Ten bucks says he'll be a peacock.* Sure enough, Mr. Track Pants increased the pace of his treadmill to match hers. Amanda choked down a grin and shoved in her earbuds to drown out his wheezy breathing. Then she increased her incline. This was going to be fun.

    Techniques and Devices Used: Metaphor, multisensory descriptions

    Resulting Effects: Characterization

FUNERAL HOME

SIGHTS
Manicured lawns, shrubs and trees, a decorative flower garden, a parking lot, a parking garage in the back (containing a hearse, a limousine, and a minivan for discreet body transfers), a **storage room** (body shipping boxes, a refrigeration unit, cleaning and embalming supplies, a workspace for transferring ashes into urns), an **embalming room** (a table and sink, an embalming machine, jugs of embalming fluid, scalpels, aneurysm hooks, eye caps, a ventilation system and UV lights), **a viewing room** (soft lighting and a wood-paneled backdrop wall, an open space around the casket, tasteful silk flower sprays in standing arrangements, patterned rugs or a carpet to minimize noise from foot traffic, chairs or benches, **a showroom floor** (displays of glossy caskets in different sizes and styles, a selection of urns, catalogues of flower arrangements, special customizations, wood inlays and designs, a funeral director and staff members on hand keeping a discreet distance, couches and tables used for consults, boxes of tissues, silk flower arrangements on stands and displayed on caskets, samples of memorial pamphlets to have printed and distributed the day of the funeral), **a chapel room** for the service (chairs or pews, a podium and stage, video and media equipment, a sound system, a piano or organ, microphones, a collection of mourners, ushers leading family members to the first few rows), **a reception room** (tables laden with food and drinks, a table of personal items belonging to the deceased for viewing)

SOUNDS
Soft music or hymns, people speaking in hushed tones, fabric rustling, quiet weeping, sniffing, blowing noses, speeches delivered through a microphone, live music and singing during the service, the creak of pews, someone's phone going off and being quickly silenced, throat clearing, laughter if a humorous past moment about the deceased is shared

SMELLS
The cloying scent of too much perfume and cologne, fresh flowers, burning candles, carpet, furniture polish

TASTES
Tears, a thick lump in the throat, breath mints or throat lozenges to keep from coughing during the service, food and drink at the reception (cookies, cheese and crackers, small cakes, coffee, tea), the smoky drag of a cigarette in the parking lot after the service is over

TEXTURES AND SENSATIONS
The feel of another's hair against the cheek as one pulls a loved one close, the soft papery or slightly moist feel of another's hand when holding it, a lump of tissue balled up in one's palm, the hard pew seat causing back stiffness as one tries to remain still, the scrape of a knuckle beneath one's eye to wipe away a tear, rubbing a hand across one's throat or breastbone in an attempt to ease the tightness there, the constriction of ill-fitting clothing or shoes that pinch and rub, stroking the silky hair of a child as she or he cries, rubbing the deeply-veined hand of an elderly relative in support, a thorny rose stem held in one's fist, the silky smoothness of the coffin lid,

one's shoes sinking into the thick carpet, curling and uncurling a program, speaking notes that are creased and damp in one's hand

POSSIBLE SOURCES OF CONFLICT
Feuds cropping up as the family gathers
A body reviving itself after being mistakenly pronounced dead (on delivery)
Worries of how to pay for the arrangements
Friends or family outliers tactlessly discussing the deceased's wealth or will
A car accident in the parking lot because emotions are high
Family secrets coming out
A person showing up to the funeral who is disliked by the surviving members of the family
Members of the press showing up to a high-profile funeral
Underestimating how many mourners will come and running out of space at the service

PEOPLE COMMONLY FOUND HERE
A funeral director, a priest or pastor, employees, mourners (family, friends, neighbors, co-workers), parking valets

RELATED SETTINGS THAT MAY TIE IN WITH THIS ONE
Rural Volume: Church (154), graveyard (164), mausoleum (172), wake (98)
Urban Volume: Morgue (90)

SETTING NOTES AND TIPS
Some funeral homes have a crematorium on site, while others do not. Note that remains are never cremated during the day, nor during active funerals out of respect for family and friends who are grieving at the loss.

SETTING DESCRIPTION EXAMPLE
I stepped through the dark wooden doors of the viewing room, grateful for the funeral director's thoughtfulness at the gentle flute melody he'd chosen as background music. As the last sister and only family member left to see Jim off, this room would be unbearable in silence. A spotlight lit up the silk rose arrangement on the casket. A pang struck my chest at the sight of those false white flowers; oh, how I wish I could've afforded fresh ones. But then I caught sight of Jim's bony features above his starched shirt and tie and the pain eased. Even in death he looked ready to crack a grin and tease me for fretting over flowers—didn't I remember he was allergic? I smiled, eyes watering, and missed him more than ever.
Techniques and Devices Used: Contrast, multisensory descriptions
Resulting Effects: Characterization, establishing mood, reinforcing emotion

GAS STATION

SIGHTS

Outside: Dingy gas pumps, wasps flying around overflowing garbage bins, slumped-shouldered gas attendants washing bug-splattered windows with squeegees, customers grumbling over the price of a fill-up, paper towel dispensers, a stack of window washer fluid on a pallet by the door, pay-at-the-pump signs, a motor oil display, a locked ice machine, bags of firewood, a giant sign showing current fuel prices, security cameras wired into the building or roof, painted yellow curb lines surrounding pump stations, grimy and graffiti-dressed restrooms for customers inside the store, window signs offering convenience store specials, giant RVs blocking access to the air hoses and dual pumps, muddy off-road trucks and motorbikes, cars and trucks, oil stains on the cracked pavement, a fuel truck pumping gas into an underground tank and making it difficult to maneuver

Inside: manual or automated doors, racks filled with food items (chips, candy bars, trail mix, cookies, pastries), a very limited grocery aisle, refrigerated coolers holding drinks (sodas, fruit juices, milk, waters, iced coffees, energy drinks, beer), a small prepared foods counter where quick meals can be bought (pizza slices, hot dogs, churros, sandwiches, fried chicken, fries), racks of magazines and newspapers, a basket of fresh fruit for sale, a checkout counter (an assistant ringing people up, a wall of tobacco products, adult magazines, lottery tickets)

SOUNDS

Outside: Gas caps being unscrewed, the metallic noise of a pump turning on or off, the gurgle of gas through the hose, music drifting out of parked cars, traffic whizzing past on the roadway, dogs barking in trucks, kids yelling at one another while being cooped up on a road trip, motorcycles revving, the ping of a cooling engine

Inside: till tape spitting out of the debit machine, coffee machines percolating, slush machines whirring, songs playing on the radio, the slap of a credit card on a plastic counter, the rustle of a chip bag being opened or a straw wrapper being removed, coins dropping into a cash register tray

SMELLS

Gasoline, dirty motor oil, trash spoiling in the hot sun, an air freshener dangling from a truck's rearview mirror, exhaust, sunbaked pavement

TASTES

Road food and drinks (energy drinks, coffee, pop, sugary slush drinks, salty chips, powdery mini doughnuts, beef jerky, chocolate bars, power bars), cigarettes or tobacco chew

TEXTURES AND SENSATIONS

The grimy feel of the rubber gas nozzle, squeezing to maintain pressure as the gas pump fills, the wet stickiness of old takeout drinks or ice cream cups as one empties the car of trash, the rough feel of a paper towel torn from a dispenser, dirty water from the squeegee dripping on one's leg or foot, chalky dust from a dirty car door or panel, shoving a credit card into the pump to pay, gasoline dripping on one's foot when the nozzle is removed, ripping one's receipt from the machine, the soft give of a car seat when one climbs back in, cool hand sanitizer applied after touching the pump

POSSIBLE SOURCES OF CONFLICT
Cars taking off without paying
A robbery
A drunk or inattentive driver angling too close to the pumps or the storefront and hitting something
Arguments between customers
A gas shortage that causes long lineups and short tempers
Rude drivers who park between pumps and restrict access to both
People trying to pay with coins and crumpled small bills
People holding up the line to buy large amounts of lottery and scratch tickets
Needing to use the restroom but being disgusted by its condition
Putting the wrong kind of gasoline in one's car
A pump that isn't working properly, so the customer has to go inside to pay and sign the receipt
A baby that screams whenever the car stops

PEOPLE COMMONLY FOUND HERE
Customers, delivery drivers, gas attendants, gas tanker drivers, kids on bikes

RELATED SETTINGS THAT MAY TIE IN WITH THIS ONE
Car wash (44), convenience store (162), parking lot (102), truck stop (284)

SETTING NOTES AND TIPS
A fact of life is that everyone needs gas, including murderers, serial killers, outpatients from mental hospitals, porn stars, soccer moms, nuns, drug addicts, and even police officers. So while a gas station might seem like a rather bland setting, in reality, it can be just the opposite. Bring together a few clashing character types, throw in a security camera or two, and you have a stage set for brilliant conflict.

SETTING DESCRIPTION EXAMPLE
Of course, the one day I was grossly late for work, all four pumps were busy. I pulled up behind a grimy yellow van and began tapping my fingers against the steering wheel in hopes the pot-bellied owner was almost through. Finally he gave the gas nozzle a tap and slid it back into the holder. I straightened, ready to shift into drive. But as he climbed into the van, the side door rolled open and half-a-dozen kids spilled out like ants fleeing a nest. They ran pell-mell, past the ice machine and racks of motor oil and through the automated convenience store doors. My head thumped back against the rest. I was going to die in this line.

    Techniques and Devices Used: Hyperbole, simile
    Resulting Effects: Passage of time, reinforcing emotion

HAIR SALON

SIGHTS

A front desk (with a computer and cash drawer, a debit machine, a display case with hair accessories), a trendy waiting area (couches, a coffee table piled with fashion magazines, a cart with glasses and a pitcher of water), glass shelving holding designer products (shampoos, conditioners, hair repair oils, gels, waxes, hairsprays and mousses), a selection of wigs and hair pieces, a wall of sinks with dark towels stacked in cubbies, large shampoo and conditioner dispensers, garbage cans, reclining chairs, hair stations (mirrors, antibacterial washes for combs and tools, a hair dryer and irons, a padded swivel chair that can be raised or lowered, a collection of products, a water bottle sprayer, different sizes of scissors, electric shears, brushes and combs), hair scattered over the floor, industrial hair dryers, a broom leaning against the wall, posters of models with designer haircuts, a display of hair extensions, books of hair color samples, bowls and brushes for mixing colors, a movable storage tower (with clips, combs, bands, rollers, and a foil dispenser for highlights), stylists dressed all in black or wearing a company apron, a restroom in the back

SOUNDS

Hair dryers blowing, the snip of scissors, music on the radio, water spraying in the sink, sheets of tin foil being torn off, customers laughing with their hairdressers, the phone ringing, aerosol spray hissing, foamy shampoo plopping into the sink, the hiss of a hydraulic chair being lowered, the *chunk chunk chunk* of a chair being raised with a foot pedal, supply drawers sliding open and closed, heels striking the tile or wood floor, stylists chatting with each other between appointments

SMELLS

Shampoo and conditioner (mint, eucalyptus, floral, citrus or herbal scents), an overheated blow dryer motor, astringent cleaners and antiseptic washes, chemical hair dyes, colors and perming agents

TASTES

Accidentally getting a spritz of hairspray in one's mouth, coffee, tea or lemon water

TEXTURES AND SENSATIONS

Hair being pulled taut and then cut, the cold slickness of water and suds washing away extra hair color or bleaching agents, the smoothness of a plastic cape covering one's body, flipping through a glossy magazine while the heat from the blow dryer causes one's scalp to prickle, the itch or burn of a hair chemical along one's hairline, cold water misting one's face and neck, shampoo being splashed into one's eyes at the sink, one's neck lying uncomfortably against the ceramic curve of the washing station, warm water and foamy shampoo being massaged into one's hair, holding one's head at an awkward angle while a stylist cuts it, heat from an iron pressing into one's scalp, the wet ends of hair slapping one's face at the end of a cut, the silky smoothness of hair that has been styled

POSSIBLE SOURCES OF CONFLICT

Receiving a bad haircut or color

Studio drama between stylists

The hairdresser being bumped or her heel twisting in the middle of a cut

Color that sits in too long and damages the hair

A client's skin reacting to a chemical and being burned

A stylist who overestimates his own abilities and can't deliver the style one requested

Having no cash and learning too late that the tip can't be placed on a credit card

Having a stylist who speaks a different language and being unable to communicate one's desires

A chatty hairdresser (or client) who won't shut up about her problems

PEOPLE COMMONLY FOUND HERE

Clients, employees and trainees, stylists

RELATED SETTINGS THAT MAY TIE IN WITH THIS ONE

Shopping mall (180)

SETTING NOTES AND TIPS

Some salons may offer other services beyond hair care like tanning booths, dermatology services (such as electrolysis and laser treatments), eyebrow threading, hair waxing, etc. Consider also that a hair salon is a place where a customer feels a bit invisible and she has a captive audience: her stylist. This may lead to someone talking about things that are overly personal or none of her business. This situation is a breeding ground for potential conflict if the wrong person was to overhear a secret being spilled under the assumption that no one knows the person being talked about.

SETTING DESCRIPTION EXAMPLE

After an hour of pulling and poking, my soggy hair was suitably spiked with foil. Anna directed me to the hair dryers and I couldn't get my head under there fast enough. Anna, in her mid-fifties, was prone to hot flashes and so kept the studio's temperature somewhere around frostbite level. She dropped a hefty stack of magazines on my lap and flicked the switch. Blissful heat blasted me, sucking away the tendrils of cold and making my long, chilly wait in the styling chair worthwhile.

    Techniques and Devices Used: Contrast, hyperbole

    Resulting Effects: Characterization

HOMELESS SHELTER

SIGHTS
A staffed check-in counter, a cafeteria-style area for eating and visiting (bare walls, tile flooring, long rows of tables with folding chairs), a buffet line with serving staff offering a balanced meal to residents, a long line of residents waiting with trays for food, steaming pots of soup and trays of meats and vegetables, vending machines in one corner stocked with toiletries, a bookcase full of used books, older computers with free Wi-Fi so residents can search for jobs, a bulletin board (with lost and found notes, volunteer opportunities and events, free education and job listings), volunteers wearing aprons and hairnets (collecting and washing dishes, wiping down tables while chatting with residents, offering assistance to people with disabilities, etc.), a water cooler with plastic cups, an industrial-sized coffee machine, community sleeping areas (one large room each for male and female residents, rows of bunk beds, garbage bags or duffle bags holding personal possessions, mismatched donated blankets and sheets), rooms of a more private nature (three to four beds or bunks each, possibly earned by residents volunteering at the shelter), simple shared bathrooms (sinks, showers, toilets), a common room lounge (a bolted down television, tables and plastic chairs, cards and board games, etc.)

SOUNDS
People talking, laugh tracks from the TV, arguments between residents, snoring, bedsprings creaking, volunteers setting freshly washed trays in stacks, the slap of food on a plate, laughter, singing and humming, muttering, knocks on the door to wake residents up, phones ringing, the crinkle of plastic sleeping mats as people toss and turn on their beds or cots, backpack zippers opening and closing, showers running, dripping bathroom sinks, the scrape of chairs, people yelling that they need to get in the bathroom, feet shuffling along the concrete floor, fights over rooms or personal items, children crying

SMELLS
Soups, pastas, gravy and vegetables cooking in the cafeteria, sour body odor, cigarette smoke, alcohol on the breath, sweat, unwashed clothing funk, plastic mattress covers and sleeping pads, coffee, a heavy bleach scent on the sheets and towels

TASTES
Typical meals from the soup kitchen or cafeteria (buns, soup, pasta that feeds a crowd, hamburgers, meat loaf, hot dogs, cooked vegetables, fresh fruit), toothpaste, mouthwash, tobacco, small sweets, pop from a vending machine

TEXTURES AND SENSATIONS
The give of an old mattress, springs poking one's back, a rickety cot that wobbles when one climbs into it, the lightweight smoothness of plastic cutlery, the pilled roughness of well-washed bedding, hard plastic food trays, mushy food in the mouth, the hardness of the floor as one tries to sleep on a thin sleeping pad, the slipperiness of soap in one's hands, knots pulling while washing and combing one's hair with cheap shampoo or a bar of soap, the tingle of clean skin

after a shower, the stiff fabric of a worn backpack that holds one's personal belongings, plunging one's hands into soapy water to clean and maintain the shelter, grit caught under one's nails, the pleasurable sweep of a tongue across clean teeth after brushing, a plastic garbage hand held firmly under one's arm

POSSIBLE SOURCES OF CONFLICT
An altercation with another resident resulting in the police being called
An injury
Running out of space or resources (food, beds, etc.)
Residents who are sick and possibly contagious
Mental illness or drug use that results in paranoia or violent psychosis
Being accused of breaking the rules and being turned out of a shelter
Having to leave the shelter because one's prescribed time is up but having no other place to go
Sneaking a dog into the shelter

PEOPLE COMMONLY FOUND HERE
Homeless residents, police and paramedics, shelter staff and security, volunteers

RELATED SETTINGS THAT MAY TIE IN WITH THIS ONE
Alley (34), city bus (256), condemned apartment building (50), underpass (128), public restroom (112), refugee camp (114), subway tunnel (276)

SETTING NOTES AND TIPS
Homeless shelters differ in population; they can be unisex or may cater specifically to men, women, or families. Some offer shelter on a first-come-first-served basis, while others allow longer term stays in exchange for a small fee or hours spent volunteering at the facility. There is no privacy in a shelter, and when demand is high, common areas such as the cafeteria hall may be converted to sleeping quarters. Drama and unrest are also common, due to the high percentage of residents struggling with mental illnesses or addictions.

SETTING DESCRIPTION EXAMPLE
Whenever the temperature dropped, the lineups started early. A stream of people shuffled in through New Hope's double doors, their faces chapped with cold and coats bristling with white. With each bowl of soup, hands trembled to cup the warmth and find a place to sit. I ran a head count as I served, hating how numbers were adding up so quickly, tables filling faster than I'd hoped. Soon, we would have to close the doors for the night, and those left outside—mothers, children, older men and women stiff with arthritis—would be forced to find another place to stay.

    Techniques and Devices Used: Multisensory descriptions, weather
    Resulting Effects: Foreshadowing, passage of time, reinforcing emotion

HOSPITAL ROOM

SIGHTS
Pale walls, plug-ins for equipment, florescent lighting, a whiteboard with specific patient information (the name of the nurse on shift, food allergies or diet restrictions, tests to be performed) written on it, boxes of gloves in holders on the wall, a large window with blinds, a bathroom (a small sink area, a shower with safety bars and a toilet), an adjustable hospital bed with a plastic cover, side rails and hospital sheets, a television set on the wall, a metal IV stand with saline bags, an LED heart monitor, a pressure cuff, a rolling table, a nightstand with drawers, a small closet for personal items, an antibacterial sink station, a garbage can, a plastic disposal for syringes, an array of get well cards and flower arrangements, a plastic cup with a straw, a well-worn visitor's chair, extra pillows, the patient's chart held in a slot on the wall, a curtain surrounding the bed or separating beds in a semi-private room, a hospital robe hanging from a peg on the bathroom door, a patient in bed with IV or chest tubes, monitoring wires leading to machines, an automatic finger clip to check a patient's pulse, nurses and doctors making the rounds, support staff cleaning and delivering meals, visiting family members who stop in, volunteers reading to patients or talking with them

SOUNDS
People being paged over the intercom, the whoosh of automatic doors between hospital wings, slippers whispering over floors as a patient takes his IV stand for a walk, the beep of a heart monitor, an alarm dinging when a medicine or saline bag needs to be checked or if a heart rate monitor falls off the patient's finger, the soft breaths of someone sleeping or snoring, laugh tracks on the television, the scrape of a fork through soggy peas and mashed potatoes, an empty water glass rattling as a patient slurps up the last of the water, the rubber snap of gloves being pulled on, the nurse asking questions while checking a patient's IV site or reading vitals, family members trying to keep the conversation positive and upbeat, the whir of the bed being adjusted, the snap of side rails locking into place, muffled creaks as the patient adjusts position in bed, running water, the automated hum as sanitizer is dispensed from a machine, the metallic slide of a curtain being pulled along its rod, a tray of unappealing food being shoved across a surface

SMELLS
Cleaning supplies, astringent hand sanitizer, soap, latex gloves, the unidentifiable odor of bland food, fresh flowers, coffee or tea, over-bleached towels, robes and sheets

TASTES
Chalky pills or plastic capsules, tasteless hospital food (fish fillets, applesauce, dry toast, hard meat loaf, mushy vegetables, fruit cups, chicken and rice, hard buns), water, weak coffee and tea, juice, fortified vitamin and mineral drinks, gelatin deserts or fruit cups

TEXTURES AND SENSATIONS
The soft give of a hospital pillow and mattress, muscles aching at restricted movement, pain or sensations that are specific to the patient's injury or illness, the cool brush of an alcohol swab, the

painful pinch of an IV needle going in, tape being pulled away from the skin, the poke of a straw as one guides it toward one's mouth, the rough feel of chapped lips, sweat-soaked hair sticking to one's forehead and neck, the cold metal of the IV stand as one pulls it closer, shakiness in the limbs as one walks across the floor in thick socks, the soft touch of a nurse pressing her finger against the wrist or inner elbow for a pulse read, the cold shock of a stethoscope against the skin, a cool breeze alerting the patient that his gown has come open in the back, grogginess from pain medication

POSSIBLE SOURCES OF CONFLICT
Medication making a patient paranoid or violent
Misdiagnoses
Picking up a staph infection
Being given the wrong medication
Becoming exhausted by nonstop visitors in the room
An emergency that causes a hospital-wide evacuation
A catheter that slips out
A loud or obnoxious roommate that makes it difficult to get rest
Having to share a room with another patient with a large family and no personal space boundaries

PEOPLE COMMONLY FOUND HERE
Cleaning staff, doctors, family members and friends, maintenance employees, medical students, nurses, patients, specialists, visiting pastors

RELATED SETTINGS THAT MAY TIE IN WITH THIS ONE
Ambulance (254), elevator (56), emergency room (58)

SETTING NOTES AND TIPS
Hospital rooms will vary depending on the type of room (standard, semi-private, or private) as well as its purpose (a maternity birthing room, an intensive care bed, general recovery, etc.). Rooms used for a specific purpose will have monitoring equipment tailored to the type of care needed.

SETTING DESCRIPTION EXAMPLE
Leda woke, squinting at the bright light overhead. Someone was rubbing something cool on the back of her hand, but the slickness quickly turned to a jab of pain. She flinched and turned her head. A nurse was securing an IV into her hand with tape. An IV? She was in the hospital? Pain slithered between her temples, fogging her thoughts, and the bleach smell wafting off the sheets turned her stomach. The last thing she remembered was dropping Caren off at her house after the basketball game. Then, nothing.
   Techniques and Devices Used: Multisensory descriptions
   Resulting Effects: Hinting at backstory, passage of time, reinforcing emotion, tension and conflict

HOTEL ROOM

SIGHTS
A numbered door with a key card entry, a fire escape plan on the wall, closets with non-removable hangers, an extra blanket and pillows folded on a shelf, a room safe, patterned carpet with muted stains, a bathroom with typical fixtures (a shower, toilet, sink area and mirror), a tiled floor with dirty grout in the corners, racks holding fluffy white towels, extra toilet paper rolls, dings and scuff marks on the walls, a cramped standing area between the shower and sink, a tray with complimentary toiletry items, a box of tissue and a paper-wrapped water glass, a hair dryer attached to the wall that may or may not work, bright overhead lighting, a robe hanging from a hook on the door, a bed (or two, with matching bedding and pillows), a nightstand with an alarm clock and bedside lamp, a TV on a console, a telephone and phone book, a service sheet (room service, laundry rates, amenities information), pamphlets for nearby takeout restaurants, a thermostat, bland artwork, a desk with stationery and a pen, a wall hookup for laptops or chargers, a small chair or love seat, a coffee maker with supplies (coffee, tea, sugar, powdered cream, coffee mugs), water glasses and an ice bucket, a minibar or fridge with a pricing chart, a trash can, the TV remote, thick drapes on the windows, a chest of drawers, a Bible in a drawer of the night stand, a *Do Not Disturb* sign hanging from the door handle

SOUNDS
The hum of air conditioning or a heater, water gurgling in the pipes within the walls, doors opening and closing, half-heard conversations from people passing in the hall, the shower or toilet running, a dripping sink, the coffee pot perking, the ding of a nearby elevator, drunk people stumbling to their rooms and talking loudly, kids running across the floor in the room overhead, traffic or construction filtering in through an open window, a phone ringing to deliver a wakeup call, canned laughter or explosions from TV shows, the suction of a fridge door giving in to pressure as one opens it, bottles clinking on the door of the fridge, a rap at the door, a couple arguing in the next room, kids crying after a long day, muffled voices through the walls, the crinkle of shopping bags, luggage zippers being pulled open or closed, the high-speed whir of the blow dryer

SMELLS
Bleach, cleaners and deodorizers, old carpet, fabric, bleached towels, aromatic shampoos, conditioners and soap, brewing coffee, alcohol, cigarette smells clinging to one's clothing, perfume, aftershave, hairspray, sweat, junk food with strong odors (tortilla chips, cheese puffs, popcorn), room service meals

TASTES
Coffee, tea, water, mouthwash, toothpaste, food brought up to the room or delivered by room service (burgers, fries, sandwiches, spaghetti, salads, soup), pop and snacks from a vending machine (chocolate bars, granola bars, gummy treats, candy, chips)

TEXTURES AND SENSATIONS

Sliding the smooth plastic card into the slot and then yanking it out to disengage the lock, the instant freeze of ice on the fingers while digging into the bucket for cubes, steam on one's face as one blows on a hot cup of coffee, the give of a mattress, the first brush of cool air on sweaty feet when one's shoes are kicked off, the shock of cold as bare feet touch the bathroom tile, a fresh towel against the skin, lather sliding down one's back in the shower, blotting a wet face with a soft towel, rummaging around in a suitcase to find items by feel, flipping through the plastic laminated room service menu, lining one's shoes up by the door, dumping shopping bags onto the bed, sliding a hand along the wall in the dark as one searches for the light switch, thick curtains being opened or closed, the rush of heat from the blow dryer, peeling back a heavy comforter

POSSIBLE SOURCES OF CONFLICT

Noisy neighbors (fighting, screaming children, babies crying, people playing the TV too loudly)
Drunk people trying to reach their rooms at night (jiggling door handles, knocking on the wrong door, being obnoxious)
Spotting bed bugs or roaches
Bad room service
Infidelity or break-ups
Building construction that wakes one early

PEOPLE COMMONLY FOUND HERE

Cleaning staff, guests, handymen

RELATED SETTINGS THAT MAY TIE IN WITH THIS ONE

Rural Volume: Tropical island (240), wedding reception (192)
Urban Volume: Ballroom (194), black-tie event (196), elevator (56), limousine (262), taxi (280)

SETTING NOTES AND TIPS

There are many different kinds of hotels, from elegant, to run-down, to full-on sleazy. Ask yourself what type of hotel your character can afford and if appearances are important in the situation. Then incorporate some conflict to create problems for your character and add zing to the setting.

SETTING DESCRIPTION EXAMPLE

I glared up at the ceiling. Never again would I stay in a hotel hosting a family reunion. First the elevator doors were dinging every ten minutes, dropping off drunks. But of course they couldn't just stagger off to their rooms—no, they had to scrape along the wall and try every door, swearing at the ones their cards refused to open. If that wasn't bad enough, a trio of old ladies got off on my floor practically shouting at each other about how wonderful it was to be with family, and that Lindy's fiancée seemed like a bit of a drunk and wasn't it just pathetic how Lee couldn't hold a job? If they didn't shut up soon, my head would explode.
Techniques and Devices Used: Hyperbole
Resulting Effects: Characterization, passage of time, tension and conflict

JUVENILE DETENTION CENTER

SIGHTS
A facility enclosed by chain link fences, narrow holding cells consisting of wall benches and a toilet, concrete or cinder block rooms with a narrow window and sturdy furnishings, metal doors with rust marks and scratches, bunk beds or rows of cots, graffiti-stained walls, a stainless steel commode and sink, thin mattresses and pillows, standard issue clothing (scrubs, jumpsuits, T-shirts, sweat suits, socks, boxers, sneakers or slip-on shoes, identification bracelets), isolation rooms, an intercom system and security cameras, a posted daily schedule that is strictly enforced, a basketball court, a grassy or concrete outdoor area, an infirmary with nurses or doctors on duty, a library, a kitchen, a multipurpose rec room (couches, tables and chairs, TVs mounted to the wall), an area with tables and seating where residents meet with visitors, facilities for group or individual therapy, a garden, classrooms with standard equipment (student desks and chairs, a teacher's desk, pencils and paper, textbooks, a dry-erase board, visual aids on the walls), sneakers left sitting outside of private rooms, computers for supervised usage, a bank of telephones that can be used during designated times

SOUNDS
Echoing hallways, amplified noises due to the concrete walls, voices and laughter, shoes squeaking on tile, doors clanging shut, electronic doors buzzing open, voices speaking over the intercom, teachers instructing in a classroom, basketballs bouncing on an indoor or outdoor court, residents playing games or watching TV in the rec room, residents arguing (exchanging insults, yelling, swearing), fistfights drawing a ring of cheering onlookers, large groups of people eating in the cafeteria, a mop swishing across the floor, pages turning as someone reads a book in her room, workers doing systematic room checks, footsteps passing by in the hallway, sounds from one's roommate (talking, reading aloud, singing, humming or whistling, snoring, shifting in bed)

SMELLS
Food from the cafeteria, floor cleaner, sweat, smells from the toilet, dry-erase markers in the classroom, the papery smell of books in the library

TASTES
Cafeteria food, toothpaste

TEXTURES AND SENSATIONS
Cold concrete walls, the stir-crazy sensation of being stuck in a small room, loose-fitting clothing, a thin mattress that does little to soften the metal or concrete bunk underneath, a cold steel toilet, a plastic or metal ID bracelet sliding up and down one's wrist, the sun or wind on the skin as one steps outside for an exercise period, nervous jitters when one is summoned by an administrator or psychologist, the feel of a letter from a loved one, sinking into a couch in the rec room, a pencil scratching over paper in the classroom, silverware scraping over a metal tray, a thin blanket

POSSIBLE SOURCES OF CONFLICT

Confrontations with other residents

Gang- or race-related conflicts

Insomnia

Worry over the future

Claustrophobia

Restlessness from not getting enough exercise

Academic difficulties that make learning difficult

Boredom

Conflict with family on visiting day

Family who refuse to visit

Therapy meetings that force a resident to confront past wounds

Peer pressures

Abuse or neglect by the staff

Budget cuts that make it difficult for the facility to acquire sufficient resources and personnel

A faulty stigma that exists about a given facility

PEOPLE COMMONLY FOUND HERE

Administrators, armed guards, doctors and dentists, janitors, kitchen staff, lawyers, nurses, psychologists, residents, social workers, teachers, visitors

RELATED SETTINGS THAT MAY TIE IN WITH THIS ONE

Rural Volume: Group foster home (58)

Urban Volume: Courtroom (54), homeless shelter (74), police car (270), police station (106), prison cell (108), psychiatric ward (110)

SETTING NOTES AND TIPS

A juvenile detention center is not a prison. It's a secure but temporary residence for juvenile offenders who are awaiting trial. Sometimes, a judge may decide that a longer stay at the center would be of benefit to a certain child, and he or she might stay for a longer period of time. If a child doesn't respond to the treatments and services provided at this level, he or she may then be transferred to a juvenile correctional facility, which is essentially a prison for youth offenders.

SETTING DESCRIPTION EXAMPLE

Mia lay on the thin mattress, the sorry excuse for a blanket pulled up over her eyes. Unfolded, it didn't reach her feet, so she might as well use it to block out the lights that never went off. Shoes squeaked along the hallway, pausing just outside her door before passing on. She had lost count of the number of people who had walked by or the hours, days, and weeks she'd been stuffed into this box. She was a mouse caught in a trap, but it didn't matter. The trap was simply part of a maze designed to make sure people like her could never find the exit, never hope for anything more than a crappy piece of cheese. One that always came with a price.

Techniques and Devices Used: Metaphor, symbolism

Resulting Effects: Establishing mood, passage of time, reinforcing emotion

LAUNDROMAT

SIGHTS

Windows facing the street, a row of uniform plastic chairs within sight of a television set that's bolted to the wall, chipped folding tables, metal laundry baskets on wheels, rows of industrial washing machines and dryers, a security camera, rotary fans on the ceiling, garbage cans (stuffed full of dryer sheets, lint, and empty jugs of laundry soap), a tile floor with the occasional clump of dryer lint, spilled detergent powdering the tiles, signs that give instructions about the facility, a vending machine for detergent and dryer sheets, coin slots on the machines (if coin-operated), kids running around, bored patrons texting or listening to music on devices, too-bright florescent lights overhead, stray socks left behind on a folding table, a laundry attendant behind a desk, candy and soda machines, a change dispensing machine, laundry spinning in machines, piles of clean laundry on tables, garbage or cloth bags of dirty laundry on the floor by an empty machine, stainless steel sinks and sprayers

SOUNDS

The whir and slurp of a washing machine, the click and clack of buttons and zippers hitting metal as they tumble in a drum, sneakers banging around as they're washed, the clang of loose coins being tumbled in a dryer, automated snaps and buzzers as machines progress through cycles, the suction seal of a machine door being opened or closed, the shimmy and squeak of metal on metal as a machine goes into a spin cycle, people laughing or talking, parents yelling at their kids to stop running or climbing on things, noises from the television, coins cascading down a chute, the click of a turnstile candy machine as a gumball or handful of candy pops out, squeaky wheels on a laundry cart, a snap as one shakes out sheets or dress shirts before folding them, a rush of traffic when the door opens, the whirling blades of overhead fans, sheets that crackle with static as they're pulled apart and folded

SMELLS

Detergent, chemicals, bleach, fake flower or citrus scents (lavender, lemon, lilac), hot fabric, the metallic scent of overworked motors, sweat, body odor, wet laundry, musty wetness from a washing machine in need of cleaning, dirty clothes sitting in a bag for too long

TASTES

Candy or gum from a mechanical vending machine, granola bars, chips, chocolate bars or pretzels from an electronic vending machine, water or pop brought into the facility

TEXTURES AND SENSATIONS

Hard plastic seats, warm quarters pulled from one's pocket, feeling the ridged edges as one inserts them into a machine slot, granules of dry detergent stuck to one's fingers, greasy liquid soap or stain remover, the cold wetness of clean clothing being pulled from a washer, hot air on one's face as one opens a dryer to collect clothing, fluffy clothes pulled right from the dryer, the shock of static electricity as one sorts and folds, slipping on a liquid detergent spill on the tile floor, the slick and hard-to-wash-off feeling of bleach on one's hands, peeling a dusty sheet of lint out of a filter and throwing it away

POSSIBLE SOURCES OF CONFLICT

Someone removing one's clothing from a dryer before it's dry

Clothing that goes missing from a folding table

A customer's children being overly rambunctious and bothering others

Air conditioners that are broken in the summer, causing tempers to flare

Someone trying to wash or dry something that ruins the equipment

Pranks that involve putting pens in dryers so they will explode all over the next load of clothing

A power outage that stops the machines in the middle of a wash cycle

Getting to the laundromat and discovering that one is out of detergent or has forgotten one's coins at home

Frustrations arising from the circumstances that have forced one to use the laundromat in the first place

PEOPLE COMMONLY FOUND HERE

College kids, customers (people living in apartments, etc.), homeowners with broken-down washers or dryers, laundromat employees, people on vacation, people with large items that won't fit in personal machines (comforters, pillows, sleeping bags, small rugs), repair men, vagrants

RELATED SETTINGS THAT MAY TIE IN WITH THIS ONE

Big city street (38), parking lot (102), small town street (120)

SETTING NOTES AND TIPS

Some laundromats are nicer than others, with newer equipment, free Wi-Fi, complimentary coffee, televisions, and a play area for children. They may also offer laundering drop-off and delivery services. Some may still use coins, but many newer laundromats involve paying an onsite cashier for usage.

SETTING DESCRIPTION EXAMPLE

Once the old lady who smelled like cat pee left, I loaded Carmichael into the metal basket and gave it a shake, testing the wheels to make sure we had a solid ride. He gripped the wire bottom and then nodded. The washing machine gurgled and slurped, mashing the load like a colorful wad of food. The noise should cover the clatter of wheels on the tile floor, but I checked to make sure no one was watching anyway. Mom was outside on the sidewalk, blowing out a gust of cigarette smoke as she gossiped with Auntie Denise on her cell. The laundry attendant had her back to us, watching anime on her mobile. I gave my brother the thumbs up and started the countdown. The only good thing about wasting a Friday night here was a game of Laundromat Derby.

Techniques and Devices Used: Multisensory descriptions, personification, simile
Resulting Effects: Characterization

LIBRARY

SIGHTS
Sturdy bookshelves (lining the walls, marching across the floor in rows, curling around reading nooks and study areas), a long front desk manned by librarians and their assistants (scanning books, checking them out, taking payments for overdue books, running searches for patrons), organizers with stickers and bookmarks for kids, pamphlets for special events and reading clubs, book carriers, pens and pencils, a reference section (filled with thick dictionaries, encyclopedias, atlases, and historical texts), students working at tables, senior citizens flipping through newspapers in cozy chairs, patrons using library computers for research or web surfing, reading rooms (for special events, peer tutoring and book club meetings), a staircase leading to a second level, reference numbers at the end of each row, a magazine corner with a variety of glossy periodicals, banners and signs about literacy and the importance of reading, bright overhead lighting or lamps on tables, a children's section with picture books on the shelves and beanbag chairs on the floor, signs reminding patrons to be quiet, filing cabinets, shelves full of movies to check out, a photocopier and laminating machine, book displays for popular authors and new releases, turnstile shelving for paperbacks, workstations with privacy barriers, crumpled paper and eraser shreds left on tables, fabric couches and easy chairs in the reading area

SOUNDS
The tick of a clock or whir of a printer or copy machine, the quiet flip of a page, coughing and throat clearing, a cell phone ringing and then being shut off, air conditioning snapping on, the ping of a text message, hushed voices as students collaborate on a school project or discuss research, toddlers laughing and singing during story time, a librarian reading to preschoolers, books dropping, hard covers slapping shut, paper tearing, sneezing, the creak of chairs or springs in an old couch as someone flops on it, shoes tapping on the staircase, footsteps thudding overhead on an upper level, the scratch of pencils and clicking of pens, a frustrated sigh or groan, the snap of a teenager's gum, tapping a pencil on a table or book, muffled music coming from a user's earbuds, the crackle of a newspaper page being straightened or folded, fingers tapping at a keyboard, the click of a mouse, backpack zippers opening and closing

SMELLS
Crisp paper, musty carpet (especially after it rains), dust, dry air conditioning, the minty breath of a librarian leaning in to speak so that no one else is disturbed, the smell of stale cigarettes wafting off smokers, leather, spicy cologne, perfume, air fresheners, cleaning products, pencil shavings

TASTES
Gum, breath mints, chewing tobacco, a wood taste from biting on pencils, ink transfer (from newspaper to hand to mouth), water from a public fountain

TEXTURES AND SENSATIONS
Slippery pages, rough leather bindings, smooth desk surfaces that are cold to the touch, scratchy seat cushions or uncomfortable plastic chairs, brushing eraser bits off a piece of homework,

pressing a finger against the edge of a plastic library card, tapping one's fingers against the keyboard to search for a book, paper cuts, running a finger over a raised book cover, gripping a smooth polished banister on the way up the steps, cold doorknobs, sticky book pages that are hard to separate, the sun's warmth shining through windows as one reads, pressing a hand against the cool glass door to exit

POSSIBLE SOURCES OF CONFLICT

Accidentally damaging a book (spilling coffee on it or tearing a page)
Being hassled by one's peers to help with projects or lend homework
Losing one's library card or misplacing one's books
Going to the library to retrieve a book only to discover that someone else has checked it out
An overly zealous librarian who will not tolerate any sort of noise
People who monopolize the computer stations
A pipe bursting and damaging the books
Overhearing a whispered secret that bothers one greatly

PEOPLE COMMONLY FOUND HERE

Historians, librarians, parents with preschoolers, readers, researchers, students, teachers

RELATED SETTINGS THAT MAY TIE IN WITH THIS ONE

Rural Volume: Elementary school classroom (112), high school hallway (118), university lecture hall (136)
Urban Volume: Bookstore (160)

SETTING NOTES AND TIPS

The bigger the library, the larger the onsite book selection generally is. Often libraries within a city are linked, so a book at one location can be requested by another, increasing a patron's access to a greater selection. Libraries are also popular places for nonprofit groups to meet, and they run a variety of social programs for their communities, making this a good location for your character to potentially run into friends or enemies.

SETTING DESCRIPTION EXAMPLE

Something pulled me out of my research and I glanced up. The entire floor, usually bustling with library-goers, stood empty. No backpacks lay on the floor as owners slouched in chairs, the always-busy computer terminals had black screens, and an utter lack of noise made the silence seem too obvious. The stacks on the floor above, usually well lit and busy with book browsers, had become a meeting point for shadows, hazy strangers huddled in the dark. I laid my pencil down on my notebook as the desk lamp hummed. I wanted to clear my throat just to hear something familiar, something human, but I didn't. A greasy flutter filled my chest. It was like one of those apocalyptic movies where a person wakes up to find everyone and everything gone.
Techniques and Devices Used: Light and shadow, multisensory descriptions, personification
Resulting Effects: Establishing mood, foreshadowing, passage of time

MECHANIC'S SHOP

SIGHTS

An assortment of damaged cars in the parking lot, open bays with vehicles on lifts and ramps, employees (wearing boots and oil-stained coveralls, with black-rimmed fingernails from grease and oil), lifts and hydraulic equipment, stacks of tires and rims, hoses dangling from the ceiling, workbenches along the walls, water hoses wound around wall spigots, tools (wrenches, screwdrivers, socket sets, drills, etc.), engine hoists, plastic envelopes containing keys and work orders, idling cars, stacked-up construction cones, large drums, oscillating fans on the walls, oil and gas cans, safety signs, garbage bins, crumpled up paper towels, grease cloths thrown onto nearby work surfaces, spare auto parts, tool chests and rolling tool carts, cars with their hoods up, mechanics on rolling creepers under cars, oil-stained concrete floors, a waiting room with chairs, a television and a coffee machine

SOUNDS

The deafening sound of electric drills and other equipment, music playing on a radio, employees whistling, car hoods creaking open and slamming shut, engines idling, mechanics yelling to be heard over the noise, customers being called on an intercom system, car engines that aren't running smoothly (clanking, revving, stalling, choking), the click of an engine that won't turn over, shrieking belts, soda cans being cracked open, heavy objects dropping into garbage cans, hydraulic ramps going up and coming down, rubber-treaded footsteps, the drip and splash of automotive liquids hitting the ground (water, oil, brake fluid, transmission fluid), the whir of heavy-duty oscillating fans, creepers rolling under cars, water dripping from hoses, keys jangling

SMELLS

Motor oil, grease, gasoline, sweat, metal, paint, rust

TASTES

Foul air laden with gas or oil, food and drink from the waiting room vending machine (candy bars, chips, gum, water, soda, coffee)

TEXTURES AND SENSATIONS

The rattle and jerk of a dying car as it rolls into the parking lot, sweat gathering on the skin as one waits for a car to be ready, a cool breeze from the oscillating fans, slipping on grease or oil that has gathered on the ground, stumbling over potholes in the parking lot, cold metal tools in one's grip, rubbing at calloused hands with towels to smear away the grease or oil, accidentally banging one's head or knee while underneath a vehicle, cuts and bashed knuckles from trying to force stuck bolts to loosen

POSSIBLE SOURCES OF CONFLICT

Being crushed by a car
Obtaining burns and serious injuries from a running engine
Hurting one's back when picking up heavy objects

Being attacked by someone wielding tools or dangerous machinery
Getting caught stealing items from a customer's car
Accidentally scratching or damaging a car and then trying to cover it up
Dealing with a dishonest mechanic
Sabotage by a jealous or angry mechanic
Having one's car fixed by an incompetent mechanic

PEOPLE COMMONLY FOUND HERE
Customers, managers, mechanics, office staff, vendors delivering supplies

RELATED SETTINGS THAT MAY TIE IN WITH THIS ONE
Rural Volume: Garage (54), salvage yard (184)
Urban Volume: Car accident (42), car wash (44), gas station (70), used car dealership (184)

SETTING NOTES AND TIPS
The inner workings of a mechanic's shop will vary depending on what kind of work the establishment does. Besides a general mechanic's shop, which has been described here, there are also auto-body shops, tire shops, and oil change and general maintenance shops. Owners of new or high-end automobiles might choose to take their cars to the dealership instead of to a mechanic when work needs to be done, especially if the car is still under warranty.

As authors, it's our job to make things difficult for our characters; once we've stressed them out, we need to stress them some more. A car breakdown in the heat of summer is a great way to start. Maybe with two small kids in the backseat in a remote location. Then a smelly cross-town drive in a tow truck to a waiting room with no air conditioning. Top it off by revealing that the work involved is more extensive and expensive than originally planned, and you've got a character with volatile emotions who is primed for explosive responses and poor decisions.

SETTING DESCRIPTION EXAMPLE
His dad was saying bad words under his breath and sweating like a gorilla, but Joey smiled as he clung to the back of the plastic chair, his breath fogging the glass. The huge tires looked heavy, but the guy in the blue uniform picked them up and tossed them around like they were nothing. Another guy was using a drill that made an awesome screeching sound while his partner banged on something under the hood of a rusty old truck. Joey bounced on his knees and wondered if maybe he could work here someday.
Techniques and Devices Used: Multisensory descriptions, simile
Resulting Effects: Characterization, reinforcing emotion

MILITARY BASE

SIGHTS

A chain link perimeter topped with razor or barbed wire, a guard station entry point with a motorized barrier, security cameras, flags flying from poles or on rooftops, a security office, intersecting roads with typical signage and streetlights, administrative offices, basic utility services (a power station, a water plant, sewage treatment facilities, etc.), a hospital, various medical offices, a post office, gas stations, the motor pool (an automotive maintenance garage, jeeps, Humvees, trucks, heavy equipment, government-issued vehicles), a commissary, the PX (Post Exchange) or BX (Base Exchange) with a wide variety of items for sale (groceries, cigarettes, sporting goods, clothing, hardware supplies), snack bars selling specialized foods (coffee, ice cream, hot dogs), security vehicles driving around the base, a barber shop, a laundromat, a dry cleaners, a bank, a recreational area (a swimming pool, ping-pong tables, a bowling alley, basketball and volleyball courts, putting greens, a gymnasium), a movie theater, a library, public parks and playgrounds, a school, religious facilities (chapels, synagogues, etc.), base housing in the form of single family homes or duplexes, the mess hall, barracks (bunk beds, pillows, sheets, blankets, shelving or lockers for uniforms and personal items, duffel bags, laptops, books, pictures of loved ones)

SOUNDS

Reveille in the morning and taps at night, chains clanking against a flagpole, traffic noises (cars starting up, engines idling at a red light, brakes screeching, sirens), people talking and walking, phones ringing, flags flapping in the breeze, doors opening and closing, dogs barking, the slap of tennis shoes from a jogger running by, children's laughter and voices coming from a school or playground, recreational noises from the center (balls bouncing, splashing noises from the pool, bowling balls crashing into pins, weights clanking in the workout room), a leash jangling as someone walks a dog, squeaking and rustling noises from sleeping in a bunk bed, aircraft taking off and landing

SMELLS

Car exhaust, blooming trees and flowers, food smells, coffee, meat cooking on a grill, rain, wet pavement

TASTES

Military bases have a large variety of choices when it comes to food and drink. Meals can be cooked at home if one lives in base housing, while those living in barracks have a wide array of choices in the mess hall. There are also small restaurants and shops where one can eat out, and a large selection of foods can be bought at the commissary.

TEXTURES AND SENSATIONS

A plastic badge dangling from one's shirt pocket, the crisp smoothness of an ironed uniform, a hat pulled low over one's forehead, car wheels rolling over a well-maintained road, running a hand across hair stubble after a regulation haircut, pushing a wobbly-wheeled cart through the grocery store, a full grocery basket tugging on the inside of one's elbow at the commissary, flopping onto a thin bunk mattress, pulling on a crisply ironed uniform

POSSIBLE SOURCES OF CONFLICT

Domestic conflicts that stem from living in a military family (frequent moves, a lack of privacy or space, rebellion against strict rules and regulations, etc.)

Being passed over for a promotion

Receiving a poor evaluation or review

Being stationed in an area where one doesn't want to live

Being away from one's spouse and worrying over his or her fidelity

Getting into the kind of trouble that permanently goes on one's record (getting into a fight, being arrested, getting a DUI or not following orders)

Personality clashes between military personnel and civilians

Suffering from post-traumatic stress disorder

PEOPLE COMMONLY FOUND HERE

Chaplains and religious support personnel, civilians and private contractors providing support services (lawn maintenance, teaching at the school, vending machine maintenance), delivery people, doctors and hospital support personnel, military personnel and their families, special dignitaries and visitors

RELATED SETTINGS THAT MAY TIE IN WITH THIS ONE

Military helicopter (266), submarine (272), tank (278)

SETTING NOTES AND TIPS

A military base is like a small town and will have many of the amenities that one would find in a self-sufficient community. The size of the base will play a part in determining which facilities are available. Bases will also vary between the different branches, between countries, and whether or not the base is located on home territory or somewhere overseas. Consider how weather, climate, location, and seasons will shift the look of this type of setting, and how buildings and home construction may look different depending on the country and the local environmental challenges.

SETTING DESCRIPTION EXAMPLE

The moving truck had barely lurched to a halt before Dad was jumping out and barking orders. I pushed my door open to catch a breeze but didn't budge from the front seat. The dark street was lit by streetlights set at a regulation distance. Lined up like a row of new recruits, the houses were small and square with tidy front yards. Groomed palm trees instead of maple trees kept watch this time, but base living was basically like shopping at different Walmarts—not much changed from one to the next. And while this late it was hard to see details, I'd bet my phone there wasn't a stray toy in sight, not a leaf out of place. I yawned, bored already.

Techniques and Devices Used: Light and shadow, simile

Resulting Effects: Establishing mood, reinforcing emotion

MORGUE

SIGHTS

Covered bodies being wheeled into or out of the facility, bright lights, secure doors with keypad or card swipe entries, a sterile room filled with metal furnishings and tools, autopsy tables with raised edges to catch bodily fluids, step stools, technicians wearing varying degrees of safety garb (scrubs, booties, gloves, a face mask, splash guard, goggles, hairnets), a cooler for holding bodies (either a large walk-in cooler or smaller cabinets where the bodies are rolled in), bodies in bags or covered with sheets, naked bodies lying on tables with toe tags attached, sinks with hoses, trays of sterilized tools, metal bins for holding organs and other evidence, hanging scales, X-ray machines, a shelf or desk where reports are written and paperwork is filled out, patient files, biohazard garbage bags, a shelf filled with binders and reference books, boxes of latex gloves, typed reminders on the wall (about hand washing, proper procedures, etc.), a whiteboard with information written on it, a computer and printer, a telephone, cameras for taking pictures of the body, clipboards with information or forms attached to them, bags holding a patient's clothing and personal items, a rack where specimens are stored to be picked up by pathologists, blood spatters on the tile floor

SOUNDS

Squeaky gurney wheels, doors buzzing or swinging open, rubber-soled shoes on a tiled floor, the shuffle of booties, phones ringing, technicians verbally recording findings during an autopsy, papers being flipped on a clipboard, music playing, the snick of scissors as clothes are cut, items being placed into a plastic bag, water running into a sink, hands being washed, surgical instruments clanking against a metal tray, slightly muffled voices speaking through face masks, the stretch and rattle of a hanging scale as something is placed in the tray, objects plopping or clanging into an evidence tray, a scalpel slicing through flesh, the rev of a surgical bone cutter or electric saw, a body bag being zipped closed, cabinet doors opening and closing, the rustle of protective wear being unfolded and put on, a pen scratching on paper, latex gloves snapping on or off

SMELLS

Antiseptic, bleach, blood, a sickly sweet decomposing or "death" smell, formalin (for preserving specimens), one's own breath being expelled into a face mask, menthol ointment spread under the nose

TASTES

Some settings have no specific tastes associated with them beyond what the character might bring into the scene (chewing gum, mints, the waxy flavor of lipstick, etc.). For scenes like these, where specific tastes are sparse, it would be best to stick to descriptors from the other four senses.

TEXTURES AND SENSATIONS

A very chilly temperature-controlled room, the dry feel of latex gloves, a paper mask chafing one's skin, an itchy hair net or cap, punching buttons on a keypad, a headset scratching one's ear or scalp, a corpse's dead weight, slightly lessened sensitivity from wearing gloves, the feel of ebbing resistance as a scalpel cuts into flesh, slippery blood on one's hands or under one's feet, squishy organs, the cooler strip of skin under one's nose where menthol has been applied, keeping a firm grip on one's scalpel, cold water on one's skin, scrubbing one's skin in an effort to remove any residual smell, a blast of cold air as one enters the cooler

POSSIBLE SOURCES OF CONFLICT
Losing a body
Misplacing the deceased's important personal items
Being unable to determine a cause of death or determining an unpopular cause of death
Circumstances that cause power sources and backups to fail
Getting stuck in the morgue
Faulty safety wear that compromises one's health
Mixing up tissue samples
Mis-labeling a body
Being embarrassed by one's job at the morgue
Difficulty separating one's emotions from one's job

PEOPLE COMMONLY FOUND HERE
Coroners, family members identifying a body, forensic technicians, grief counselors, medical examiners, medical students or law enforcement personnel doing a tour, nurses, pathologists

RELATED SETTINGS THAT MAY TIE IN WITH THIS ONE
Rural Volume: Graveyard (164), mausoleum (172)
Urban Volume: Ambulance (254), emergency room (58), funeral home (68), hospital room (76), police station (106)

SETTING NOTES AND TIPS
When you think of a morgue, a set group of services usually come to mind: conducting autopsies, collecting and sending off samples for testing, holding bodies, and identifying the bodies of loved ones. However, not all morgue facilities offer all of these services. Some hospitals, depending on their size and funding, may use morgues as basic storage facilities until the bodies can be taken offsite for autopsy, usually to a medical examiner's or coroner's office. In some cases, autopsies can also take place at the funeral home (though the morgue here is usually called a mortuary); if so, procedures here are typically performed by a private pathologist and come at a cost. When family members need to identify a body, this can take place at any location along the way, depending on when this step occurs in the overall process.

SETTING DESCRIPTION EXAMPLE
Julia opened the door, glad to see that maintenance had finally oiled the hinges, and escorted the grieving husband into the room. The smell always hit her first—the faintest sickly sweet odor disguised by liters of antiseptic. It was so subtle that no one else seemed to notice, not the desensitized technicians and certainly not the destroyed family members. The woman's husband stifled a sob as he stared at her covered body on the metal gurney. Julia placed a hand on his shoulder and waited for him to take that first impossible step.
Techniques and Devices Used: Multisensory descriptions
Resulting Effects: Establishing mood, reinforcing emotion, tension and conflict

NEWSROOM

SIGHTS

General Floor: A reception desk, **a workspace area** (desks, computers, file cabinets, phones, pads of paper, pens and office supplies, water bottles and drink cups, stacks of paper and files, reference books and binders, newspapers), computer monitors with sticky notes plastered on them, journalists eating lunch at their desks, jackets thrown over chairs, mounted TV monitors, police scanners, workstation pods where many reporters work in close proximity to each other, whiteboards where schedules and upcoming events are recorded, **an intake area** filled with computers and servers that store incoming transmissions, **a conference room** (sparse décor, plain chairs in rows, a lectern), **a control room** (mixers, control boards, microphones, multiple monitors, headphones, audio equipment), printers, potted plants, **a break room** (tables and chairs, a microwave, etc.)

Broadcast Room: anchors sitting behind a long desk, loose papers and pens, chairs that roll and swivel, textured walls to help with acoustics, interactive flat screen monitors, green screens, teleprompters, studio cameras, lighting, lighting boards, cords crossing the floor, monitors for the anchors to see, a digital clock

SOUNDS

Computer keys clicking, cell and office phones ringing, phones being hung up, papers being shuffled, the white noise of many people talking in low voices, the grainy sound of voices coming over a police scanner, file cabinets sliding open and closed, the rustle of newspapers, printers printing, chairs rolling and squeaking, footsteps, silence in the broadcast room as the cameras prepare to roll, producers calling orders

SMELLS

Coffee, heated-up food from home, delivery food brought in

TASTES

A bagged lunch from home, food that has been picked up or delivered, birthday cake, doughnuts, coffee, soda, energy drinks, bottled water

TEXTURES AND SENSATIONS

A sore back from sitting for long hours in a desk chair, swiveling back and forth while thinking, blurry eyes from staring at a computer screen all day, warm paper fresh out of the printer, tapping a pen against a desk or one's leg in thought, wolfing down food, an adrenaline rush from working under a deadline, a crick in one's neck from cradling a phone between the ear and shoulder, pacing across the floor, holding a mug of hot coffee to one's lips, heartburn from poor food choices

POSSIBLE SOURCES OF CONFLICT

Running a story without properly checking the facts
Paper cuts

Getting scooped by another reporter or station

Being pressured by influential people who oppose the story one is trying to pitch

Having inner conflict over the story one has been assigned

Untrustworthy sources

Death threats

Writer's block

Unrealistic deadlines

Fearing that one's career is being threatened by younger or more attractive co-workers

An ailment that makes it difficult to remember one's lines or read a teleprompter

A disfiguring injury that threatens one's position as an anchor

Embarrassing oneself on camera

Being asked a question during a live recording that one has trouble answering

PEOPLE COMMONLY FOUND HERE

Camera operators, editors, graphic designers, makeup artists, meteorologists, news directors, photographers, producers, production assistants, receptionists, reporters and journalists, sound and lighting technicians, TV anchors

RELATED SETTINGS THAT MAY TIE IN WITH THIS ONE

Car accident (42), courtroom (54), emergency room (58), green room (208), police station (106)

SETTING NOTES AND TIPS

Journalism is a high-energy career that can add a lot of conflict to a story line. But the newsroom is home to many interesting people, too—ones who can impact the main character or act as main characters themselves. When writing your story, don't forget the editors, camera operators, photographers, makeup artists, and other people who frequent this setting.

SETTING DESCRIPTION EXAMPLE

Ella clamped the phone between her ear and shoulder, taking notes with one hand and verifying facts on her computer with the other. The digital clock screamed 4:42 in bleeding red letters. Her heart hammered; she had three minutes, tops, before the broadcast would start. With a rushed "Thank you," she let the phone drop, grabbed her notes, and ran for the editor's desk like her shoes were on fire.

Techniques and Devices Used: Simile

Resulting Effects: Tension and conflict

NURSING HOME

SIGHTS

General: A sign-in desk and hand sanitizer stations, homey commons areas with couches and chairs for family members and residents, wide hallways conducive to wheelchairs, a special events board, cheerful paper and foil decorations during a holiday (Easter, Christmas, Chinese New Year), railings along each wall, curio cabinets holding china dishes or antique plates, silk flower arrangements, a fish tank, a piano, a small chapel, a cafeteria with widely spaced tables, physiotherapy equipment, staff rolling past with drink and snack carts (water, juice, coffee, easy-to-digest cookies), a music player with a variety of music from earlier eras, large central tables where residents can park their wheelchairs and visit, a group TV room with a few chairs but mostly open spaces for parking wheelchairs, a games room with tables (set up with cards, puzzles or checkers), residents (in wheelchairs, sleeping, watching TV in the television room, using walkers, sitting attached to IV machines or oxygen tanks, holding dolls or other mementos, staring off into space, ranting at staff or talking to themselves, having one-sided conversations with an unresponsive companion), support staff (helping residents eat, go to the bathroom, take a shower, get dressed), custodial staff making beds and wiping down bathrooms, a nurse bringing medication and engaging residents in conversation

Residents' Rooms: a narrow space with an adjustable hospital bed and side rails, a thin closet (filled with a few changes of clothing, nightgowns, a box of adult pull-ups, socks and incidentals), an end table (with a bedside light, a phone, a water glass, hand cream, a clock), a laundry basket with the resident's name on it, slippers tucked under the bed, pulley equipment attached to the ceiling to help those who have limited mobility, call buttons to alert the staff, windows with heavy drapes, a privacy curtain in rooms with multiple occupants, framed pictures of family, a corkboard holding greeting cards and a calendar of events

SOUNDS

Music, humming, residents talking or muttering accusations, attendants asking questions to engage residents, the creak of wheelchair wheels, a loud rap when a resident bumps into doors or tables, water running in bathrooms, the hiss and grind of air flow machines, heaters and air conditioning units turning on, laugh soundtracks on the TV, people calling out for help or crying, footsteps in the hall, the bubbling of a fish tank, wheelchair brakes snapping into place, toilets flushing, phones ringing

SMELLS

Bleach, cleaners, fresh laundry, food cooking, urine and feces

TASTES

Easy-to-chew food, water, juice, chalky medicine, warm tea or coffee, snacks (soft cookies, banana bread, etc.), high calorie supplemental drinks

TEXTURES AND SENSATIONS

The cold wetness of antiseptic foam against one's palms, lumpy beds, wiping crumbs off one's hands or face, a brush pulling through one's hair, chewing mushy or bland food, smearing on greasy face cream, the slight give of a wheelchair seat as one settles into it, a splash of cold if one spills a drink, the uncomfortable lump of a pill stuck in the back of the throat, soft sheets, the glossy sleekness of old photographs, the painful prick of an IV being inserted, bumps, scuffs and falls that cause pain, the warm embrace of a loved one

POSSIBLE SOURCES OF CONFLICT
Personal items going missing
Mistakes in medication
Rude or dangerous roommates suffering from dementia
Residents who steal the TV remote
Falling and injuring oneself
Caregivers who ignore patients' pleas or requests
Toilet accidents
Having a disturbing visit from one's family

PEOPLE COMMONLY FOUND HERE
Family members, nurses and support staff, residents, visiting doctors and preachers, volunteers and entertainers for special events

RELATED SETTINGS THAT MAY TIE IN WITH THIS ONE
Ambulance (254), hospital room (76), waiting room (132)

SETTING NOTES AND TIPS
Nursing homes run the gamut. Some are excellent facilities, providing healthy meals, trained nursing staff, social programs and activities, and regular medical care. Others may have cramped quarters, poor sanitation and cleanliness, staff that are lazy or even abusive, and an environment that provides little mental or physical stimulation to keep the residents active and happy. Private or public funding may make a difference, as well as location, size, and age of the facility in question.

SETTING DESCRIPTION EXAMPLE
Visiting Uncle Joe at the Winding Hills Center was hard, but I made myself go every second Sunday. It was an unfortunate preview of my own future; sooner or later, we'd all end up in a place like this. Between the stained carpet, worn furniture, and doors that didn't quite close, the care center had seen better days. I waved at the nurse behind the desk and then made my way through the hallway gauntlet of wheelchair-bound seniors watching orange guppies circle the fish tank or sleeping with their heads slumped against their chests. The worst ones, the saddest ones, were those who sat tucked against a big empty table, staring at nothing. They were ghosts, their minds caught on a train heading for somewhere else while their bodies waited at the station like unclaimed luggage.

    Techniques and Devices Used: Simile, symbolism
    Resulting Effects: Establishing mood, reinforcing emotion

OFFICE CUBICLE

SIGHTS
Soft-sided dividing walls, a name plate on the desk or fastened to the wall, a computer and headset, electrical cords dangling off the edge of the desk, a wastebasket, a rolling desk chair, a seat cushion, office supplies (a stapler, scissors, pens, highlighters, notepads), personal pictures in frames, a phone, a coffee mug or water bottle, snacks, file cabinets with magnets and reminders stuck to them, an inbox with stacks of papers or files, knickknacks and personal items, a child's crayon drawings pinned to the wall, a college banner, postcards and posters tacked up to the dividing walls, sticky notes stuck to the desk or computer screen, a box of tissues, a desktop oscillating fan, a space heater on the floor, a sweater or jacket draped over the back of the chair, shelves filled with binders and manuals, a potted plant, seasonal decorations, a bulletin board with photos and memorabilia, a calendar, a dry-erase board

SOUNDS
Voices from the other cubicles, laughter as other office workers gather to talk, phones ringing or beeping, the tap of fingers against keyboards, printers shuttling out paper, chairs rolling or squeaking, the click of a stapler, tinny music from someone's headset, the crackle of snack bags being torn open, the pop of a soda can, file cabinet doors sliding shut, papers being shuffled or crumpled or torn from pads, muted music from a computer, someone tapping or clicking a pen, buttons being punched on an adding machine, the whir of a fan, book pages being flipped, carts rolling down the aisles, footsteps, the ding of an elevator, a vacuum cleaner, a member of the maintenance crew running a sweeper over the carpets, water gently splashing into a potted plant

SMELLS
Markers and highlighters, old files, potpourri and air fresheners, scented candle warmers, carpet, cleaning supplies, hand sanitizer, perfume and cologne, hairspray, paper, cardboard boxes, microwaved lunches, coffee, birthday cake

TASTES
The gummy taste of a licked stamp or envelope, a plastic pen that is being chewed, coffee, tea, soda, water, snacks from the vending machine, homemade snacks, lunches from home (sandwiches, fruit, yogurt, cheese and crackers, salads), doughnuts, birthday cupcakes, delivered pizza, takeout food

TEXTURES AND SENSATIONS
The rough padded fabric of a wall divider, the give of a chair when one leans back in it, a cushioned seat, aching wrists and finger joints from too much typing, a crick in the neck from holding the phone between one's ear and shoulder, an aching back, changing position to keep one's feet from falling asleep, cold fingers and toes, the radiating warmth of a space heater under the desk, the intermittent gust of air from an oscillating fan, antsy movements (tapping a pen on the desk, drumming fingers, jiggling a foot), standing up to stretch, the satisfying scratch of one's

favorite pen on paper, slippery condensation from a cold bottle of water or can of soda, huddling into one's sweater for warmth, the nick of a paper cut, a fresh cup of tea or coffee warming one's hands

POSSIBLE SOURCES OF CONFLICT
Co-workers who don't respect one's space
Brownnosing co-workers sucking up to employers and making others who don't look bad
Power struggles and clashes between employees
Overbearing or inept bosses
A neighbor whose cubicle emits offensive smells (garlic, cologne, body odor) or irritating noises (pen clicking)
A co-worker stealing one's ideas or clients
Being paired with an incompetent or irresponsible co-worker
Annoying or hurtful practical jokes
Sexual harassment
Having to work with substandard or faulty equipment
Conflicts between one's work and home life
Overhearing a nearby conversation about oneself

PEOPLE COMMONLY FOUND HERE
Clients, delivery people, employees and bosses, lawyers and public relations people, maintenance staff, members of the cleaning crew, professionals from other companies attending a business meeting

RELATED SETTINGS THAT MAY TIE IN WITH THIS ONE
Boardroom (40), elevator (56)

SETTING NOTES AND TIPS
Because an employee spends so much time in her cubicle, the space can be a strong indicator of her personality. What kind of memorabilia does she keep? Is the area neat or sloppy? Is it sterile and plain or over-decorated? How protective is she of her things? The answers to questions like these will determine what kind of cubicle the character would have and will enable authors to create workspaces that are as unique as their characters.

SETTING DESCRIPTION EXAMPLE
The fluorescents flicked off, leaving just the computer's glow and the dim light of the desk lamp. A cleaning cart rolled by on well-oiled wheels. The scents of bleach and glass cleaner made Mike's nose twitch, but he kept working, his fingers scurrying across the keyboard like termites racing to erect a mound before the flood came.

> **Techniques and Devices Used:** Light and shadow, multisensory descriptions, simile
> **Resulting Effects:** Characterization

PARK

SIGHTS
Mature trees and meandering paths, grassy areas populated with people enjoying the outdoors (dog walkers, people laying out on blankets and reading books, youths throwing a football or playing Frisbee, kids playing tag, a couple having their wedding photos taken), fallen leaves carpeting the walkways and lawns, benches for sitting, pull-up bars and other equipment at an exercise station along the path, a gazebo, covered pavilions with picnic tables, a pond or river with geese nibbling the grass along the edge, walking bridges, decorative rock formations, a playground or baseball diamond, chipmunks or squirrels leaping from branch to branch or scampering across the grass, dogs on leashes, birds splashing in a fountain, ants trundling through the grass, flies and gnats buzzing around one's head, butterflies flitting among the flowers, mosquitoes whining, ducks and swans paddling in a pond, signs indicating the names of plants and trees, streetlamps, garbage cans, a flagpole, a child's lost cap or baby shoe left on a bench, runners and cyclists using the pathway system for exercise

SOUNDS
People talking as they walk or hang out, the steady slap of a jogger's footsteps, kids laughing and yelling, dogs barking, birds chirping, squirrels chattering and rustling through the bushes, the thump of a ball landing in a mitt, the crack of a baseball bat, a splashing fountain, adults calling to children, the crumpling sound of snack bags being torn open or wadded up, water gurgling from a river or spurting from a fountain, flies buzzing, geese honking and hissing, distant city sounds (sirens, car horns, traffic), cell phones going off, rain pattering against the leaves, a crack of thunder, wind sighing through the canopy and causing tall trees to creak, planes flying overhead, a squeaky bicycle rolling by

SMELLS
Fresh-cut grass, rain, flowering trees and plants, wood, dirt, coffee, sunblock, garbage cans in need of changing

TASTES
Picnic foods (sandwiches, fruit, chips, pretzels), fast food, water, coffee, soda, beer, snacks (candy bars, peanuts, granola bars, trail mix)

TEXTURES AND SENSATIONS
Sitting on a warm blanket or towel, prickly grass against one's skin, the heat from a metal park bench, getting headachy from the sun's glare, the dry feel of a book's pages, bare feet shuffling through the grass and toeing the dirt, the sun's warmth on one's face, uneven cobblestone walkways, a runner's feet jarring against the path, wading barefoot into a pond or stream, mist blowing from a fountain on a windy day, sun-warmed rocks, the rough wooden railing of a bridge that spans a stream, the tension of a lunging dog's leash in one's grip, a football thumping against one's chest, a Frisbee slipping through one's fingers, gnats buzzing around one's face, flies landing on one's skin, a sensation of complete relaxation as one is able to be still and rest, cool

water from a bottle, leaves crunching under one's shoes, sunglasses slipping down the nose, sweat trickling

POSSIBLE SOURCES OF CONFLICT
Getting mugged at night
Being hit by a stray baseball or Frisbee
A child wandering away or falling into the water and not being able to swim
Eating food that's gone bad in the heat
A lover's quarrel
Bullies who follow one around the park to intimidate
Accidentally sitting on an anthill
Wearing inappropriate clothing and being too hot or too cold
Being bitten by an unleashed dog
Stepping in dog poop
A child abduction
Being stung by a wasp and suffering an allergic reaction

PEOPLE COMMONLY FOUND HERE
Bikers, dog walkers, families, garbage collectors, landscapers and groundskeepers, maintenance crews, picnickers, runners and walkers, school groups, security people, sunbathers

RELATED SETTINGS THAT MAY TIE IN WITH THIS ONE
Rural Volume: Forest (212), hiking trail (216), lake (220), meadow (224), playground (122), pond (232), river (236)
Urban Volume: Outdoor skating rink (220), parking lot (102), public restroom (112), skate park (236)

SETTING NOTES AND TIPS
The items found in a park will vary depending on its size and location. Because Central Park is large, it has the usual amenities, plus an ice-skating rink, horse-drawn carriages, and snack vendors, among other things. On the other end of the scale, very small parks may simply consist of an expanse of grass and a tree or two. Urban parks will have all the natural sounds, plus the usual city noises of traffic and mass population. Rural parks may be truly subdued, with only the sounds of nature as a backdrop. Seasons and weather will also greatly affect the description, so remember to think about the specific elements of your park and filter them through the senses of your POV character to reinforce realism.

SETTING DESCRIPTION EXAMPLE
Trees lined the path, branches weaving together to support a thick, yellowing canopy. Squirrels leapt from tree to tree, traveling along their own private highway around the mirror-calm lake, collecting bits and bobs for nests and winter storage. Every so often, a leaf would glide down to join the others on the walkway bed. Every time a runner or cyclist roared past, they stirred and twisted, briefly alive once more, before settling back to sleep.
Techniques and Devices Used: Metaphor, personification, seasons
Resulting Effects: Establishing mood, passage of time

PARKING GARAGE

SIGHTS
Gray concrete pillars, a low roof, exit signs, stripes painted on the pitted pavement, oil stains, cigarette butts, pea gravel or mud clumps scattered across the ground, scuff marks along the walls of the exit ramps, glass or metal doors leading to a stairwell and automated payment machines, shoe marks on the pillars and walls, brown water stains on the concrete roof, signage (turning arrows, exit and stop signs, numbers or letters pinned to posts for orientation), rows of cars and trucks parked carefully within the lines, brake lights coming on, people heading to and from their cars (holding store bags, packages, or briefcases), cars circling for a spot, a flickering light overhead that casts odd shadows as the bulb starts to die, areas that are cordoned off for maintenance with wooden blockades or tape, a collection of maintenance supplies (painting or plaster buckets, ladders, other repair supplies) sitting in a parking space behind chain link fencing

SOUNDS
Brakes squealing, motors rumbling, a car horn echoing sharply off the walls, voices, arguments cut off by a door slamming shut, engines revving, motors pinging as they cool, the blowing whir of giant fans clearing out exhaust, backfiring and gears grinding, people talking on their phones as they walk to their car, a lightbulb buzzing, sticky stains creating suction noises as one walks over them, elevator doors dinging and then closing shut, the clink of keys as one pulls them out of a pocket or purse, beeps as cars are locked and unlocked by remote, the echo of footsteps crossing the cement, the clank of a chain from a rolling door on the entrance and exit

SMELLS
Motor oil, exhaust, smoke, dirt and stone, spilled antifreeze, road salt

TASTES
No food is associated with this setting, however characters may bring food or drink with them (like a bag of popcorn after watching a movie, for example).

TEXTURES AND SENSATIONS
Sticky pavement pulling at one's shoes, the smoothness of a polished doorknob one twists or pulls to access the stairwell or elevator, punching the plastic buttons in the elevator to reach different parking levels, the points of cold metal as one selects the correct key for one's vehicle, accidentally nudging a dirty post as one gets into the car and then brushing the dust from one's sleeve

POSSIBLE SOURCES OF CONFLICT
Feeling fearful at discovering a homeless person using the garage for a warm place to sit or sleep
Walking to one's car and feeling followed
A section of lights going out
Getting to one's car and being unable to find one's keys
A carjacking or abduction
Being approached by someone asking for help

Arriving at one's car to discover it has been damaged (paint scrapes, a dented bumper, a break-in, etc.)
Forgetting where one parked

PEOPLE COMMONLY FOUND HERE

The people using an underground or multi-level parking garage (also known as a parkade) will
depend on where it is located. Working professionals and people employed within a high density
location would be the most likely to use a parkade situated in a busy business district downtown,
while shoppers and mall employees would use one attached to a mall. If underground parking is
part of an apartment building, only those living there would have access to it. Often maintenance
people doing work in the building have a storage area in the parking garage, and so they too may
be seen coming and going.

RELATED SETTINGS THAT MAY TIE IN WITH THIS ONE

Big city street (38), elevator (56), parking lot (102), shopping mall (180)

SETTING NOTES AND TIPS

Many business buildings have underground parking, as do apartments and malls. Freestanding
parking structures at hospitals, airports, train stations and other busy locations are also common
sights in bigger cities. The size and lighting of a parking garage will vary, and the time of day or
night will dictate how busy the parking garage is. Some are patrolled or have a security booth, but
as automation increases, these are becoming more and more rare.

Parking garages cause many people discomfort, especially those who have been victimized in
some way, or who suffer from anxiety. The low ceilings, packed-in cars and narrow lanes can also
cause a bit of claustrophobia to emerge, making this a great setting to bring out tension. Not only
can you build a sense of stress or unease in your character as they interact with this setting, you
will at the same time trigger emotional memories in your readers as they are reminded of their
own past experiences in parking garages.

SETTING DESCRIPTION EXAMPLE

Halfway to her Grand Cherokee, the lights overhead started to flicker. Mary stopped, her heel
skidding against the dirty cement in a sandy rasp. The rows of parked cars, mud-splattered
cement posts and faded yellow paint strips came and went in rapid flashes. *In a movie, this would
be the point when a deranged escaped convict would jump out between parked cars and axe me to
death.* The thought broke her paralysis and she ran the last twenty feet to her truck, jamming the
button on her key fob to unlock the door.

    Techniques and Devices Used: Light and shadow, multisensory descriptions
    Resulting Effects: Establishing mood, reinforcing emotion, tension and conflict

PARKING LOT

SIGHTS

Black or gray pavement with the occasional pothole, yellow parking blocks, white lines to mark the spaces, blue paint to designate handicapped spots, parked cars and trucks, vehicles pulling up to the curb to let people out, lights, trees and greenery framing the lot, signs (handicapped parking, stop signs, 30-minute parking, loading area signs), arrows painted on the asphalt to indicate traffic flow, sidewalks littered with fallen leaves, mulch and twigs blown up against the curb, trash (wadded papers, crushed soda cans, Styrofoam cups, cigarette butts), fire hydrants in the grassy areas, in-ground sprinklers, neon signs in the windows of nearby stores, garbage cans on the sidewalks chained to a light post, speed bumps, shopping carts, security cars or golf carts paroling the area, people walking to and from nearby stores, groups standing on the sidewalk or gathered near cars, parents holding their children's hands as they walk, customers putting bags in their trunks, a car with its blinker on to claim a spot, kids walking the curbs like balance beams, people placing flyers under windshield wipers, seasonal vendors offering fresh produce or local goods out of the back of a truck at harvest time (corn, apples, cherries, honey, etc.), an awning set up to do windshield repairs on the spot

SOUNDS

Birds chattering, traffic, people talking, the beep of a car door being locked or unlocked with a remote, car doors slamming, vehicles idling, screeching tires as cars turn corners, horns honking, the clacking sound of heels on asphalt, a child's running footsteps and a parent yelling at her to wait, brakes squealing, a bus beeping as it backs up, the rattle of a shopping cart over the asphalt, music from outdoor speakers attached to a store

SMELLS

Pavement, wet asphalt, food from nearby restaurants, grass, exhaust, rain, cigarette smoke

TASTES

Some settings have no specific tastes associated with them beyond what the character might bring into the scene (chewing gum, mints, lipstick, cigarettes, etc.). For scenes like these, where specific tastes are sparse, it would be best to stick to descriptors from the other four senses.

TEXTURES AND SENSATIONS

The wind tugging at one's clothing and hair, the wet pelt of rain, hard concrete underfoot, heat rising from the asphalt making the air unbearably hot to breathe, the shock of moving from a cool car to a hot parking lot (or vice versa), the weight of a cumbersome key ring in one's hand, juggling many things while crossing the parking lot (a purse, shopping bags, keys), the vibration of a shopping cart handle when pushing it across uneven ground, having to squeeze out of the car to avoid too-close vehicles, the resistant pull of gum that has been stepped in

POSSIBLE SOURCES OF CONFLICT

Getting into a car accident or having one's car door dinged
Difficulty finding a spot

Waiting for a spot only to have someone else take it

Forgetting where one's car is parked

Being hit by a car as it's backing out

Someone driving the wrong way down the one-way lane

Children running and not paying attention

Being mugged or attacked at night

Needing a handicapped spot and finding them occupied by non-handicapped drivers

Drivers texting or talking on the phone and not paying attention

Stepping in gum or a sticky patch of unidentifiable dried liquid

Dropping one's purchases in the street

Carts that have been left out instead of taken to the designated drop-off spots

Leaving one's purse or phone in a shopping cart by accident

PEOPLE COMMONLY FOUND HERE

Consumers, employees, parents and children, parking lot maintenance workers, police officers, residents (if the parking lot is connected to residential building), seasonal vendors, security guards, teenagers

RELATED SETTINGS THAT MAY TIE IN WITH THIS ONE

Airport (252), grocery store (166), parking garage (100), shopping mall (180)

SETTING NOTES AND TIPS

Parking lots are often overlooked as a potential setting because they're so ordinary. But they can be very convenient, since they're found in so many places. People often become less observant in parking lots because they're intent on one thing: getting to the car or store. This lack of attention means that people are more easily targeted and are less likely to notice private things that may be going down, like clandestine meetings, teenage make-out sessions, abductions, or quiet vandalism, making a parking lot an ideal spot for all kinds of conflict.

SETTING DESCRIPTION EXAMPLE

The automatic doors swooshed open, and the heat from the parking lot hit me with a heavy, wet slap. My hair immediately frizzed and I scraped it into a pony, blowing the stinging smell of new tar out of my nose. Heat waves shimmered over the newly paved lot, one that seemed so much bigger in the afternoon heat at the end of my shift. Shoppers were everywhere, pushing their grocery carts to their cars, loading up bags and corralling kids into vans. The loud clash of metal on metal as carts were rammed into the collection wicket clawed at my ears. I picked up speed, thinking of that glorious blast of air conditioning waiting for me in my car, of the soft music ready to flow from the speakers, helping to shut the rest of the world out.

    Techniques and Devices Used: Multisensory descriptions, weather

    Resulting Effects: Characterization, reinforcing emotion

PENTHOUSE SUITE

SIGHTS

A private elevator or entrance, a security system with motion sensors, a spacious entryway (high ceilings, marble floor, mirrors, decorative embellishments) which opens up to a large living area (custom furniture that fits the owner's sense of style, a state of the art sound system and TV, an opulent fireplace, floor-to-ceiling windows that boast skyline views, etc.), rooms branching off from the main living area (guest bedrooms, a laundry, a sauna, a workout room with high-end equipment, an office or library, an elegant dining room, bathrooms), displays of artwork (paintings by one's favorite artists, statues or glasswork, collections that align with one's interests), a few signature antiques or pieces with historical significance (a bed frame from the White House, an Egyptian handmade window screen, etc.), sophisticated technological sensors for optimal temperature and lighting, electronic shades or awnings for one's private terrace, top-of-the-line kitchen appliances and granite countertops, rare imported flooring, custom moldings, cabinetry and fixtures, a wine fridge or temperature-controlled wine pantry, a sprawling master bedroom (sometimes on its own level with luxury carpeting and bedding), throw rugs and pillows, freshly cut flowers, staff (a housekeeper, maids, a nanny), French doors leading to a tiled patio (loungers, an umbrella, a small private pool or spa, a bar and outdoor sitting area, a barbeque, security railing, ambiance lighting)

SOUNDS

Soft music from a sound system, the ding from one's private floor elevator, the click of shoes over marble or wood floors, the slide of the door opening or closing, the electronic whir of shades being positioned, the soft *whump* of a gas fireplace turning on, kitchen sounds (preparing meals, glassware and cutlery clinking, plates being set out on a table, the pop of a cork, wine glugging through an aerator, voices and laughter while entertaining others, water rushing out of a faucet), splashes coming from the private pool or spa, the creak and scrape of patio furniture, an occasional helicopter or plane flying past, the wind sliding through the leaves of potted plants on the outdoor patio, street sounds (traffic, sirens, music) from far below

SMELLS

Fragrant woods and oils, fresh-cut flowers, cleaning products, cooking smells, aftershave or perfume from the occupants, air freshening products, clean linen

TASTES

Good quality wine and other alcoholic beverages, bottled water (sparkling and still), food prepared at home or brought in by caterers for entertaining

TEXTURES AND SENSATIONS

The smoothness and weight of quality bedding, one's feet sinking into a plush carpet or throw rug, the feel of the night air sliding over one's skin while on the terrace, the silkiness of one's favorite wine after a long day, tucking one's feet up in an overstuffed chair or lounger to read or watch TV, the slide of water on one's skin in the pool, hot sun that turns the patio's tile warm, always-clean surfaces

POSSIBLE SOURCES OF CONFLICT

A home invasion

Financial troubles that lead to unpaid rent

Booking a penthouse suite (if in a signature hotel) and discovering it was double-booked and now unavailable

A building fire that shuts down all the elevators

A guest who drinks too much and ruins an expensive antique or irreplaceable furnishing

An embarrassing theft (of an item belonging to one's guest) that occurs while hosting a party

RELATED SETTINGS THAT MAY TIE IN WITH THIS ONE

Black-tie event (196), elevator (56), limousine (262)

PEOPLE COMMONLY FOUND HERE

A chef, a doorman, a housekeeper, a nanny, caterers, cleaning staff, interior designers and their employees, maintenance personnel and delivery people, the owner or renter

SETTING NOTES AND TIPS

Penthouse suites are at the top floor of a building and include stunning city skyline views. Perceived to be the height of luxury, these suites are expansive, opulent, and have all the amenities a person might need. Penthouse suites may be rented short-term or long-term, or even purchased outright, and will be styled according to the tastes of the owner (either the building owner if it is a rental space, or the actual owner if it belongs to someone else). If this is a hotel penthouse suite, the furnishings will lean toward a more "clean" design with less personal touches, but it will still have all the modern amenities and be a suitable space for both relaxation and entertaining. When using this setting, think about how the furnishings and the character's interactions with them can reveal his or her personality to readers, either through comparison or contrast.

SETTING DESCRIPTION EXAMPLE

Neda smiled, throwing me a half-wave as she chatted with two paunchy men about the painting above the fireplace, a gift from her parents. I took the wave to mean she'd be over in a minute, after her father's pot-bellied friends snuck a few more glances down her dress while she gestured at the crayon-esque artwork. It was a Guston, whoever the hell that was, and I thought my nephew could draw a little better, frankly, but Neda had lit up when she'd unwrapped it. The gift, I was sure, was more for me than Neda—a message from her sharp-eyed father telling me I wasn't good enough for his daughter. I sipped at my tart wine, wishing it was lager, and realized he was right. I didn't belong in this world of white custom sofas, trendy seagrass throw pillows, and marble statues of women holding water jugs. This whole apartment was stuffed with expensive things I could never afford.

    Techniques and Devices Used: Contrast, symbolism

    Resulting Effects: Characterization, reinforcing emotion

POLICE STATION

SIGHTS

A **waiting area** with chairs, a flag, statuary, a map of the city or county, Rotary Club plaques, restrooms, a water fountain, a glass partition that has to be spoken through to gain entrance to the station, a bell to be rung for service, doors with electronic locks and keypads, **the dispatch room** (computers, phones, TVs), a **secure armory** filled with weapons, **interview rooms** (table and chairs, handcuffs, pens and pads of paper), **holding cells** (concrete walls, a door with a window in it, a steel table and stools attached to the floor), **a recording room** (computers that record interviews and witness accounts, a TV screen that shows what's happening in an interview room, pens and paper, table and chairs), **transcription rooms** (cubicles, officers dictating reports into recording devices, transcribers entering recorded reports into computers), **debriefing rooms** for bringing officers up to speed on current cases (a large table and chairs, a dry-erase board, a bulletin board, boxes of files, pens and notepads), **an evidence room** (baggies filled with evidence, a rolling cart filled with labelled baggies, crowded shelves, evidence lockers, boxes of spare evidence bags, an officer logging evidence and recording visitors), **offices** (for sergeants and detectives, the SWAT team and their equipment, a community service office), **a kids' area** where children can wait or be interviewed (soft furniture, coloring books and crayons, board games, blocks, books, toys), **a garage** used for searching a vehicle for evidence or for prepping a vehicle that will be used for undercover work (tools, automotive equipment) as well as for the secure transport of prisoners in and out of police vehicles, **a chain link impound cage** for bicycles, witnesses giving statements, suspects being interviewed, children and family members waiting in the waiting area, police officers doing desk work, a break room

SOUNDS

People shifting about in the waiting room, officers discussing cases behind the glass, phones ringing, doors buzzing, keys jingling, electronic doors clicking open, the quiet murmur of dispatchers speaking into headsets, officers interviewing a suspect, the rattle of a suspect's handcuffs as he answers questions, keyboards clicking, papers being flipped, music playing from a player, shoes squeaking on tile floors, file cabinets sliding open, police radios squawking, people arguing, babies crying, sirens sounding from outside, voices coming over an intercom system, whistling and humming, doors opening and closing, officers chatting and joking in the break room, printers spitting out rap sheets, TV and microwave noises from the break room

SMELLS

Old coffee, cleaning chemicals, metal, sweat, cigarette smoke wafting off the clothing of smokers

TASTES

Coffee, soda, delivery food or a lunch brought from home

TEXTURES AND SENSATIONS

The claustrophobic sensation of being brought into a locked facility, pacing the length of a tiny holding cell, cold handcuffs confining one's wrists, a hard plastic chair, sweat trickling down one's back, the powdery feel of latex gloves as one handles evidence, stretching or getting up to walk around after bending over a file or keyboard for a long period of time, a headset that scratches the ears, sore wrists and fingers from sitting at a computer and typing, the weight of a gun at one's hip, leaning back in a rolling chair as one listens to a debriefing

POSSIBLE SOURCES OF CONFLICT
Uncooperative suspects
High or inebriated suspects
Paperwork and red tape that slows the process
Dishonest or untrustworthy witnesses
Unethical or incompetent police officers
Political posturing within the department
Pressure being applied from higher-ups
An officer losing his keys or access card
Pushy lawyers making things difficult
A power failure that disables the electronic locking mechanisms
Misplaced evidence
Conflicts of interest (family members or friends brought in for questioning, etc.)

PEOPLE COMMONLY FOUND HERE
Citizens who want to file a report, delivery people, detectives, dispatchers, friends and family members of suspects, lawyers, police officers, reporters, suspects and criminals

RELATED SETTINGS THAT MAY TIE IN WITH THIS ONE
Courtroom (54), police car (270), prison cell (108)

SETTING NOTES AND TIPS
Police stations have come a long way since the days of *Andy Griffith*. While some remain small, others are sprawling, taking up an entire multi-level building. Many factors will determine the environment of a station, including its budget and the size of the area it services. A low-traffic station might be clean and sterile, while a station in a high-crime area may be less tidy. There may be a large waiting area filled with restless people, or an empty waiting room that consists of just a few chairs. The holding cells could be numerous and spacious enough to fit large numbers of people, or there might be just one or two meant to hold a single suspect.

SETTING DESCRIPTION EXAMPLE
Ms. Minas perched on the edge of her plastic seat, pinching her pocketbook in a death grip. It had been two hours since they'd called about Brian. Ninety minutes she'd been sitting in this chair, surrounded by Meritorious Medal winners and posters of dimpled police officers—none of whom seemed to care that her grandson had been arrested and was being held somewhere behind that glass partition against his will.

    Techniques and Devices Used: Contrast
    Resulting Effects: Reinforcing emotion

PRISON CELL

SIGHTS
Iron bars shiny in places where hands have gripped them, cement walls, furniture that is firmly fastened to the wall or floor, single or bunk beds, a metal locker, a desk and chair, a barred window, thin mattresses and pillows, old sheets, rough blankets, a toilet and sink, stuff written on or carved into the walls, a painted cement floor that is worn in places (from pacing, pushups, etc.), prison-issue clothing and shoes, a few toiletries (toothpaste, a comb, soap), a lightbulb with a cage surrounding it, a reading table, books or magazines, photos taped to the walls, contraband hidden out of sight (cigarettes, drugs, bladed weapons, money, syringes, electronics, lighters, food, cutting tools), inmates (pacing, reading, sleeping, staring at the wall, doing sit-ups and push-ups, writing letters), the underside of the bunk above one's mattress with photos tucked into the springs

SOUNDS
Footsteps echoing along the walkways, coughing, an inmate whispering to his neighbor, whistling and humming, swearing, inmates muttering to themselves, shoes squeaking or shuffling, pages turning, water turning on and off, toilets flushing, grunting or panting while one exercises, mattresses squeaking, guards speaking to or yelling at the inmates, door buzzers going off, an iron door swinging open, mechanical doors sliding shut, locks mechanically opening or closing, voices coming over loudspeakers, sirens sounding, riots or fights breaking out, the jingle of chain from handcuffs and leg irons, the methodical sound of footsteps pacing the length of a cell

SMELLS
Sweat, metal, mildew, cleaning products, soap, air conditioning, food cooking in the mess hall, dust, dirt

TASTES
Water, contraband items, approved items purchased through the prison confectionery (cookies, chips, instant coffee, chocolate), strict meals from the mess hall

TEXTURES AND SENSATIONS
Cold metal bars and stainless steel sinks, a pitted concrete wall with gouged spots or messages scratched into it, a saggy mattress with no back support, springs digging into one's back, lumpy pillows, scratchy blankets, pilled sheets rubbing at one's skin, running a finger over a loved one's face in a photo, slick magazine pages, a pen held tightly in one's fingers while writing a letter, bruising and muscle soreness from a run-in with an inmate or guard, a hard concrete floor, sweat dripping down one's face while exercising in the cell, sunlight coming through a high window, the chafe of handcuffs or ankle cuffs, uncomfortable shoes rubbing at one's feet, pants that are constantly falling down and having to be yanked up or cinched tighter, one's forehead pressing against the cold metal bars

POSSIBLE SOURCES OF CONFLICT

Confrontations with inmates and guards

Despair and thoughts of suicide

Boredom

Prejudicial guards who decide to make an inmate's life difficult

Being assigned a difficult roommate (one who snores or talks incessantly, makes unappreciated advances, is violent, is a snitch, has disgusting habits)

A guard or roommate finding one's contraband stash

Being afraid to leave one's cell for fear of violence or retribution from another inmate

A broken toilet

Overcrowding

Getting caught up in a prison riot

Meeting an inmate who one truly believes to be innocent

PEOPLE COMMONLY FOUND HERE

Guards, inmates, officials on tour

RELATED SETTINGS THAT MAY TIE IN WITH THIS ONE

Ambulance (254), courtroom (54), police car (270), psychiatric ward (110), therapist's office (126)

SETTING NOTES AND TIPS

Prisons have changed quite a bit over the years, making it difficult to identify a standard for this setting. Modern prisons have solid walls and doors instead of the age-old iron bars, and stainless steel furniture has replaced porcelain commodities. Doors are largely mechanized, opening and closing with a buzzer and the press of a button, making jingling keys a thing of the past. However, modernization is costly; while some prisons are updated, others retain the accoutrements of the past or contain a mixture of the two. The type of prison will also determine what may be found in its cells. Maximum security cells house individuals rather than pairs of inmates and may have only the bare essentials in regards to furniture.

SETTING DESCRIPTION EXAMPLE

A guard stood to the side of the door waiting as I glanced one last time at the barren walls that had housed me for seven years. The room was straightened—toothpaste scum washed down the cracked sink, table cleared off, bed neatly made. I didn't need to do those things, but habits are hard to break. In my hands, I carried three items: a copy of Orwell's *1984*, a photo of my wife and kid, and my toothbrush. Maybe it was stupid to bring the toothbrush, but I didn't want to leave anything personal in this place. I turned my back on the room and followed the guard into the maze of hallways and gates that would lead me outside to where my family waited. A strange feeling swelled in my chest, something absent so long I almost didn't recognize it: hope.

    Techniques and Devices Used: Metaphor, symbolism

    Resulting Effects: Characterization, reinforcing emotion

PSYCHIATRIC WARD

SIGHTS

General Ward: (hospital-like hallways with plain walls and flooring, double doors between wards with security pads for exiting, rooms with nameplates (laundry room, medication room, therapy room, cafeteria, etc.), a common "day" room (magazine and books on a shelf, tables and chairs, games), wheelchairs, orderlies checking on patients and monitoring them, nurses and doctors making the rounds and distributing medications, security personnel walking the ward or working out of security stations, bubble mirrors at hallway intersections so personnel can see down each hallway, trays with paper medication cups holding pills, locked doors, secured drawers and cupboards, a crisis stabilization unit for emergencies, patients wearing color-coded wrist bands that indicate possible risk factors (a history of assault, an eating disorder, a flight risk) with a scannable code containing information about medication, meals served with plastic utensils, animals brought in for supervised pet therapy sessions, a basic fitness room and outside recreational area that can be utilized, personal counseling sessions

Patient Rooms: Doors with a small window insert, covered lights (with a dim setting for overnight monitoring purposes), a hospital bed (with a plastic mattress cover, white sheets, blanket, and padded restraints if necessary), a basic set of drawers and a desk, journal books with no spiral bindings, extra thick pencils that cannot be broken and used to harm oneself, heavy curtains pulled across a secured window, a bathroom (shower, tiled floors, a sink and mirror, a toilet, some may also have bubble mirrors for monitoring high risk patients), orderlies searching drawers for contraband or dangerous materials, patients being checked on the first few nights with a flashlight or woken up by a nurse with a needle as she takes blood for testing

SOUNDS

Doors opening and closing, fists banging on doors, echoing footsteps, a squeaky laundry cart being pushed down the hall, the beeps of monitoring equipment, the exhale of a blood pressure cuff, a plastic mattress cover crinkling as one shifts at bedtime, buzzing florescent lights, people (talking to themselves, humming, singing, muttering, crying or screaming), arguments between patients, music used to calm patients during certain sessions (like art therapy), the whisper of cloth (if shoes are not allowed on a ward), air conditioning or heaters that click and rattle, coughing, codes being called over a speaker system, the calming voice of a nurse, orderly or therapist, patients making repetitive noises (throat clearing, clicking, or swearing) associated with certain disorders, secure doors opening with a click as a nurse swipes an access card over a reader

SMELLS

Food smells around mealtimes (gravies, oils, bread, spices, meats), disinfectants, sweat, deodorant, bleach-scented sheets and towels, astringent hand sanitizer foam, urine, vomit, alcohol swabs, musty air conditioning

TASTES

Bland hospital food (meals that meet nutritional values but lack flavor), juice, water, vending machine pop or chocolate (if one has obtained special privileges for progress and good behavior), chalky or plastic-tasting pills

TEXTURES AND SENSATIONS

Soft towels, a scratchy paper towel from a bathroom dispenser, the rub of a hospital bracelet against one's wrist, a cool glass window, gripping a plastic fork at mealtimes, the pain of self-inflicted pinches or scratches, thick cotton socks, footwear without shoelaces that slide loose during monitored exercise sessions, scratching at surfaces (a desktop, scraping paint off a pencil) out of boredom, gagging on a pill, the cool swab of alcohol and a pinch of a needle, gloved hands probing at skin during examinations to look for signs of self-harm, the clammy feel of wet hair that must air dry after a shower, the sense of release that comes from cutting oneself, running a finger along a hemline for comforting repetition, soft clay or cold paint during art therapy

POSSIBLE SOURCES OF CONFLICT

Receiving a medication in error
Arguments over favoritism (real or imagined)
Medication side effects (zoning out, food tasting bland, difficulty sleeping, hallucinations)
Refusing medications or needing to be restrained or isolated
Needing to use the bathroom but finding it locked due to special precautions (like guarding against purging)

PEOPLE COMMONLY FOUND HERE

Chaplains, doctors, janitorial staff, mentally ill patients, nurses, orderlies, psychologists, therapists, visitors (state-appointed guardians, family, and close friends)

RELATED SETTINGS THAT MAY TIE IN WITH THIS ONE

Ambulance (254), emergency room (58), hospital room (76), police car (270)

SETTING NOTES AND TIPS

Some psychiatric facilities exist within a regular hospital (a ward), while others are independent institutions. Patients may admit themselves, or if they're believed to be in immediate danger of harming themselves or others, they can be admitted by a psychiatrist or legal caregiver. Some mental hospitals may also have outpatient programs for low-risk patients. As with many settings, the rules and procedures will vary, as will the conditions of the facility.

SETTING DESCRIPTION EXAMPLE

A foul stench coated the hallway, and Cam was not the least bit surprised to smell it the strongest outside room 34. William Rand was a long-term schizophrenic who was known for regurgitating his meds and tossing them away. He was also known for his habit of smearing feces across the safety glass in his door. Sure enough, William had decorated his window, this time adding a smiley face flourish. Cam's gag reflex kicked in and he rushed to the custodial room's sink. He'd had it with this place. Time to get a new job.

    Techniques and Devices Used: Multisensory descriptions
    Resulting Effects: Establishing mood, foreshadowing

PUBLIC RESTROOM

SIGHTS

Small stalls against one wall, dented doors or missing lock holes sprouting wads of white toilet paper, a set of sinks with drippy faucets, rust rings around the drains, hair strands clinging to the white sinks, urinals with pink or blue sanitary cakes near the drain, a condom or tampon machine, messages written on the walls and in the stalls, advertisements on the interior stall door, toilet paper dispensers (sometimes broken or out of paper), urine on the seats or floor, a sanitary garbage box and a tissue seat cover dispenser, dirt and ripped-up toilet paper on the floor, a hook for a coat or purse in the stall, a garbage bin overflowing with brown paper towel wads, bits of soggy paper towels littering the countertop, pink soap oozing out of dispensers and streaking the sinks, hand dryers that may or may not work, aged mirrors that are losing their silver, water-speckled counters, a fold-down diaper changing station attached to one wall

SOUNDS

Water dripping from faucets that won't shut off, toilets flushing, girls laughing and fixing their makeup and hair, the whir of the hand dryer, the tear and crinkle of paper towels being pulled from a wall dispenser and used, the gurgling of a toilet refilling, echoing voices, stall doors slamming shut, locks clicking into place, people talking on their phones, bodily function noises that one typically associates with a restroom, parents ordering small children not to touch anything, babies crying

SMELLS

Cleaner, soap, bleach, cloying perfume, hairspray, bathroom smells

TASTES

Some settings have no specific tastes associated with them beyond what the character might bring into the scene (chewing gum, mints, lipstick, cigarettes, etc.). For scenes like these, where specific tastes are sparse, it would be best to stick to descriptors from the other four senses.

TEXTURES AND SENSATIONS

Sitting on a tissue-thin seat cover, holding a foot against the door to keep it closed when the lock is broken, using a foot to flush the toilet, using one's elbows or forearms to open a door, slippery soap, wet hands from washing, foamy lather, a scratchy paper towel used to dry one's hands, smoothing on lipstick or plucking at one's hair, rubbing a finger under the eyes to remove makeup smudges, being embarrassed about doing one's business in public and trying to do so quietly, shoving one's sleeves up to keep them from getting wet while washing, water from the counter dampening the front of one's shirt, struggling to keep one's clothing from touching the floor while using the toilet, toilet paper that's rough and thin

POSSIBLE SOURCES OF CONFLICT

Someone lying in wait in a stall
Running out of toilet paper or soap

Discovering that all the toilets are plugged up
Being followed by bullies who block the exit
Overhearing a conversation that puts oneself in danger
Witnessing a brutal crime while in a stall
Gastrointestinal issues
Being a germaphobe and having to use a public restroom
Seeking privacy but finding the restroom occupied
Not being able to get into the restroom when one really needs to

PEOPLE COMMONLY FOUND HERE
Cleaning staff, visitors

RELATED SETTINGS THAT MAY TIE IN WITH THIS ONE
Airport (252), amusement park (188), bazaar (158), convenience store (162), gas station (70), homeless shelter (74), park (98), shopping mall (180), sporting event stands (240), water park (244), zoo (246)

SETTING NOTES AND TIPS
Some public restrooms are well kept and post a sheet near the door that shows frequent cleanings, while others are rarely visited by custodial staff or restocked for supplies. If your scene uses this location, think about the character's reason for being here and what will take place. Which type of restroom will create strong contrast, add tension, or offer symbolism opportunities?

SETTING DESCRIPTION EXAMPLE
Amy shouldered open the rest stop door, wishing she hadn't ordered that extra-large soda with her hamburger at lunch. A draft stirred crumpled wisps of toilet paper against the dirty tile and the overhead florescent light flickered and buzzed, threatening to go out. Dead bugs decorated the single cracked sink, but water dripped from that faucet, so at least it worked. Two stalls were missing doors, and the third hung askew. She headed for it, praying that it held a square or two of toilet paper and no passed-out drug addicts.

Techniques and Devices Used: Contrast, multisensory descriptions
Resulting Effects: Establishing mood, tension and conflict

REFUGEE CAMP

SIGHTS
A fenced-in area with security gates, dry and sandy ground, flags flying, dwellings local to the area (thatched huts with tarp roofs, mud huts, a labyrinth of makeshift tents, rows of tin or cinderblock shacks), a registration building (with desks, computers, office supplies), a large tent for food storage, other storage areas where rations are distributed (clothing, bedding, heating materials), a hospital (with rows of cots, mosquito netting, bedding, bins of medical supplies), a playground or small open field, communal toilet facilities, fires burning in pits, plastic jugs and bottles of water, empty buckets and baskets, large bowls for washing clothes or food, pots and pans, clothing hanging to dry on roofs or bushes, a pumping system where refugees can fill up water jugs, people walking on foot or riding bicycles, wooden wagons drawn by refugees that carry supplies around the camp, trucks arriving piled high with bags of food (flour, rice, wheat, lentils) and medical supplies, long lines of refugees waiting to be registered or receive supplies, single-room schools (with student desks, textbooks, chalkboards), women carrying bundles on their heads, men walking with sacks slung over their shoulders, UN trucks and vehicles, jeeps carrying military personnel, stacks of debris (water containers, empty sacks, cloth scraps, pieces of wood, tin cups), graffiti-marked structures, children playing with makeshift toys (rocks, scrap metal, flat balls), children working alongside parents, idle children, water dripping into shelters and pooling on the ground, flies, people fixing broken items or repurposing them when they're beyond repair

SOUNDS
Announcements delivered through a megaphone or speaker system, the chain link fence rattling from people holding onto it, tarp roofs and curtained doorways fluttering in the breeze, people talking, coughing, singing, babies crying, children playing (kickball, chasing games, etc.), dogs barking, footsteps shuffling along the dusty ground, dry rice or beans rattling into a pot, small snaps from a burning cook fire, raised voices, wind whistling through a shack or hut, tent flaps fluttering, tires crunching over gravel, a squeaky bicycle rattling over the rough ground, mosquitoes buzzing, dirty water being dumped out, water splashing into a jug or bottle, spoons clanging against cooking pots, sacks being dropped to the ground, the noise of a large quantity of people living in a small area, the squeaking of brakes that signals the arrival of a supply truck, children reciting lessons or singing together in the school area, a radio playing news broadcasts

SMELLS
Sweat, body odor, unwashed bodies and clothes, urine and feces, dust, a cooking fire, flatbread being baked on a hot stone, boiling water

TASTES
Bland food (rice, beans, bread), lukewarm water, sweat

TEXTURES AND SENSATIONS
Stiff clothing that has been washed in unclean water, limp and sweat-stained clothing that hasn't been washed in some time, bug bites, sleeping on the hard ground in extreme hot or cold

weather, hunger pangs and desperate thirst, water that tastes stale and has grit in it, dirt getting into everything (clothes, bedding, food), constantly being sweaty, wiping oneself clean with a wet rag, the weight of a sack of food over the shoulder or a bundle balanced on the head, symptoms specific to certain illnesses (cholera, malaria, jaundice, hepatitis, tuberculosis, HIV, typhoid, parasites), water splashing over one's hands or feet while a jug is filled, stepping into a shelter and out of the sun or wind, sitting against a rough hut wall, water slaking one's thirst, relief at eating something, sitting on a rock or log, dust on the skin, feet shuffling through the dirt, lank hair that itches the scalp, lethargy, boredom, the numbness of despair

POSSIBLE SOURCES OF CONFLICT
Attacks from violent people outside of the camp

Altercations between refugees from opposing cultures or religions

Fights over supplies and food

Attacks on women

Children with too much idle time on their hands

Illness and disease

Post-traumatic stress disorder

Prejudice or judgment from those in charge who are supposed to be impartial

Shifts in the political climate that could affect a camp's existence

PEOPLE COMMONLY FOUND HERE
Administrators, armed guards, celebrities on a goodwill tour, doctors and nurses, psychologists and therapists, refugees, reporters and journalists, teachers, United Nations representatives

SETTING NOTES AND TIPS
There are over seven hundred refugee camps around the world that cumulatively serve tens of millions of displaced people. Some camps are better funded and are therefore more habitable, offering more (and nicer) amenities than others. But regardless of the facility, every camp eventually fills, becoming overcrowded with people and families who would rather be living somewhere else but have nowhere left to go. Further problems arise as many of the people who inhabit these camps have been exposed to horrific atrocities and hardships, and adequate counseling is rarely available. This can lead to emotional volatility, rash decisions, and personal conflicts that may escalate quickly.

SETTING DESCRIPTION EXAMPLE
The line inched forward and I followed, craning my neck to see how much farther we had to go. Flies buzzed around my eyes and I shrugged a shoulder, my hands full with both water jugs. I'd been in line since dawn, and the sun was directly overhead. Worry over Natalya and the baby, alone in our hut, stabbed at me. I shuffled my feet in the dust, willing the never-ending line to move faster.

Techniques and Devices Used: Weather

Resulting Effects: Establishing mood, passage of time

RUN-DOWN APARTMENT

SIGHTS
Small rooms with low and water-stained ceilings, grimy windows, peeling linoleum floors, ripped wallpaper, chipped cabinet doors that hang askew, a rust-stained sink, cluttered surfaces, clothes thrown over furniture or lying on the floor, dishes piled in the sink, discolored walls and cabinetry, drawers that don't close all the way, mismatched furniture and sparse décor, outdated appliances, dirty baseboards, cobwebby corners, crooked or broken blinds, a window air conditioning unit, radiators that don't work, windows (that don't open, have torn screens, have no screens, are propped open with a book), threadbare curtains and bed linens, bare bulb lighting fixtures crisscrossed with spiderwebs, exposed plumbing and holes in the wall, blackened grout lines in the bathroom, chipped shower tiles, shower doors covered in hard water film, floors that slant or buckle, cracks in the ceiling, rickety stairs, thin or discolored carpets, a balcony (with clothes hanging to dry, holding bags of trash or recycling items), a mostly-empty fridge containing odds and ends, cockroaches and ants in the kitchen, rat and mouse droppings along the floorboards, belongings stacked in piles or in old boxes, trash littering the floor, pictures hanging crookedly on the walls

SOUNDS
A dripping faucet, creaking floors, voices and TV noises coming clearly through thin walls, neighbors yelling and fighting, babies crying, dogs barking, feet clattering up and down the stairs, footsteps shuffling along the hallway, warped doors scraping open or slamming shut, sirens and other traffic noise, people knocking on doors in the hall, phones ringing, the squeak of a drawer being pulled open, the hum of an old refrigerator, rats and mice scurrying in the walls, an air conditioning unit clanking on or off, the wooden screech of an old window being forced open, water pipes banging, the whir and rattle of a ceiling fan, curtains rustling in a breeze, bed springs squeaking, normally quiet noises that can be heard throughout the small apartment (food sizzling on the stove, someone rummaging through a drawer, silverware scraping over a plate, a ticking clock, someone talking on a phone, the shower running)

SMELLS
Mildew and mold, dust, the rusty smell of hard water, urine in the stairwells, a wet dog, spoiled food, sweat, body odor, food cooking, grease and oil smells from the kitchen, unwashed clothes, garbage that needs to be taken out, dirty diapers, old cigarette smoke

TASTES
Stale air, food that is inexpensive and easy to make, cigarettes, alcohol, water from the faucet

TEXTURES AND SENSATIONS
Heavy metal locks on the door, water dripping from a shower head with low pressure, a cold shower, floorboards that give and bend under one's weight, walking on a sloped floor, having to tug on a tight drawer to get it open, sinking into a saggy couch or mattress, sweating in an apartment with no air conditioning, occasional breezes from a ceiling or oscillating fan, shoving

open a sticky window, washing dishes by hand, sitting in a broken chair carefully so it doesn't fall apart, scratchy blankets on the skin, thin pillows that cause pain in the neck, jumping as a mouse or cockroach crawls out of a cabinet, walking over a carpet so thin the hard floor can be felt underneath it, a cold floor under one's bare feet, banging on the wall or ceiling to tell neighbors to quiet down, allergy symptoms due to dust or mold

POSSIBLE SOURCES OF CONFLICT
Broken appliances the landlord refuses to fix
Shady neighbors and illegal activity in one's apartment building
Not being able to make rent
Dictatorial landlords
Faulty sprinkler systems and fire escapes
Diseases from vermin
Robbers looking for money or drugs
Drive-by shootings and stray bullets
Unreliable or dangerous roommates

PEOPLE COMMONLY FOUND HERE
Guests, landlords, managers, tenants

RELATED SETTINGS THAT MAY TIE IN WITH THIS ONE
Rural Volume: Bathroom (40), child's bedroom (50), kitchen (66), living room (68), teenager's bedroom (86)
Urban Volume: Alley (34), elevator (56), old pick-up truck (268), parking garage (100), parking lot (102)

SETTING NOTES AND TIPS
Run-down apartments are often part and parcel of a run-down apartment building (though this isn't always the case) and are usually inhabited by people who are struggling to make ends meet. But this doesn't mean that these residences are devoid of personality. Even a seedy dwelling should tell the reader something about the people living there, from items collected, to artwork on the walls, to its state of cleanliness. As with any home dwelling, a few well-chosen details about a character's living space can tell the reader a lot about who lives there.

SETTING DESCRIPTION EXAMPLE
Ben jerked, blinking shadows from his eyes and kicking off the damp sheet. His heart thrummed a bass beat in his chest, making it hard to hear what had woken him. Sirens, or the dude in 312 yelling at his wife? His next door neighbor's sorry excuse for a dog whining out on the balcony? No, all of that was outside. His room was a tomb—not a clock ticking, not a cockroach stirring, not a wheeze from the . . . his gaze darted upward. The warped overhead fan blades drifted silently clockwise, taking forever to hobble through a final rotation before dying. Great. Ben yanked his sweat-drenched T-shirt over his head and scrubbed his face with it. Now he'd never get back to sleep.
   Techniques and Devices Used: Metaphor, multisensory descriptions, personification
   Resulting Effects: Establishing mood, foreshadowing, tension and conflict

SEWERS

SIGHTS

Curved cement walls, rusted metal grates, pipes, mesh debris collectors, standing water, canals and tunnels, larger reservoirs, raised walkways, center channels in large pipes for water flow, manhole access points, ladders leading up to the street, graffiti on the walls, oily water peppered with waterlogged garbage, clots of water foam and other slimy buildup, access chambers and tunnels that branch off the main line, shadows, mold and algae, dripping water, rats, spiders, cockroaches, beetles, centipedes, drug paraphernalia, weak light shining down from street level grates, aqueducts, slimy walls, dead rodents floating in the water, air vents, overflow lines high up on the walls, discolored brick walls, debris caught in grates (sodden plastic bags and fabric, leaves, branches, remnants of cardboard boxes), cracked cement, rust trails bleeding from pipe access points on the wall, paint-blistered signs leading work crews to designated areas, bobbing flashlight beams from work crews or other visitors

SOUNDS

Dripping water, splashes and odd echoes, the squeak and click of rats congregating, sloshing footsteps, urban sounds from above (traffic, street sounds, voices), the roar of subway trains causing the pipes to vibrate, manmade waterfalls to create drainage flow, gurgling water in the pipes, roaring water at high capacity (during or after storms), running water, debris scraping along the edges of pipes and catching on grates, the high-pitched squeal of brakes from nearby subway lines

SMELLS

Stagnant, dirty water, an overpowering odor of sewage (if the sewer is used partially for sewage), decomposition, pollutants (motor oil, grease, other lubricants that wash in with the street water), the tang of wet stone, mold, rust

TASTES

Some settings have no specific tastes associated with them beyond what the character might bring into the scene (chewing gum, mints, lipstick, cigarettes, etc.). For scenes like these, where specific tastes are sparse, it would be best to stick to descriptors from the other four senses.

TEXTURES AND SENSATIONS

Water seeping into one's boots, cold water soaking through one's clothing, rats that bump into or run over one's boots while on a walkway, sliding a hand along a slimy wall, the cold iron rungs of a ladder, being bumped by unseen debris in knee-deep murky water, feeling things brush against one's rubber boots, nausea rising in one's throat, claustrophobia, arms wind-milling in an attempt to keep one's balance on a dry ledge, swinging a flashlight from side to side or up and down, a back or neck ache from bending over in a narrow passage, jerking away to avoid something nasty floating in the water, rubbing sweat off the face with the back of the hand, drips of water falling on one's head or sliding down one's neck, stepping on mushy debris underwater, sweating inside a protective suit, the pinch of facemask straps

POSSIBLE SOURCES OF CONFLICT

Having to flee to a sewer as a means of escape

Getting stuck in a sewer during a storm or some other time when the water runs quickly

Rats and snakes

Falling into the water

Claustrophobia

A fear of drowning

Ingesting dirty water

A wound getting infected from contaminated water

Losing one's light source

Running into strangers underground when one is far from help

Getting lost and being unable to find an exit point in the dark

Hypothermia

RELATED SETTINGS THAT MAY TIE IN WITH THIS ONE

Subway tunnel (276)

PEOPLE COMMONLY FOUND HERE

Civil engineers, inspectors, maintenance workers, urban explorers, vagrants

SETTING NOTES AND TIPS

While sewers are often used in video games and movies to house hidden rooms and provide privacy for clandestine meetings, in reality, they're hard to access and are usually uninhabitable. That said, sewers differ depending on where they are located. Some are so confined that they are difficult for city workers to navigate much less a character in a novel, while others are expansive and surprisingly well kept as they once functioned as a channel to transport supplies into a growing city. Unless your novel takes place in a specific contemporary location, you have some creative license; just make sure to pull in enough realistic sensory detail (especially smell) to make the setting feel real and vivid to readers. If your sewer setting takes place in a real location, do some legwork and see what information you can find about the sewer system.

SETTING DESCRIPTION EXAMPLE

The beam of my flashlight played off the filth-encrusted walls, the tide line showing where the water had gone down a good four feet. Claws ticked against metal and I jumped. My light caught the tail end of something scurrying along a rusty pipe. A shudder ran through me. I hated it down here. Hated it. Cold water pressed against my waterproof gear, and I nudged unseen debris with each step. Near the entrance of the offshoot tunnel, an unholy stench slammed into me. I pressed a sleeve to my nose; the blockage was close. After a week's worth of rain in half a dozen neighborhoods, there were sure to be a few deceased pets or other animals caught in the grates. I hoped that would be all I found.

Techniques and Devices Used: Light and shadow, multisensory descriptions, weather

Resulting Effects: Establishing mood, reinforcing emotion, tension and conflict

SMALL TOWN STREET

SIGHTS
Parked cars, striped awnings, colorful and welcoming displays in storefront windows, mom-and-pop businesses (such as a locally-owned deli, coffeehouse, a flower shop, a bakery, an ice cream parlor, etc.), personal residences on the second floor above the stores, other municipal standards (a post office, a police station, a small fire house, a library), tree-lined sidewalks, colorful flower boxes or potted plants outside shops, pedestrians strolling along and then stopping to talk to people they know, streetlights or four-way stops, single lane traffic with faded pavement markings, crosswalks, light posts with a hook for a hanging flower basket, sapling trees spaced along the sidewalk, garbage cans painted by local artists to be more appealing, turnstile parking meters, people walking their dogs or pushing strollers, kids on bikes or skateboards, cracked sidewalks, clean gutters, water bowls placed by a business' entrance for thirsty dogs, window shoppers, someone on a lunch break sitting on a bench to people watch

SOUNDS
Cars driving past, brakes squealing or tail pipes backfiring, older trucks with chugging engines, the occasional honk of a horn, a driver calling out and waving to someone walking past, chimes ringing as doors are opened, people chatting as they walk, dogs barking or panting in the heat, leaves skittering along sidewalks, the breeze fluttering an awning, customers chatting at an outdoor table, water splattering the sidewalk as someone hoses off the plants

SMELLS
Yeasty bread browning in bakery ovens, fresh flowers, sunshine, green leaves, spices, hamburgers cooking, frying grease, car exhaust

TASTES
The sugary coldness of an ice cream cone, the bitterness of coffee, water, a slush drink from the local gas station convenience store

TEXTURES AND SENSATIONS
Uneven ground when walking over cracked sidewalks, the bumpy hardness of a brick storefront wall while leaning against it, pulling on the smooth door handle of a shop, the searing heat of sitting down on a leather car seat after it's been parked in the hot sun, placing the arch of one's palm against the glass store window to see inside, the tug of a dog leash during a morning walk, a metal bench that has been warmed in the sun, a cool breeze lifting one's hair, kids skateboarding or riding scooters across bumpy sidewalk slabs, heavy bags full of purchases causing arm strain

POSSIBLE SOURCES OF CONFLICT
Intoxicated altercations near a pub or liquor store
Rivals or enemies running into one another
Small town gossip being aired
Cars parking poorly and taking up too much room

A driver cutting someone off

A pedestrian or cyclist being hit by a car

A dog slipping its leash and running into traffic

Finding a dog or baby left in a car while the owner is shopping

Experiencing a public humiliation that everyone knows about (losing an election, being arrested, getting fired)

A chain restaurant or retail store coming to town and threatening one's small business

Being at odds with an important person who can make one's life difficult (the mayor, the sheriff, a building inspector)

PEOPLE COMMONLY FOUND HERE

A street cleaning crew, locals, police officers, shopkeepers, tourists

RELATED SETTINGS THAT MAY TIE IN WITH THIS ONE

Antiques shop (156), bank (36), bookstore (160), grocery store (166), hair salon (72), hardware store (168), laundromat (82), library (84), parade (222), park (98), parking lot (102), police station (106)

SETTING NOTES AND TIPS

Small towns often have generic mom-and-pop stores rather than big box franchises, and everyone seems to know everyone else. Criminal activity still exists (especially if the town has seasonal tourists), but infractions tend to be less serious than the ones seen in a bigger city. For the most part, locals involved in criminal activity are known to the police, and a smaller population allows those in charge to better control troublemakers.

SETTING DESCRIPTION EXAMPLE

Ten feet from The Big Grind I could tell Sarah was on shift. Not only was there a flower-filled welcome message drawn in chalk on the sandwich board outside, but soft jazz, her favorite, seeped out the propped-open door alongside the scent of fresh-roasted coffee.

    Techniques and Devices Used: Multisensory descriptions

    Resulting Effects: Characterization, establishing mood

SPA

SIGHTS

A reception area, comfortable chairs and sofas, warm décor (dark wood, thick carpeting, plush seating, lamps, cozy colors), cosmetics and beauty products for sale, brochures for spa products and services, bowls of potpourri, incense burners, lit candles, glasses and a pitcher of water with lemon or cucumber slices floating in it, complimentary coffee or tea, magazines fanned out on a table, a public telephone with pens and paper, potted plants, **a dressing area** (lockers and changing rooms, mirrors, hair products and other toiletries, cushioned benches, towels, robes, showers), **private massage rooms** with supplies (massage tables, a hamper for towels, a swivel stool, a tray of lotions and oils, a music player, hot stones, tissues, a towel-warming machine, thermostat controls and switches for adjustable lighting, **a treatment room** (disposable cloth tube bra and underwear, therapeutic muds and exfoliating scrubs, a sink, a bed ensconced in plastic within a low-sided tub, a rinsing sprayer, hot towels, aromatic lotions), clients walking around in robes and sandals, **manicure and pedicure rooms** with supplies (foot baths, towels, a rack of polishes on the wall, polish remover, lotion, cotton balls, nail clippers, pumice stones, cuticle pushers, files, buffers), **a hair salon** (shampooing sinks, reclining chairs, dryers, hair products, combs and brushes in jars of disinfectant, adjustable chairs, smocks, scissors, irons, hair coloring supplies)

SOUNDS

Nature sounds or sensory music (chimes, flutes, running water), footsteps in thick carpet, doors closing softly, air whooshing through vents, a phone buzzing in the waiting area, receptionists answering questions, water being poured from a pitcher or dispenser, groans from massage patients, lotion being pumped from a bottle, water splashing into a sink, magazine pages being flipped, timers going off, the snick of hair scissors and nail clippers, hair dryers humming, hair trimmers buzzing, the swish of a broom as hair is swept up and thrown away, guests chatting and laughing

SMELLS

Musky incense, oils and lotions, herbal aromas (lavender, rosemary, grapefruit, sandalwood, eucalyptus, lemongrass), fresh-cut flowers, aromatic soaps, acetone, nail polish, shampoos and conditioners, the chemical smell of hair dye, hot air from a dryer, essential oils and mists during a massage or treatment

TASTES

Tea or coffee, water, mints

TEXTURES AND SENSATIONS

Being ensconced in a fluffy robe, a thick towel against one's skin, plush carpet under one's feet, a cushioned chair, a firm massage table, the knead and pull of a massage therapist's hands during a session, discomfort in the muscles as they're being stretched, a euphoric sensation of relaxation, warm stones on one's back, oil being rubbed into the skin, lotion that has been warmed being smoothed onto one's arms and legs, a mud mask stiffening and tightening over one's face, stinging skin from an acid peel, cold cucumbers on the eyes, being tickled as someone touches one's foot during a pedicure, rough scrubbers and files being rubbed against the heel, dust from filed nails powdering one's skin, a cold slick of polish dampening a nail, cold lotion, heated towels being wrapped around one's body, scalp massages during a shampoo, cut hair ends making one's skin itchy, heat from an iron or blow dryer, hair being blown into one's face, tension in the back and shoulders from sitting still for long periods of time, rushing to change in the locker room before other clients come in, not wanting to leave when one's appointment is over

POSSIBLE SOURCES OF CONFLICT
Embarrassment at having to remove one's clothing
Sensitive skin and sore muscles
An allergic reaction to the chemicals in a skin or hair treatment
Being burned or temporarily disfigured from a treatment that was left on for too long
Disappointment over the haircut that one was given
Difficult clients
Having to administer peace and tranquility when one's mind or spirit is in a state of turmoil
Trying to speak quietly to a client who is hard of hearing
Getting stiffed on a tip
An entitled client expecting special service

PEOPLE COMMONLY FOUND HERE
Clients, hair stylists, makeup artists, manicurists and pedicurists, massage therapists, receptionists

RELATED SETTINGS THAT MAY TIE IN WITH THIS ONE
Hair salon (72), hotel room (78), waiting room (132)

SETTING NOTES AND TIPS
Spa services often depend on the venue. Hotel and resort spas will offer a large variety of services in a luxurious environment. Local spas have less space and may choose to specialize in one or two areas, such as massage and skin care. Regardless of the services that are available, the spa "feel" is fairly standard wherever the location, providing an atmosphere of peacefulness, pampering, and tranquility for all who visit.

SETTING DESCRIPTION EXAMPLE
I sank into the couch, pulling the warm robe more firmly around my legs. The air was heady with some aromatic scent (eucalyptus? sandalwood?) that soothed my breathing and calmed my thoughts. A receptionist placed a cup of mint tea on the table by my chair and slipped back to her desk. Soft music played overhead and my eyes drifted closed. If this is what the waiting room felt like, the hot stone massage was going to be outstanding.

Techniques and Devices Used: Multisensory descriptions, symbolism
Resulting Effects: Establishing mood

TATTOO PARLOR

SIGHTS
Neon signage out front, a seating area for waiting guests, coat racks, tattoo portfolios in binders, tattoo drawings on the walls, eclectic artwork for sale (paintings, pottery, jewelry, sculptures and knickknacks), promotional merchandise (T-shirts, mugs, key chains, bumper stickers), hanging mirrors, a TV, a drawing area with sketching supplies (tables, sketchpads, pens and pencils, markers), a reception counter, curtained-off rooms that reflect each tattoo artist's personality (via décor, memorabilia, pictures, artwork, the choice of music that's playing), licenses posted on the wall, clients reclining in chairs or beds, tattoo sketches tacked to the wall, boxes of disposable gloves, tattoo machines, inks and ink caps, needles, stacks of towels, a discolored towel that is being used to wipe away ink, thermal papers with tattoo stencils on them, ointments and bandages, headband magnifiers that allow the artist to better see the tattoo he's working on, adjustable lights, biohazard and sharps containers, autoclaves for sterilizing tools, sinks, aftercare products for sale, a break room area

SOUNDS
Music playing from a sound system, voices coming from the television, the buzz of the tattoo machine, background chatter, the receptionist welcoming clients, a client's footsteps as she is taken to a back room, clients shifting on a chair or bed, a rolling chair skating closer to a reclining client, sanitary wrappers being removed from equipment, water splashing in a sink while an employee washes his or her hands, pages turning as a customer flips through portfolios, the crumple of paper unfolding as a client produces original artwork for a potential tattoo, clothes being removed, a receipt machine printing a receipt, the crackle of paper as one sits on a covered chair, a client's indrawn hiss of pain when the process begins, exclamations of excitement and happiness as the client sees the finished product

SMELLS
Disinfectant, stale cigarette smoke, paint, microwaved or delivery food from the break area

TASTES
Some settings have no specific tastes associated with them beyond what the character might bring into the scene (chewing gum, mints, lipstick, etc.). For scenes like these, where specific tastes are sparse, it would be best to stick to descriptors from the other four senses.

TEXTURES AND SENSATIONS
Flipping and touching pages as one browses potential designs, sinking into a cushioned chair or bed, tense muscles and apprehension over the oncoming pain, feeling one's legs or head raising or lowering as the chair is adjusted, gloved hands touching one's skin, the press of a razor and the coolness of shaving foam, holding one's clothing out of the way as a tattoo is applied, lying or sitting in an unusual position, pain, deep breaths being drawn in and out, a towel swiping the tattoo site, tacky ointment, twisting one's body to catch sight of a finished tattoo, the pull of a taped-on bandage

POSSIBLE SOURCES OF CONFLICT
A client passing out from fear or nerves

Underage customers trying to obtain a tattoo

A parlor coming under fire for unsanitary practices

Tattoo artists stealing each other's designs

Getting a tattoo that doesn't look like what one requested

Being assigned to a surly or uncommunicative artist

Trying to work on a client with a low pain threshold

Indecisive clients

Running out of supplies in the middle of an application

Clients who come in drunk or high in a preemptive attempt to manage their pain

Customers lying about medical conditions that could create complications (pregnancy, the use of blood thinners, drugs recently taken)

A customer wanting a tattoo that is taboo (a swastika or racial slur, etc.)

PEOPLE COMMONLY FOUND HERE
Apprentices, customers, guests accompanying those getting tattoos, health inspectors, local artists hoping to sell goods on consignment, parlor owners, tattoo artists

RELATED SETTINGS THAT MAY TIE IN WITH THIS ONE
Big city street (38), shopping mall (180), waiting room (132)

SETTING NOTES AND TIPS
Tattooing has become an art form for many who engage in the practice. Individual shops will reflect the owner's philosophy and personal preferences. Some parlors will be artsy, while others might have a gritty and dark atmosphere. Regardless of the environment, licensed parlors must adhere to standard health regulations and are subject to regular inspections to ensure they're following sanitary procedures. Unfortunately, many unlicensed artists still find work by lowering their rates, targeting underage clients, and giving tattoos out of their own homes or at parties. These artists put people at risk by not adhering to proper sanitary procedures.

SETTING DESCRIPTION EXAMPLE
Macy perched on the edge of the couch and tried not to crumple the paper in her hand. Her boyfriend had designed the hummingbird himself—small, delicate, the perfect choice for her first tattoo. Her stomach cramped and she mashed a fist against it. Zeke had promised the pain wasn't too bad, but the thought of all those needles . . . she closed her eyes and breathed through her nose, noting the antiseptic smell of the air. It was clean. Safe. People got tattoos all the time. She could do this.

    Techniques and Devices Used: Multisensory descriptions, symbolism

    Resulting Effects: Characterization, reinforcing emotion

THERAPIST'S OFFICE

SIGHTS
Couches and soft chairs, throw pillows, cozy décor (soft lighting, throw rugs, warm colors), a dish of candy or mints, boxes of tissues, a small wastebasket, a bookcase filled with books and personal memorabilia, an office desk covered with the usual supplies (an inbox, a phone, stacks of files, paper pads and pens, a computer and printer, open reference books, a coffee mug, knickknacks), a burning candle, artwork on the walls, inspirational plaques, windows with the blinds or curtains drawn, potted plants or cut flowers, a corner or desktop water feature

SOUNDS
Muffled voices in the hallway or behind closed doors, a therapist's soft voice, the trickle of a fountain, soothing background music, people arguing, clients crying and sniffling, noses being blown, tissues being ripped from boxes, someone shifting awkwardly on a sofa, carpeted footsteps, the scratch of the therapist's pen as notes are taken, repetitive sounds made by nervous clients (clicking a pen, drumming fingers, twisting the cap on a bottle of water), the crinkle of a candy wrapper, awkward or stubborn silence, voices that raise or climb over one another during couple's therapy

SMELLS
Upholstery, coffee, tea, scented candles, air freshener

TASTES
Salty tears, bottled water, candy or mints, coffee, tea

TEXTURES AND SENSATIONS
A comfortable chair or squeezable pillow, shrinking away from someone at the other end of the sofa, a spine that is ramrod-straight or slumped in despair, jittery or tense muscles, tears trickling down the back of one's throat, sniffing back tears and snot, a hard wad in one's throat from the effort of holding emotion in, eyes prickling as tears begin to form, a dry mouth, taking deep breaths and rapidly blinking in an effort not to cry, a knotted stomach, soft tissues, dampness on the cheeks, blurred vision, the fight-or-flight response kicking in, clenching fists and jaws, leaning in to emphasize one's point, a muscle jumping in the face or jaw, clearing one's throat, fiddling with a watch or other piece of jewelry to have something to do with one's hands, scraping the heels of one's hands down the front of one's jeans as if to push bad feelings away, crossing one's arms and angling the body away from one's partner or the therapist, taking a swig of water to stall after a difficult question has been asked

POSSIBLE SOURCES OF CONFLICT
Clients who are in denial
Clients who are repressing memories and emotions
Seeing an inexperienced therapist who is unable to help
A therapist who is physically or emotionally involved with a patient

Dishonest clients

Meddling family members

A scenario in which one's therapist abruptly becomes unavailable (an injury, a family emergency that calls her out of town, personal issues, a sabbatical)

Side effects from one's medication

A client who refuses to speak or engage

An inattentive therapist

A therapist with personal experiences and emotional wounds that bring personal bias into sessions

PEOPLE COMMONLY FOUND HERE

A cleaning crew, clients, office staff, therapists

RELATED SETTINGS THAT MAY TIE IN WITH THIS ONE

Courtroom (54), hospital room (76), police station (106), psychiatric ward (110)

SETTING NOTES AND TIPS

Character wounds should be deep and hurtful, forming flaws and inhibiting the hero's ability to achieve his goals. Therapy is often helpful to get to the root of the problem and bring about self-revelation. A common problem with this setting is that the scenes leading up to this epiphany are often inactive ones and can slow the pace of the story. To alleviate this problem, be careful with the length of these scenes; don't let them drag out. Make sure that each scene is necessary to the overall story, and engage readers through the sharing of new information or the raising of new questions. Utilize body language in this setting as it can be especially revealing when characters are reluctant to speak or are bottling up their emotions.

SETTING DESCRIPTION EXAMPLE

Jake slouched on the end of the couch, as far from the therapist as he could get. He hadn't said a word yet and she was already making notes on her pad. The scratch of ink sawed at his ears, making him want to stab something with her pen. And that box of tissues. They pissed him off, sitting on the coffee table, all perky and within reach. You know, in case he felt the need to burst into tears. What a joke. And all this because he'd yelled at the coach and slapped that pushy reporter's camera out of his hand. He'd barely grazed the guy, and now he was stuck doing this stint to avoid "further repercussions." What a load of crap.

    Techniques and Devices Used: Multisensory descriptions

    Resulting Effects: Characterization, reinforcing emotion, tension and conflict

UNDERPASS

SIGHTS

A concrete or tiled tunnel going under a road or train track, vehicles using the road overhead or passing through the tunnel itself, pedestrians or cyclists sticking closely to the side, a floor made of concrete or pavers, light fixtures in longer passages, daylight shining from the far end of a very short underpass, colorful graffiti or murals, posters or ads hanging on the walls, water (running down the walls in rivulets, dripping from the ceiling, puddling on the ground), people turned into silhouettes from the light shining behind them, structural pillars or arches in a particularly wide underpass, stairs at the ends of pedestrian underpasses, burned-out lights that produce shadowy places, cobwebs and spiders, moths and other bugs fluttering around the lights, bird droppings splattering the ground, strands of dry grass and twigs spilling out of holes or ledges at the top of supports where birds nest, homeless people sleeping in sheets of plastic, blown leaves and dirt gathering in piles, water-damaged ceilings, debris in gutters (crumpled newspapers, discarded flyers, cigarette butts, plastic bags), fences or painted lines to separate motorized vehicles from pedestrians, cracked curbs, wild animals passing through (deer, bears, raccoons, possums) in rural areas, low spots that flood during heavy rains, grass growing up through cracks in the concrete

SOUNDS

Echoes, wind whistling or howling during wind storms, the hollow tock of footsteps, traffic thundering overhead, the amplified sound of cars driving through, water dripping from the ceiling and trickling along the floor, bicycles whirring by, wheels bumping over cracks in the concrete, humming lights, insects and moths buzzing around the light fixtures, distant sirens, people talking, small animals moving through debris at the edge of an underpass, leaves being blown by the wind and scuttling along the underpass's wall, pedestrians talking on cell phones as they walk, splashing through a puddle, the squawk of a bird, the hiss of a feral cat or wild animal

SMELLS

Rain, mildew, wet concrete, hot pavement, exhaust, urine, stale water

TASTES

Some settings have no specific tastes associated with them beyond what the character might bring into the scene (chewing gum, mints, lipstick, cigarettes, etc.). For scenes like these, where specific tastes are sparse, it would be best to stick to descriptors from the other four senses.

TEXTURES AND SENSATIONS

Being buffeted by the wind as one walks through the underpass, the air suddenly turning cooler as one enters the shade, hard concrete under one's feet, a blast of air as a car drives by, still and stuffy air in the middle of a long underpass, the stomach-tightening apprehension of entering an isolated place where danger may lurk, a slick metal handrail, solid brick walls, leaves crunching underfoot, water dripping onto one's head or sleeve, splashing through a puddle, uneven pavers that trip one up, a sticky spiderweb clinging to one's skin, moving into the other lane to avoid a questionable person or dark area, stumbling over debris or accidentally kicking a bottle or pop can in the dark, being startled by a bird flying out of a nest, jumping at the sound of something rustling through the debris, rat claws scraping the concrete

POSSIBLE SOURCES OF CONFLICT
Being attacked in the dark
A pedestrian being hit by a cyclist or driver
Dangerous debris (broken glass, used needles, etc.)
An underpass collapsing
Being caught in an underpass during an earthquake
Tripping over uneven concrete
Having to meet someone at an underpass late at night
Coming across a wild animal while in an underpass (in a rural area)

PEOPLE COMMONLY FOUND HERE
Cyclists, joggers and runners, motorists, pedestrians, vagrants

RELATED SETTINGS THAT MAY TIE IN WITH THIS ONE
Big city street (38), park (98), small town street (120), subway tunnel (276)

SETTING NOTES AND TIPS
Underpasses come in a wide range of sizes, from the length of a footbridge to multiple acres long. Some are dingy and damp (especially those that go under a body of water), while others are well lit and brightly painted. Certain underpasses are meant for vehicle use, some only accommodate foot and bicycle traffic, and still others cater to both. Many urban underpasses, once a haven for vagrants and troublemakers, have been turned into productive spaces, such as skate parks, flea markets, theaters, and homeless shelters, making this a versatile setting that can be used for many different scenarios.

SETTING DESCRIPTION EXAMPLE
Cyclists whizzed past Marjorie in the bike line, their wheels humming loudly against the pavement as the sound bounced off cement walls. Other pedestrians brushed past, intent on crossing the half-mile underpass and getting to work on time. But unlike them, Marjorie strolled. In the dim light, painted murals brightened the arches, their colors vibrant. Textured. She traced the brush strokes with her finger, wondering who had painted them, and when.

    Techniques and Devices Used: Multisensory descriptions
    Resulting Effects: Characterization, establishing mood

VET CLINIC

SIGHTS

A waiting room and reception area, tiled floors, cats in carriers and dogs on leashes, owners leafing through magazines or soothing nervous pets, racks of pet food displayed in a corner, drool spots and stray hairs on the floor, pet supplies for sale (shampoos, leashes and collars, tags, toys, skin treatments, vitamins, stain treatment systems, house training supplies, nail and hair clippers), flyers for upcoming fundraisers and events, animal-themed posters on the walls, individual exam rooms (a set of scales, a sink, a computer, assistants taking notes on clipboards, files, an exam table, medical instruments, garbage cans, sharps containers, assistants wearing scrubs and latex gloves, veterinarians in lab coats, posters depicting common animal anatomy such as digestive tracts or the heart and lungs), an in-house lab (an X-ray machine, an ultrasound machine, lead vests and aprons, a centrifuge, a microscope), a pharmacy, surgical rooms (an operating table, lights, trays of surgical instruments, anesthesia machines, IVs and catheters, blood pressure monitors, an autoclave, an oxygen machine), a kennel area (stacked cages, blankets, bowls of food and water, toys, pets lying down or standing and barking), a washer and dryer

SOUNDS

Animals verbalizing (barking, meowing, growling, chirping, squawking, squeaking, hissing, whining, crying), a dog's tail thumping the table or floor, owners chatting as they wait to be called to the back, phones ringing, assistants calling for patients to be seen, claws clicking on tile floors, shoes squeaking, doors opening and closing, the snap of latex gloves being pulled off, foot-operated garbage can lids clanging open and closed, muffled voices behind a closed exam room door, the buzz of hair clippers, water pouring into a metal sink, claws scrabbling on the metal surface of an exam table, the hydraulic sound of weight scale being lowered or raised, water being lapped from a bowl and splashing to the floor, kibble rattling into a metal bowl, hard treats being chomped, an animal obsessively licking a wound site until reprimanded by the owner

SMELLS

Disinfectant, bleach, animal dander, urine, feces, blood, wet fur, pet food, pet musk

TASTES

Some settings have no specific tastes associated with them beyond what the character might bring into the scene (chewing gum, mints, lipstick, etc.). For scenes like these, where specific tastes are sparse, it would be best to stick to descriptors from the other four senses.

TEXTURES AND SENSATIONS

A nervous dog twining between one's legs or climbing into one's lap, a rough leash in one's grip, a purring cat, the prick of a cat's claws as she kneads one's pant leg, the weight of a heavy pet carrier, trying to hold onto an excitable pet while filling out paperwork, a leash being wrapped around one's legs, pet hair on one's skin, dog drool dripping onto one's foot or arm, the tug of a dog on a leash, feeling a small pet's growl as another animal enters the room, a dog that is shivering in one's lap, the nip of a small dog's bite, smoothing a pet's fur in an effort to calm it down, being licked by a nervous dog, a slick floor that has recently been mopped, a cold metal exam table, dusty-feeling latex gloves, the rough texture of a doggy treat, a knot in one's stomach when waiting for a diagnosis

POSSIBLE SOURCES OF CONFLICT
Animal fights in the waiting room
Owners letting their animals run rampant
Being peed on by a nervous pet
Having to give or receive bad news about a pet
Outrage at the cost of services rendered
A veterinarian who is good with animals but terrible with people
Examining a pet that one suspects is being abused or mistreated in some way
A mystery illness that is difficult to diagnose
Being bitten by an animal during the examination
Having one's leg humped by an amorous dog
Being covered in animal hair prior to an important meeting or appointment
The difficult decision of whether or not to put a pet down

PEOPLE COMMONLY FOUND HERE
Animal rescue workers, assistants, children, pet owners, receptionists, veterinarians

RELATED SETTINGS THAT MAY TIE IN WITH THIS ONE
Pet store (176)

SETTING NOTES AND TIPS
Like medical clinics, vet clinics differ in size, cleanliness, services offered, and décor. Some maintain a sterile environment with colorless walls and metal accessories. Others are as warm and welcoming as any medical practitioner's office. Still others are animal-centric to the extreme, with murals, poster-covered walls, and pet play areas. The clinic tends to match its occupants, so the environment and level of customer service can say a lot about the veterinarian in a particular practice.

NOTE: If your character has an exotic pet such as a guinea pig, lizard, ferret or snake, she would need to take it to a veterinarian that specializes in exotic pets, since most general vet clinics aren't qualified to treat these animals.

SETTING DESCRIPTION EXAMPLE
Juggling the clipboard, my purse, and an overgrown cocker spaniel, I staggered to the nearest seat. I put Quincy in the chair next to me, but he clambered into my lap and proceeded to shed hair all over my sweater. With a sigh, I balanced the clipboard on his back. His trembling turned my neat handwriting into an illegible scrawl. My teeth ground together. You'd think we were here to discuss his final days instead of just getting his nails clipped.
    Techniques and Devices Used: Multisensory descriptions
    Resulting Effects: Establishing mood

WAITING ROOM

SIGHTS
A coffee table covered with glossy magazines and travel books, cardboard holders with pamphlets covering topics that might interest the clientele, posters on the walls, framed artwork, advertisements for services or temporary specials, a water cooler on a stand, a receptionist's desk, a sign-in sheet, clipboards with paperwork to be filled out, empty forms, a jar of pens, a machine dispensing numbers and an LED wall readout (if the business caters to walk-ins), rows of thin-padded seats, a toy corner for children (containing blocks, books, a coloring table, trucks, etc.), professionals in uniform (nurses in scrubs, bankers in suits), a business card holder with employees' cards, people waiting (checking cell phones, watching TV, reading a magazine or book, bouncing a baby, wrangling children, staring into space), a wall-mounted TV tuned to a news network or soap opera, boxes of tissues on the tables, signs pointing to the restroom, a sign reminding people to take their valuables with them, fake plants in the corners or on an end table, a wastebasket, a complimentary coffee machine, a door and hallway leading to individual rooms

SOUNDS
Magazine pages being carefully turned, people clicking keys on their cell phones, sounds from a gaming device, low whispers, coughing, throat clearing, heavy breathing, the rustle of clothing, the office phone ringing or beeping, doors opening and closing, the receptionist calling out a name, staplers banging, cell phone ringtones going off, the scratch of a pen as a visitor fills out forms, complaints about the long wait, creaking chairs, heels clicking across the floor, a printer or fax machine spitting out paper, children asking questions or expressing boredom, the hiss of air conditioning or heat, a glass partition sliding open when the receptionist is ready to see the next visitor, TV sounds or piped-in music, chairs creaking and scraping on the floor, the staff discussing work or laughing in the break room

SMELLS
Cologne, perfume, dust, room deodorizers, cleaning products, hand sanitizer, a bouquet of flowers sitting at the reception desk, old carpet

TASTES
Water, candy, cough drops, medicine, gum, mints, complimentary coffee

TEXTURES AND SENSATIONS
A dry throat, crossing and uncrossing one's legs, padded seat cushions against the back of one's legs, shifting to get comfortable, a pen gripped in one's hand, shaking a pen to get it to release ink, the dry feel of paperwork, warm paper fresh from the copy machine, a crinkly candy wrapper, rolling the neck to loosen a kink, bumping elbows with the person sitting in the next seat, heels tapping the metal chair legs, being nudged by purses or bags as someone walks past one's chair in a tight space, running one's hands impatiently through the hair, a cold brass door handle, shoes that scuff against the carpet or tile floor, nervous jitters in the belly as one waits to be called, checking one's phone for the time or to surf the internet, the slipperiness of glossy magazines, gooseflesh if the air is uncomfortably cold, a warm cup of coffee in one's hand

POSSIBLE SOURCES OF CONFLICT

A long wait time

Showing up only to discover that there is no record of one's appointment

An uncomfortably hot or cold waiting room

Having to wait with someone who is annoyingly talkative or nosy

Rude or inept receptionists

Guests gaining entry out of the order in which they arrived

Another guest talking loudly on a cell phone

Not being able to keep one's appointment (due to an insurance or payment glitch, lost paperwork, or broken equipment that requires one to reschedule)

PEOPLE COMMONLY FOUND HERE

Couriers, delivery men and women, friends or family members who have come for moral support, receptionists and other office staff, visitors (clients, patients, customers, etc.)

RELATED SETTINGS THAT MAY TIE IN WITH THIS ONE

Rural Volume: Principal's office (126)

Urban Volume: Bank (36), emergency room (58), hair salon (72), police station (106), therapist's office (126)

SETTING NOTES AND TIPS

Waiting rooms vary according to type but most are fairly standard. The level of expense in a waiting room is often an indicator of the quality of the provider. But what if the quality of the waiting room meant something else entirely? A shabby doctor's office waiting room might not indicate a shabby physician; it might be the sign of a medical professional who invests every possible penny into the welfare of his patients. On the other hand, an impressive waiting room at a law office may be the result of a talented interior decorator rather than a top-notch lawyer. Subtext can be just as useful for settings as it is for dialogue. Use it as a way to mix things up and say something extra about your characters.

SETTING DESCRIPTION EXAMPLE

While Mother was in with the doctor, I selected a magazine from the wall rack near reception but quickly found I couldn't concentrate. Who could in a place like this? I flipped pages to give my hands something to do, snatching glances at other patients occupying the blue plastic chairs. The woman with the headscarf and the man with the ball cap pulled low—it was obvious why they were waiting to see this particular doctor. Other patients broke my heart though, like the little girl whose hands were clenched around a glossy picture book, the cover unopened, and the teenage boy who looked lost and vulnerable in clothes that billowed around his shrunken body. I blinked back tears. Cancer had a lot to answer for.

Techniques and Devices Used: Symbolism

Resulting Effects: Characterization, reinforcing emotion

Restaurants

BAKERY

SIGHTS
Tall glass cases filled with doughnuts (glazed, sugared, powdered, garnished with nuts and sprinkles, drizzled with frosting and filled with cream), paper-wrapped muffins (carrot, banana nut, chocolate chip, blueberry and bran), a selection of cookies on red plastic trays, golden loaves of bread in bins or wrapped in bags, colorful fruit tarts and glazed flans, Danishes, chocolate squares, macaroons and éclairs, a selection of cakes in white boxes, a stainless steel counter with a cash register and debit machine, daily specials written on a black chalkboard on the wall, a small mini cooler for bottled drinks (pop, juice, milk, iced tea), a sitting area with small tables or booths where patrons can enjoy their gooey confections, an open doorway to the kitchen (flour dusting the counters, bagels being pulled from giant ovens, berry pies cooling as their juices ooze through decorative slits in the crust), a freshly washed tile floor, bakery employees rushing about in white uniforms and aprons covered in chocolate streaks and flour, a whirring bread machine mixing batter, a lineup of metal pans that are greased and ready for bread dough, a large stainless steel sink, a stack of crumb-smeared plates waiting to go into an industrial-sized dishwasher, shelves holding cans of yeast

SOUNDS
Dough mixing in an industrial mixer, the slide and catch of the cash register, oven timers going off with a beep, a roomful of customers chatting as they eat, the crackle of wax paper as one grabs doughnuts or muffins, the clatter of cutlery and plates, the crunch of crusty bread, people murmuring their appreciation, the creak of an oven hinge as the door is opened or closed, the gentle sawing of a knife cutting through a bagel or bun, the watery slosh of the dishwasher, the clunk of garbage dropping into trash bins, the chime of a bell as the front door opens, cell phones ringing, the crackle of a paper bag being folded down and handed to a customer

SMELLS
Yeasty dough rising and then baking, sugar, melted butter, coffee, toasted bread, roasted nuts, maple or honey, tea, savory spices, garlic, cinnamon, cardamom, ginger, lemon, chocolate, cheese-topped croissants and bagels browning in the oven

TASTES
Soft fresh bread dripping with melted butter, the spicy zing of ginger, sugary glaze dissolving on the tongue, crunchy nuts, grains and seeds, fudgy cream-filled doughnuts, billowy whipped cream, rich chocolate, bitter coffee, water, seedy jams, smooth cream cheese, lemon zest decorating a loaf, maple glazes, tea, salt, crumbly pie crust with sweet berry or apple filling

TEXTURES AND SENSATIONS
Cool jam or lemon filling squirting out of a doughnut and sticking to one's cheek, sugar crumbs sticking to fingertips, a dry smudge of powdered sugar on the lips, sticky glaze on one's fingers, a papery napkin swiped across one's mouth, a glass beaded with condensation, the slight singe of hot coffee through a mug, carrying a plate warm from the dishwasher to one's table, ripping

moist rolls in half to slather on butter, biting into the light crispy layers of puff pastry or chewy bread, butter or melting jam oozing onto one's fingers, shaking a sugar packet before ripping it open, tugging a paper napkin from a dispenser, pressing one's fingertip against the plate to gather the last few crumbs of a savored treat

POSSIBLE SOURCES OF CONFLICT
Slipping on a wet floor
A kitchen fire
An employee being burned while using the oven or fryer
Being confronted by a rival in the crowded seating area and being accused of something embarrassing
An infestation of bugs
Bioterrorism (an agent such as Anthrax being mixed with powdered sugar to kill a large group of people)
A health inspector with a bone to pick
Eating something that triggers an allergic reaction
Hair in one's food

PEOPLE COMMONLY FOUND HERE
Bakers, customers, delivery personnel, employees, health inspectors

RELATED SETTINGS THAT MAY TIE IN WITH THIS ONE
Rural Volume: Kitchen (66)
Urban Volume: Coffeehouse (142), deli (144), diner (146)

SETTING NOTES AND TIPS
Selections may vary depending on whether your bakery is commercial or a small mom-and-pop store. Some bakeries are strictly for the sale of baked goods and there is no seating, while others have a café atmosphere, offering a place for customers to sit and eat, drink coffee, and meet friends. Bakeries can be specialized, selling a specific product like cakes or doughnuts, while others may have a variety of baked goods and cake decorating services. If you wish to bring a multicultural element to your novel why not make it a German, Chinese, or Swedish bakery that specializes in cultural confections?

SETTING DESCRIPTION EXAMPLE
Regina wiped her hand on her apron and lowered several doughy rings into the vat of oil. In mere seconds the doughnuts ballooned to twice their size, floating in their glistening bath like little brown life preservers. Her brain tallying calories, she lifted the doughnuts out and tossed them into the bowl of sugar, careful to keep from touching the tempting powder. She examined her resolve and found it strong, like a castle wall meant to repel enemies. If she could make her weight-loss goal while working here, she could do it anywhere.
Techniques and Devices Used: Simile
Resulting Effects: Characterization

BAR

SIGHTS
Wooden stools butting up against a brass foot rail at a high counter, crowded tables and booths, patrons (laughing with friends, hitting on strangers, watching a TV affixed to the wall or staring into their drinks), a bartender with rolled-up sleeves freshening drinks and filling orders being delivered by wait staff, stacks of highball glasses in green-gray dishwasher racks, a sink with a sprayer, bags of ice in a tray or sink, draining trays, beer kegs being switched out, straws and stirrers, plastic skewers and straws, blenders whirring with colorful icy concoctions, several multi-button soda dispensers, a wall of alcohol bottles, upside-down stem glasses in racks above the bartender's head, plastic tubs of lime and lemon wedges, fridges with juices, milk and cream under the counter, an automatic coffee maker, a small computer station for servers to process payments, draft beer dispensers with brand logos on each tap, a mirrored wall behind the bar throwing back reflections of neon beer signs, servers weaving through the room with trays held high to avoid collisions, a line of highball drinks placed on square napkins or cardboard beer coasters along the bar, green or brown glass beer bottles wet with condensation, dim lighting, water rings on tabletops, several cardboard menu stands with drink specials on them, a scattering of pretzel bowls, a dingy hallway leading to restrooms at the end, flashing gambling machines, tables covered in a collection of shot glasses, half-empty cocktails or wine glasses, a wall phone for calling a cab, ads and advertisements for special events, restrooms

SOUNDS
Customers (talking, arguing over sports, complaining about work or spouses), laughter, the clink of ice in a highball glass as someone drinks from it, the murmur of low voices from people who don't want to be overheard, a patron telling his story to the bartender, the scuff of barstools being dragged or moved, a game or fight on the TV, piped-in or live music, the glug of beer in a bottle, the rustle of dollar bills, the thump of a bottle or glass on the bar, the occasional sound of glass shattering, the squeak of door hinges opening and closing, rattling air in the tubes when a keg goes dry, the whir of a blender, inebriated patrons swearing or yelling, tables and chairs being knocked down in a bar fight

SMELLS
Beer, cloying perfume, salt, sweat, citrus, bar food (nachos, hot wings, dry ribs, sliders, poutine, hot dips, fried pickles)

TASTES
The burn of straight alcohol shots (tequila, whiskey, etc.), yeasty or bitter beer, fruity drink mixes, bubbly soda water or pop, the zing of sour lime or lemon wedges, salt or sugar from a rimmed glass, spicy tomato Caesars, the burst of sweetness from biting into a maraschino cherry, the sour taste from drinking too much and then throwing up

TEXTURES AND SENSATIONS
Slippery beer labels covered in condensation, hard bar stools, slowly spinning a highball glass between one's hands while lost in thought, absently picking at a beer label, awkwardly trying to

open doors or flush a toilet without touching handles, the wooden counter pressing against one's elbows as one leans in to talk, papery napkins or sugar packets, knees touching another person at the bar as one shows interest, a bumpy lime wedge in one's fingers, a stray squirt of lemon or lime that stings one's eye, thin napkins being used to mop up a spill, a floaty or spinning sensation at drinking too much

POSSIBLE SOURCES OF CONFLICT
A bar fight
A drunken patron getting too friendly or acting aggressive with servers
A breakup
Not having enough money to pay the bill
Someone passing out
Getting carded as a minor
A bouncer gravely injuring or killing someone
A drunken customer who refuses to listen to reason and gets behind the wheel

PEOPLE COMMONLY FOUND HERE
Bartenders, bouncers, cab drivers, patrons, police, the bar owner, wait staff

RELATED SETTINGS THAT MAY TIE IN WITH THIS ONE
Rural Volume: Wine cellar (100), winery (194)
Urban Volume: Nightclub (216), pub (152)

SETTING NOTES AND TIPS
Bars can be dingy dives, sports hangouts, or upscale hot spots, any of which may leave your character feeling like he's in his element or just the opposite. Some may have dance floors and bring in live bands on certain nights. Look at your character's personality and experiences and think carefully about your goal for this scene. Which type of bar will set the mood and offer the best opportunity to create conflict and tension or to encourage your character to let loose?

SETTING DESCRIPTION EXAMPLE
The businessman hunched at the end of the bar grunted for a refill. Russell obliged, staring at him like he was a tricky jigsaw puzzle. He'd tried already to pull the man into conversation and was met with silence, and while this place attracted its fair share of solo drinkers, his tailored suit and carefully knotted silk tie said he didn't belong here. Throughout the night, the guy was indifferent to the people cramming in next to him to order, and he didn't seem to notice the makeup-caked cougars who kept trying to hit on him. His mission seemed to be one that Russell had seen many times before: to dull the pain as quickly as possible. And that left one question that no barman worth his bourbon could turn away from: why?
Techniques and Devices Used: Multisensory descriptions, simile
Resulting Effects: Characterization, foreshadowing

CASUAL DINING RESTAURANT

SIGHTS
A trendy chalkboard with specials written on it, customers sitting on benches while they wait, a hostess stand with menus and silverware roll-ups, crayons and coloring paper for the kids, ambiance lighting and décor that ties into the restaurant's theme (rustic, trendy, etc.) or the specific type of food served (**Italian:** jars of decorative oils, dried pastas and hot peppers; **Seafood:** nautical decorations, saltwater aquariums, lobsters in a tank; **Japanese:** sushi rolls, silk fans, room dividers, Japanese art, sake bottles), pictures or paintings on the walls, a bar with a mirrored wall behind it, drinks sitting on paper napkins, wine and liquor bottles, low-hanging lights, people swiveling on stools, booths with cushioned benches, high top tables, a dining room with booths and standard tables and chairs, bare tables or tables covered in paper cloths, a selection of condiments (salt and pepper shakers, ketchup, mustard, sugar packets), complimentary bread baskets, waiters and waitresses rushing by in aprons with pens and pads sticking out of their pockets, steaming trays of food, customers seated at tables, kids turning around in their seats, empty tables with dirty dishes, restroos in the back, mints placed on top of a bill, busboys and busgirls carrying bins of dishes, managers stopping to chat, credit card signs at the cash register, the pained expression on a guest's face at the sight of a high bill

SOUNDS
People murmuring and talking, loud laughter and shouts from the bar, sporting events and news anchors on the televisions, silverware clinking, dishes breaking, doors swinging open, servers taking orders, children fussing and crying, the sound of children's feet as they run to and from the restroom, the squeak of swiveling bar stools, glasses being filled at the bar, knives scraping against plates, drinks being slurped through a straw, menus snapping shut, receipts printing at servers' stations, servers and cooks yelling back and forth, the sizzle of cooking food, a soft scrape as cheese or pepper is grated onto food, people sliding into booths, employees singing to a customer, waitresses reciting specials, chairs scraping the floor, the hiss of draft beer or pop pouring out of the spout, the crunch of crusty bread being cut at the table, the sawing of steak, the clink of keys being pulled from pockets as customers prepare to leave

SMELLS
Prepared food, steam, spices, yeast, beer, robust wines, perfume, cologne, grease, air freshener, cleaning products, garlic, bad breath, minty breath

TASTES
Prepared food (in line with the restaurant's type of cuisine), coffee, tea, water, wine, beer and other alcoholic beverages, bubbly pop, ice, mints, gum, lipstick or lip gloss, garlic, butter, oil, grease, salt, pepper

TEXTURES AND SENSATIONS
Crunching salad, plastic or fabric seat covers sticking to the legs, bumping knees or stepping on someone's feet under the table, the wobble of a table with uneven legs, hard tile or wood floors,

cold silverware and dishes, rough paper or soft cloth napkins, a smooth tabletop, warmth from low-hung lamps, shoulders and hips touching in a too-small booth, warm bread, hot plates, burning the roof of the mouth on hot food, the air conditioner set too cold, air stirring one's hair as it wafts down from ceiling fans, sauce dribbling onto one's lap, bread crumbs sticking to one's fingers, food stuck in one's teeth

POSSIBLE SOURCES OF CONFLICT
Receiving the wrong food and being allergic to it
Cheapskates who skimp on the tip
Spiteful waiters and waitresses
Finding something unpleasant in one's food
Being waited on by someone who is clearly sick
Being stood up by a dinner companion
Running into a frazzled waiter and having food or drink spilled on oneself
A lost reservation
Waiters and waitresses having to deal with other employees who are unethical or lazy
Rude or demanding customers
Sexual harassment

PEOPLE COMMONLY FOUND HERE
A host or hostess, busboys and busgirls, business people holding a working lunch, couples on a date, customers, friends and families celebrating a special occasion (anniversary, birthday, engagement, rehearsal dinner), managers, wait staff

RELATED SETTINGS THAT MAY TIE IN WITH THIS ONE
Diner (146), parking lot (102)

SETTING NOTES AND TIPS
Eating out is a common leisurely activity in many cultures, so a restaurant is a likely place for characters to interact in a story. Because casual dining restaurants cater to a more distinguished customer than a fast food joint, the conflict that arises will look a little different in each venue. But wherever people gather, strife is inevitable—particularly with large-ego types who want to impress others—giving authors myriad opportunities to stir up trouble in their stories.

SETTING DESCRIPTION EXAMPLE
I slid into the booth, approving more and more of Rob's choice of restaurant. Candles flickered on the tables and the lights were nicely dim. A server approached on noiseless shoes, bearing a basket that smelled like a baker's oven. My stomach rolled over as he placed it and a plateful of butter curls on the pristine white tablecloth. I was a touch early, but hopefully Rob wouldn't be long or there wouldn't be a stitch of bread left for him. It would be nice to finally meet him face to face . . . provided he was honest in his dating profile and I could recognize him.

    Techniques and Devices Used: Multisensory descriptions, simile
    Resulting Effects: Characterization, establishing mood

COFFEEHOUSE

SIGHTS
A long counter stacked with chrome espresso and frothing machines, bean grinders, coffee carafes filled with aromatic coffee blends, bottles of coffee flavorings and toppings (a silver whipped cream canister, caramel and chocolate drizzles, shakers of toffee bits, etc.), a blender, metal thermometers, jugs of milk in fridges under the counter, coffee pots percolating, damp mugs hot from the dishwasher stacked on trays, towers of paper cups and lids, a tip jar near the cash register, a glass case holding a selection of snacks (breakfast muffins, sandwiches, pastries, cookies), spaced-out bistro tables with trendy wrought iron chairs and padded seats, a few comfy leather chairs around a coffee table, stray newspapers or magazines that have been left behind, customers (working on their laptops or tablets, reading books or visiting with friends), shopping bags and purses that dangle off the backs of chairs, wall shelving and displays for merchandise (artisan mugs, tinned cookies, coffee grinders, travel mugs, bags of coffee or tea, coffee machines, tea pots, gift baskets), giant glass windows with a view of the street, long lines to the cash register, a chalkboard with specials written on it (smoothies, teas, frozen blended drinks, lattes, cappuccinos, and espresso drinks), a wall of coffee bean drawers with labels, plates and cutlery, sandwiches and wraps, garbage left on tables, a condiment trolley (carrying sugar packets, fake sweeteners, and creams), stir sticks, extra lids, napkins and cinnamon shakers, a set of garbage and recycling bins

SOUNDS
Coffee beans in a grinder, employees calling out orders, the murmur of voices, laughter, dishes clattering, spoons clinking against the side of a mug, the thick whir of a frothing machine, metal scraping on metal, the ding of a cash register, the shuttering sound of till tape printing, a barista tapping out used grounds from a filter, coins clinking into a tip jar, the airy slurp of an empty whipping cream canister, people sipping and murmuring appreciation, the crinkle of paper as cookies and Danishes are withdrawn, foil bags of coffee being ripped open, ice grating in the blender, the hum of machines, a radio station playing music in the background, the chime of the door being opened or closed, the flap and flutter of newspapers, the swish of a mop against the floor, the thump of unfinished coffees being thrown in the trash

SMELLS
Freshly brewed coffee and ground beans, the aromatic scent of espresso, acrid burned coffee, warm caramel or chocolate, the tingle of spices (cinnamon, chai teas, mulled ciders), fresh-baked cookies and muffins, the fruity aroma from a steaming cup of herbal tea, mingling perfume scents, vanilla

TASTES
Sweet or bitter coffee, milky lattes, chai spices and teas, whipped cream laced with a chocolate drizzle, a warm and nutty cookie, hearty sandwiches with the zing of mustard or mayo, spicy soups, the numbing cold of a blended drink or iced coffee, lemon or mint

TEXTURES AND SENSATIONS

A warm mug in the hands, scalding coffee or tea burning the tongue, warmth cascading down one's throat, licking crumbs or foam from one's lips, sticky counters from spilled food or coffee, slipping on a wet floor, steam warming one's face and misting up one's glasses, the puff of heat from blowing on a hot drink, the icy relief of a smoothie in the throat on a hot day, a sudden scalding pain at slopping coffee on one's wrist, feeling infused by warmth as the coffee fills one's stomach, brushing one's lips with a paper napkin, a glossy magazine balanced on one's knee, smooth keyboard keys against the fingertips, a cozy reading chair, the dig of hard metal from the back of a bistro chair, tingling fingers after releasing a hot paper cup of coffee

POSSIBLE SOURCES OF CONFLICT

Not having enough money to pay
Being bumped and spilling one's coffee
A solitary person nursing his coffee at a large table when another customer needs the table for a big group
Having one's order served incorrectly
The Wi-Fi being down
Jitters from too much coffee leading to a quick temper
Waiting for a date who never shows
Wanting to sit and enjoy the ambience but discovering that all the tables are full

PEOPLE COMMONLY FOUND HERE

A manager, baristas and other serving and food prep staff, customers, delivery people

RELATED SETTINGS THAT MAY TIE IN WITH THIS ONE

Bakery (136), big city street (38), diner (146), parking lot (102), small town street (120)

SETTING NOTES AND TIPS

Chain coffeehouses will have a very similar layout and feel from one store to the other, whereas independently owned locations will look unique and even follow a special style or theme to play to a specific clientele: trendy and upscale, an old-fashioned diner feel, one that appeals to creative types, or even a "green" focus to draw the environmentally-conscious crowd.

SETTING DESCRIPTION EXAMPLE

I sipped the last of my black coffee and signaled for more. Several teenage couples leaned over cappuccinos at the chic chrome bistro tables, while laughing groups crowded the booths at the back. My own table partner, the only empty chair, silently encouraged me to get a life and leave so others could fill the table with conversation.

    Techniques and Devices Used: Contrast, symbolism
    Resulting Effects: Establishing mood

DELI

SIGHTS
An expansive glass case filled with cured meats (pastrami, pepperoni, salami, garlic roast beef, smoked chicken and turkey, ham, chorizo, pepperoni sticks), sandwich fixings (lettuce, several types of cheese, pickles, onions, tomatoes, hot peppers, olives) and condiments (grainy and hot mustards, chipotle mayo or garlic mayo, hot sauce, oil and vinegar), a fridge and cooler behind the counter, a stainless steel scale, deli slicers, trays of baguettes and fresh sandwich bread, plastic trays lined with wax paper, a case for sides (coleslaw, salads, mashed potatoes, cooked peppers, baked beans), multiple soup tureens, single servings of desserts (cookies, brownies, slices of cake) wrapped in cellophane, murky jars of pickled eggs and sausages, a jar of pickles, thick sandwiches being packed into takeout containers, a glass-doored cooler holding drinks (sodas, water, juices, iced teas), a rack filled with bags of potato chips, a line of customers, a cash register, money exchanging hands, trash bins, a few small tables and chairs with extra condiments and napkin holders, an eating counter along the front window with stools

SOUNDS
The chime of the door opening, people placing orders and chatting with friends, an employee calling back for items that are running low, glass doors sliding open, the ding of a microwave, an alarm on the oven going off when bread is finished toasting, hot oven sheets sliding onto a counter to cool, a knife softly slicing through a bread loaf, crackly wax paper, a frying pan hissing on the stove, a spatula scraping a pan as warm sandwich ingredients are made, the burp and squirt of a condiment bottle, music playing on the radio, the whirring blade of the meat slicer, shaved meat thumping onto a scale, the ding of the cash register, coins dropping into a tip jar, the fizzy sound of water mist spraying meats in the display case to keep them fresh, orders being called out, people talking with their mouths full, cellophane being unwrapped, a chip bag being torn open, biting into a crunchy pickle

SMELLS
Cured meats, spicy mustard and cayenne, vinegar, pepper, yeast from freshly baked bread

TASTES
Smoky meat, peppercorns and other spices, soft yet crusty bread, tangy mustard, hot peppers, mayonnaise, vinegary pickles, steaming soups, sweet desserts, sour pickles

TEXTURES AND SENSATIONS
The edge of the counter pressing one's chest as one leans in to place an order, a plastic tray holding a heavy sandwich, a blob of mustard sticking to the corner of one's mouth, biting into a crisp pickle, the heat of spices on the tongue, crumpling up a napkin, crusty bread that's soft on the inside, a full takeout bag in one's arms, arranging one's items on a tiny table, chip salt dusting one's fingers, warm soup on the tongue, chewy bread, flavors bursting in one's mouth as meats, fresh fixings and condiment layers meld together

POSSIBLE SOURCES OF CONFLICT

An argument with the deli owner over an order

Running into someone one does not want to see (an ex-partner, a one-night stand, an old boss one despises)

Long lines during a short lunch break

A customer who takes a long time to order

A health or safety violation

Meat that smells or tastes bad

A holdup

Criminals trying to extort protection money from a business owner who is barely able to get by

Dealing with an unethical health inspector

The landlord raising one's rent with little notice

Being threatened when a popular chain store moves into the neighborhood

Hiring relatives who are lazy or incompetent and not being able to get rid of them

PEOPLE COMMONLY FOUND HERE

A manager, customers, delivery personnel, employees, health and safety inspectors, suppliers, the owner

RELATED SETTINGS THAT MAY TIE IN WITH THIS ONE

Bakery (136), diner (146), fast food restaurant (148)

SETTING NOTES AND TIPS

Delis are popular whether they're in a spacious mall or crammed into a small rental spot along a city street. Unlike most eateries, the long counters create a lack of space, meaning the focus is more on getting a sandwich to go rather than eating one's food there. Some delis make fresh sandwiches and also sell meat by weight for customers to take home, while others sell only fresh food or sliced meats. If you choose a deli for your setting, think about how you might use the tight space to your advantage. For instance, a character might be able to hide in the bustle of a crowd, or he could choose this as a meeting point because it would be easy to hand something off without being noticed.

SETTING DESCRIPTION EXAMPLE

I pulled on the glass door to Ed's Deli, a small strip of a store on the main drag. Bells jangled, and the scents of fresh rye bread, smoked meat, and spicy mustard sent my stomach into a joyful flurry. People stood shoulder-to-shoulder in a long line that snaked along the counter and there was nowhere to sit, but I didn't care. I was tired of everyone bringing Ed's sandwiches into their cubicles at lunch and hearing the groans of delight as they tucked in. Time for me to have one of these heavenly creations for myself.

Techniques and Devices Used: Multisensory descriptions

Resulting Effects: Establishing mood, reinforcing emotion

DINER

SIGHTS

Booths nestled against smudged windows with a view of the street or parking lot, a long counter with stools spaced along it, laminated menus offering staple diner food (bacon and eggs, pancakes, burgers and fries, meat loaf, grilled cheese, patty melts, etc.), several fruit and meringue pies displayed under glass domes, metal napkin holders on each table along with salt and pepper shakers and a bottle of ketchup, well-scratched tabletops with chips around the edges and gum stuck to the bottom, dull metal cutlery with fork tines that may be slightly bent, a checkered tile floor, dingy curtains or dusty blinds, white coffee mugs, plates and bowls, a hard-looking waitress in uniform setting down a gravy-laden plate of food or baskets of fries, another waitress pouring coffee and jotting down orders, a cash register, a whiteboard with daily specials written on it, fry cooks wearing stained white aprons turning burgers on a grill, a jar for tips by the cash register, a not-too-clean public restroom, newspapers left on the counter, salt spilled on tables, bored customers (stacking creamers, folding up their paper placemats, nursing coffees), truckers wearing grease-stained ball caps and plaid shirts tucking into a large breakfast, stressed parents with loud children who are impatient for their food to arrive

SOUNDS

Cutlery clinking on tables and scratching against plates, the bubbly squish of a ketchup bottle, a waitress drawling out orders to the fry cook in diner-slang, a hacking smoker's cough, stools that creak, truckers taking that first slurp of coffee to wake them up, waitresses rushing to get food orders out and dropping plates on the table with a thump, the gurgle of a water glass being filled, the clatter of change hitting the tabletop, a spoon clinking as it stirs sugar into coffee, the sizzle of burgers on the grill or fries being lowered into hot oil, the cook calling an order up, doors swinging open to a blast of outside traffic noise, bells on the doors ringing when a customer comes in, big trucks rumbling outside in the parking lot, a radio belting out music, the clunk of a coffee pot sliding back into the urn slot, the burp and hiss of a coffee machine brewing a fresh pot, customers asking for refills, friends talking and laughing, a customer grumbling over the bill or service

SMELLS

Meat grilling, onions frying, hot oil from the deep fryer, salty hot dogs, bacon grease, fragrant coffee, spices, tangy vinegar wafting off fresh coleslaw, melted butter, gravy, pine cleaner from a freshly washed floor, body odor and sweat

TASTES

Coffee, greasy fries, hamburgers, hot dogs, breakfast meals (steak and eggs, bacon, sausage, pancakes, grits, buttered toast, omelets), spicy chili, ketchup, mustard, hot sauce, pepper, pies (blueberry, apple, strawberry, rhubarb, peach, lemon meringue), grilled cheese sandwiches, soups, saltine crackers, spices, water, carbonated pop, juice, milk, salads, milk shakes

TEXTURES AND SENSATIONS

A sticky spot on the counter, a greasy menu, spilled salt or sugar granules on the tabletop, the warmth of cutlery that has just come from the dishwasher, a hot mug of coffee on a cold day, the burst of steam against one's face when blowing on coffee, trying to pull a napkin from an overstuffed holder and having it rip, bright light coming in the window which makes one squint, scraping a piece of dried food off a knife with a fingernail, a glob of food stuck to the corner of one's mouth, squeezing a condiment bottle, a cold glass or can of pop against the palm, dragging fries through a puddle of gravy, a knife sawing through a piece of steak, warm plates, the resistance of metal when bending a mangled fork tine back into place, slouching back after a big meal, fake leather seat cushions sticking to one's bare legs

POSSIBLE SOURCES OF CONFLICT

Being the victim of a dine and dash
Couples arguing during a night out
Another waitress stealing one's tips
The cook quitting mid-shift
Someone complaining loudly about an order and disrupting everyone in the restaurant
A customer coming on to a waitress by grabbing at her
People who pay in change and don't tip

PEOPLE COMMONLY FOUND HERE

Customers, dishwashers, fry cooks, police officers, the owner, waitresses

RELATED SETTINGS THAT MAY TIE IN WITH THIS ONE

Urban Volume: Bakery (136), coffeehouse (142), deli (144), fast food restaurant (148), truck stop (284)

SETTING NOTES AND TIPS

Because of a diner's long hours (often they never shut down), these places can contain an eclectic mix of people. Locals in for a serving of their favorite food mingle with on-duty police officers, truckers and salesmen who live on the road, young adults grabbing some late-night grease after a stint of bar hopping, and homeless people needing a break from the streets. Think of the varied conversations one might overhear and how different personalities could clash in such an environment.

SETTING DESCRIPTION EXAMPLE

The man stumbled in just after three a.m. and made for the back, the air in his wake as yeasty and sour as a spilled beer keg. At the halfway point, he lurched to the left just enough to hook a stool at the counter and a short tussle ensued. He almost went down for the count twice, but finally escaped the stool's wrestling move and fell into a booth. I grabbed the extra strong pot of coffee, wishing for the hundredth time that I hadn't agreed to switch shifts with Bethany.

Techniques and Devices Used: Multisensory descriptions, simile
Resulting Effects: Characterization, reinforcing emotion

FAST FOOD RESTAURANT

SIGHTS

A front counter with cashiers manning registers, a kitchen in the back, a drive-thru window, menu boards containing products and prices, customers handing over cash or credit cards, people carrying trays of food and drinks, a condiment station (offering packets of ketchup and mustard, napkins, plastic cutlery), a soda dispenser with beverage supplies (cups, straws, lids), a children's play area, posters on the walls advertising different products, images of a mascot or some other symbol for the restaurant, garbage cans hidden in cabinets, stacks of used trays, tables and booths spaced at equal distances, rolling high chairs, stacks of booster seats, stray wrappers and receipts on the floor, dirty tables with crumbs and ketchup smudges, caution cones to indicate a spill on the floor, restrooms, workers wiping tables or mopping floors, managers supervising, kids running to the restroom

SOUNDS

The sizzle of burgers and fries cooking, customers giving orders, cashiers calling corrections back to the kitchen employees, receipt machines spitting out paper, fryers and ovens beeping, salt being shaken over fries, the scrape of a scoop through the fry bin, the drive-thru worker talking into a headset, drink machines dispensing gurgling soda, fridge doors closing, the crinkle of cellophane-wrapped plastic cutlery, food being placed in bags, straw wrappers being ripped open, ice falling into a cup, squeaking swivel chairs, chairs scraping over the tile floor, running feet, kids laughing or yelling, babies crying, parents reprimanding too-loud children, customers greeting each other, people talking on cell phones, noisy eaters chewing their food, someone slurping drink through a straw or shaking ice in a cup, shrieks and shouts coming from the play area

SMELLS

Meat cooking, oil and grease, tart dressings on salads, hand wipes, ketchup

TASTES

Burgers and fries, fried and grilled chicken, onion rings, fruit, sandwiches and wraps, salads and dressings, milk shakes, ice cream, cookies, soda, water, coffee, fruit juice, mayonnaise, mustard, ketchup, barbeque and other sauces, ice

TEXTURES AND SENSATIONS

Greasy hands, licking sauce off one's fingers, brushing crumbs of salt from a table, slurping a cold liquid through a straw, ice cream melting over the edge of a cone, sticky ketchup, condensation on a cup wetting one's palm when one grips it, balancing a tray full of food and drinks, soda overflowing onto one's hands, too-hot food burning the mouth, wiping at one's mouth with a paper napkin, crumpling a sandwich wrapper and tossing it onto the tray, struggling to cut a child's meat with a plastic knife

POSSIBLE SOURCES OF CONFLICT

Customers who can't make up their minds or who have a long list of customizations
Long lines and understaffed counters

Food taking forever to be served
Employees getting one's order wrong
The kitchen running out of things and being unable to serve certain menu items
Unclean restrooms
Rude or inept employees
Parents letting their kids run riot
Kids throwing fits
Attending the restaurant at someone else's request when it isn't one's favorite place
Liking the food but not liking the calories or ingredients that go along with it
A car dying in the drive-thru lane
A loud children's birthday party that disturbs the entire restaurant
A diaper explosion in the play area

RELATED SETTINGS THAT MAY TIE IN WITH THIS ONE
Deli (144), shopping mall (180)

PEOPLE COMMONLY FOUND HERE
Children attending a birthday party, families with kids, members of an athletic team hanging out after an event, retirees gathering to socialize over coffee and breakfast, road crews and construction workers on lunch break, single diners

SETTING NOTES AND TIPS
Because people spend a fair amount of their time eating, both in real life and in stories, it's natural to write scenes that happen around the dinner table. But because mealtime scenes are sedentary and low-action, they can slow the pace of the story or become dumping grounds for chunks of backstory. When writing a scene that unfolds at the table, whether it's in the kitchen of a house or at a restaurant, keep it upbeat by including some action. Children running, people excusing themselves from the table, someone getting up to refill a drink—interspersing the dialogue with movement will give the scene an active feel, and it will read as less passive. Also ensure that you have a good reason for choosing this particular setting, and that this chaotic, busy space makes sense for the important events about to take place.

SETTING DESCRIPTION EXAMPLE
Ed grabbed a table in the corner for us, but this was one scenario where location didn't seem to matter. Kids' shouting in the play area vied with the volume of noise of the crowded dining room. The floor shook with the stomp of little feet, accompanying the headache that had started thumping in my skull. I stood at the counter and scanned the menu, but the smell of sweaty kids killed whatever appetite I'd come in with. When the bored cashier asked if I'd made up my mind, I rubbed at the ache behind my eye. "Beer?" I asked, without much hope.

Techniques and Devices Used: Multisensory descriptions

Resulting Effects: Establishing mood, reinforcing emotion

ICE CREAM PARLOR

SIGHTS
A chalkboard menu high on the wall listing specialty desserts and their corresponding prices, a long line of customers excitedly discussing what they plan on getting, bright posters advertising house specialties, a long glass case with dozens of ice cream buckets, flavor labels attached to the glass or sticking out of the buckets (chocolate, vanilla, strawberry, coffee, rocky road, birthday cake, mint chocolate chip, cookies and cream, fudge ripple, peanut butter cup, butter pecan, praline, pistachio, cherry), a selection of sherbets (orange, lemon, raspberry, lime, cherry, rainbow), a stack of waffle cones, bowls and cups ready to be filled, empty cups for milk shakes, bright plastic spoons and striped straws, napkin dispensers, tubs of toppings (crushed nuts, sprinkles, candies, chopped berries, marshmallows, cookie chunks, cut-up fruit, chocolate chips, gummy bears, coconut, whipped cream), syrup dispensers (chocolate, caramel, strawberry), employees plying metal scoops, a sink with scoopers soaking in it, a blender and several cutting boards, a cash register, tables and chairs

SOUNDS
The whir of the blender, a knife chopping up bananas or other toppings, the tap of a scoop against the side of the sink, a cone cracking when too much ice cream is forced in, the last rattle of milk shake through a straw, people sighing as those ahead of them take too long to order, the jingle of the cash register opening, the rattle of a spoon scooping through sprinkles, syrup squirting out of a dispenser, excited children squealing as cones are handed out, the thump of a scoop against the interior of an almost empty bucket of ice cream, the click of coins going into the register

SMELLS
The sugary scent of waffle cones being pressed and cooked, warm chocolate, fresh strawberries and bananas, ozone smells from refrigeration units, toasted nuts, caramel sauce

TASTES
Sugary cold ice cream, the burst of a tart berry, half-frozen banana chunks, caramel and chocolate syrups, crunchy toasted nuts, a crispy wafer cone, swapping cone licks with a friend or family member, pop, water, fizzy ice cream floats, creamy milk shakes

TEXTURES AND SENSATIONS
The cold smoothness of ice cream on the tongue, licking a cold drip off one's wrist, a bumpy waffle cone under one's fingers, too-thin napkins quickly becoming soggy when one tries to wipe up an ice cream spill, sticky fingers, biting through a hard chocolate shell to taste the soft ice cream beneath, the mix of smooth ice cream and crunchy nuts or cookie bits in the same bite, sitting outside at a picnic table in the warm sun, slurping a shake through a straw, a brain freeze, a plastic spoon scraping the bottom of a bowl, a plastic spoon breaking when one tries to dig too forcefully into one's ice cream

POSSIBLE SOURCES OF CONFLICT

Refrigeration units going on the fritz

Late deliveries causing ice cream shortages

Hot weather creating customers with short tempers

Assembling an ice cream cone, then the customer changing his mind

Little kids who drop their cones and begin to wail

Having to serve someone that one detests

Inner conflict over cheating on one's diet

Being served by an employee who licks a spoon or scratches his hair while he works

Employees who eat the product and increase one's food costs

Teenaged employees treating their friends to free ice cream

Ordering and eating ice cream despite a known dairy allergy

PEOPLE COMMONLY FOUND HERE

Customers (parents and grandparents with children, couples on dates, tourists), delivery people, employees, the store owner

RELATED SETTINGS THAT MAY TIE IN WITH THIS ONE

Rural Volume: Beach (202)

Urban Volume: Big city street (38), convenience store (162), park (98), shopping mall (180), small town street (120)

SETTING NOTES AND TIPS

Some ice cream shops are built around a theme, like a '50s ice cream parlor, and furnishings will align with this theme. Others may be little more than a long glass case and counter, encouraging customers to order and then eat their treat elsewhere. If the ice cream store is part of a box chain, then the employees will wear uniforms, and likely the cups, napkins, and posters will all carry the chain's logo. Ice cream shops are often found near tourist locations and malls, and some in cooler climates are only open seasonally. The latter type is especially popular with students needing a summer job.

SETTING DESCRIPTION EXAMPLE

My daughter stood on tiptoe, her black braid swishing across her back as she gazed at the long line of colorful ice creams and sherbets. The kid behind the counter joked how she looked like the fate of the world was at stake, and I laughed. It was true. But no matter how long Lorena tormented herself, she always ended up getting the same thing. The customers in line behind us started to shift and grow tellingly quiet. After prompting her with three throat clearings, Lorena poked the case with a frantic tap, her breath fogging the glass. I swiped at the wet mist to read the tag. Sure enough, Bubblegum had won out yet again.

Techniques and Devices Used: Multisensory descriptions

Resulting Effects: Characterization

PUB

SIGHTS
Wooden paneling, wall-mounted flat screen TVs over the bar and spaced around the room, a themed décor that often is affiliated with a specific country (Ireland, Scotland, Germany, etc.), décor that represent that culture (pictures, antiques, flags, colors, symbols), heavy wooden tables, bench seats or sturdy chairs, low lighting, windows with stained glass inserts, waitresses dressed in short black skirts and mini pouch aprons holding pens and notepads, a long wooden bar with local craft beer taps and a selection of international beers, a computer for placing orders, stemmed glasses inverted in racks above the bar, a tray holding drink embellishments (straws, stirrers, plastic swords, umbrellas, orange sections, lime and lemon wedges, pineapple chunks, olives, pearl onions), beer drains, full ice trays, sinks with dirty blenders and mixers waiting to be rinsed, bottles of alcohol, a stack of menus, a bartender passing out drinks and placing orders on trays, tables cluttered with drinks (in bottles, mugs, highball and shot glasses), drink coasters and crumpled napkins, plates of pub food and appetizers, a waitress clearing a table and wiping it down with a cloth so new patrons can be seated, tipsy customers weaving their way to the restroom, a dartboard on the wall

SOUNDS
Friends talking and laughing, voices growing louder the more people drink, sports fanatics shouting at the TV or cheering, glasses clinking together, the thump of a beer glass against a wooden table top, forks and knives scraping a plate, chairs dragging over the floor, the sigh of a plastic cushioned seat as someone sits down heavily, the creak of restroom doors opening, a gurgle of foam spitting out of a tap attached to a near-empty keg, the sizzle of hot food (like fajita meat and peppers) brought straight from the kitchen, the crunch of nacho chips, the chime of a text on someone's phone, a hand banging the table to emphasize what one is saying

SMELLS
Hamburger meat and grilled steak, the deep fryer, spices, yeasty beer, cologne and perfume, cigarette odors wafting off a smoker's clothing, stale beer breath, sweat, body odor, citrusy coolers, strong licorice-scented or nutty liqueurs, coffee

TASTES
Beer, distinctive alcohol flavors (tequila, rum, whisky, wine, vodka), salty ribs and spicy chicken wings, a burst of vinegar at biting down on a deep fried pickle, cheesy dips and spreads, pop, coffee, flavored lip balm or lipstick, sugary mixed drinks, a sour lemon or lime wedge, a sugar or salt rim

TEXTURES AND SENSATIONS
Cushioned seats, the ridges of a roughhewn table, being crammed into a booth with others, greasy chicken wings turning one's fingers slick, the weight of someone's arm across one's shoulders, wet condensation from a glass against one's palm, playfully or nervously biting the smooth plastic stir stick or drink spear, a warm plate of food, the smooth texture of a cheesy dip

against the tongue, a dry paper napkin, dusting gritty salt from one's fingers, increased nudges and touches between people as alcohol flows freely, an ache in the lower back from sitting on a stool with no support, the slight spin of a swiveling stool, the burn of a shot doing down one's throat

POSSIBLE SOURCES OF CONFLICT

Drunken patrons
Food poisoning or allergies
Spotting one's ex with someone new
Drinks that taste too weak or too strong
Arguments or fights over a sports match on the TV
Being hit on by someone who is drunk or otherwise unappealing
A creepy pub patron whose continual staring makes one uncomfortable
Being followed out into the parking lot by a stranger
The temptation to drink and drive because cabs can't be found
Being ditched by friends while one is in the restroom
Trying to impress others by treating them to drinks when one can't afford it

PEOPLE COMMONLY FOUND HERE

Bartenders, cooks, customers, delivery people, managers, patrons, police, sales reps from liquor companies

RELATED SETTINGS THAT MAY TIE IN WITH THIS ONE

Bar (138), nightclub (216), pool hall (226)

SETTING NOTES AND TIPS

Pubs and bars are similar, but there are a few notable differences. The emphasis at a pub is more on sitting down for a few drinks, eating fattening or hearty foods, and socializing with friends, while bars tend to be about drinking, picking up dates, or watching the game. When a band is brought in to play at a pub, patrons mostly remain seated and enjoy the show from their tables rather than getting up and dancing.

SETTING DESCRIPTION EXAMPLE

I scanned the packed room, hoping to find Josie and the others quickly so I didn't look like a friendless waif, or worse, attract a half-loaded guy determined to buy me a drink. A curvy server passed me with a platter of nachos roughly the size of the Goodyear blimp and my stomach growled. She went up a half-hidden staircase, and I remembered Lisa saying something about the top floor being quieter. Sure enough, when I crested the second floor landing, a cheer went up. My crew sat at a high table in the corner, hands raised in greeting and an impressive collection of empty beer pitchers and glasses between them. I squeezed into a chair and ordered a coffee, because someone would have to drive this drunken lot of soccer moms home.

Techniques and Devices Used: Hyperbole, multisensory descriptions
Resulting Effects: Characterization, establishing mood

Retail Stores

ANTIQUES SHOP

SIGHTS
A vintage welcome sign, narrow walking aisles with table displays on both sides, sunlight glimmering off silver and crystal, oil paintings in elaborately carved frames hanging on the walls, a display of gilded mirrors worn with age or partly de-silvered, antique wood cabinets (filled with dainty figurines, collectible plates, china cups, thimble collections), display surfaces covered in knickknacks and antique costume jewelry, intricate handmade floor rugs hanging from display clips, glittering crystal chandeliers and lamps dangling overhead, rusted and paint-distressed signs from iconic businesses (Coca-Cola, Pepsi, Gerber), statues, masks and carvings from different cultures and countries, exotic wood jewelry and cigar boxes with polished stone inlays, hand-carved dressers with slightly warped drawers, a collection of framed black and white portraits, pitted metal oil lanterns, carved and lacquered chairs, stained glass pieces, dolls, collector buttons, coins and wartime paraphernalia (medals, propaganda posters, pistols, clothing, berets), silver and bronze candlesticks, old chests with worn leather straps, vintage hair brushes, shaving razors, folding knives, clocks, clothing, lace, old farm tools and washboards, wooden spindles, sewing machines, crates of records, handcrafted cushions with silky fringes, vases, musical instruments, grandfather clocks, stacks of vintage books and comics, watches, old cameras, salt shaker collections, a crowded front counter with rare items under glass

SOUNDS
The chime of bells as the shop door opens, voices of customers discussing pieces, the tick of a grandfather clock, vintage records playing in the background, a chord ringing out as a customer tests an old guitar, out-of-tune notes from a piano, floorboards creaking, soft clinks and thumps as items are sorted or moved, a creak of hinges as a cabinet or trunk is opened, the scrape of a warped desk drawer pulling open, gasps of surprise or wonder, the crinkle and rustle of paper as purchases are carefully wrapped

SMELLS
Oil paint, wood, lacquer, musty cloth, potpourri, leather, paper, dust

TASTES
Peppermints from a complimentary bowl on the counter, gum or other items brought into the store by customers (although most places actively discourage food and drink)

TEXTURES AND SENSATIONS
The uneven texture of chipped paint on a distressed cabinet or mirror frame, lacquered wood, satiny brocades and fabrics from furniture cushions, crisp starched lace, the pitted roughness of cast metal, glazed figurines that are cold to the touch, bumping a table or chest with one's hip, moving from a hard wood floor to a plush rug, the papery feel of money in the hands as one pays for an item, fingering lace or cloth to gain a sense of quality, running fingers over decorative inlays on serving trays or cigar boxes, the cold weight of a brass candlestick in one's hand, feeling the notches on a carved mask, sliding one's fingertips over the wood grain of a handmade chessboard or humidor

POSSIBLE SOURCES OF CONFLICT

A break-in

Discovering a haunted object

An earthquake or nearby building construction shaking valuables and causing breakage

Finding an object that belongs to one's family but the owner refuses to sell

Scouring for a collectable only to have someone else snap it up first

Accidentally knocking something over that is quite valuable

Faulty wiring that starts a fire

Discovering a fake art piece

Someone wanting to sell something that is taboo, such as a Nazi uniform or a carved rhinoceros horn

PEOPLE COMMONLY FOUND HERE

Antique dealers, customers, delivery people, employees, sellers looking to trade heirlooms for quick cash, the store owner or manager, window shoppers

RELATED SETTINGS THAT MAY TIE IN WITH THIS ONE

Art gallery (190), pawn shop (174), thrift store (182)

SETTING NOTES AND TIPS

Antiques stores may be a hodgepodge of anything and everything, or they may specialize in certain time periods or types of antiques. Some stores are laid out so furniture and displays are grouped by room (kitchen antiques piled on an old pot-bellied stove and kitchen nook, for example), while others are arranged by theme (World War II memorabilia, etc.). If you're attempting to utilize antiques in your story, choose those that offer symbolism opportunities for your character, giving meaning to the challenges or personal issues he or she must face.

SETTING DESCRIPTION EXAMPLE

The doll didn't belong here. She was clearly a German doll from the 1800s, but while the other pre-war toys in the cabinet appeared worn and well loved, she did not. She sat off to the side, away from the other toys, although Alice remembered placing her between the wooden blocks and the hand-carved marionette. The customers had starting asking about a curious smell when they were near the cabinet—the smell of fabric burning. One person had crossed herself after mentioning it, saying she felt watched by the doll. So she'd moved her into the glass case. It was nonsense, of course. Yet as she stood here, Alice did get a whiff of a faint smoky odor. She rubbed her arms, then stopped when she realized what she was doing. Good grief, listening to superstitious old ladies now? Her smile wavered. Still, it might not hurt to lower the doll's price and see if she couldn't encourage someone to buy it.

> **Techniques and Devices Used:** Contrast, multisensory descriptions
> **Resulting Effects:** Establishing mood, foreshadowing, hinting at backstory, tension and conflict

BAZAAR

SIGHTS
Sun-faded striped fabric or blue tarps strung above rickety wooden stalls, smiling shopkeepers wearing money belts bustling forward to help customers, portable fans being snapped on to offer customers a respite from the heat, uneven dirt pathways between rows of merchants, children begging or walking among the crowd selling cool drinks and inexpensive trinkets, hundreds of people browsing for goods or haggling over prices, vendors calling out to shoppers to entice them to their stalls, a stray dog wandering about and begging for morsels, people eating nuts or sweets from a bag or meat from a skewer, people sitting at tables sipping drinks (tea, beer, water, or other local beverages), steam rising from cooking pots and kettles, policeman or militia strolling through the market to keep an eye on things, handmade signs in foreign languages, tables and shelves crammed with a variety of colorful and unique items (clothing, flags, hats, rugs, pots and pans, shoes, tablecloths, lace, raw fabrics, wall art, pottery, musical instruments, children's toys, giant seashells, incense burners, religious relics, collectible books, lights, candles and paper lanterns), small knickknacks and handmade items that represent a specific culture (lacquered boxes, jewelry and beadwork, pillow covers, hand-stitched bags and leather goods, carvings), edible goods (locally grown spices, specialty jams, butters, honey, teas, coffees, candy, smoked fish, nuts, fresh fruits and vegetables)

SOUNDS
Shopkeepers calling out to visitors and describing what they sell while promising the best prices, dogs barking, the sizzle of cooking meat, the rattle of bags and newspaper as purchases are wrapped and given to customers, local music on portable radios, the whir of a fan firing up when customers enter a shopkeeper's booth, customers quietly discussing whether or not to make a purchase and how much to offer, wind chimes jangling in the breeze, tarps snapping in the wind, feet shuffling along the dirt path, a musical instrument being strummed by a customer

SMELLS
Local spices, meat cooking, yeasty breads, sweat, body odor, dust, musty fabric, incense, coffee beans, smoke, stale air, garlic, mint, scented soaps and potpourri, spices local to the area

TASTES
The blissful shock of a refrigerated drink on a hot day, the unusual flavors of local street food, biting into ripe fruit, snacking on a sugary candy, fried bread or cake, licking icing off one's fingertips, the unpleasant sour reaction to a new food that one does not care for, the bitter yet pleasant taste of a street vendor's brewed tea samples

TEXTURES AND SENSATIONS
The weight of a glazed pot or figurine in one's hands, fingering different types of woven fabrics, a breeze cooling the sweat at the back of one's neck, prickling sunburn, a blast of cold air from a fan, smooth silver, hot metal pots lying in the sun, brushing crumbs off one's hands and shirt after eating, the condensation on a cold bottle of water, holding a cold drink against one's

forehead or neck to cool down, bumpy beadwork or embroidery on clothing or cloth, a silky fringe falling through one's fingers, sorting through a hodgepodge of bracelets or other jewelry, plucking or flapping at one's clothes to let air in, accidentally bumping a table or in a tight space, knocking one's head on a hanging shell mobile, sore feet from walking over uneven ground, blisters forming from sandals or new shoes, heavy bags pulling one's arms down and causing fatigue, light-headedness from too much sun or dehydration

POSSIBLE SOURCES OF CONFLICT

Pickpockets

A cultural misunderstanding (such as unknowingly making an obscene gesture and causing offense)

Getting lost

Language barriers

Miscalculating currency conversions and overpaying

Shopping with an incompatible partner (being someone who hates shopping, yet being stuck with someone who will do it all day)

Desperately needing an item and not being able to find it

PEOPLE COMMONLY FOUND HERE

Beggars, criminals, local police, locals, merchants, orphans, tourists, tourism planners operating out of tour excursion booths

RELATED SETTINGS THAT MAY TIE IN WITH THIS ONE

Rural Volume: Farmer's market (162)

SETTING NOTES AND TIPS

If your bazaar is in a real place, research the goods commonly made and sold in that region. If you're going strictly from your imagination, think about what the area might be famous for, what foods they might grow and raise locally, and the colors they would use that represent that country's traditions, holiday celebrations, and artistic expressions.

SETTING DESCRIPTION EXAMPLE

I strolled down the first row of the bazaar, dazzled by the colors and chaotic movement of such a huge crowd. Bolts of fabric, handmade pillows, beaded bags, fringed shawls, and small silver trinkets crowded every stall. I stopped at a table to admire the stitch work on a pillowcase but quickly moved on when the owner started speaking to me in a language I couldn't understand and shoving different pieces at me. Pushing deeper into the crowd, I turned a corner and the air turned rich and fragrant. This row was quieter, each table a collection of wooden bowls filled with mounds of freshly ground spices. The women didn't speak, but their smiles were welcoming, so I made sure to spread my purchases around, buying a bag of vanilla beans from one and delicate saffron threads at the next.

Techniques and Devices Used: Contrast, multisensory descriptions

Resulting Effects: Establishing mood, tension and conflict

BOOKSTORE

SIGHTS
Shoulder-high bookshelves on the floor and walls, round tables holding books on display, corner and end displays holding popular books, posters displaying bestselling book covers or announcing an author signing event, signs for different book categories, ads for store loyalty cards, an author at a table doing a book signing, an in-store coffeehouse with tables and chairs, a collection of reading chairs and couches, windows letting light in, colorful book spines, novelty gifts (cards, mini-books, bookmarks, CDs, DVDs, chocolates, pens, candy, seasonal gift items), a massive wall displaying bestsellers with discount stickers, employees at a front desk ringing up purchases for customers, computers and registers, a colorful children's section filled with novelty books, a selection of board games and puzzles and plush toys, a section devoted to staff picks, gift cards on a turnstile, calendars, storefront displays, magazine racks, customers (scanning shelves, standing in line to pay, tugging a book off the shelf to read the back or fan the pages, standing still with heads bent as they read an opening page, relaxing in cushioned reading chairs, wandering the aisles, stalking the discount tables, sitting at a table enjoying a coffee and a scone), a pair of teens sharing a magazine and discussing the contents, a lone reader sitting on the floor with her back to a shelf

SOUNDS
Customers (talking, murmuring, asking employees questions), the crisp ruffle of pages being turned or fanned, the slick slide of magazine pages, coffeehouse noises (blending, grinding, foaming, gurgling, tapping, steaming), people blowing on or slurping coffee, the low-level musical spillover from a book-browser's earbuds, shoes clicking or tapping against the floor, the click of keys on a keyboard as someone writes or studies, scanner beeps, till tape spitting out, the slide of a bank card, slapping another book onto one's pile, the sigh of regret as one puts a book back on the shelf, an excited intake of breath at finding exactly the right book, easy-listening music playing from store speakers, knees cracking when one rises after sitting or squatting too long, cardboard boxes being cut open as an employee stocks the shelves, kids' voices coming from the children's section

SMELLS
The dry scent of paper and cardboard, coffee and spices (cinnamon, nutmeg, cocoa) from an internal coffee bar, old carpet, hair products, cologne or perfume, magazine ink, the ozone-like tang of air conditioning, outdoor scents drifting through an open door (grass, cigarette smoke, car exhaust), pine shelving, cleaning products (lemon, ammonia, pine)

TASTES
Hot coffee or tea sipped from a cardboard to-go cup, fruit or coffee smoothies sucked through a straw, nibbling on a treat (giant cookie, muffin, scone, roll, or biscotti) while paging through a book, sugary icing, water, gum, mints, cinnamon-flavored foam from a specialty coffee

TEXTURES AND SENSATIONS
A leathery or paper book spine, tugging the top of the book spine to pull it off the shelf, squatting to read titles on a low shelf, sinking into a soft reading chair, paging through a book

or magazine, running fingers over the raised bumps on a book cover, tilting the book to see a hologram or iridescent image on the cover, juggling a stack of books, a heavy basket of books digging into one's arm, bumping into or squeezing past another customer to get to a shelf, breaking off tidbits of a treat and popping them into one's mouth, a coffee cup warming one's hand, a paper napkin used to wipe one's lips

POSSIBLE SOURCES OF CONFLICT
Impatient or demanding customers
Running out of a popular book
Accidentally spilling one's drink in the store
A needy or entitled author at a book signing
Being short-staffed during the holidays
Customers who don't pick up on the subtle hints that the store is now closed
Catching a shoplifter

PEOPLE COMMONLY FOUND HERE
Authors signing books, book reps, customers, delivery people, janitorial staff (if the store has hired a service to maintain the store rather than its own employees), store management and employees

RELATED SETTINGS THAT MAY TIE IN WITH THIS ONE
Library (84)

SETTING NOTES AND TIPS
Chain bookstores will have a very similar look and feel. On the other hand, indie stores will be typically smaller but have details that add more personality, such as a store cat, a display of steampunk devices, or a collection of healing crystals, Celtic symbols, and incense. These are examples of how the owner might fill the store with personalized items to give it a specific feel. Think about the type of vibe you're going for and how symbolism in the store's décor could bring about a specific mood or feeling for scenes in this location.

SETTING DESCRIPTION EXAMPLE
With the excitement of a six-year-old discovering one last present under the Christmas tree, I scampered over to the empty armchair in the reading nook and sunk into its soft, plush folds. Across from me, an elderly woman glanced over the cover of a shockingly steamy romance novel and took in my bulging bookstore bag. She nudged her own, nestled at the foot of her chair, and we shared a secret smile. After settling in, I took a sip of my London Fog and pulled out my newest purchase, a gothic mystery. I peeled back the cover and inhaled its dusty scent before losing myself in the pages.

 Techniques and Devices Used: Contrast, multisensory descriptions
 Resulting Effects: Characterization, establishing mood, reinforcing emotion

CONVENIENCE STORE

SIGHTS
A wall of built-in coolers (containing milk, butter, other dairy products, different sizes of soft drinks, vitamin water, juices, plain water, and energy drinks), tile floors, shelving units lined up to form aisles, a section for medicinal items (pain remedies, stomach aids, cold pills), personal products (tampons, condoms, deodorant, shampoo, hand cream, hand sanitation wipes, travel packs of diapers), canned goods (beans, ravioli, soups, etc.), outdoor items (bug spray, sunscreen, etc.), car products such as motor oil and air fresheners, an assortment of snacks (candy, gum, chocolate bars, chips, granola bars, doughnuts), a self-serve beverage station (soda machines, coffee dispensers, coffee condiments, cups, lids, straws, napkins), a rack of bread loaves, a lottery center for filling out lottery tickets, a beverage counter (with coffee, hot chocolate and slush machines), an open cooler holding fresh fruit and prepackaged sandwiches, security mirrors and cameras throughout the store, a newspaper and magazine stand, a front counter (with a cash register, a display of lighters, lottery scratch tickets, adult magazines, a bin of pepperoni and beef jerky, energy shots, almanacs, and other impulse buys), a wall of cigarettes and tobacco products, an automated lottery machine, advertisements on the walls or hung from the ceiling, hand-written signs for sale items and special deals, a hallway at the back that leads to an employee's room that doubles as a storage and janitorial area, an office, a set of restrooms

SOUNDS
The jingle or buzz of the door opening, the vacuum seal on a refrigerated case breaking as a door opens, drink bottles clinking together, bottles or cans sliding forward when the first one in the row is removed, kids asking for candy, ice clanging into a cup, soda being dispensed, someone tapping a straw on the counter to break the wrapper, the whirring of the slush machine, coffee percolating, the crinkle of potato chip bags, an attendant talking with a customer, change being dropped to the counter, the chime of the cash register opening, drawers opening and closing, the rattle of a plastic bag, till tape spitting out of the debit machine

SMELLS
Air conditioning, coffee brewing, pine or lemon cleaner, gasoline, grease from a countertop rotary hot dog machine, cleaning supplies

TASTES
A sugary sip from a slushy drink, swigging back a gulp of water or pop while waiting in line, taking a sip of coffee to make sure it has enough cream or sugar before tossing the stir stick

TEXTURES AND SENSATIONS
The slight give when squeezing a loaf of bread to test its freshness, a slush cup's shocking coldness, condensation on a refrigerated beverage, the glossy cover of a magazine, the tap of a sugar packet against the fingers as one shakes it before tearing it open, running one's fingers over the bumpy numbers on a debit card while waiting to pay, balancing a bunch of items in the crook of one's arm, walking over a sticky spot on the floor, foaming soda spilling from an overfilled cup

POSSIBLE SOURCES OF CONFLICT
Shoplifters
Teenagers or shady-looking people loitering at the entrance
Working alone and seeing a customer acting oddly (looking around a lot, appearing secretive)
A robbery
Having to take a small child into an unclean restroom
Having too many people in the store at once to monitor
An employee who quits mid-shift
A sugar-loaded child that throws up all over the floor
Teenagers trying to purchase beer or cigarettes
A customer locking her keys in the car while a baby or dog is inside
A carjacking in the parking lot

PEOPLE COMMONLY FOUND HERE
Adult customers, delivery people, store employees, teenagers and children

RELATED SETTINGS THAT MAY TIE IN WITH THIS ONE
Gas station (70), grocery store (166), truck stop (284)

SETTING NOTES AND TIPS
Some convenience stores, especially those with gas stations, may have a small takeout counter or even a mini-restaurant as part of the store. These add-ons have limited offerings that are attractive to people looking for a quick bite to eat on the road or for those taking a pit stop during a trip. Many stores have extended hours or even operate twenty-four hours a day, and some will also sell a limited supply of liquor (usually a few brands of beer and coolers).

Another way to make your convenience store setting stand out is to stock it with products the locals need and want. If it's near a lake, likely there will be a small section for fishing tackle and even a cooler with live bait. A store popular with campers and hikers may offer easy-to-forget camping supplies and trail-ready food. If your store is close to a tourist site like a waterpark, it may have a good selection of sunscreens, blow-up pool toys, sunglasses, hats, and even souvenir trinkets bearing the park's name. Adding a few extras to a familiar setting like a convenience store can turn a commonplace location into something fresh and unique.

SETTING DESCRIPTION EXAMPLE
Randall shoved open the door and his sweat-soaked shirt instantly cooled. He tipped his head back and closed his eyes. Sweet, blissful air conditioning. He only had a couple of bucks, but he took his time wandering the aisles before finally selecting a drink from the cooler and bringing it to the front counter. He'd barely made it here from the bus stop and wanted to be as cool as possible before returning to the oven outside for his walk home.

    Techniques and Devices Used: Contrast, metaphor, weather
    Resulting Effects: Establishing mood

FLOWER SHOP

SIGHTS
Bright colors and cheerful displays, ivy plants, silk arrangements in baskets or vases, live houseplants on shelves, home décor plaques with cute or homey sayings on them, a card rack, small knickknacks, boxes of chocolate, tall glass coolers filled with fresh flower arrangements, a walk-in cooler for bulk flowers and storage, a staging area for creating arrangements (spools of ribbon, lace and wire, green florist tape, flower wrap, crystal vases, packets of flower food, bows, spray glitter, blank cards on sticks, and seasonal embellishments for special holidays or occasions), Mylar balloons and helium tanks, hardier flowers sitting out in water pails, shoppers browsing for an arrangement or flipping through wedding catalogues

SOUNDS
The rustle of florist plastic or tissue paper, the ding of a cash register opening, the suctioned whoosh of a display case door being opened, refrigeration motors, the hiss of the helium tank, the owner chatting with customers, sheets of florist paper being torn from a roll, the snip of scissors as flower stems are trimmed, water droplets falling as flower bunches are pulled from hydration buckets, water pouring into a vase, leaves rustling against flower stems, the phone ringing as someone calls in an order, a broom sweeping up stems and leaf fragments

SMELLS
Fresh flowers, greenery, earthy scents as sunlight from the window warms plant soil, glue, lacquer, plastic, chemicals from spray glitter or glue

TASTES
Coffee, smoothies, water or pop brought into the store by employees, fast food grabbed for lunch or leftovers reheated from home

TEXTURES AND SENSATIONS
The powdery smoothness of a flower petal, a painful prick from accidentally snagging one's finger on a thorn, slippery floral paper being wrapped around a purchase, twisting an arrangement to see it from every side before making a decision, the blast of cold on one's arms and face when opening the cooler, wrapping stems in rubber bands to keep a bouquet together in a water pail, moist soil from a potted tropical houseplant, wiping bits of ferny leaves and flower clippings off the counter, the rhythmic sweeping motion as one cleans up for the night

POSSIBLE SOURCES OF CONFLICT
A cooler breaking down
A flower shipment being delayed
Not being able to order a specific flower for a customer because of supply issues beyond one's control
A delivery mix-up
A forgotten order

Having an employee quit right before a big function like a wedding or anniversary party

Vandalism

Losing power to one's refrigeration units for an extended period of time

Receiving an order of flowers that are diseased or contain pests

A shop owner developing allergies to flowers later in life

An arrangement from one's shop being used in a terrorist attack

PEOPLE COMMONLY FOUND HERE

Commercial supply delivery people, drivers delivering arrangements, employees, the storeowner, wedding and event planners

RELATED SETTINGS THAT MAY TIE IN WITH THIS ONE

Rural Volume: Farmer's market (162)

Urban Volume Big city street (38), grocery store (166), small town street (120)

SETTING NOTES AND TIPS

Some flower shops are freestanding, while others are part of a larger business (such as a floral department in a chain grocery store). Most also sell a variety of household potted plants, fertilizer and vases, and also double as a gift store.

SETTING DESCRIPTION EXAMPLE

Greg unwrapped the last miniature orchid and placed it near the register. Perfect. He stepped back to take in the colorful silk arrangements, vibrant potted plants, and eclectic giftware decorating the shelves and display counters. Everything was ready for tomorrow's opening day. He took a deep breath, inhaling the sweetness of greenery, soil, and petals, a mixture that had captivated him since opening his first flower store ten years ago. A swell of warmth gathered in his chest at how far he'd come. The dyslexic boy too shy to raise his hand in class—the one who no one believed would amount to much—was about to open his third store.

Techniques and Devices Used: Multisensory descriptions

Resulting Effects: Establishing mood, hinting at backstory, reinforcing emotion

GROCERY STORE

SIGHTS

Aisles of cream-painted metal shelving, bright florescent lighting, towering end displays of popular or sale products (soup cans, chips, barbeque sauce, cereal), sale signs, banners with store mottoes, signs on each aisle indicating which products are located there, rows of household products (toilet tissue, cleaners, dish washing liquid, laundry soap), canned foods (soup, tuna, beans, tomatoes, corn), boxes and bagged goods (macaroni and cheese, rice mixes, chips, sugar, flour, cereal, etc.), sample stations offering tastes of featured products, pallets of restocking boxes blocking the aisles, customers browsing shelves, kids hanging off their mom's carts or being pushed in kid-friendly carts, a **floral department** with ready-made arrangements and gifts, **a bakery** (with packaged bread products, cakes, doughnuts, and other confections), **a deli cooler** filled with chubs of smoked meats and prepared artisan salads), **a meat counter** (with steak, hamburger, pork, and chicken in trays), **a seafood counter** (crab legs, shrimp, salmon and swordfish steaks, halibut, trout, scallops, whole fish, oysters in their shells, tanks of fresh lobsters, prepared seafood items), **a frozen food aisle** (with cooler cases filled with ice creams, frozen vegetables, pizzas, and convenience dinners), **a produce area** with colorful mounds of fresh fruit and vegetables in baskets and bins (oranges, melons, apples, peppers, sacks of potatoes, onions, grapes, bananas, and berries), **a bulk department** with foods in square bins (dried fruits, nuts, grains, baking supplies, candy, etc.), **a checkout area** (black conveyer belts, cashiers ringing up purchases, shelving with impulse items like batteries and mints, a selection of candies, a magazine rack, reusable bags for sale), managers walking around with clipboards, a steam cleaner rental stand

SOUNDS

Easy-listening music playing from store speakers, the rattle of bags, cashiers calling for price checks on the intercom, the bleep of items being scanned at checkouts, squeaky cart wheels, the whoosh of air conditioning and electronic doors opening and closing, bags being torn off the roll in the produce and bulk departments, phones ringing, cans clanking into a metal cart, the rattle of a box of dry pasta, flats of pop and other heavy items being thumped onto the conveyor belt, coupons being torn out of a flyer, kids whining and crying when shopping trips go on too long, people talking on cell phones as they shop

SMELLS

The yeasty scent of warm bread from the bakery, cinnamon buns hot from the oven, savory chicken roasting on a spit, brine from the fish department, pungent tomato vines, fresh-cut flowers, air conditioning, spiced sausage grilling at a sample station, the clean scent of dryer sheets and detergent in the household products aisle, papery cardboard as boxes are cut open, metallic shelving, the tang of ozone from frost and dry ice in the frozen department, rotting fruit or veggies that have not been disposed of by staff

TASTES

Samples from sample booths (sausage, cinnamon buns or other sweets, pastries, drink samples, yogurts), opening a bag of chips or crackers to snack on while shopping, gum, mints, candies, coffee

TEXTURES AND SENSATIONS

The cold metal of a shopping cart, squeezing a loaf of bread, a dusty potato, lightly squeezing fruit to test ripeness, a cold bag of peas from a cooler, cool air rushing into one's face when one opens a frozen food case, a tickling in the nose from too many scents in the fabric softener aisle, a bulky bag of dog food, pushing a heavy cart, maneuvering corners with an overloaded cart, frilly herbs (cilantro, parsley, etc.), wet hands from recently sprayed produce, meat trays that stick together, spongy mushrooms, cellophane bags that crinkle at the touch, grocery bags pulling at one's hands and arms

POSSIBLE SOURCES OF CONFLICT

A holdup
Screaming toddlers on sugar highs
Long lines and too few cashiers
Forgetting one's wallet at home and discovering it after groceries are bagged
Cashiers who bag one's purchases poorly, leading to crushed produce or bread
A bag tearing open in the parking lot
A runaway cart dinging one's door
Not being able to find the ingredients one needs

PEOPLE COMMONLY FOUND HERE

Customers, delivery people, inventory specialists, people holding raffles or selling cookies out front, price checkers for other grocery store chains, secret shoppers, store staff and management

RELATED SETTINGS THAT MAY TIE IN WITH THIS ONE

Rural Volume: Farmer's market (162)
Urban Volume: Bazaar (158), convenience store (162), parking lot (102)

SETTING NOTES AND TIPS

Grocery stores are often part of a larger chain and will follow a similar design from store to store. The inventory will vary depending on where one is, but even smaller independent stores will have the basic departments. Because people tend to shop at stores in their own neighborhoods, you could easily throw a nosy neighbor or ex-boyfriend into the mix to add tension and conflict for your character.

SETTING DESCRIPTION EXAMPLE

If Hell had a grocery store, it would only sell one thing: candy. How do I know? Because regardless of the time or day, when I wheel my overflowing cart past the colorful containers of licorice and jelly beans, I see the same thing: a hysterical toddler clawing at his mom's pant leg, screeching for that bag of gummy bears or bar of chocolate. It's almost enough to put me off sugar. It's definitely enough to put me off having kids.

Techniques and Devices Used: Multisensory descriptions
Resulting Effects: Characterization

HARDWARE STORE

SIGHTS
A display window filled with seasonal or themed displays such as gardening (seed packets, seed starter kits, soil, gardening gloves, a trowel, a watering can) or painting and décor (paint swatches, a paint tray and roller, wall decals and crown molding samples, a painted child's chair or table), narrow rows with high shelving filled with items for the home, cans of spray paint, caulking and other sealants, rolls of tape, poisons and traps for local pests, small plastic boxes (of washers, nuts, bolts, screws and fasteners), kitchen gadgets and supplies, camping products (plastic dishware, hot dog sticks, foil containers, grills, bug spray and sunscreen, propane canisters, flashlights, tarps), bags of home and gardening supplies (lawn seed, fertilizer, potting soil, and road salt) stacked near the entrance, coils of garden hose, spools of rope and twine, a selection of sprayers and sprinklers, a bin full of different sized dowel rods, a tool section with common house tools (drill bits, screwdriver and socket sets, sandpaper, hammers, levels), car accessories (cleaning products, lubricants, oils, fluids, air fresheners), a back door or hallway (leading to a break room, restroom, storage room, an office), a crowded counter area with a key tree and key cutting machine, a cash register and other odds and ends for sale (mini tape measures, bins of super glue, key chain flashlights, lighters), a selection of batteries, a rack of propane tanks outside, bundles of firewood

SOUNDS
The chime of the bell on the front door as a customer enters or exits, the friendly greeting of the employee at the cash register, the shrill grind of metal being shaped into a key, an employee blowing on the key to remove the metal filings, the ding of the cash drawer opening, beeps from barcodes being scanned, the shake of kernels in a seed packet, the metal clink and scrape of a customer tossing handfuls of bulk nails into a bag, a box cutter slicing through cardboard, the crinkle of items being loaded into a plastic bag

SMELLS
Soil and fertilizer, metal, chemicals from pest repellent canisters, citronella candles and mosquito coils, rubber, cut wood, pine-scented cleaning supplies

TASTES
Some settings have no specific tastes associated with them beyond what the character might bring into the scene (chewing gum, mints, lipstick, cigarettes, etc.). For scenes like these, where specific tastes are sparse, it would be best to stick to descriptors from the other four senses.

TEXTURES AND SENSATIONS
The plastic handle of a carrying basket digging into the crook of one's arm, the bumps and clefts of a freshly cut key, the heavy weight of a bag filled with soil or salt, the soft cotton of a new pair of gardening gloves, a container of grease or oil that has spilled, sawdust underfoot from wood that has been cut

POSSIBLE SOURCES OF CONFLICT
Lifting a bag of soil or fertilizer and having it tear open
Shoplifting
A customer misjudging the distance when backing up his truck and hitting the storefront
Customers wanting to return used items
A customer buying a combination of items that causes concern for the employees
Dropping a heavy tool on one's foot
Reaching for an item on a high shelf and collapsing the entire shelving unit

PEOPLE COMMONLY FOUND HERE
Customers, delivery people, employees, the storeowner

RELATED SETTINGS THAT MAY TIE IN WITH THIS ONE
Rural Volume: Tool shed (88), workshop (102)
Urban Volume: Parking lot (102), small town street (120)

SETTING NOTES AND TIPS
Chain hardware centers are much larger than smaller, independent stores and carry a greater selection of goods. In a smaller store setting, customers are usually local and loyal, meaning they would be known to the owners, and they might hang around longer to visit while shopping.

If your character needs to pick up items for committing a crime (such as chemicals that can be mixed to create an explosion), it would be in his best interest to spread out purchases between several locations or go to a big, anonymous store. However, playing to the opposite scenario, it might be comical for your character to have innocent intentions, but because of his purchases, be singled out and have to talk his way out of the situation.

SETTING DESCRIPTION EXAMPLE
I asked the matronly redhead at the checkout for directions, and she motioned to the aisle on the far side of the paint counter. My cart rolled over the cement floor, one loose wheel rattling and twisting as if it couldn't decide which way to go. The display was right where she'd said, and one of the better ones I'd seen, almost as if the person who had built it had me in mind. A thrill loosed itself across my skin as I touched each rope sample, feeling the different textures, gauging the quality. The lengths provided enough slack to tie a knot, enough to tell me what I needed to know. I gave the blue nylon a tug, admiring its strength. Perfection. The color didn't matter, of course. Usually women cared about such things, but not with this. When the rope came out, they understood it had only a single job to do, and they weren't too concerned with how it looked after that.
Techniques and Devices Used: Multisensory descriptions
Resulting Effects: Characterization, foreshadowing

JEWELRY STORE

SIGHTS
Bright lighting, locked display cases, posters displaying signature items of popular jewelry brands, long counters, gleaming glass display cases, engagement and wedding rings, bracelets, earrings made with precious stones (rubies, diamonds, emeralds, opals, sapphires, black diamonds), watches and cufflinks, pendants, crystal collectible figurines, a computerized cash register, velvet pads for customers to place jewelry on, polishing cloths, well-dressed and well-groomed sales associates, turnstile displays full of gold and silver earrings, mirrors, jeweler tools, a watch band display, a consultation desk, expensive wall clocks, designer costume jewelry pieces, decorative flourishes in the displays (bracelet bangles displayed on silk scarves, a scatter of sequins or semi-precious stones lying on velvet, etc.), a security guard standing or sitting on a stool by the exit

SOUNDS
Peaceful background music, a sales associate's heels clacking across the floor, drawers sliding open, the jingle of keys as the associate opens a display case, the chatter of till tape spitting out of the debit machine, the tap of a manicured nail against the glass display, customers discussing a purchase, a sales associate reviewing the qualities of each piece or notable facts about the manufacturing, traffic rushing by outside, a cell phone ring tone, mall traffic (if the store is part of an indoor mall complex), bangle bracelets jingling together

SMELLS
Air freshener, ammonia from glass cleaner, perfume or cologne from the sales associate

TASTES
Some settings have no specific tastes associated with them beyond what the character might bring into the scene (chewing gum, mints, lipstick, cigarettes, etc.). For scenes like these, where specific tastes are sparse, it would be best to stick to descriptors from the other four senses.

TEXTURES AND SENSATIONS
The cold smoothness of a gold ring sliding over one's finger, leaning against the cool glass case while browsing, the slight tickle of a fine chain being placed around one's neck, the heaviness of a locket settling into place, twisting a bracelet or watchband on one's wrist, holding a dangling earring up to one's ear before looking in a mirror, digging through one's purse or wallet for a credit card

POSSIBLE SOURCES OF CONFLICT
Angry customers disappointed with the quality of a purchase
Shoplifting or burglaries
An employee firing that turns explosive, drawing attention and embarrassing store management
Discovering that a shipment has been tampered with
A sales associate stealing a customer from a co-worker in order to gain a commission
Discovering that the jewelry one purchased from the store is fake

A storeowner learning that his jewelry is being made with blood diamonds or through other unethical manufacturing methods

An engaged couple arguing over rings and calling off their wedding in the store

Bringing in a piece of jewelry to have it cleaned and it being damaged in the process

Having an engagement ring sized after saying *yes* and learning the diamonds are actually cubic zirconia

PEOPLE COMMONLY FOUND HERE

A security guard stationed at the door, customers, delivery people, jewelry appraisers, sales associates, store management

RELATED SETTINGS THAT MAY TIE IN WITH THIS ONE

Antiques shop (156), pawn shop (174)

SETTING NOTES AND TIPS

The caliber of a jewelry store can greatly influence the style, layout, and service a customer receives. Lower-end shops have sales associates that tend to be less knowledgeable regarding the items because price is more of a determining factor for the customer. Much of the jewelry will be of lower quality and have generic branding. As such, these types of stores often have flashy sale signs to try and draw people in with the lure of a good deal. Other stores cater specifically to a more knowledgeable customer, and the brands carried are well-known, speaking for themselves. Sales associates are well trained and can provide detailed information regarding the piece's quality and manufacturing. Prices are fairly standard in higher-end stores, and they may carry less product, relying instead on catalogues for customers who wish to see a slightly different model of jewelry that is on display.

SETTING DESCRIPTION EXAMPLE

Beneath the case, diamonds glittered, winking under the bright lights like paparazzi snapping pictures of a celebrity. The sales associate, a pretty thing with her hair pulled back to show off ruby drop earrings, smiled and nodded toward the ring sets. Tony squeezed my hand, and that's when it finally felt real. We were getting married.

Techniques and Devices Used: Simile

Resulting Effects: Reinforcing emotion

LIQUOR STORE

SIGHTS

Barrels on display, wood floors with mud mats, whiteboards with specials written on them, posters advertising liquor brands, grocery baskets for carrying one's purchases, pricing signs, trendy décor plaques (*There's always time for a glass of wine!*), display cases holding bottles of liquor, floor-to-ceiling racks filled with bottles (whiskey, bourbon, vodka, wine, beer, tequila, fruit mixers, rum, gin, port, cognac), a sliding ladder for reaching the top shelves, a refrigerated case holding six-packs of beer, open crates with liquor bottles in them, boxes of wine stacked up as sale displays, wine bottles arranged by certain criteria (brand, the location of the winery, types of wine), a wall map of vineyards around the world, a wine tasting table (bottles of wine, a pail of ice, a corkscrew, wine glasses, an employee pouring samples, customers swirling wine and sniffing it), a delivery area in the back, a checkout desk with accessories for sale (corkscrews, champagne stoppers, stem tags, shot glasses, pour spouts, tall gift bags, flashing freezable ice cubes and gel glassware), liquor-themed books for sale

SOUNDS

A chime sounding as the door opens, customers asking questions, an office phone ringing, shoes clacking across the floor, bottles clinking together as customers turn labels or remove product from the shelf, crates scraping over the floor, the whoosh of motion sensor doors leading into the cooler room, music playing over the store speakers, a ladder sliding along its rails, wine being poured into a glass, an employee telling a customer about the wine that's being tasted, plastic bags rustling, the ding of a cash register, traffic noise from the sidewalk outside (a skateboard rolling by, shoes on the pavement, conversation between employees on a smoke break, shrill children's voices)

SMELLS

Wine being poured into a bottle, the sour smell of beer when a bottle is broken, cleaning supplies, muddy floor mats on a rainy day

TASTES

Besides a wine being tasted, this setting has no specific tastes associated with it beyond what the character might bring into the scene (chewing gum, mints, lipstick, cigarettes, etc.). For scenes like these, where specific tastes are sparse, it would be best to stick to descriptors from the other four senses.

TEXTURES AND SENSATIONS

Shoes clacking over the wood or tile floor, the weight of a grocery basket pulling on one's arm, smooth liquor bottles, swirling a glass of wine during a tasting, bulbous cognac bottles, heavy boxes of wine, carrying a bottle of wine by its long neck, balancing a few bottles in the crook of one's arm, stepping carefully around a spill, tugging on cooler case handles to grab a six-pack of cold beer, dropping a wine bottle and being sprayed with liquid and glass pieces

POSSIBLE SOURCES OF CONFLICT
Dropping an expensive bottle of wine or port
Knocking over a display
Inner conflict in the form of guilt as one battles an addiction
Being in charge of bringing the wine to an event and buying the wrong kind
An armed robbery
Employees sampling the goods
An earthquake that causes widespread breakage
Employee theft being passed off as bottle breakage
Minors paying an adult to buy alcohol for them and getting caught

PEOPLE COMMONLY FOUND HERE
A manager, customers, delivery people, liquor reps, store employees, the storeowner

RELATED SETTINGS THAT MAY TIE IN WITH THIS ONE
Rural Volume: Winery (194), wine cellar (100)

SETTING NOTES AND TIPS
Liquor stores come in various sizes and conditions. Some are high-end, with expensive products and décor. Others are smaller and shabbier with little floor space and simple inventories. Still others might focus on a certain product like wines or specialty spirits or deal in low-end bulk sales. Liquor stores can be located in trendy neighborhoods or on seedy side streets; some may hold special events such as wine or port tastings, liquor infusions, or cocktail mixing. As with so many settings, the kind of store you choose for your story will depend largely on your character. Consider her needs and the kind of store she might frequent when choosing this setting.

SETTING DESCRIPTION EXAMPLE
The door jingled and I looked up, barely catching a glimpse of frizzy brown hair as a customer I'd never seen barreled toward the back of the store. A flash of sequins, heels pounding the tile like pissed off post drivers, and that was it. The door to the refrigerated case slid open, then slammed shut so hard, the Merlots on the shelf next to it rattled. Both her footsteps and her muttering grew louder before she reappeared, sliding a six-pack of beer and a bottle of Jose Cuervo on the counter. Her cheeks were flushed and tears had tracked mascara all down her face. I opened my mouth to make sure she was okay but snapped it shut as she leveled a glare at me.
Techniques and Devices Used: Multisensory descriptions, simile
Resulting Effects: Hinting at backstory, reinforcing emotion

PAWN SHOP

SIGHTS
Tinted windows, bright interior lighting, a long mirror along the back wall, narrow aisles, shelves holding a variety of merchandise (radios, TVs, microwaves, toaster ovens, humidifiers, sewing machines, vacuum cleaners, purses, leather jackets and fur coats, hard drives, laptops, DVD players, stacks of old records), merchandise hanging on pegs on the walls (sunglasses, binoculars, headphones), a glass-top counter containing more expensive goods (watches, rings, chains, cell phones, cameras, tablets, e-readers, gaming systems), musical instruments and equipment (guitars, drums, amplifiers, keyboards, equalizers, brass instruments, harmonicas), framed and signed sports memorabilia, a variety of sporting equipment (fishing rods, surfboards, an archery bow, in-line skates, bicycles and helmets), dolls in collectible boxes, swords and tactical knives, remote-controlled vehicles, larger items (hubcaps, tires and rims, chainsaws, lawn mowers and leaf blowers, car stereo equipment), tools (saws, drills, sanders, air compressors), computers and laptops, a locked safe behind the counter, a magnifying lens for examining merchandise, jewelry cleaner and cloths, wires running up and down the walls so various items can be plugged in, security cameras

SOUNDS
Background music or a muffled sounds from a television show an employee is watching behind the front desk, people talking, customers and employees haggling, phones ringing, a bell chiming when the door opens, footsteps, keyboards clicking, shoes squeaking on the tile floor, employees working on merchandise in the back room, items being pushed aside to make room for new goods, keys jingling as cases are unlocked, heavy goods being removed from shelves and set on the floor for inspection by customers, sound quality tests for customers (TVs being turned up, keyboards played, guitars plucked, microwaves turned on)

SMELLS
Dust, grease and oil (near the tools and machinery), musty air

TASTES
Some settings have no specific tastes associated with them beyond what the character might bring into the scene (chewing gum, mints, lipstick, cigarettes, etc.). For scenes like these, where specific tastes are sparse, it would be best to stick to descriptors from the other four senses.

TEXTURES AND SENSATIONS
Dusty boxes, grimy lawn tools, power buttons on electrical devices that stick, carrying something heavy to the back counter so it can be examined, a scratched glass countertop under one's fingers, the feel of worn bills in one's hand, tugging at taut guitar strings, running one's hand along the soft fur of a coat, the heft of a fishing rod in one's grip, sitting and balancing on a bike to test its size, a supple leather jacket or pair of gloves, hanging a purse over one's shoulder to see if it's the right length, flipping through a stack of vinyl records, slipping one's feet into a pair of skates to test the size

POSSIBLE SOURCES OF CONFLICT

Being accused of buying or selling stolen goods

Being a terrible haggler

Dealing with a crook

Desperately needing money and not receiving enough in exchange for the item one is selling

Shady characters that make one feel uncomfortable

Being sold an item that one discovers is broken

Trying to sell an item that doesn't work or is in some way inadequate and hoping it won't be noticed

Bumping into someone one knows while trying to surreptitiously deal with a pawnbroker

Accidentally dropping merchandise or knocking over a stack of shelves

A robbery

The pawn shop being a front for criminal activity

The pawn shop owner buying a piece of merchandise and discovering that it was stolen or used in a crime

PEOPLE COMMONLY FOUND HERE

Customers, employees

RELATED SETTINGS THAT MAY TIE IN WITH THIS ONE

Antiques shop (156), thrift store (182)

SETTING NOTES AND TIPS

Pawn shops provide a service to the public that enables people who need cash to get it quickly. In one scenario, customers can sell an item that is in good working order to a pawn shop for an agreed-upon price, and the pawnbroker then turns around and sells it in his shop. Another option is to take out a loan on the object; the customer loans a product to the broker for a period of time. In exchange, the broker gives the customer a set amount of money. The customer must return within the specified time period and pay back the loan, plus interest, to get back their item or risk losing it altogether.

SETTING DESCRIPTION EXAMPLE

Jake pulled a slip of paper from his pocket as he passed the scratched-up jewelry counter and wall of DVDs. This was the third pawn shop he'd checked, and each one smelled the same—a combination of old carpet, motor oil, and takeout food. The latter he expected wafted off the mountain of a man doing his best to murder a helpless stool behind the counter as he tracked customers on a surveillance screen. Jake headed toward the back. Past a lawn mower and a pair of electric guitars, he found what he was looking for: audio equipment. He quickly catalogued brands, dismissing pieces until he came to a small black Bose sound wave speaker with a dinged-in corner. Flipping it over, he compared the serial number to the one written on his paper. A match. His lips flattened. He was going to kill Paul.

    Techniques and Devices Used: Metaphor, multisensory descriptions

    Resulting Effects: Characterization, hinting at backstory

PET STORE

SIGHTS
Rows of pet food and treats, toys, bags of litter, clothing, dental and hair care products, leashes and other training devices, stacks of colorful dog beds of different sizes, boxes of crates and pet carriers, scratching posts for cats, glass-sided viewing displays running along the outer wall for puppies (sleeping, wrestling, jumping at the glass, tails wagging) and kittens (mewing, batting at plastic balls, jumping on one another and play-fighting), an open-topped hutch containing rabbits or ferrets (eating, burrowing into the shavings, hiding under bridges or in hidey-houses), a section for fish supplies (tanks or bowls, lightbulbs, water features and fake plants, colorful gravel or glass stones, water treatments, salt, nets, filters and hoses), smaller terrariums for different breeds of animals (containing food and water dishes, exercise wheels, wood shavings and toys), a penned-in area with a gate where customers can visit with puppies or kittens one-on-one, large bird cages for twittering cockatiels or brightly-plumaged parrots, smaller cages with green or blue budgies and other exotic small birds, reptile tanks (for snakes, lizards and spiders), an area with low light filled with fish tanks (goldfish, tiger, tetras, catfish, lionfish, clownfish, piranha), a shelf full of small containers for beta fish, tanks containing sea horses or turtles, a grooming department with dogs being bathed and trimmed, special displays and seasonal items, bright sale signage, a dog tag engraving machine, a checkout area, patrons with dogs (or other animals) on leashes

SOUNDS
Dogs barking or howling, the click of nails across the floor, food cans or crinkly bags of dog food being dropping into a cart, animals bumping against metal pens, customers cooing at the animals, kids jumping around in excitement or racing around the store, bubbles cascading through fish tanks, wood shavings rustling as an animal burrows into them, the hum of motors in the fish tank area, birds squawking and biting at the metal bars of their cages, the rattle and squeak of a plastic wheel as a mouse or hamster runs on it, bells dinging, shoes squeaking on the floor, rattling shopping cart wheels, beeping and chimes from the checkout counter, till tape spitting out of a machine

SMELLS
Pine litter shavings, dog fur, scented shampoo (if a grooming station is close by), dry dog food and treats, algae, animal feces and urine

TASTES
This setting will typically have no tastes associated with it. However, some pet stores will host children's birthday parties; in these instances, cake and other treats may be brought in for the guests by the parents of the birthday child.

TEXTURES AND SENSATIONS
Soft kitten or rabbit fur, the wet licks and kisses of an excited puppy, gently holding an animal and feeling its heart race within one's palm, the squirmy wiggling of a puppy, the nip of a

puppy or cat, the misty wetness on one's skin from a dog's sneeze, wood shavings falling from an animal's feet or fur, slippery bags of pet food and treat bags, the cold metal of a food can, knobby twists of rawhide treats, bumpy knotted rope toys, spongy balls and smooth nylon leashes and collars, rubbery toys, a cold metal water bowl, the weight of a fish inside a water-filled plastic bag

POSSIBLE SOURCES OF CONFLICT
Animals escaping their cages—especially a snake, spider or bird
A disease that spreads among the animals
A power outage that puts delicate fish in jeopardy
A customer caught intentionally trying to harm an animal
A guest at a birthday party having a phobia of animals
An animal that has not had appropriate shots biting a customer
Protests by animal rights groups
A store manager's inner conflict at discovering a litter of puppies came from a puppy mill

PEOPLE COMMONLY FOUND HERE
Customers, delivery people, groomers, pet store employees

RELATED SETTINGS THAT MAY TIE IN WITH THIS ONE
Vet clinic (130)

SETTING NOTES AND TIPS
Pet stores are a source of joy for most people, and it is common to visit them occasionally for fun, even if one is not actively looking for a pet. Big box stores have a larger selection, while smaller ones may deal only in dogs and cats and carry minimal supplies for exotic animals. It should also be noted that many stores are discontinuing the purchase of puppies and kittens due to the bad press and social pressures associated with puppy and kitten mills, so stores won't always have these animals in-house. However, some stores run pet adoptions for local rescue groups and are able to make the animals available to the public through these events.

SETTING DESCRIPTION EXAMPLE
Levi tugged my hand, pulling me past the leashes, dog sweaters, and chew toys, eager to show me what he and Grandpa had found on their last outing together. My steps were slow, and I was still upset with Dad, promising to buy a four-year-old a pet "but only if his mom and dad agreed." That was my father in a nutshell, always passing the responsibility buck onto someone else. Thankfully Levi didn't swerve toward the wall of cats and dogs in their glass-sided display kennels; my allergies could never handle something like that. Wood shavings and the ammonia stench of urine tickled my nose as we passed the rabbits and mice, and I tensed, but again Levi didn't stop. I was starting to hold out hope that this wouldn't be too bad—that we'd end up with a colorful beta fish or something—when my hand was jerked to the left, toward the reptile section.

    Techniques and Devices Used: Multisensory descriptions

    Resulting Effects: Characterization, foreshadowing, hinting at backstory, reinforcing emotion

PSYCHIC'S SHOP

SIGHTS

Main Shop: strings of lights around the ceiling, color-shaded lamps on tables, burning candles, potted plants decorating the corners, celestial pictures on the walls, a seating area with a sofa and plush chairs, a terrarium full of plants, a dog or cat wandering the shop, a refreshment cart offering tea and fruit-infused water, a small wishing fountain with coins in the bottom, a cashier's station, flyers for upcoming seminars and classes, a sign-in book, private rooms in the back for psychic readings, glassed-in cases with items for sale (jewelry, crystals, dream catchers, figurines and statues of dragons, unicorns, angels, and saints), shelving and tables displaying tea sets and herbal teas, packets of herbs (comfrey root, feverfew, hyssop, calendula), mirrors, charms, essential oils, candles, relaxation CDs, plaques embossed with inspirational messages, a collection of spell candles (to bring money, harmony, friendship, good health), books, tarot cards, wands, rune stones, incense, pendulums, prayer boxes, vials for carrying ashes or herbs, mortar and pestles, Tibetan bowls

Private Rooms: folding doors for privacy, a round table with a fringed cloth, cushioned chairs, a storage chest, a lamp, tarot cards spread on the table, crystals in a bowl, a tea cup, an incense burner, a box of tissues, statuary, a potted plant, curtains draped from the ceiling and walls, paintings on the walls, business cards, pens and paper, candles

SOUNDS

Ethereal music playing, customers murmuring to each other, a bubbling fountain, chimes jingling when the front door opens, the phone ringing, the click of a dog's toenails on the floor (if they have a store pet), tea being poured into a cup, the rustle of a plastic bag filled with herbs, coins splashing into the fountain, glass doors sliding open so merchandise can be examined, a cash register drawer shooting open or clicking closed, the whir of a receipt being printed, a match being struck to light a candle, tarot or angel cards slipping from a deck and onto a tabletop, murmurs from the private rooms, the tinkle of crystals bumping against each other, sniffling or weeping, the soft swish of tissues being pulled from a box

SMELLS

Incense, herbs, scented candles, essential oils

TASTES

Herbal tea, water

TEXTURES AND SENSATIONS

The tickle of incense in the nose, a cup of tea warming the hands, sweaty palms as one nervously awaits a reading, impending tears, relaxing into a cushioned chair, smooth crystals, a pet rubbing against one's leg, feathery dream catchers, metal and glass figurines, papery tea packets, steam rising from a tea cup as one takes a sip

POSSIBLE SOURCES OF CONFLICT

Hearing bad news from a psychic

Encountering a charlatan

A psychic shop being picketed or publicly opposed in some way

Hearing conflicting news that adds to one's confusion

Breaking a piece of merchandise and fearing a negative psychic response

Being asked to do a reading for a skeptic

Superstitions that make a customer closed-minded or irrational

A customer who wants the psychic to make choices for her and tell her what to do

Family members who oppose one's work as a psychic

Temporarily or permanently losing one's psychic abilities

Being attracted to a customer and not wanting to give him bad news

Having one's energy depleted when toxic people enter one's space

Feeling drained after giving an especially taxing reading to a client

PEOPLE COMMONLY FOUND HERE

A cashier, alternative healing practitioners, customers seeking answers to questions, delivery men and women, people facing big decisions, people grieving the loss of loved ones and wanting reassurance, psychics, spiritually-minded people

RELATED SETTINGS THAT MAY TIE IN WITH THIS ONE

Parking lot (102), shopping mall (180), small town street (120)

SETTING NOTES AND TIPS

Psychic readings can be given by utilizing a variety of methods: tea leaves, palms, auras, tarot or angel cards, star charts, runes, numerology (the use of numbers), crystals, or psychometrics (the use of personal items). Most psychics are specialized in one or more of these areas. Besides offering readings, many psychics also sell merchandise through their place of business; customers entering a psychic shop may do so for the purpose of obtaining a reading or because they want to buy their own supplies.

SETTING DESCRIPTION EXAMPLE

The door jingled as I walked in, ruining my attempt at a subtle entrance. Someone was burning incense strong enough to make me cough. Haunting chimes and watery flute notes drifted from the store speakers, and voices murmured in the back behind a divider as someone sat for a reading. While I waited, I walked around the store. Crystals, spell candles, dream catchers, tarot decks . . . if my devoutly Catholic grandparents knew what I was up to, they would schedule an exorcism before I could blink. I jammed my hands in my pockets, thinking I'd officially lost my mind. But it had been twenty-two days since Dad left—a week longer than any of the other times. I needed to know if he'd stay gone this time.

> **Techniques and Devices Used:** Contrast, multisensory descriptions
> **Resulting Effects:** Hinting at backstory, tension and conflict

SHOPPING MALL

SIGHTS
People carrying branded store bags and sipping on to-go coffees, bright store signs, glass doors and windows, well-tended public restrooms, food courts with a central dining area, benches with people resting or checking their phones, specialty item kiosks, escalators and stairways, glass-sided elevators, cash machines, sales staff, parents pushing baby strollers, retail stores specializing in a variety of products (clothing, housewares, cigars, coffee, furniture, books, purses and luggage, artwork, electronics and music, games and toys, jewelry, health food, maternity wares, baby items, knickknacks, makeup), banks, travel stores, lines of people waiting at checkout counters, changing rooms piled with clothing that was tried on and discarded, sculptures and artwork, water fountains, exit signs, vending machines, an information desk, lounge areas (with comfortable chairs, TVs, and electronic device charging stations), bright lighting, skylights, glass and brass railings, receipts dropped on the floor, special events in open areas (charity raffles, fashion shows), teens sitting and texting, people walking and talking on their cells, kids dragging parents into stores and toward displays, coin machines that carry items catering to children (gum balls, small cheap toys in plastic bubbles, costume jewelry, tattoos), large parking lots or garages

SOUNDS
Boots and shoes on the tile floor, people talking and laughing, echoes, a mishmash of voices, people calling out to friends spotted in the crowd, cell phones ringing, cash registers printing receipts, the crackle of a security radio, plastic bags crinkling, zippers on purses and jackets being pulled, someone slurping through a straw, kids asking questions and begging for purchases, store security alarms going off, customer announcements in stores (regarding specials, demo locations, or lost children), cashiers calling over the store speakers for a manager, scanners bleeping as they pick up bar codes, the click and clack of hangers rubbing against each other, elevator doors dinging, running children, a half-full coffee dropping into a trash can with a soft thud, parents calling to children, a fountain's splashing, soothing background music floating out of mall speakers

SMELLS
Food from the food court (meat grilling, grease, the yeasty smell of fresh bread products, cinnamon, salt, spicy foods, barbeque, hot dogs, burgers), bad breath, body odor, perfume, hairspray and products, strong perfumes and body sprays from beauty product counters, popcorn, cleaning supplies, coffee, wet shoes and boots during poor weather, air fresheners, floor wax

TASTES
Water, coffee, pop, mints, gum, multicultural choices from the food court, snacks bought at stores or from vending machines (cookies, candy, chocolate, chips, ice cream), cough drops, tobacco chew

TEXTURES AND SENSATIONS
Balancing carefully on an escalator step, brushing by other shoppers, being jostled in a crowd at a food court restaurant, a cool drink in one's hand, sucking on a straw, heavy shopping bags biting

into one's palms, shopping bags bumping against one's legs, crumpling up a receipt, sitting on a hard food court chair, dropping gratefully onto a bench to rest, soft fabrics, cool metal railings, hot coffee or food, feet that are sore from walking, arms that feel heavy and strained, tapping a glass showcase with a fingernail, a child's sweaty hand in one's grip, struggling to carry bags while answering one's phone and corralling children

POSSIBLE SOURCES OF CONFLICT
An item ringing up for more than the tag indicates
A sales associate who won't refund one's purchase
Not being able to find the item one wants in the right size
Crowds and long lines
Stores running out of hot-ticket items
Buyer's remorse or overspending
Wanting to leave but being stuck at the mall with an avid shopper
Being in a big rush with hyper children or sullen teenagers in tow

PEOPLE COMMONLY FOUND HERE
Delivery people, maintenance workers, mall employees, moms and dads with small children, salespeople, security guards, shoppers, teenagers, walkers getting their exercise

RELATED SETTINGS THAT MAY TIE IN WITH THIS ONE
Bookstore (160), coffeehouse (142), deli (144), elevator (56), fast food restaurant (148), hair salon (72), ice cream parlor (150), jewelry store (170), movie theater (212), parking garage (100), parking lot (102), pet store (176)

SETTING NOTES AND TIPS
Shopping malls are as different as the communities where they are found. High-end malls cater to a wealthier clientele with expensive stores and restaurants. Some malls try to reach a younger crowd by including movie theaters, children's play areas, and kid-friendly stores, or they bring on big brand outlet stores popular with the price-conscious shopper who still wants designer products. Many malls are closing their doors, which doesn't happen overnight; these malls remain open while their stores slowly go out of business, creating a very different shopping experience for consumers.

SETTING DESCRIPTION EXAMPLE
Marcy hopped on the escalator and rode up to the second level. As she rose, she watched the mass crowd below shrink to the size of bugs. Groups of teenagers bounced against one another like popcorn, laughing as they ricocheted down the corridor. Older couples marched side by side, clearly on a mission to snap up the best Boxing Day deals. More than a few young families pushed strollers despite the early hour, but most held cups of coffee for a much needed caffeine boost. She tapped the pocket of her jeans, making sure her fifty dollar gift card was still in place. Time to do some damage at the music store.
    Techniques and Devices Used: Contrast, simile
    Resulting Effects: Characterization, establishing mood

THRIFT STORE

SIGHTS

Racks of crowded clothing arranged in a variety of ways (by size, type, or color), hat pegs holding hats and purses, racks of shoes and sandals in varying condition, stacks of DVDs and VHS movies, bookcases filled with books, floor-length wall mirrors on dressing room doors, stacks of blankets and sheets, furniture (desks, file cabinets, bookshelves, chairs, sofas and couches, dining room tables and chairs, lamps, headboards, coffee tables, end tables, folding tables), mismatched throw pillows, artwork hanging on the walls or leaning in a stack against the wall, birdcages, chandeliers, knickknacks, old TVs and other electronics, luggage, stacks of baskets, sporting equipment (tennis rackets, dartboards, bike helmets, skates, golf clubs), crutches, bins of picture frames, stacks of records, old silk flower arrangements, a toy section (dolls, a rocking horse, board games, stuffed animals), baby equipment (high chairs, playpens, cribs, toys), metal racks of housewares (dishes, vases, pots and pans, canisters, recipe books, serving utensils), small appliances (microwave ovens, small fridges, waffle irons, coffee makers, blenders, mixers, fondue pots), ugly holiday décor, narrow aisles blocked by people with shopping carts or baskets, caution cones for wet areas, a checkout counter, employees restocking shelves and putting away clothing, stray hangers, posters and flyers advertising other services (employment services, adult daycare, skills training programs), employees wearing back supports, a drop-off area with large bins for donations, employees with handcarts for transporting heavy boxes and furniture, cars and trucks unloading furniture

SOUNDS

Rattling shopping cart wheels, shoes squeaking on tile floors, hangers scraping on metal racks as people browse through the clothing, doors opening and closing, people talking, employees laughing, customers leafing through books or lifting lids on pots, desk drawers sliding open and closed, items shifting in a shopping cart, customers calling to one another between dressing rooms, an empty hanger swinging on a rack, the rattle of merchandise as customers pick things up and move them around, rustling plastic bags, an office chair rolling back and forth as someone waits for a friend to finish shopping, cell phones ringing, the clap of shoes hitting the floor as one drops them to try them on

SMELLS

Musty clothing and upholstery, floor cleaner, dust, old paper

TASTES

Some settings have no specific tastes associated with them beyond what the character might bring into the scene (chewing gum, mints, lipstick, cigarettes, etc.). For scenes like these, where specific tastes are sparse, it would be best to stick to descriptors from the other four senses.

TEXTURES AND SENSATIONS

Gently pushing past people in narrow aisles, a rattling shopping cart that doesn't roll quite straight, soft clothing, well-worn shoes, testing a couch to see if it's comfortable, smooth wooden finishes, lumpy throw pillows, ratty stuffed animals, the heft of a jam-packed box, working with a partner to lift and move a heavy piece of furniture, sliding hangers along a metal rack, paperback books curling at the edges, dusty record sleeves

POSSIBLE SOURCES OF CONFLICT

Being short on time and not finding what one wants
A disorganized store
Difficulty finding the clothing one needs in one's size
Embarrassment over having to shop at the thrift store
Accidentally donating something to the thrift store that was meant to be kept
Customers fighting over merchandise
Running into someone one would like to avoid
Precariously stacked merchandise that is likely to topple if disturbed
Being teased for shopping at the thrift store
A customer hogging the single dressing room

PEOPLE COMMONLY FOUND HERE

Employees, people dropping off donation items, shoppers (individuals, whole families)

RELATED SETTINGS THAT MAY TIE IN WITH THIS ONE

Antiques shop (156), homeless shelter (74), pawn shop (174)

SETTING NOTES AND TIPS

For purposes of clarity, a thrift store can be defined as a retail establishment that sells used goods and is often run by a charity. Because the items have usually been donated, there is often a stigma associated with shopping at these stores. Other more socially acceptable thrift stores are ones that only re-sell designer brands. Vintage stores are closely related to the thrift store but vary in that they specialize in clothing and items from the past. Their merchandise is considered "retro" and cool rather than simply old and used.

SETTING DESCRIPTION EXAMPLE

Jackie's sandals slapped the tile floor as she edged past a lady with a piled-high cart to get to a rack of fancy dresses. Some smelled a bit musty, but it was nothing a good wash couldn't fix. The hangers scraped along the metal rod as she rejected one after another, and as the selection narrowed, she knew she'd have to stop being so picky. Every cent she saved on a prom dress went straight toward her neighbor's beat up Ford, and she was determined to claim it before someone else bought it. It would take a good year to restore, but once it was done, the beauty of it would make all this scrimping and saving worth it. A strapless blue silk swished against the floor, and she held it up, giving it a closer look. It would need alterations, definitely. But, considering her lofty goal, this just might be the dress for her.

    Techniques and Devices Used: Multisensory descriptions, symbolism
    Resulting Effects: Characterization

USED CAR DEALERSHIP

SIGHTS
Rows of vehicles (cars, trucks and minivans) in various colors and models, price placards propped against the dashboard or written on a window sticker, shiny paint and chrome glimmering in the sun, strings of colorful plastic flags that flap in the wind, clusters of balloons tethered to antennas or posts, a rare or antique car on a raised platform to showcase it better, inflatable tubes that flap and dance as air flows through them, blow-up mascot characters that tower over the lot to draw the attention of those driving by, a building with glass walls, taglines (*The best deals in town!* or *Drive off with an incredible bargain today!*) written on the glass windows in florescent paint, salespeople taking customers through the lot or arranging for test drives, big sale signs announcing financing deals, a paved entry and exit, a car wash area, a mechanic's bay, a customer parking area, a few flower pots or other generic landscaping touches, oil stains on the pavement

SOUNDS
Vehicles firing up in various conditions (slow starting chugs, grinding or squealing that gives way to a steady rumble, the tinny rattle of the heat shield vibrating as a truck idles), the wind causing flags and air socks to flutter and flap, the hum and rush of traffic from an adjoining street, customers discussing a vehicle with a salesman, the squeak of a door hinge, doors and trunks slamming closed, tires rolling across pavement or gravel, the sputter of exhaust, music floating out of store speakers, a voice over the intercom calling someone to the front desk, metal clanking, the high-pitched whine of air tools and hydraulics lifting and lowering from the mechanic's bay

SMELLS
Car exhaust, hot pavement tar, oil stains baking in the sun, sweat and cologne from salespeople and customers, cigarette smoke

TASTES
Some settings have no specific tastes associated with them beyond what the character might bring into the scene (chewing gum, mints, lipstick, cigarettes, etc.). For scenes like these, where specific tastes are sparse, it would be best to stick to descriptors from the other four senses.

TEXTURES AND SENSATIONS
The sun beating down on one's head, heat rising from the pavement, opening a car door and feeling the heat rush out, running a finger along the ridge of a hood or spoiler, scraping at a rust spot with a fingernail to test if it will flake, rubbing at a scratch to see if it is just a line of dust, lifting a car hood, brushing hands together to loosen the dust, the give of an older car's front seat, gripping onto the steering wheel to see how it feels, pressing buttons and fiddling with knobs, the rush of air from a heating or cooling vent, the painful bounce of a car that needs its shocks replaced

POSSIBLE SOURCES OF CONFLICT
Fraudulent claims regarding a vehicle's condition
Buying a vehicle only to discover filed-off serial numbers and other signs of illegal activity

Discovering there's a bank lien on one's used vehicle

Taking one's car to a mechanic only to find out it was in an undisclosed accident

Driving a car off the lot and having it break down

Lot vandalism (cars spray painted, windshields smashed in)

Weather that destroys one's car, such as a hailstorm or tornado

Dealing with a pushy salesperson

Being talked into spending more money than one intended to spend

Spilling a drink on the cloth seat of one of the cars

The dealership acquiring a car and finding something disturbing inside (blood stains in the trunk, etc.)

PEOPLE COMMONLY FOUND HERE

Administrative clerks, car salespeople, customers, mechanics, support staff

RELATED SETTINGS THAT MAY TIE IN WITH THIS ONE

Rural Volume: Salvage yard (184)

Urban Volume: Mechanic's shop (86), parking lot (102)

SETTING NOTES AND TIPS

Used car dealerships are often portrayed as being shady or full of con-artist salesmen, but if this was always the case, the industry wouldn't stay afloat for long. Be aware of the clichés associated with this setting so you can steer clear of them. This doesn't mean that your dealership can't be a front for money laundering or one that engages in fraud; just fill it out with details that feel authentic, and stay away from balding, cigar-puffing salesmen wearing bad suits.

SETTING DESCRIPTION EXAMPLE

When Tracey drove the dealership's new acquisition into the bay, I didn't even need to look up from my toolbox. From the laborious rattle of the engine's struggling breath, I knew I'd be here all weekend trying to resurrect the dead.

Techniques and Devices Used: Personification

Resulting Effects: Sometimes description needs to be economical. Here, specific word choice and vivid imagery convey the setting concisely in an efficient manner.

Sports, Entertainment, and Art Venues

AMUSEMENT PARK

SIGHTS
Amusement rides (a giant spinning Ferris wheel, colorful looping roller coasters, a two-story haunted house painted in gloomy colors, a log ride racing down metal rails to land with a giant splash, a tea cup ride, a swinging pirate ship see-sawing back and forth against a bright blue sky, a slow moving airplane ride for kids, pony rides, paddlewheel boat rides), long lines for rides, bumper boats and cars, bumpy slides, a kiddie ball pit and climbing area, rows of carnival games (ring toss with giant stuffed animals hanging from the ceiling as prizes, floating duck games, a basketball-through-the-hoop toss for prizes, a dumbbell strength meter, a shooting gallery with pop-up targets and flashing lights, hanging tires one must throw a football through, dart and balloon popping games), people carrying off their prizes (long stuffed snakes, glittery hats, giant bears, cheap toys and small-sized stuffed animals), mazes filled with fun house mirrors and laughing teenagers, smiling employees in uniform manning the rides, food vendors (selling pizza, giant turkey legs, ice cream and slushes, burgers and fries), fast food restaurants where customers can sit down to eat, litter in the gutters (wrappers, tags from toys, cigarette butts, receipts), gift shops selling park-themed merchandise (stuffed animals and dolls, books, picture frames, key chains, coffee mugs, pens and pencils, toys, decks of cards), people carrying cranky toddlers and pushing strollers, water bottles forgotten on benches, crushed pop cans lying near a recycle bin, the wind blowing around flyers and other litter, balloons drifting up into the sky, birds swooping to eat dropped food on the ground

SOUNDS
Loud music, screams, laughter, cheering, bells dinging to signal the end of a game, clanking ride chains, the whoosh of air brakes, chugging machinery, squealing brakes, feet running on hot pavement, people calling out to each other, fries or doughnuts sizzling in vats of oil, the dinging sound of pinball machines in an arcade, balls rolling and thudding down game chutes or hitting the booth backdrop, balloons popping, the jingle of change, cash registers sliding open, till tape spitting out, clapping and cheering after a stage show, the click of seat belts on rides, doors snapping shut or safety bars thudding into place, spooky theatrical noises coming from the haunted house (evil laughter, creaking, bats squeaking, ghosts moaning), tired toddlers crying, the splatter of vomit against the ground, the scrape of a broom as trash is swept up, the distant sound of a musical number from a live show, fireworks going off at night

SMELLS
Cigarettes, deep fry oil, hot pavement, oiled machinery, babies with full diapers, hot garbage, body odor, sweat, bad breath, sunscreen, vomit

TASTES
Amusement park food (burgers, corn dogs, doughnuts, ice cream, chocolate, French fries, popcorn, chips, rock candy, dipping dots, elephant ears) and drinks (pop, slushes, water, lemonade, snow cones, milk shakes)

TEXTURES AND SENSATIONS

A paint-chipped safety bar on a ride, cracks on a padded cushion seat scraping or pinching one's skin, a seat belt tugging tightly across one's lap, jamming a foot against the gas pedal in a bumper car, the smoothness of a ball in the hand before throwing it, grease sliding down one's palm from a juicy burger, ice cream that drips onto one's skin in cold blobs, swiping dry paper napkins at a smear of ketchup on one's shirt, crinkling up a hamburger wrapper or chip bag, the numbing sensation of holding an icy cold water bottle or pop, holding a child's sweaty or sticky hand to keep them close, water-soaked clothes sticking to one's skin after the log ride, water dripping off one's hair and face after a blast from a water cannon, the bottomless feeling in the stomach on a rollercoaster, light-headedness and nausea from too much sun and fast rides

POSSIBLE SOURCES OF CONFLICT

Losing a child in the throng of people
Witnessing corruption or a crime
Having one's money stolen by a pickpocket
Feeling one-upped by a rival who wins all the games
Feeling watched or stalked
Wanting to stay but having someone in one's group feel sick and need to be taken home

PEOPLE COMMONLY FOUND HERE

Amusement ride and game operators, attendees, drivers and mechanics, janitorial staff, park management, performers, security personnel, show performers

RELATED SETTINGS THAT MAY TIE IN WITH THIS ONE

Rural Volume: County fair (158)
Urban Volume: Carnival funhouse (200), circus (204), waterpark (244), zoo (246)

SETTING NOTES AND TIPS

Some amusement parks may follow a specific theme or have mascots (Walt Disney World comes to mind), while others are a hodge-podge of rides and games for all ages. Amusement parks are different from carnivals in that they are stationary; they also may open seasonally or be available year-round, depending on the location and climate.

SETTING DESCRIPTION EXAMPLE

Joel shoved his broom against the dirty concrete, collecting crumpled napkins, cigarette butts, and bottle tops. After the rides were grounded and the music silenced, the park showed its true colors. Not many saw it as he did, when the wind brushed hot dog wrappers up against dirt-smeared tent flaps and the moonlight gleamed over peeling paint. But that's what the public never understood about this world. Once the laughter disappeared and the park wiped its makeup off, it wasn't so pretty underneath.

    Techniques and Devices Used: Contrast, personification
    Resulting Effects: Establishing mood

ART GALLERY

SIGHTS
A welcoming and open-concept entrance showcasing a few signature pieces that will intrigue and encourage patrons to explore, a sparse reception desk with an artistic silk arrangement, business cards and a register on the desk, plain walls to ensure the focus is solely on the art, strategic lighting, room dividers that encourage patrons to wander, group collections (that fit a specific theme, style or artist), plain viewing benches or chairs facing a feature piece under spotlight, clean floors (often covered with thin carpet to muffle sound), tables with smaller pieces (such as blown glasswork, sculptures, or stone carvings), framed paintings and textured artwork with title cards (informing customers of the artist's name and price), art patrons admiring pieces and checking price tags, open doorways to each room, lots of open space between pieces, few or no windows, high ceilings, the gallery owner or curator discussing pieces with potential buyers or looking through a new artist's portfolio, an artist greeting guests during a showing

SOUNDS
People discussing the works in low voices, soft background music or themed sounds (running water, chimes, bells) that fit the mood of the gallery, the muffled clack or scuff of shoes crossing the floor, sounds echoing off the bare walls and high ceilings, people chatting in an entryway or near the reception area, a desk phone ringing, patrons telling an artist what they appreciate about her work, the soothing sound of a small fountain or water feature

SMELLS
Paint, disinfectant, wood polish, polyurethane, cedar, plaster, leather, aromatics brought in to create an olfactory experience for patrons (blends of sweet grass, sage, lavender, citruses, essential oils)

TASTES
None are associated with this setting unless a special showing or event is taking place. For these type gallery events, wine, sparkling water, imported beers and a selection of easy to eat, one-bite appetizers (a fine cheese selection, herb and citrus-crusted olives, marinated beef on skewers, etc.) may be offered.

TEXTURES AND SENSATIONS
As patrons are encouraged not to touch artwork, there are minimal opportunities to bring textures into a gallery description setting. During an event, people might hold wine glasses, pinching the stem or using palms to cup the glass, they may also feel the weight of a plate or napkin laden with simple appetizers to nibble on. Otherwise, think about textures associated with the character, such as touching a necklace while contemplating a piece or selecting a business card from a holder to remind oneself of an artist's name.

POSSIBLE SOURCES OF CONFLICT
Accidentally bumping into an art piece and damaging it
An earthquake or burst pipe ruining someone's art piece

A bidding war over a particular piece

Being present as a patron criticizes one's own artwork

Approaching the gallery owner for representation and being shot down

Wanting to approach a gallery owner to become a featured artist but having a personal conflict with one of the employees

Having a low turnout for one's art show

A gallery owner who is passing off frauds as authentic pieces

Receiving poor reviews from an art critic

Being accused of copying a famous artist due to the similarities in one's own work

PEOPLE COMMONLY FOUND HERE

Art patrons and customers, artists, framers and delivery people, gallery employees and owners

RELATED SETTINGS THAT MAY TIE IN WITH THIS ONE

Art studio (192), black-tie event (196), museum (214)

SETTING NOTES AND TIPS

There are many different types of galleries. Some are cooperatives, run by the artists themselves, while others are owned and operated by fine art and design businesses. Depending on the type and finances of the gallery, the space may be small and sparse with poor lighting, or it could be larger, well lit, and designed to attract an elite clientele. Many also do in-house framing; in this case, there will be a workroom and storage area attached with framing materials, and customers coming in specifically to have pieces framed rather than buying new ones.

SETTING DESCRIPTION EXAMPLE

Red wandered along the freestanding walls that guided guests from area to area, sipping from a flute of champagne. He stopped at each lit display but found he enjoyed the oddest pieces the most, especially ones where metal and wire were the medium. As soon as the thought occurred to him, he chuckled. Could it be? Was he was starting to collect some culture on these outings of his? The upscale crowd attending the showing flowed around him, filling the air with expensive perfumes. Flaunting sequined designer handbags and expensive shoes, they *ooh*-ed and *ahh*-ed over several chunky textured paintings that, to his uneducated eye, appeared to be made from vomit. Not that it mattered. Red was really only an expert in one type of art and so he did what he did best: worked the crowd. A smile, a word, the touch of a wrist . . . his pockets grew heavier by two wallets, a Rolex, and a pearl bracelet.

Techniques and Devices Used: Multisensory descriptions

Resulting Effects: Characterization

ART STUDIO

SIGHTS
Wall shelving for color-coded paint tubes, an adjustable easel for sketching or painting, clear bins and totes with labels for one's supplies, paintings or pictures on the wall that inspire the studio's artist, natural lighting (skylights or an uncovered window) as well as strong lighting for focused work (a moveable lamp, etc.), a table area (sketch or graph paper, a jar of artist pencils, markers, pencil crayons, or whatever medium one likes to brainstorm and sketch with), stools, jars for paintbrushes, a wall mural, stacks of panels and canvases, paint rags and rolls of paper towel, a ventilation source (a window that opens or a special built-in ventilation system), a bookshelf filled with books in one's field (painting techniques, sketching, comics, sculpting), a shelf for still life objects (a pottery jug, an antique tea set, an old doll or wine bottle), a pile of practice paintings or gray scales leaning against the wall, panel frames, clips, rolls of tape, a paint-splattered board on the easel, drawings or photos taped to the wall or pinned to a clipboard, a palette, a bucket of paint thinner, solvents, empty coffee mugs scattered about, plastic or cloth sheeting on the floor, paint splatters and stains, a camera to take pictures at different stages

SOUNDS
Music that the artist likes, outside noises drifting through an open window (traffic noise, kids playing in their yard, a lawn mower), a fan or air conditioning unit, the swipe of the brush over a new canvas, a brush clinking against a glass mason jar full of water, the scratch of a pencil on paper, using one's hand to sweep aside eraser dust, the artist muttering or humming, the ripping sound of tape, a sheet of paper towel tearing away from the roll, drafting paper being balled up and tossed in a wastebasket, the clink of brushes bumping against each other as one sorts through a jar for the right one, artists conferring over a painting (if the studio houses several artists), a coffee mug being set onto a table top, the click of a light switch, the rattle of paper, the shuffle of feet, the crack of a plastic seal breaking on a tub of compound or glue

SMELLS
Paints, oils, solvents, paint thinner, tape, plastic, pencil shavings

TASTES
Some settings have no specific tastes associated with them beyond what the character might bring into the scene (chewing gum, mints, lipstick, cigarettes, etc.). For scenes like these, where specific tastes are sparse, it would be best to stick to descriptors from the other four senses.

TEXTURES AND SENSATIONS
The smooth spindle of a paint brush, squeezing a pencil between the fingertips, the chalky grease of pastels on the fingertips, a cold slick or dab of paint on the skin, the heft of objects as one places still life pieces in a dark box area or arranges them on a display surface, tucking a dry brush or pencil behind the ear, the bumpiness of eraser dust as one brushes it off one's workspace, the smooth glide of paint being applied to a surface, the touch of air as a breeze drifts through a window, opening and closing drawers, leafing through glossy art books, rubbing one's hands clean

using a paint cloth, a dry and scratchy paper towel, the resistance of a lid screwed too tightly onto a tube, soft paint bristles, a smear of paint that tightens the skin as it dries

POSSIBLE SOURCES OF CONFLICT
Vandalism
An earthquake or fire that damages or destroys years of work
Mentoring another artist only to have them copy one's technique or style and call it their own
Poor ventilation that causes lung damage
A theft of one's paintings as they are being prepped to send to an art gallery or buyer
An illness or condition that causes body tremors (such as Parkinson's)
Losing faith in one's work after several pieces don't turn out as one hoped
Preparing for a show that is unexpectedly canceled (due to the gallery going out of business, the owner changing his mind due to poor reviews, or an emergency at the gallery)

PEOPLE COMMONLY FOUND HERE
An art teacher, art enthusiasts, artists, family or friends of the artist invited within the space

RELATED SETTINGS THAT MAY TIE IN WITH THIS ONE
Art gallery (190)

SETTING NOTES AND TIPS
Art studios may be a simple, tucked-away room in one's home or apartment, a large open space used by art schools to teach multiple students, or anything in between. The supplies within the studio will align with the type of art being made, such as paintings, sketches, drawings, comics, pastel work, or other more modern or unusual mediums. When using this setting, think about how the space is organized, the quality of supplies, and the items of inspiration the character keeps, and how each detail will help characterize him or her to the reader.

SETTING DESCRIPTION EXAMPLE
Reed selected the red as he always did when he was angry, and he slashed at the white canvas. He pictured her, his muse, his Lorna. The line was a blade through her creamy skin—skin that lied, skin that betrayed. His rage sliced and splattered the painting again and again, his breath coming in short, hard rasps. By the time he finished, red smeared the easel, spotted the drop sheets, and covered his white shirt. Fortunately Reed had the foresight to lay down plastic before meeting up with her this last time, something he'd learned from their three years together. Their relationship had always been ripe with friction, and the flame of his rage was messy. Now that he'd discovered her affair, that friction, and the flame, would come to an end.

    Techniques and Devices Used: Contrast, symbolism

    Resulting Effects: Establishing mood, hinting at backstory, reinforcing emotion, tension and conflict

BALLROOM

SIGHTS

Vaulted ceilings (embellished with scalloped edging, plaster medallions, custom moldings, painted artwork), glossy hardwood or marble floors suitable for dancing, thick velvet drapes over large French windows, high walls with crown molding, curved observation balconies on an upper level, massive tiered crystal chandeliers glittering in the soft light, indoor fluted columns with gold leaf accents and scrollwork, archway entries, panel moldings, decorative inserts and sconces, a spiral staircase and balustrade to the second level, a small orchestra or live band, a baby grand piano, guests wearing tuxedos and gowns, women with updos and expensive jewelry, circular dining tables (with white tablecloths, napkin puffs in wine glasses, perfectly polished and spaced silverware, gold-edged china place settings, candle or flower centerpieces), wait staff circulating the crowd to offer canapés or to exchange empty glasses for fresh ones, golden bubbles rising in flutes of champagne, dancers swirling on the floor, elegant floral arrangements and sprays, large ornate doors manned by white-gloved staff, ruby carpet runners flowing down the stairs, metal-framed mirrors spaced along the walls, the sparkle of jewelry, sequins, and expensive watches, black dress shoes polished to a bright gleam

SOUNDS

Musical instruments harmonizing, the murmur of many voices, the clink of glasses and cutlery, laughter, the rustle of dress fabric while one dances, heels crossing the marble floor or climbing the stairs, people calling out to one another, echoes (especially when there are less people in the room)

SMELLS

Food odors, perfume and cologne, sweat after too much dancing, polish or wood oil, smokers with bad breath or who carry an odor of stale cigarettes, fresh floral arrangements

TASTES

Food being served at the event (tenderloin steak, fish, elegant pastas and artisan salads, wild game dishes, creamy tiered desserts), beverages (bubbly champagne, appetizers, wine, water), lipstick, breath mints

TEXTURES AND SENSATIONS

A smooth banister on the stairway, heels sinking into a thick carpet in the foyer, pushing open a heavy door into the ballroom, holding a clutch purse under one's arm, air-kissing a friend so as not to smear one's lipstick, a glass champagne flute pinched between one's fingers, the silky fabric of one's dress, clasping hands with a partner during a dance, the pressure of a hand at one's back, cool silverware in one's hand, the heat of a tuxedo in a crowded room, the pinch of tight shoes, hairspray and pins pulling one's hair into a stiff arrangement, sitting carefully in a tight dress, an expensive necklace lying heavily against one's throat, the pinch of heels or new shoes, a bowtie constricting one's neck

POSSIBLE SOURCES OF CONFLICT
People drinking too much and becoming obnoxious or clumsy
Rivals meeting and getting into a heated argument or fight
A pickpocket working the crowd
Losing one's invitation and being denied entry
Two women wearing the same dress
Wardrobe malfunctions
Falling off a riser or down the stairs
Dating more than one person and having them both show up at the same event
Dangerous political maneuvering—especially if one is playing to opposing sides of a conflict
Having one's borrowed jewelry stolen
Saying something that one should not and having the wrong people overhear it

PEOPLE COMMONLY FOUND HERE
An event coordinator, attendees, guest dignitaries or celebrities, hotel or establishment staff (waiters, musicians, bartenders, kitchen staff, caterers)

RELATED SETTINGS THAT MAY TIE IN WITH THIS ONE
Rural Volume: Mansion (72), prom (128), wedding reception (192)
Urban Volume: Black-tie event (196), limousine (262)

SETTING NOTES AND TIPS
Ballrooms are often found in opulent hotels, wealthy private residences, and in certain state buildings. In an older location, they may be carefully restored to protect the historic nature of the room; newer ballrooms may be designed in a specific architectural style.

SETTING DESCRIPTION EXAMPLE
It was a night of flickering candlelight, soft music, and tastefully decorated tables holding blue rose centerpieces. Attentive white-gloved servers held trays of sparkling champagne flutes aloft, filtering through the crowd as they waited for the final donation tally to be read. It was also the night that Belinda, the forty-something charity organizer for the McMann Arts Center, discovered she was not a size nine. In truth, she was not a ten either, but something closer to a twelve or perhaps a fourteen. The size of her didn't matter, at least not to those who knew and loved her. The only one who really cared was her sleek green satin dress. As she ascended the stage for the announcement, her outfit chose to protest that second piece of blackberry tart from dessert. A mighty tearing sound rang through the chamber—a herald trumpeting the announcement that her form-fitting dress could take no more. Splitting right up the backside, the slit showed the crowd more than Belinda intended, including her propensity for going commando.

Techniques and Devices Used: Metaphor, multisensory descriptions, personification
Resulting Effects: Characterization, establishing mood, tension and conflict

BLACK-TIE EVENT

SIGHTS
Limousines and expensive cars queuing up around a circular driveway, valet parking, a red carpet-type entry, ladies wearing black dresses or gowns and glittering jewelry, men in tuxedoes, hosts greeting the guests as they enter, someone checking coats and wraps, a posh environment with expensive décor, an ice sculpture, hanging chandeliers or charming paper lanterns, displays announcing keynote speakers or charity opportunities, wait staff dressed in black and white and carrying trays, tall tables for guests to gather around while hors d'oeuvres are being served, guests mingling and sipping wine or champagne, tables covered in black cloths, covered chairs, name cards to designate who will sit where, gift bags, flickering candles on the tables, floral centerpieces, crystal dishware, fine china, cloth napkins, gourmet meals, ladies checking their makeup in hand mirrors and reapplying lipstick or powder, a DJ or chamber quartet playing music, guests dancing on a dance floor, friends taking selfies together, an attendee asking a celebrity or keynote speaker for an autograph or a picture

SOUNDS
Guests being announced upon arrival, outside noises coming in as exterior doors open and close, classical or instrumental background music, high heels clacking against marble floors, coats and wraps being removed, squeaky dress shoes, people calling out to one another, laughter and chatter, cell phones ringing, waiters quietly sharing hors d'oeuvres, the quiet drip of an ice sculpture that is beginning to melt, the scrape of chairs being pulled out, silverware clinking against plates, ice knocking against a highball glass, water being poured, the amplified voice of a keynote speaker coming over the sound system, applause, the murmur of wait staff asking questions about wine selections as they pour

SMELLS
Furniture polish, floor cleaner, air fresheners, scented candles, essential oils, fresh flowers, perfume and cologne, hairspray, lotion, soap, food smells, mouthwash, alcohol on someone's breath

TASTES
Gourmet food (scallops, shrimp, salmon, prime rib, fillet mignon), champagne, wine, water, delicate and flavorful desserts

TEXTURES AND SENSATIONS
Satin or silk sliding across one's skin, itchy lace, a too-tight dress or shirt collar, heavy earrings pulling at the earlobes, new shoes that need breaking in, feeling too cool in a strapless dress, heat coming from warming pans and candles, a date's hand on the elbow or at the small of the back, hair that is unnaturally stiff from hairspray, bobby pins scratching the scalp, struggling to juggle glasses and little plates while eating appetizers, feeling tipsy, touching up lipstick in the restroom, slow dancing with a partner, feeling unsteady on high heels

POSSIBLE SOURCES OF CONFLICT

Offending someone with one's political or religious opinions

Calling someone by the wrong name

Wanting to leave before one's date is ready to go

Having food restrictions that limit what one can eat

Getting stuck with someone who won't stop talking

Being seated next to an enemy

Being allergic to the centerpiece or something in one's meal

Having to attend the event against one's will (due to a work requirement or spouse's request)

Discovering that one has no cash with which to tip the coat-check attendant or valet

Learning disturbing information about one's host

Being the victim of vicious gossip

Being pressured by one's host (to go to a future event that one really has no desire to attend, to make a hefty charitable donation to a cause, to volunteer time that one does not have, etc.)

Discovering that the nonprofit organization running the event is not what it proclaims to be

PEOPLE COMMONLY FOUND HERE

A DJ, auctioneers, bartenders, celebrity guests, chauffeurs, guests, keynote speakers, valets, vendors and delivery people, waiters and waitresses

RELATED SETTINGS THAT MAY TIE IN WITH THIS ONE

Rural Volume: Mansion (72), prom (128)

Urban Volume: Art gallery (190), ballroom (194), cruise ship (258), limousine (262), penthouse suite (104), performing arts theater (224), yacht (286)

SETTING NOTES AND TIPS

Black-tie events can be thrown for a variety of reasons: to celebrate a birthday or anniversary, to raise money for a charity, as a social event for one's work or club, etc. The purpose of the event, as well as the location and time of year it's given, will determine the décor, type of food served, and clothing choices. An outside venue may find women holding on to their wraps and choosing hairstyles that will defy the wind. If a guest knows the host personally, he or she may choose to be a little less formal while still adhering to black-tie guidelines. All of these things should be taken into consideration when characters are dressing for a formal event.

SETTING DESCRIPTION EXAMPLE

The room had grown hot with so many people, and thankfully someone had thought to open the doors leading to the veranda. A breeze skated inside, heavy with the promise of rain, tickling the candles and scattering the tabletop confetti. My shawl fluttered against my arms and my hair swayed, but with so much spray, it'd take a monsoon to do any serious damage.

Techniques and Devices Used: Hyperbole, weather

Resulting Effects: Characterization

BOWLING ALLEY

SIGHTS
An attendant spraying shoes with deodorizer behind the check-in counter, a cubby hole cupboard filled with ugly shoes, merchandise for sale (bowling balls, bags, shirts, etc.), dim lighting, neon lights for glow-in-the-dark bowling, glossy wooden bowling lanes with black gutters, inflatable or plastic bumpers for amateurs and children, molded plastic chairs and electronic score boards, a ball return machine filled with marble-textured bowling balls, arrows and lines on the floor to help players with starting positions and where to aim, white pins covered in black scuff marks, a concession area and tables (holding plastic drink cups, beer bottles, water bottles, fast food trays filled with fries or hot dogs), an arcade area with video games and pinball machines, restrooms, a water fountain, garbage cans, emergency exit doors, bowlers (trying on shoes, selecting balls, cheering on whoever is taking their turn), staff clearing pins when the pinsetter malfunctions, bowling teams in matching shirts high fiving one another when a member does well, advertisements on the walls, kids with cake-smeared faces and birthday hats attending a party

SOUNDS
Balls dropping and rolling along the wooden floor, pins clattering against one another, the whir of a ball returning through the machine and clunking into the other balls, the distant clank of the pinsetter machine, people laughing and shouting, music blaring from the loudspeakers, children running around and asking if it's their turn yet, bowlers jumping up and down after a good shot or slouching to their seats to wait for their next turn, shoes rubbing against the floor, games bleeping and dinging, the rattle of candy bar wrappers, the slurp of soda through a straw, chips crunching, families singing to a child at a birthday party, friendly trash talk between competitive friends

SMELLS
Floor polish, leather gloves and bags, disinfectant, stale cigarette smoke wafting off people who smoke, perfume or cologne, the salty scent of hot dogs, a deep fryer bubbling as it cooks a fresh batch of French fries, yeasty spilled beer, sweat, smelly feet

TASTES
Chips, nachos with fake cheese, hot dogs, French fries, water, soda, pizzas, beer, birthday cake, candy from machines

TEXTURES AND SENSATIONS
Smooth balls, fingers slipping into cold holes, the blast of a dryer on the hands, tight leather gloves, the ball's weight in one's grip, the moist feel of used shoes that have recently been worn by someone else, frayed shoelaces, slippery soles on the wooden floor, the vibration of the ball return machine as it does its job, hard plastic chairs, cold drinks, the smack of a high-five when one gets a strike, cold air conditioning, bass from loud music, crumpled dollar bills, a smooth tabletop peppered with food crumbs, the silkiness of a new bowling shirt, sweat dampening one's hair, sticky candy, salty nachos, a pizza's hot cheese burning the roof of one's mouth, cold fountain water splashing one's shirt, slipping on the slick floor when one steps over the foul line

POSSIBLE SOURCES OF CONFLICT

A competitive rivalry that devolves into a fight

Damage caused by people goofing off

A kid getting decked on someone's backswing

Food poisoning

A pinsetter malfunction that screws up a player's shot (especially on the competitive circuit)

An inattentive bowler throwing his ball before the gate has gone up and breaking the machine

A thumb getting stuck in a hole

Dropping a ball on one's foot

Losing money in the arcade games

Breaking under pressure and losing an important game

PEOPLE COMMONLY FOUND HERE

Birthday party attendees, bowling club members, bowling enthusiasts, employees, professional bowlers

RELATED SETTINGS THAT MAY TIE IN WITH THIS ONE

Movie theater (212)

SETTING NOTES AND TIPS

Some bowling alleys may have glow-in-the-dark lanes where backlights are used, lighting up reflective paint décor and glowing pins. This can be a fun way to transform your bowling setting into an unusual and unique landscape that allows you to make use of light and shadow contrasts.

When you're looking for characters for your hero to interact with, it's easy to settle back on the standard archetypes: the love interest, the sidekick, the mentor. But the wonderful thing about settings is that each one can provide you with interesting and unique opportunities in the form of peripheral characters. Think about the kinds of people your hero might find in a bowling alley: a semi-professional bowler, a single dad throwing his son's party, the maintenance guy clearing pins and bringing out kiddie ramps—all of these people can share meaningful interactions with your character, providing opportunities for conflict, reflection, and growth.

SETTING DESCRIPTION EXAMPLE

I scanned the remaining two pins, the ball heavy in my grip. A split. Tough shot, and with us down by five, I'd need to hit both. I tuned out the *whump-whump* of the bass-heavy music, the shouting kids in the next lane, and the lights glaring off the alley's high sheen until all I could see was my target: the inch-square spot on the 10 pin's right side.

Techniques and Devices Used: Multisensory descriptions

Resulting Effects: Tension and conflict

CARNIVAL FUNHOUSE

SIGHTS
Flashing lightbulbs around a multi-colored sign, a bored attendant taking tickets at the entrance, a floor heaving and moving in odd directions, stairs that shake or tilt, safety handrails with chipped paint, twisting disks that must be walked across, a huge barrel that rolls while one is inside, spray-painted cartoon pictures (clowns, balloons, kids listening to music and having fun), bright graffiti on the walls, twisting ladders with unbalanced rungs, safety netting, curly slides, swinging wooden step bridges, escalator stairs that go down while one climbs up, a floor that bucks when one stands on it, narrow hallways, balconies at intervals providing fresh air and giving a view of the rest of the carnival grounds, scratched or chipped mirrors on the walls which create misshapen reflections, flashing lightbulbs, optical illusions and spinning disks that can make a person dizzy, laughing teens and kids, trash on the floor, strobe lights, spills from drinks, steam or smoke spilling out of holes for effect

SOUNDS
Loud music, recorded clown laughter, the clanking of shoes on metal floors, machinery grinding and spinning, a chugging motor powering the ride, noise from the carnival, chains squeaking and swinging, friends yelling or screaming with one another, the shuffle and bumping of people caught in the barrel yet trying to get up, voices echoing in the tight hallways

SMELLS
Carnival food cooked in hot oil (corn dogs, mini doughnuts, deep fried Oreos, etc.), popcorn, fresh cotton candy, sweat, dirt, stale beer, sunbaked plastic, hot machinery, gasoline exhaust

TASTES
Food and drinks from the carnival (pop, cotton candy, fries, candy apples, funnel cakes, hot dogs, etc.), candy, gum, mints, a swig of water from a water bottle

TEXTURES AND SENSATIONS
A papery ticket held between the fingers, sliding one's hand along the paint-chipped safety railing, trying to steady oneself as the floor shifts and heaves, the vibration of the funhouse's running motor sliding up one's legs and down one's arms, touching the wall for balance and then wiping one's hand on a pant leg, crawling on one's knees through the rolling barrel, bumping into the people ahead and being bumped from behind when the ride is crowded, grabbing onto a friend's warm arm to steady oneself, being poked by a friend for being too slow as one is trying to cross the shaking floor, sticky or dirty fingers

POSSIBLE SOURCES OF CONFLICT
The ride breaking down
Meeting a rival or bully in the funhouse
Overhearing other people talking about oneself
Having one's so-called friends take off while one is inside

Falling and being injured

Getting one's clothing stuck between moving metal plates in the floor

Claustrophobia

Being shoved or pushed by an aggressor in the dark

PEOPLE COMMONLY FOUND HERE

Carnival management, customers, maintenance people, safety inspectors

RELATED SETTINGS THAT MAY TIE IN WITH THIS ONE

Amusement park (188), circus (204)

SETTING NOTES AND TIPS

If the carnival is a traveling one, the funhouse will be crowded, since all rides have to be transported on truck beds from town to town, meaning it will be quite small overall. If the carnival is a year-round one in a fixed building, then the ride may be much more elaborate with several different levels. Either way, to maximize profit, carnies will try to cram as many bodies through as possible. Some funhouses follow a theme (popular video games to attract younger kids, zombies, aliens, creepy clowns, Arabian nights) but classic (stationary) ones may have the entrance depicted as the mouth of a giant clown or monster.

SETTING DESCRIPTION EXAMPLE

Megan darted down the dark hallway, leaving me by myself. Demented clown laughter roared out of the speakers and a blast of compressed air slapped my face, stealing several years off my life. I clutched the safety railing as the floor bucked and heaved. My sister knew I hated this ride, especially at night, and she'd ditched me on purpose. If her plan was to jump out and grab me like she did back in the Haunted House, I would murder her in her sleep.

Techniques and Devices Used: Hyperbole, multisensory descriptions

Resulting Effects: Establishing mood, foreshadowing, tension and conflict

CASINO

SIGHTS

High arched ceilings spotted with dome security cameras, flashing lights and hundreds of backlit gambling machines, a rolling patterned carpet, players sitting on stools (pressing buttons, drinking, smoking, printing cash-out receipts), mirrored walls that reflect lights and increase the dazzle of the machines, uniformed casino workers, servers and table dealers, blackjack and other card tables, roulette wheels, crap tables, trays of chips and dice, security guards in suits, roped-off high stakes poker tables and gaming areas, giant TV monitor screens for online gambling, scrolling displays announcing jackpots, bank machines, boutique stores (selling high-end jewelry, handbags, cigars, watches and clothing), trendy restaurants and bars, a reinforced glass cash-out counter, half-empty drinks left behind on tables and near machines, flashy posters and glitzy artwork, drunk patrons, prostitutes, poker players wearing sunglasses, tourists taking pictures, luxury prizes on display (spinning cars and custom motor bikes), casino workers handing out coupons for the buffet or shows affiliated with the casino, elevators leading to other hotel levels

SOUNDS

The swish of automatic doors leading outside, the warble of slot machines rotating electronically, buttons being punched, people muttering or swearing at machines, dinging alarms when someone wins, people laughing and talking, customers placing drink orders as they gamble, cards being electronically shuffled, the click of chips as poker players fidget before bidding, the click of the roulette ball, the dealer calling for bids, chatter feedback from the staff's walkie-talkies, the tumble of dice across felt, the squeak of stools, ice clinking as it melts in drinks, music or live singing filtering in from another room, canned voices from video display dealers, phones ringing, guests cheering as someone wins big

SMELLS

Cigarette or cigar smoke, old carpet, perfume, cologne, aftershave, sweat, food smells, money, hot machinery, air deodorizer, air conditioning, beer breath

TASTES

Water, soda, alcoholic beverages, chewing gum, mints, tobacco, flavored smokeless cigarette vapor

TEXTURES AND SENSATIONS

Thin carpet underfoot, cool air-conditioning, padded stools and chairs, slick cards, plastic chips, felt tabletops, wooden table rims, warm dice, metal slot machine arms, smooth plastic buttons, a trickle of sweat when extending oneself too far on a bet, too-warm clothing, sunglasses sliding down one's nose, the bustle of the crowd, stepping in beer spills, sticky slot machines, a sleeve dragging on felt as one reaches for one's chips, dice rattling in one's palm or in a cup, rubbing sweaty hands on a pant leg, a cold drink against one's lips, blowing on the dice for luck, chips weighing down one's shirt or jacket pocket, tearing a receipt from a slot machine at cash out

POSSIBLE SOURCES OF CONFLICT

Drunk people who lose at poker and cause a scene

Guys who paw the wait staff

Pickpockets

Spilled drinks

People drinking too much and needing to be assisted to their rooms

Feeling sick after eating at the buffet

A celebrity whose security team gets a little too aggressive

Gambling a weekend's worth of money in a single evening

Being ditched by one's friends

Underage teens trying to gamble

Trying to count cards and not get caught by security

Gamblers secretly working as a team against the house

Arguments between addicts and loved ones who want them to see reason

Unknowingly picking up a prostitute

PEOPLE COMMONLY FOUND HERE

Bartenders and servers, celebrities, criminals, gambling addicts, hotel and casino staff, patrons, security and police, vacationers

RELATED SETTINGS THAT MAY TIE IN WITH THIS ONE

Cruise ship (258), racetrack (horses) (228), Vegas stage show (242)

SETTING NOTES AND TIPS

Casinos that are part of a hotel will be decorated in the same style and level of grandeur. Ceilings may be low or high, and the air quality varies based on the age of the building and how effective their air filtering system is. If a person has visited several casinos, they all start to look and feel the same, but gambling enthusiasts often get a feel for one and believe their luck is tied to that establishment. Large sprawling casinos can make a person feel lost, since they look very similar in every direction, so having a few landmarks (a spinning car on a platform that is the grand prize for a poker game, wax statues of past performers, signs hanging from the ceiling that indicate which direction the lobby or buffet is) will not only help characters navigate, it will help make the experience feel authentic for readers.

SETTING DESCRIPTION EXAMPLE

I dealt the cards, trying to keep disdain from my face. Every night, losers wearing too much cologne would sit at my table, all puffed up with the belief that their pathetic internet gambling forays had turned them into big league players. By the end of the night they looked like the people the cops scraped off the street for a police lineup . . . stooped shoulders, broody eyes, and, thanks to their pride, empty pockets.

    Techniques and Devices Used: Multisensory descriptions

    Resulting Effects: Characterization

CIRCUS

SIGHTS

Outside: Colorfully painted train cars or tractor trailers, striped tents with flags flying, a midway filled with games and prizes, a carousel and other kiddie rides, sideshow acts (the bearded lady, the tattooed man, fire eaters, the human cannonball), a petting zoo or menagerie, concession booths, dirt and clumps of grass, fenced-off areas, floodlights, overflowing garbage cans, small bits of litter on the ground (popcorn kernels, crumpled napkins, cigarette butts, a plastic fork)

Under the Big Top: a circular or oval floor in the center of the structure, tiered seating, dim lighting cut by spotlights to highlight certain areas, a ringmaster speaking to the audience, multiple rings where various acts are performed (trapeze art, acrobatics, gymnastics, animal acts, motorcycle stunt driving, the wheel of death), trainers working with wild and domesticated animals (tigers, lions, horses, dogs, birds), clowns and towering stilt walkers, glittering costumes, gymnasts jumping on trampolines, colored spotlights swirling across the rings, acrobats utilizing aerial equipment (trapezes, bungees, silks, rings), cast members walking on tightropes, air made foggy by smoke or dry ice, dance troops, juggling unicyclists, neon lighting, pyrotechnics, loose helium balloons hovering at the top of the tent, wide-eyed children eating popcorn and cotton candy

SOUNDS

Announcements being made over an intercom system, the circus theme music playing, trainers speaking to their animals, the ringmaster's voice being amplified throughout the space, gasps from the audience, applause, acrobats calling out to each other, animals vocalizing (roars, bleats, barks, hisses, trumpets), the thud of horse hooves on the floor, the drum roll and cymbal crash that accompanies a stunt, shoes scuffling against metal stairs, a cannon booming, balloons popping, clown horns blowing, a carousel calliope, bells and alarms ringing on the midway, music blaring, hawkers calling out to people passing by, people talking and laughing, cell phones ringing, kids laughing or crying

SMELLS

Animals, sweat, circus food, fryer vats, hay, smoke, urine, manure, dust

TASTES

Popcorn, peanuts, cotton candy, snow cones, hot dogs, pizza, fries, nachos and cheese, ice cream, soft pretzels, soda, water, lemonade

TEXTURES AND SENSATIONS

Air-conditioning within the tent, the gradual adjustment of one's vision when moving from the bright sunlight into a darkened tent, ridged metal steps leading up to one's seat, touching those sitting on either side when the place is packed, hard metal or plastic seats, hands stinging from avid applause, tightening muscles as one watches a dangerous act, a sudden intake of air as one gasps, sticky cotton candy, a cold drink on a hot day, greasy fries or pizza

POSSIBLE SOURCES OF CONFLICT

A train or highway accident that destroys equipment or harms performers and animals

A collapsing tent

Rampaging animals

Animal rights groups protesting outside

Cruel handlers

A trapeze artist falling to her death

A trainer being mauled by an animal

Being shut down by the health department

A pivotal performer falling ill and being unable to perform

An attendee who is afraid of clowns or a particular animal

A child going missing in the crowds

PEOPLE COMMONLY FOUND HERE

A circus director, a ringmaster, acrobats, animal trainers and handlers, clowns, concession vendors, customers, dancers, groundskeepers, gymnasts, jugglers, midway hawkers, sideshow performers, stilt walkers

RELATED SETTINGS THAT MAY TIE IN WITH THIS ONE

Rural Volume: County fair (158)

Urban Volume: Amusement park (188), carnival funhouse (200), parking lot (102)

SETTING NOTES AND TIPS

Circuses have been around for centuries, and as one might expect, much has changed over those years. Many circuses are held in permanent arena structures now, rather than in tents that must be erected and taken down. Likewise, it's often more convenient for the circus to travel via semi-trucks and tractor-trailers instead of by train. Animal activism has shown the spotlight on the historically inhumane treatment of animals by their handlers, and many locales have banned the use of some wild animals, particularly elephants and bears, at the circus. As always, thorough research and consistency are important when building a believable setting.

SETTING DESCRIPTION EXAMPLE

Jimmy's eyes were as wide as Frisbees as they followed the roving red spotlights from one act to another. In one ring, horses trotted in figure eights, their hooves kicking up dust and tails swishing side-to-side. He craned his neck to see the trapeze artists at the top of tent, flying through the air in time with the drumroll, barely grabbing each other at the last minute. To his left, a sequined performer juggled a chainsaw, a scimitar, two dinner plates, and a cantaloupe. Ice cream was melting on his hand, and his eyes stung from staring so hard. He was scared to blink or move, sure he'd miss the coolest thing yet.

Techniques and Devices Used: Light and shadow, simile

Resulting Effects: Establishing mood

GOLF COURSE

SIGHTS
A parking lot filled with vehicles and golfers (swapping street shoes for golf shoes, loading and unloading golf bags from the car's trunk, setting up carts, organizing tees and golf balls, slathering on sunscreen, stowing water bottles in one's bag, tugging on a golf glove), off-white carts buzzing along paths and queuing by the pro shop, greenery and well-tended landscaping, **a driving range** (stalls with rubber tees and baskets of balls, a field pocked with range balls, distance markers and targets, an employee driving a motorized ball collector), **a putting green** (golfers practicing using one of the holes placed at intervals on a small green), **a pro shop** (selling golf clothing, brand name golfing equipment and supplies, rulebooks and handbooks, giftware and items with the golf course's name and logo on them), **a clubhouse locker room** (a changing area with lockers and benches), **a lounge** for after-round gatherings (often decorated with retro golf paraphernalia, trophies and framed pictures from past tournaments, the course's flag or emblem), **a patio area** with umbrellas and chairs, course marshals in golf carts keeping tabs on the place, golfers carrying their bags to **the first hole** (tee-off areas marked with sand-filled divots, broken tees lying in the grass, a sign displaying the hole's yardage and placement of hazards, distant flags marking the holes), carts buzzing along the fairway, freestanding bathrooms, reed-ensconced water hazards, ducks and other waterfowl, sand traps of various depths and sizes, frustrated golfers searching through the rough to find their ball, a deer bounding across the course and into the tree line, a concession cart pulling up to offer snacks and cold beverages

SOUNDS
The electronic whir of a golf cart, players talking as they walk the fairway, the *tock* of a ball hitting a tree, swearing and muttering, a golfer overdriving his shot and yelling "fore!" to the group ahead, a shout going up as someone in one's group makes eagle, the rattle of clubs hitting one another as a bag is jostled on a cart, the tab popping on a soda or beer can, the drag of a rake through a sand trap, a golfer tromping around in the tree line in his spiked shoes, maintenance equipment (mowers, leaf blowers, etc.), the patterned spritzing of automatic sprinklers

SMELLS
Fresh-mown grass, cologne, sweat, body odor and deodorant, stale beer breath, freshness after a rainfall, exhaust near the parking lot or maintenance shed area, cooking smells (steak, pizza, burgers) from the lounge kitchen

TASTES
Cold beer, fizzy pop, water, hot dogs and chips from the concession cart, food ordered in the lounge (pizza, fries, calamari, chicken wings, steak, and other clubhouse fare)

TEXTURES AND SENSATIONS
A golf glove fitted snugly to one's hand, shoes sinking into the spongy turf, pulling knitted head covers from a set of clubs, playing with a ball while waiting to tee off, fitting one's hand firmly around the club's grip, widening one's stance when readying for a shot, the back and forth motion

of a practice swing, pressing the ball and tee into the turf, slapping at mosquitoes, the bumpiness of a fast golf cart zipping down the fairway, being scratched by branches while making a shot along the tree line, using a GPS device to check the distance to the hole, lifting a flag from its placement so others can finish their shots, sand from a trap getting into one's shoes and pant cuffs

POSSIBLE SOURCES OF CONFLICT

A golf partner with poor etiquette (playing out of turn, talking while others shoot, cheating, etc.)
Alcohol-fueled cart driving that ends in injury or property damage
Being struck by lightning
Coming across a mother bear and her cub when retrieving a ball from the woods
Friction between neighbors or office workers spilling over to the golf course
Overhearing a golfer in the locker room bragging about conquests and discovering that the woman involved is one's own wife

PEOPLE COMMONLY FOUND HERE

Course marshals, golf pros, golfers, greenkeepers, maintenance workers, pro shop staff and administration

RELATED SETTINGS THAT MAY TIE IN WITH THIS ONE

Rural Volume: Forest (212), lake (220), pond (232)
Urban Volume: Parking lot (102), sporting event stands (240)

SETTING NOTES AND TIPS

Most golf courses have eighteen holes of varying lengths and difficulty, but there are also simpler par-three courses more suited to families and amateur golfers, as well as courses with twenty-seven holes. Most are open to the public, but some are private; the latter are generally better kept as the membership dues pay for newer equipment. The clubhouse may be sparse, no more than a functional meet-up place before and after a game, or it could be an opulent rec center acting as a symbol of the financial status of its members.

SETTING DESCRIPTION EXAMPLE

Argo, my co-worker and best-ball partner, strutted up to the first hole, his blindingly yellow and pink tartan sweater vest and red pants bleaching out the lush turf. We traded friendly hellos, but it was all I could do not to cry. Someone back at the office was having a good laugh, pairing us together for this tournament. When our turn came, I motioned for Argo to tee off first so I'd know what I was dealing with. *Please let him be a bad dresser and a good golfer.* But when he drew out his sand wedge instead of his driver, I knew it would be a very long eighteen holes.

Techniques and Devices Used: Contrast
Resulting Effects: Characterization, foreshadowing

GREEN ROOM

SIGHTS
Clean and appealing décor, comfortable chairs and sofas to lounge on, throw pillows, a coffee table, a stocked bar holding bottled waters and staple liquors (rum, whisky, scotch, vodka, gin, wine), sodas and mix in the fridge, fruit in a bowl, a bucket of ice, platters (vegetable, fruit, cheese, shrimp) lining the counter, a small buffet table (with finger foods and sandwich fixings, plates and napkins, coffee, candies, chips, ice cream), a flat screen TV (tuned to a show or showing what's happening onstage where the celebrity will be appearing), framed wall portraits and posters of famous celebrities who have performed or been interviewed at this venue or studio, a stereo system playing soft music or ambient sounds, a few popular magazines, a telephone, artwork and décor that reinforces a chic and relaxing atmosphere, an attached bathroom with well-lit mirrors for applying makeup, celebrities reviewing speech cue cards and itineraries before going onstage, stylists touching up one's hair or makeup

SOUNDS
Soft music (or music that suits the venue and people), the squeak of a leather couch as someone sits on it, ice clinking in a glass, laughter, a TV playing in the background, support staff prepping celebrities for the event, candy wrappers or chip bags crinkling, crunchy snack foods being eaten, the pop of a champagne cork, the hiss of a soda being opened, the grind and whir of an espresso machine, musicians warming up their voices, a stylist spraying hairspray, reporters asking questions in an interview prior to one's event, celebrities meeting with fans and signing autographs after an event

SMELLS
Warm food, air freshener, cologne, perfume, sweat, coffee, citrus, beer

TASTES
Food and drinks provided to green room users (alcohol, snacks and sweets, meat, cheese and fruit trays, shrimp cocktail, easy-to-eat appetizers or special requests from celebrity guests)

TEXTURES AND SENSATIONS
Leaning back into a cushy seat, flipping through a glossy magazine to settle one's nerves before performing, pacing the length of the room, stretching or performing relaxation rituals before an interview or stage appearance, holding tightly to a pen or marker as one signs something for fans with backstage passes, dabbing a soft cloth napkin at the lips after eating, straightening one's silk tie or plucking at one's costume or clothing, scraping a hand through one's hair, smoothing down one's shirt or dress, picking at one's nails or engaging in another bad habit to try and settle one's nerves, a makeup artist dabbing at one's face, a stylist fussing with one's hair, sweat gathering along one's back and under the arms, hot and sweaty hands, a dropping sensation in the pit of one's belly, the beginnings of stage fright

POSSIBLE SOURCES OF CONFLICT
Celebrities with personal conflicts using a shared green room
A celebrity making a special green room request (a specific style of décor, food, beverage, ambiance elements) that isn't fulfilled
Stage fright kicking in
A band member showing up late or intoxicated
Drunk or high celebrities trashing the green room
Illegal activities happening in the green room (drugs being used, prostitutes being brought in)
Underage fans and groupies trying to get into the space
A security guard dropping the ball and allowing a deranged fan or other threat inside

PEOPLE COMMONLY FOUND HERE
Celebrities and their handlers, event coordinators for the studio or venue, groupies, special guests of the celebrities (contest winners, family members brought on tour, an entourage), the local host at the studio or location, TV reporters invited to speak with the celebrity or performer

RELATED SETTINGS THAT MAY TIE IN WITH THIS ONE
Rural Volume: Mansion (72)
Urban Volume: Cruise ship (258), limousine (262), penthouse suite (104), performing arts theater (224), rock concert (234), Vegas stage show (242), yacht (286)

SETTING NOTES AND TIPS
Some green rooms are very basic: a simple room where celebrities can wait before going on air with a host or on stage at an event. The standard rooms—with comfortable couches, a live feed of the studio playing on the TV, a table of refreshments and bathroom facilities—are fine for a short in-and-out interview. However, when celebrities are putting on an intense live performance with intermissions or time in the beginning where a cover band plays, they may have specific requests for their relaxation space. From non-animal-byproduct furniture and vegan refreshments to a specific brand of imported bottled water, celebrity requests can make green room management especially challenging. If you have this setting in your story, think about how specific requests might characterize your celebrity and the possible conflict that might arise if those requests are not fulfilled.

SETTING DESCRIPTION EXAMPLE
Martin grabbed the remote and cued up some jazz, then fluffed the plum-colored pillows on the white chaise and matching overstuffed chairs. The requirements for this room had been very specific: white and purple décor only, three types of chilled Prosecco in individual ice buckets, soft jazz, and, oddly enough, lime jelly beans. He'd scoured the internet hoping to find lime-flavored beans that came in purple or white but had no luck. Rather than disappoint, he'd placed green ones in a purple glass dish and hoped for the best.
Techniques and Devices Used: Contrast, multisensory descriptions
Resulting Effects: Characterization, establishing mood

INDOOR SHOOTING RANGE

SIGHTS
Sales Floor: racks of guns on the wall or within glass displays, legalized self-defense items (pepper spray, keychain alarms, electronic whistles, mace), holsters and gun cases, cleaning kits, gun vaults, tripods, boxes of ammunition, T-shirts and caps bearing the range's logo, duffels and bags for carrying weapons, protective ear muffs, paper targets (silhouettes, generic human shapes, bull's-eyes), a gun rental area for people needing to rent a weapon for the range, brochures and cards for local businesses, a waiting area (couches, tables and chairs, magazines, a TV), posted rules and regulations, posters, restrooms, water fountains, double-paned viewing windows into the range

Shooting Range: foam walls to absorb sound, a wall made of rubber at the back of the range to stop projectiles, numbered lanes, bulletproof glass partitions between each lane, a metal track running along the top of each lane that carries a paper target, buttons that move one's target forward or backward, a digital readout that displays the distance to one's target, a tripod to stabilize larger weapons while shooting, patrons holding guns and wearing headphones and protective eye gear, folding chairs for those who wish to sit while shooting, posted notices (rules and regulations, safety tips, etc.), tables to hold shooters' cases and duffels, a fire extinguisher, a garbage can for discarding used targets, shiny casings scattered across the floor, range marshals dressed in fatigues assisting shooters and monitoring weapon handling, a red do-not-cross line on the cement floor, bits of cardboard or paper drifting down as a target is shot

SOUNDS
Loud and sharp bangs as guns are fired, the tinkle of metal casings hitting the floor, the whir of a target moving along the metal track, muffled sounds through one's headphones, the zip of a case or duffel being opened, bullets sliding into a gun, the click of a mag being loaded, paper rustling as a target is examined or rolled up to take home, footsteps on the concrete floor, casings being kicked aside by boots, shooters talking to each other in loud voices, the door to the range opening and closing, range marshals loading and prepping weapons belonging to the range and running through safety protocols with each shooter

SMELLS
Air conditioning, cement, lead, gunpowder

TASTES
Some settings have no specific tastes associated with them beyond what the character might bring into the scene (chewing gum, mints, lipstick, cigarettes, etc.). For scenes like these, where specific tastes are sparse, it would be best to stick to descriptors from the other four senses.

TEXTURES AND SENSATIONS
The heft of the weapon in one's hand, the smoothness of a wood stock, the rough grid of a plastic or rubber grip, brushing the trigger before committing to pulling it, resistance from the trigger, shifting one's weight to find the right balance, a sense of calm as one steadies one's breathing to

take a shot, an instinctive eye blink when the gunshot sounds, a jerk of pressure in one's shoulder that may be painful, a concussive thud in the chest from the sound of a gunshot, cool climate-controlled air, a tingling rush of adrenaline at firing a powerful weapon, protective muffs cupping one's ears and muting hearing

POSSIBLE SOURCES OF CONFLICT
An old or improperly maintained gun that misfires
An argument between shooters
Conflict between patrons and anti-gun rights activists
A faulty air filtration system that allows shooters to inhale lead residue
Discovering that the range is run by criminals
Discovering that a long-time patron has been connected with a shooting crime
A customer who uses his weapon to commit suicide

PEOPLE COMMONLY FOUND HERE
Ex-military personnel, gun enthusiasts, gun owners, hunters, police officers, survivalists, tourists

RELATED SETTINGS THAT MAY TIE IN WITH THIS ONE
Rural Volume: Archery range (146)
Urban Volume: Military base (88)

SETTING NOTES AND TIPS
Shooting ranges can be inside, as the one described here, or outside, with shooters firing longer distances (and often with more powerful weapons). Modern facilities should have air filtration systems that pull the lead residue away from shooters and allow for a rapid cool down. As with any venue, older ranges will be seedier and more dangerous, without modern-day safety and security features. Keep in mind that the weapons available to rent will align with the laws of the country, province or state where your shooting range is located. Weapons that are illegal will not be for sale or allowed on the range for use.

SETTING DESCRIPTION EXAMPLE
I leaned against the cement wall of the viewing area, rubbing my bare arms to keep warm. The air conditioning blew a steady stream of cold, and I was freezing. Shell casings covered the floor behind the stalls, and every time someone started shooting, a new batch went flying, ricocheting off dividers and bouncing off the steel-toed boots of the range marshals. My heart slammed in my chest at the noise and I crushed my ear protection against my head to try and drown it out. Tom grinned like an idiot when the range marshal handed him something called an AR-15, one of the weapons from the "Call of Duty" package he'd paid for. All I knew is after having to endure this, I'd better not hear a single word about him having to go with me to pick up my paints at the art supply store.
Techniques and Devices Used: Multisensory descriptions
Resulting Effects: Characterization, reinforcing emotion

MOVIE THEATER

SIGHTS

A white marquee with black letters listing movies that are currently playing, movie posters displayed out front, kids being dropped off at the curb, a glassed-in box office with cashiers sitting on chairs, lots of doors to enter through, tile floors in the foyer area, an LED display showing all the movies and show times, electronic ticket machines, customers waiting in line to pay, a brightly lit foyer, an arcade area with video games and token machines, caution cones to alert customers to spills, cutouts of actors, displays advertising future releases, ropes separating the ticketing area from the concession stand, a concession counter with neon lighting and pricing boards, popcorn and soda machines, boxes of candy, straw and napkin dispensers, a condiment station, garbage cans, stacks of booster seats, water fountains, restrooms, a party room, an employee checking tickets and directing moviegoers to their theaters, bins of 3-D glasses, dimly lit hallways leading to the theaters, a marquee outside each theater showing the title of the movie playing, carpeted stairs inside the theaters, a big screen with curtains on either side, speakers on the walls, track lighting along the stairs, cell phones glowing in the dark, tiered rows of cushioned seats, cup holders, popcorn and straw wrappers on the floor, a scatter of colorful candy spilled on the steps, crumpled napkins on the floor, rows of attendees focused on the screen

SOUNDS

People arguing over what movie to see, car doors slamming as people get out at the curb, the tinny sound of a cashier's voice coming through a microphone, shoes clacking or scuffling over tile floors, workers talking, popcorn popping, soda splashing into cups, the scrape of a popcorn scoop in the machine, echoing voices and footsteps, dings and alarms from the video games, kids laughing and running, the sweep of a broom, seats creaking and squeaking in the theaters, people murmuring while waiting for the movie to start, the crackle of candy wrappers being opened, the crunch of popcorn and nachos, phones ringing, deafening previews, laughter, whispers, neighbors who are loud chewers

SMELLS

Popcorn, salt, musty carpets

TASTES

Water, soda, popcorn, butter, nachos, pretzels, hot dogs, candy

TEXTURES AND SENSATIONS

Wind rushing in through an open door, frigid air-conditioned air, metal stair railings, the rock of a seat, a broken chair with a seat that angles forward or a back that reclines too far, arms brushing against each other on the armrests, fingers greasy from popcorn or messy from melting chocolate, wet condensation clinging to a drinking cup, one's seat being bumped by restless children, scrubbing away butter from one's lips and fingers with a napkin, tacky spots on the arm rests from spilled soda, sticky floors, wincing away from sounds that are too loud, the sensation of trying not to cry, feeling too hot or too cold in the theater, a throat that tingles with the onset of a coughing fit

POSSIBLE SOURCES OF CONFLICT

Choking on a Milk Dud or other candy

Aggravation over not getting to see the movie of one's choice

Teenagers making out in front of one's kids

Sitting next to someone who ruins the enjoyable experience (by snoring, hogging the armrest, eating in a messy fashion, talking, laughing at the wrong time, getting up multiple times before and during the movie)

Arriving late to a packed theater and having to sit on the front row

Spilling one's refreshments

Seeing the movie with someone who criticizes it the whole way through

Someone kicking the back of one's seat

People talking loudly throughout the movie

Hecklers

Viewing an uncomfortable sex scene with a first date or one's parents

Feeling anxiety because of crowds, the dark, loud noises, or possible exposure to germs

PEOPLE COMMONLY FOUND HERE

Cashiers, custodial staff and maintenance workers, customers, managers, other employees

RELATED SETTINGS THAT MAY TIE IN WITH THIS ONE

Parking garage (100), parking lot (102), performing arts theater (224), shopping mall (180)

SETTING NOTES AND TIPS

Most movie theaters are similar in size and venue, but there are exceptions. While the multiplex has become popular, some theaters remain small in both size and number of movies shown. There's also the dinner-and-a-movie venue, where people sit at tables rather than in rows of seats and eat dinner while viewing a new release instead of munching on snacks. Drive-in theaters are an endangered species, but you can still find them here and there. And independent theaters cater to the artsy crowd, showing classic, indie, or second-run movies in intimate theaters with historic roots or art-deco décor.

SETTING DESCRIPTION EXAMPLE

The other girls threw themselves into the saggy seats, laughing like a gaggle of demented geese. Janelle, on the other hand, was trying not to freak out. She could feel her shoes sticking to the floor from ten years' worth of soda that had never been cleaned up. Bits of popcorn—popcorn fondled by gross buttery hands and drenched in saliva—filled the nooks and crannies in the seats. And what on earth was that smell? Mold? Mildew? She gingerly sat down, trying to touch as little as possible. She hated the movies.

    Techniques and Devices Used: Hyperbole, multisensory descriptions, simile

    Resulting Effects: Characterization, reinforcing emotion, tension and conflict

MUSEUM

SIGHTS
Long hallways, high ceilings being supported by columns, bright lighting, historical pieces behind and under glass, displays that are roped off from public access, items standing on raised platforms and pedestals, placards with information about the various pieces, framed artwork on the walls, hieroglyphics (on actual stone pieces or depicted in photographs), faded tapestries, dinosaur skeletons arranged throughout the room, sculptures and statuary, busts of famous people from history, mummies in glass cases, tribal masks, dolls and toys from another time period, old airplanes and other vehicles, ancient books and scrolls, costumes and headdresses, suits of armor, a display of weapons from a certain culture or time period, jewelry and gems, cracked and chipped dishes, re-creations of extinct animals, urns and pottery, crowns and diadems, figurines, people studying the artifacts and leaning close to read placards, guests sitting on benches to rest, groups of school children, tour groups moving through with a docent, people taking pictures (without flashes), artists drawing inspiration from the items (sketching, writing about them, etc.)

SOUNDS
Whispers, people discussing the displays in quiet voices, echoes, footsteps on tile or marble floors, the carrying voice of a docent giving a tour, the scratch of pens on paper as people take notes, children laughing and running, voices narrating short films in closed rooms at the top of each hour, ambient sounds playing over a speaker in a themed area or room (battle sounds in a room dedicated to World War II, desert noises in a room depicting life in ancient Mesopotamia), teachers shushing children, the squeak of stroller wheels, babies fussing, the hum of a vacuum cleaner or floor polisher, the rattle of paper as maps are opened and folded

SMELLS
Cleaning chemicals, the smell of old items (however carefully maintained they are), must, dust, leather, stone, the papery smell of old books, fabric that is slowly decaying

TASTES
Some settings have no specific tastes associated with them beyond what the character might bring into the scene (chewing gum, mints, lipstick, cigarettes, etc.). For scenes like these, where specific tastes are sparse, it would be best to stick to descriptors from the other four senses.

TEXTURES AND SENSATIONS
The hard floor under one's feet, smooth glass under one's fingertips, leaning in to see an exhibit and feeling the press of a velvet rope against one's thighs, sitting on a hard bench, the glossy feel of a museum map, the smoothness of a dinosaur bone or fossil on display for the purpose of tactile exploration, a child's hand in one's grip

POSSIBLE SOURCES OF CONFLICT
Tripping and falling into a display
Accidentally damaging one of the pieces

Seeing an inaccuracy in an exhibit and feeling compelled to challenge it

Being in charge of a child who insists on touching everything

Attending with a pokey friend who must see every artifact and read every placard

Attending with someone who criticizes each exhibit or makes a show of wanting to be anywhere else

Visiting with the intent of seeing a specific exhibit only to find it closed to the public

Being bored but unable to leave

A break-in or theft

A bomb threat

Reports of items moving themselves or another supernatural event taking place

Being present during a heist or lockdown

Malfunctioning sprinklers that damage the exhibits

PEOPLE COMMONLY FOUND HERE

Art aficionados, conservators, curators, directors, docents, guests, historians, museum donors, school groups (children, teachers, and chaperones), tour groups, vacationers

RELATED SETTINGS THAT MAY TIE IN WITH THIS ONE

Rural Volume: Ancient ruins (144)

Urban Volume: Antiques shop (156), art gallery (190)

SETTING NOTES AND TIPS

This entry contains references to items found in history or science museums, since these are the most common. But museums have become quite specialized, dedicated to sports, specific pastimes, children's interests, arts and crafts, indigenous peoples, famous or notorious people, specific regions, time periods, military interests, entertainment, oddities, the supernatural, and many more areas of focus. Museums are also becoming more virtual and interactive, so keep that in mind as an option. To enhance a scene set in a museum, consider one that highlights an out-of-the-ordinary topic—or even one that is a figment of the author's imagination.

SETTING DESCRIPTION EXAMPLE

Our shoes shuffled and echoed as we walked into the small room dedicated to statuary from ancient Ephesus. The docent's voice faded as I studied the headless sculptures, trying to figure out how the sculptors had achieved such detail: the folds in the robes, the flawless hands and feet. My fingers itched, wanting to touch the fingernails and sandals and feel the fine cracks that ran through the stone.

Techniques and Devices Used: Multisensory descriptions

Resulting Effects: Reinforcing emotion

NIGHTCLUB

SIGHTS
A line of people waiting outside the establishment to be let in, people lingering or smoking outside, cabs dropping people off at the curb, well-muscled bouncers checking IDs and turning people away, a girl taking cover fees and stamping hands with the club's logo, strobe lights pulsing from inside, colored lights, speakers, a stage, bars with bar stools, small round tables with stools around the perimeter, waitresses dressed skimpily with glowing trays of drinks or shooters, shots lined up at the bar, bartenders filling orders, bottles of booze lining the mirrored wall behind the bar, lemon and lime wedges, multi-colored straws, empty beer cans and bottles, sprayers and beer taps, layered drinks, martini glasses, coffee mugs, spilled drinks on the floor, a line at the restroom, people dancing (on the floor, on speakers, or atop special platforms), black or dark-hued walls, a few themed décor pieces (country, rock-and-roll, Hollywood, heavy metal), neon lights, dance poles on the stage, a DJ booth, groups of friends hanging out together, bachelor and bachelorette parties, people (making out uninhibitedly, taking pictures with their phones, swapping contact numbers, drinking too much and staggering), drug tabs being exchanged for cash

SOUNDS
Loud music, people screaming in each other's ears to be heard, laughter, come-ons, hooting, yelling, swearing, breaking glass, whistling, DJ announcements coming over the loudspeaker, glasses clunking against a table, the hiss of pop filling a glass at the bar, the spray of soda or water filling a glass, phones ringing and buzzing

SMELLS
Sweat, beer breath, cologne, perfume, hairspray and hair products, body spray, stale air, vomit, smoke or pot wafting off clothing, fruity drinks and coolers, body odor, overheating electronics (speakers, sound system, lights, etc.)

TASTES
Beer, coolers, martinis, rum and Coke, gin and tonic, cosmos, mojitos, coffee, water, shooters (Dirty Hookers, Sex on the Beach, Dr. Pepper, China White, Snakebite, B52, Irish Car Bomb, Sambuca, etc.), energy drinks, pop, fruit mixes, spritzes, lemon slices, salt, lime slices, whipped cream, gum, mints

TEXTURES AND SENSATIONS
Hot stuffy air, beer or other cold drink sliding down a parched throat, crunchy ice cubes, applying lipstick or gloss, fanning oneself, sweat trickling down the neck and back, sweaty clothes sticking to one's skin, aching calves and feet from dancing in high heels, having a foot stepped on in a crowd, pressing against people to move past them, cold glass against one's fingertips, fidgeting with napkins or drink coasters on a table, constantly touching one's hair to make sure it's in place, adjusting cleavage, the papery feel of money, using hand and body language to communicate (pointing, waving, nodding), warm breath against the neck as someone speaks

directly into one's ear, the bass thumping in one's chest, light-headedness from too much alcohol or drugs, nausea making one's stomach roil, sliding a hand along the wall or grabbing at a railing to stay upright

POSSIBLE SOURCES OF CONFLICT

Being hit on by someone creepy who refuses to take the hint
Alcohol poisoning
Patrons being drugged
Underage patrons trying to get in the bar
Being vomited on
A friend hooking up with a shady stranger
Being deserted by one's designated driver
Being assigned the role of designated driver against one's will
A bouncer taking his job a bit too seriously

PEOPLE COMMONLY FOUND HERE

Bartenders, bouncers, cougars (older women going after younger men), customers, DJs, drug dealers, drunk people, strippers and hookers (male and female), underage customers with fake IDs, wait staff

RELATED SETTINGS THAT MAY TIE IN WITH THIS ONE

Rural Volume: Beach party (150), house party (64)
Urban Volume: Bar (138), pub (152)

SETTING NOTES AND TIPS

Late night party venues have certain similarities and differences. A nightclub is a large location with a bar, and while it serves alcoholic beverages, it is primarily a place to dance. It may bring in popular live bands, host special events, apply special effects (fog or foam machines, strobe lighting, spotlights, etc.), and have paid dancers on platforms to entertain crowds and keep the energy levels up. A bar is mostly about drinking and may cater to a specific crowd (biker bars, wine bars, etc.), and the centerpiece is the bar and its alcoholic offerings. Pubs are places to socialize with friends, hang out to play pool, eat hearty pub food, drink craft beers, and watch a game on one of the many TV screens.

SETTING DESCRIPTION EXAMPLE

Strobe lights worked the crowd, turning their smooth, practiced movements into a thrashing collection of jerks and bumps. I surveyed from the outer edge, trying to spot Tom or Derek, but the music blaring from the speakers was giving me a headache and the red exit sign to the left shone like a beacon of sanity. I tugged on Allie's arm to get her attention, then pointed at the door and pantomimed me taking a smoke. She nodded vacantly, like you do when you can't actually hear what someone just said. I didn't have the energy to try again, so I shook my head and took off.

Techniques and Devices Used: Light and shadow, simile
Resulting Effects: Establishing mood

OUTDOOR POOL

SIGHTS
Sun-dappled water, kids (splashing and swimming, plugging their noses while jumping into the pool, adjusting goggles, slapping at the water with pool noodles, paddling, kicking their feet, spitting out water and swiping wet hair off the face, wiggling a finger in the ear, adjusting swim suits), swimming equipment (water wings, nose plugs, bathing caps, goggles), Band-Aids and hair ties floating in the water, wet towels lying in clumps or stretched out on grass or cement, piles of clothing atop sandals or shoes, sun-bleached lockers along the wall, slatted wooden benches, rows of lawn chairs dotted with backpacks and bags, picnic blankets, a concession stand, a grassy area with a few small trees, bathrooms with showers and changing stalls, babies wearing wide hats and sitting in floaty seats, parents corralling kids or throwing dive sticks, water slides, mothers sitting on the edge with their feet dangling in the water, a first aid station, life preservers and life jackets, lifeguards wearing sunglasses and sitting on covered stands, diving boards, wet cement with puddles of water and rapidly drying footprints, flies, beach umbrellas, water toys (water guns, foam footballs, floaty toys, and balls), flip-flops, teen boys showing off, teen girls with raccoon eyes, water level markings showing pool depth, a floating deep end divider, vents, drains, filters

SOUNDS
Kids laughing and shrieking, parents and teens chatting, swimmers gasping for air, stuttering voices as people try to catch their breath, moms yelling at their kids, a lifeguard's whistle, rustling leaves, water splashing, the spray of a shower, the smack of a belly flop, feet slapping the wet concrete, pool toys hitting the water's surface, plunging dives, scavenger birds squawking as they steal food left on blankets, waterlogged noises from plugged ears, coughing and choking when one has swallowed too much water, the crinkle of chip bags and ice cream wrappers, cell phones going off, music playing over a loudspeaker, the gurgle of pool filters

SMELLS
Chlorine, sunscreen and suntan lotion, bug spray, oil and grease from fries at the concession stand, salt, freshly mowed grass, fabric softener from clean towels

TASTES
Concession foods (pop, juice, water, slushes, ice cream, chips, nachos, fries, hot dogs, chocolate bars, popsicles), gum, food brought from home (sandwiches, fruit or berries, crackers or pretzels, granola bars), chlorinated water, sunscreen dripping into the mouth

TEXTURES AND SENSATIONS
Gritty concrete underfoot, slippery tiles, cool water against the skin, drizzles sliding down the face and legs when one emerges from the pool, drips of water landing on one's feet, hot walkways, clean towels rubbing against the skin, prickly grass sticking to one's swimsuit and skin, snakes of hair clinging to the neck and shoulders, hair hanging in one's face, pinching goggle straps, hot metal handrails, chlorine stinging one's eyes, wrinkly fingertips and toes, the hot sun drying one's skin, plucking out a wedgie, sunburn, chip crumbs sticking to wet legs, bumping against other

swimmers, brushing the rough sides of the pool, toes gripping the pebbly surface at the bottom of the pool, a shock of cold water splashing a sunbather, walking through warm puddles, the burn of water in the nose, shivering with wet as the sun goes behind the clouds on a windy day

POSSIBLE SOURCES OF CONFLICT
Poor swimmers slipping into the deep end
Tyrannical lifeguards
Body image issues making people self-conscious
Inappropriately dressed sunbathers
Mean girls
A sudden downpour
Something suspicious floating in the pool
Arriving at the pool and finding it closed for repairs
Slips and falls and other injuries
A swimsuit strap breaking or slipping down
An unwelcome critter in the pool first thing in the morning (a snake, alligator, etc.)
A play date that ends prematurely due to squabbling

PEOPLE COMMONLY FOUND HERE
Birthday party attendees, children, concession stand employees, divers, lifeguards, maintenance workers, nannies, parents, swimmers, teens, young children and grown-ups taking swim lessons

RELATED SETTINGS THAT MAY TIE IN WITH THIS ONE
Rural Volume: Lake (220), summer camp (188)
Urban Volume: Cheap motel (46), hotel room (78), public restroom (112), rec center (230), water park (244)

SETTING NOTES AND TIPS
While this entry has been dedicated to the outdoor pool, many public pools are located indoors, where the weather and climate can't limit the swim season. This location also tends to bring a large mix of people together, and because many will feel "on display," it can cause them to alter their behavior to fit in, or if they feel threatened, to show their true colors. Perhaps the young mother new to the neighborhood is a bit too strict with her child, worrying that other mothers will see any friction as a sign of bad parenting. Or maybe a new friend made over the summer suddenly ignores your character when the popular girls show up to tan and check out the local boys. Whatever her age, when a character feels watched and judged by others, she can doubt herself and her own worth and may do things outside of her nature to fit in.

SETTING DESCRIPTION EXAMPLE
After pulling myself out of the pool, I plodded across the gritty cement to where my crumpled towel lay. I shook the striped fabric to get rid of the loose grass, and water cascaded off me like rain. A few minutes lying in the afternoon sun and I'd be dry enough to bike home.
Techniques and Devices Used: Multisensory descriptions, simile, weather
Resulting Effects: Establishing mood

OUTDOOR SKATING RINK

SIGHTS
An oblong ice rink with a low wall or railing around the perimeter, winter sights surrounding the rink (frost-dusted trees, snowdrifts, a street with shops and restaurants, skyscrapers, light poles, traffic zipping past and sending up plumes of exhaust), a facilities building (holding restrooms, equipment rentals, lockers, and concessions), outdoor seats and tables, floodlights for night skating, hockey nets and markings within the ice, a Zamboni cruising along and leaving a slick trail of smooth ice in its wake, skaters with ice-frosted pants, children making their way around the rink by holding onto the wall, kids using walkers or sleds, hockey teams practicing during designated time periods, breath trails lifting away from everyone's faces, confident skaters making sweeping turns and twirls, couples holding onto each other's hands, cones set up to demarcate a figure-skating area in the middle of the rink, figure skaters in costume practicing their routines, maintenance crews spraying the rink with water or shoveling the ice, falling snow, lone skaters racing around the rink, crowds of skaters moving slowly across the ice

SOUNDS
Blades slicing across the ice or scraping to a stop, people laughing and talking, kids squealing or crying, music playing over a stereo system, a hockey stick slapping the ice, a puck thumping into a goalie's glove, a puck hitting the boards, coaches shouting to their players, the fast-moving blades of skaters racing around the rink, the clatter of skates tangling and people falling to the ground, wind blowing through the trees or whistling between buildings, flags or decorations fluttering in a breeze, the hum of a Zamboni moving across the ice, shovels scraping up loose snow, a child sipping at a steaming hot chocolate, the crinkle of jackets and snow pants stiff with cold

SMELLS
Ozone, ice, coffee, hot chocolate, tea, food smells from nearby eating establishments, hot dogs cooking at the concession stand

TASTES
Cold air, lip balm, coffee, hot chocolate, water, concession food (nachos, pizza, hot dogs, fries, sandwiches), vending machine food (chips, candy, chocolate, cookies)

TEXTURES AND SENSATIONS
Squinting away from the sun's bright glare on the ice, the over-bright white of the snow giving one a headache, numb fingers and toes, mittens catching splinters as one holds onto the wall, trying to balance on two thin blades, being jostled by other skaters, throwing oneself off-balance to avoid hitting someone, skates painfully tight on one's feet and ankles, too-loose skates that cause fatigue and aches in the ankles and instep, landing on hard ice, falling and scraping one's palms or face, hitting one's head on the boards, shivering in the cold, sweating in one's winter clothes, the bulky feeling of being bundled up in heavy clothing, a skater sliding to a stop and showering one with ice, a frigid wind blowing into one's face, stray hair sticking to one's lip balm,

static cling from a fuzzy winter hat, shocking oneself on the metal railing, turning an ankle and having to limp off the ice

POSSIBLE SOURCES OF CONFLICT

Skaters of different experience levels sharing a small area

Lack of supervision

Weak ankles

Not being dressed appropriately

Reckless skaters

Flying pucks

Unhealthy competition between skaters

Falling tree limbs

An unmaintained skating surface full of pocks, troughs, holes, or gouges

Injuries (falls, scrapes, bruises, bumps)

A parent forgetting to pick a child up

Being the last skater around at night and feeling unsafe

PEOPLE COMMONLY FOUND HERE

Casual skaters, children, employees working at the concession or rental booth, families, figure skaters, figure skating or hockey coaches, hockey players, maintenance workers, volunteers, Zamboni drivers

RELATED SETTINGS THAT MAY TIE IN WITH THIS ONE

Rural Volume: Lake (220), pond (232)

Urban Volume: Park (98), rec center (230), ski resort (238)

SETTING NOTES AND TIPS

While this entry has focused largely on the manufactured skating rink, there are other outdoor skating venues. In northern climates, frozen ponds and lakes provide a more natural skating experience. Devoid of walls, floodlights, and concession stands, these venues have an organic, back-to-nature atmosphere, providing a different feel than man-made rinks. It is also common for families who are into winter activities to flood their backyards or a section of their property to create a small rink, allowing their kids to play with their friends or learn how to skate. Snow shoveled from the surface creates a bank around the sides both to create a perimeter for wayward pucks and to provide a soft landing for new skaters.

SETTING DESCRIPTION EXAMPLE

Lenny squeezed his daddy's hand in his two mittened fists. He tried to stand, but the skates slipped and slid beneath him like metal snakes. He eyed the hard ice and squeezed his eyes shut, but that only made the slip-and-slide feeling worse. Abandoning the hand in his grip, he threw his arms around his daddy's legs and buried his face in the ice-crusted fabric.

Techniques and Devices Used: Multisensory descriptions, simile

Resulting Effects: Reinforcing emotion, tension and conflict

PARADE

SIGHTS
Crowds lining the street on both sides, viewers (packed together, standing side by side, sitting on the curb, spread out in lawn chairs, sitting in truck beds), police cars or fire trucks driving at the head of the parade, floats with giant balloon arches, stray balloons flying away into the sky, mascots and themed displays, marching bands, decorated trucks and cars, horse-drawn wagons or carriages, camera crews and reporters, cameras flashing, viewers recording the parade with their cell phones, classic cars or shiny convertibles containing people of interest (politicians, celebrities, beauty queens) who wave to the crowd, fireworks going off, confetti glittering in the air and on the ground, parade participants in glitzy costumes, flags flying on floats, banners and signs attached to vehicles, people on horseback, dance troops, cheerleaders stopping to perform a cheer, acrobats walking on hands or performing a sequence of flips, clowns working the crowd, military personnel, people on stilts, policemen standing guard and watching the crowd for disruptions, lines of caution tape or sawhorses designating the parade route, people throwing candy into the crowd, dads holding children on their shoulders so they can see, baby strollers, dogs on leashes, a cleanup crew sweeping up horse manure, stray candy and bits of decorations lining the curb

SOUNDS
Fire truck or police sirens, marching band music, recorded music coming from the floats, people shouting and hooting, applause, an emcee speaking through a microphone or loudspeaker, babies screaming, kids yelling and laughing, car engines revving, horns honking, the *clip-clop* of horse hooves, balloons popping, air horns and other noise makers, people singing on the floats, a dance troop leader or drum major calling out directions, flags flapping in the wind, the shuffle of feet as large groups in the parade march in time with one another, rumbling motorcycle engines, dogs barking, a police officer's whistle, a horse snorting as it plods along, the whine of tiny motorized clown cars, news helicopters flying overhead, the boom of fireworks

SMELLS
Car exhaust, snacks, coffee, wet asphalt, sweat, manure, street food from venders

TASTES
Snacks bought from a vendor (popcorn, peanuts, soft pretzels, candy, cotton candy, hot dogs), water, soda, coffee

TEXTURES AND SENSATIONS
Bodies being crammed together, being bumped and jostled by people standing too close, rough asphalt underfoot, confetti drifting over the skin and landing in one's hair, bass drums reverberating in one's chest, the jerk of a leash as a dog strains against it, the weight of a child on one's shoulders, a nervous or fearful child crawling into one's lap, sweat dampening the hair and trickling along the skin, sticky cotton candy, hands being warmed or cooled by hot and cold drinks, the heat of the sun beating down on the back of the neck

POSSIBLE SOURCES OF CONFLICT

Being attacked or kidnapped in the chaos

A fear of clowns

Heatstroke

Being injured by a runaway car or float

Being pelted with candy

Inclement weather

Losing a child

Difficulty finding a parking space

Sensory overload that leads to a panic attack

A fire or explosion that creates chaos with so many people packed together in the streets

A dog getting loose and taking off down the parade route

PEOPLE COMMONLY FOUND HERE

Acrobats, announcers, baton and flag twirlers, children, clowns, criminals looking to take advantage, dancers, drivers, float riders and entertainers, horse riders, marching band members, news crews, parade viewers, photographers, police officers, snack vendors, stilt walkers, the grand marshal

RELATED SETTINGS THAT MAY TIE IN WITH THIS ONE

Amusement park (188), big city street (38), parking lot (102), small town street (120)

SETTING NOTES AND TIPS

A parade can be useful because it's such an active setting; with all the noise and visual chaos, parades provide a lot of natural background activity that can complement or contrast with what's happening in the story. Because everyone's attention is on the parade, characters can find their way into off-limit places or do things that aren't noticed because of the distraction. Be aware, though, of stereotypical ways that parades have been used in past stories, such as a means of escaping pursuers (*The Fugitive*) or an attention-grabbing opportunity for the hero (*Ferris Bueller's Day Off*). If your story contains any of these elements, make sure to convey the action in a fresh way.

SETTING DESCRIPTION EXAMPLE

Lights outlined the floats as they drifted past, moving along with the tinny music. Across the street, people lined the curb, their glow bands and flashing neon lights brightening their faces and hands as they hooted and danced to the music. Grandma sat in her chair, hands held over her ears against each firework boom, but her eyes were wide and a slim smile lifted her cheeks. An evening breeze cooled my skin and I closed my eyes, grateful we'd been able to get her here. Parades had been an important part of her life with Poppy. I hadn't known how she would respond to her first one since his passing, but my instincts had been right. This was good for her.

    Techniques and Devices Used: Contrast, light and shadow, multisensory descriptions

    Resulting Effects: Establishing mood, hinting at backstory, reinforcing emotion

PERFORMING ARTS THEATER

SIGHTS

External: a bright marquee with the name of the show or its famous performers, posters advertising the production being given, a box office where tickets are bought, scalpers on the sidewalk, rope lines indicating where people waiting should stand, lines of people waiting to get in, patrons smoking last-minute cigarettes before a show

Internal: a lobby with people milling about, attendants selling programs and merchandise, a coat check counter, a bar or concession counter with snacks and beverages for purchase (candy, water, sodas, alcoholic drinks), a set of restrooms, stairways leading up to the balcony seating areas and private boxes, multiple sets of doors that open into the seating area, rows of cushioned seats, viewers reading programs and chatting with neighbors, children sitting on booster seats, carpeted aisles with dim lights, balconies and boxes overhead, ushers with flashlights directing guests to their seats, an orchestra pit, a stage that is partially-hidden by a heavy curtain, a control booth for lighting and audio mixing, catwalks at the ceiling level, lights hanging from the ceiling, members of the stage crew dressed in black, lights flickering to indicate when the show is about to start, the lights dimming as the show begins, curtains opening or closing, backdrops and scenery on the stage, props being used, the stars of the show (singing, dancing, delivering lines, acting), show-appropriate costumes, spotlights highlighting various parts of the stage, flashlights bobbing down the aisles as ushers make their way in the darkness, the glow of a patron's cell phone

SOUNDS

People speaking in quiet voices, muffled footsteps on the carpeted stairs, murmured apologies as patrons step past those already seated to get to their own spots, the crackle of snack bags being opened, creaky seats, announcements being made over the loudspeaker, the cessation of voices as the show begins, the whir of curtains being drawn open, music from the orchestra, laughter and gasps from the audience, applause, people shifting in their seats, actors speaking and moving around the stage, sound effects, patrons getting up to go to the restroom, a cell phone ringing and then quickly being silenced

SMELLS

Perfume and cologne, alcohol on someone's breath, mouthwash or mints

TASTES

Candy concessions, water, pop, wine and beer (if alcohol is served), chewing gum

TEXTURES AND SENSATIONS

Huddling into a jacket or shawl for warmth when air-conditioning is set too high, the slick pages of a playbill or program in one's hands, the soft cushion and gentle rock of an auditorium seat, an elbow brushing against a neighbor's on the arm rest, carpeted stairs, taking careful steps up or down the stairs in the dim lighting, brimming tears at an emotional moment on the stage, the reverberation of drums deep in one's chest, startling from unexpected music or sound effects, a thrill of anticipation as the show is about to start

POSSIBLE SOURCES OF CONFLICT
Tripping on the stairs
Falling from a box or balcony
The house collapsing
Sitting next to someone who causes trouble (through intoxication, constant talking, being confrontational or argumentative)
Nearsightedness that impairs one's view of the stage
Having naturally heightened senses and being overwhelmed by the sights and sounds
Having a seat with an obstructed view (sitting behind a tall guest, being seated behind a pole or pillar)
Frequent interruptions during the show (via a crying child, technical difficulties, having to repeatedly get up to use the restroom)
Paying a steep price for the tickets and being disappointed by the performance

PEOPLE COMMONLY FOUND HERE
Actors, box office attendants, coat check attendants, dancers, directors, merchandise vendors, musicians, patrons, scalpers, singers, stage crew, talent scouts, the orchestra conductor, ushers

RELATED SETTINGS THAT MAY TIE IN WITH THIS ONE
Art gallery (190), black-tie event (196), green room (208), movie theater (212), Vegas stage show (242)

SETTING NOTES AND TIPS
Theaters can be used for a variety of artistic performances: musicals, operas, ballets, concerts, plays, stand-up comedy routines, etc. These venues can be upscale and grandiose or intimate and casual. They can be located in popular places like Broadway or hidden away in isolated spots. Some theaters do not allow food and drink during the performance; to compensate, they will often have intermissions where patrons can visit the lobby bar for refreshments or a snack.

SETTING DESCRIPTION EXAMPLE
My heels clacked a frantic rhythm against the sidewalk while the wind snatched at my hair. The marquee blazed against the night sky, easily three blocks away. I knotted my scarf and broke into a run. Snagging tickets had been about as easy as corralling an endangered animal, and there was no way I was going to miss this play.
    Techniques and Devices Used: Light and shadow, multisensory descriptions, simile
    Resulting Effects: Tension and conflict

POOL HALL

SIGHTS
Neon beer signs on the walls and over the bar, tinted windows running along the front, rows of pool tables with balls on them, wall racks holding wooden cues, chalk squares (blue being the most common) sitting on table edges, triangular ball racks hanging under a table or laying on the floor underneath it, a bar with stools, drinks (shot glasses, beer bottles, highballs) on small tables around the room's perimeter, jackets slung on chairs and stools, cues leaning against the walls, pub food being served, a waitress or two in tight clothing taking away empty drinks and bringing fresh ones, a juke box or sound system, TVs bolted in the corners, an ATM machine near the door, video games and pinball machines in the back, dartboards on the wall, a foosball table, a set of restrooms, a small kitchen, bottles of different types of alcohol lining the mirrored wall behind the bar, lime and lemon wedges, money changing hands, signs prohibiting minors, a liquor license displayed near the bar, alcohol sponsor signage, advertisements and sports paraphernalia, beer taps, racks of glasses, crumpled bills on tables, dirty glasses waiting to be picked up, lights hanging over each pool table, people leaning across a pool table to line up a shot, posters and framed pictures of famous pool players, couches and overstuffed chairs in the corner

SOUNDS
Balls knocking into each other, balls shuttling into the pockets or banking against the sides, a ball bouncing over the side and hitting the floor, the squeak of a cue being twisted into a chalk square, cries of disappointment, swearing, crowing and cheering at a good shot, good-natured ribbing, drinkers talking loudly over the noise as they watch the players, glasses and bottles being set on tables, the screech and scuff of a chair leg or stool being pushed back, shot glasses chinking together, noise from the TV, music from the sound system, laughter, slapping down a bet on the felt, darts thunking into the dartboard, a waitress calling orders to the bartender or cook, cash register tape spitting out a bill, noise from the kitchen, balls tumbling rapidly into the tray of a coin-operated table, restroom doors squeaking open and shut

SMELLS
Beer and other alcoholic beverages, chalk, felt, food from the kitchen, sweat, cologne, perfume, body odor, beer breath, cigarette smoke clinging to clothing and hair, leather, oiled wood

TASTES
Beer, pop, vodka, rum, shots of straight liquor (rye, whiskey, tequila), water, crunching ice cubes, pub food (nachos, fries, wings, pizza, burgers), coffee, salt, limes, pretzels

TEXTURES AND SENSATIONS
The slide of a pool cue shaft along the crook of one's hand, scraping the chalk cube against tip, the weight of a server's tray loaded with drinks, felt against the fingertips, the satisfying smack as the tip of one's cue connects with a ball, a rough or chipped tabletop, metallic quarters sliding into a slot, crumpled bills, the cool press of a beer bottle or glass in one's hand, cold beer wetting the lips and sliding down one's throat, smooth pool balls, sliding the white ball along the felt after

a scratch, high-fiving another player, twirling a cue stick between the fingers, leaning on a stick while awaiting one's turn, stretching along the table to make a difficult shot, the twisting motion of a swiveling stool, warmth emanating from lights over the tables

POSSIBLE SOURCES OF CONFLICT
Discovering that one has been rooked by a pool shark
Waiting for a table where amateurs are taking forever to finish their game
Partnering with someone whose ability level doesn't match one's own
Betting money that one doesn't have
Getting splashed with beer
Being ogled or harassed
Banging one's head on the hanging lights
Being jabbed with a stick from behind
Having one's fingers smashed by a ball
Annoyingly loud music
Someone playing the same song over and over on a jukebox

PEOPLE COMMONLY FOUND HERE
Bartenders, management, pool players, pool sharks, wait staff

RELATED SETTINGS THAT MAY TIE IN WITH THIS ONE
Bar (138), nightclub (216), pub (152)

SETTING NOTES AND TIPS
Pool halls are generally noisy, sociable places where people who like billiard games go to hang out with likeminded friends. As with any sporting activity, there will be people of varying abilities and seriousness involved, ranging from the semi-pro with a regular table to the group of college students just looking to goof off. Some pool halls don't sell alcohol and are able to cater to customers of all ages. But age limits will vary at establishments that sell certain kinds of liquor, so keep this in mind when choosing the background characters for a scene.

SETTING DESCRIPTION EXAMPLE
Arlen hitched the collar of his jean jacket and leaned against the wall, unobtrusive. I smiled, watching him scan the dingy room and finally head for a table in the corner. Arlen had a nose for weekend tough guys—dentists or accountants who came by to slum, sloughing off their wives for the night. None of them had the sense to say no when we asked them for a friendly game of pool, and by the time they left with a gut full of beer, their wallets were much lighter.

    Techniques and Devices Used: Light and shadow
    Resulting Effects: Characterization, foreshadowing

RACE TRACK (HORSES)

SIGHTS

Outside: an oval-shaped dirt track surrounded by a fence, flags flapping in the breeze, ads attached to the track rail, striped poles at measured intervals around the track, floodlights for night races, a grassy infield, numbered starting gates, a JumboTron, rows of benches in the apron area, picnic table seating, tiered grandstand seating for those wishing to sit outside for the race, racehorses wearing saddle cloths and saddles, jockeys wearing colorful silks and helmets, an electronic board that displays odds, the backstretch area (stables, dormitories, paddocks, a kitchen and recreational area for stable workers), a clearly marked finish line, water trucks and graders prepping the track before a race, dirt flying up from a running horse's hooves, spectators fanning themselves with programs

Inside: walls of glass that overlook the racetrack, booths or tables for placing bets, rows of seats for indoor viewing, spaced-out tables and chairs, clubhouse or box seating for a premium price, racing monitors, spectators peering through binoculars, cafeteria-style seating with concession foods for those who wish to grab a quick bite before a race, elevators and escalators, restrooms, vending machines, ATM machines, restrooms

SOUNDS

People chatting or placing bets, the snap of a beer bottle being opened, the crinkle of a food wrapper, sodas being slurped, doors opening and closing, a spectator flipping the pages of a program, announcements being made over an intercom, a bugle or other horn playing *Call to the Post*, a bell that signals the start of a race, starting gates clanging open, the thundering of horses' hooves, trainers yelling, sounds dimming as horses run along the far side of the track and getting louder as they come back around, a running commentary over the loudspeaker, spectators yelling or swearing, applause, spectator voices escalating as the race progresses, hurried footsteps as a spectator rushes to collect a bet, a losing ticket being crumpled up, people jumping up and down at the race's end

SMELLS

Food cooking, sweat, sunscreen, sun-warmed dirt, cigarette smoke, horses, manure, fresh-cut grass, the fresh flowers from a victor's wreath

TASTES

Concession food (hot dogs, pretzels, popcorn, burgers, nachos), higher-end food from the restaurants inside, soda, beer, wine, water, snacks

TEXTURES AND SENSATIONS

The flutter of anticipation as one places a bet, gripping a ticket tightly in one's fist, a metal seat or wooden bench pressing into the back of one's legs, sitting on the edge of one's seat, jumping to one's feet during the race, the sun beating down on one's skin, sweat trickling, a breeze stirring one's hair, flies buzzing around one's head, a can or bottle cooling one's palm, the kiss of air-conditioning on the skin when indoors, squinting into the sun's glare, sweat causing one's sunglasses to slide down one's nose, shading one's eyes with a program, hard binoculars pressed to one's eyes

POSSIBLE SOURCES OF CONFLICT
Too much drinking
Losing a sizable bet
Sore losers kicking up a fuss
Discovering that a race has been fixed
Snootiness in the form of old school racetrack aficionados looking down on newcomers
A horse being hurt in a race
Sabotage
Drama between jockeys
Disagreeing with the outcome of a close finish
Too much concession food
A pickpocket working the crowd
Inner conflict as one battles an addiction

PEOPLE COMMONLY FOUND HERE
Cashiers, grooms, hard-core gamblers, horse owners, horse trainers, janitors, jockeys, maintenance workers, newscasters, spectators, veterinarians

RELATED SETTINGS THAT MAY TIE IN WITH THIS ONE
Casino (202), parking lot (102)

SETTING NOTES AND TIPS
Racetracks vary, from the smaller, seedy tracks to the grand historical ones like Saratoga and Churchill Downs. What doesn't differ is the variety in clientele. Each venue will attract the career gambler, the gambling addict, couples out for a fun date, old school race fans, and casual attendees—all with their own run-of-the-mill baggage. Instead of assuming that racetrack drama must center around a gambler or addict, take a good look at the other people in attendance. Ask yourself what their stories are and what they might do that can cause trouble for your main character. Introducing believable conflict from an unsuspecting source is a great way to keep the story from growing stale.

SETTING DESCRIPTION EXAMPLE
My footsteps crunched into the warm dirt as I followed Merry in the Morning across the track. A wind blew and some of the gathering clouds had ugly gray bellies, but my gut told me the storm would hold off. In the other starting gate, crewmembers were murmuring to their horses, but Merry was doing just fine and I didn't want to spook her. She entered the Number Two gate, meek as a newborn calf, and I closed the door without so much as a squeak.
    Techniques and Devices Used: Multisensory descriptions, simile
    Resulting Effects: Characterization, establishing mood

REC CENTER

SIGHTS
An outdoor basketball court, a grassy area for soccer or flag football games, a playground with the usual equipment (slides, swings, jungle gyms, monkey bars, a rock wall), tennis courts, an outdoor pool, bike racks next to the sidewalk, heat waves shimmering on the asphalt, a wide cement path leading to the front doors, a reception desk just inside the entrance where people sign in or register for classes and events, an indoor gymnasium with bleachers, a small weight room, locker rooms and public restrooms, water fountains, administrative offices, motivational posters on the walls, children or adults participating in different classes (dance, painting, ceramics, tumbling, karate, gymnastics, Pilates, yoga, self-defense, swim lessons), children engaged in various after-school activities (doing homework, eating snacks, playing board games or sports), children running, parents arriving to pick up kids, adults walking alone or in pairs to a class, water spots on the floor from swimmers exiting through the building, people paying for a class at the information desk, vending machines, a waiting area with couches and chairs

SOUNDS
Echoes emanating from the gymnasium, squeaking sneakers, people yelling, balls bouncing, referee whistles blowing, children yelling and laughing, pounding feet, doors opening and closing, a breeze from an open door fluttering announcements pinned to a bulletin board, people chatting as they head to a class, keys jingling, people talking on phones, administrative phones ringing, people asking for directions, music coming from a dance class, teachers calling out instructions, splashing from the pool area, water-logged ears making sounds seem muffled, soda cans clunking out of a vending machine, people cheering or clapping at a sporting event, parents yelling at coaches, a whistle shrilling, heavy doors swinging closed, the *thwack* of tennis racquets hitting balls outside, the clattery shake of a ball hitting the chain link court fence

SMELLS
Chlorine from the pool, wet towels, sweaty kids, paints, hot asphalt, disinfectant, hand sanitizer, cleaning supplies, floor wax, rubber

TASTES
Vending machine food, water, after-school snacks, pizza and cake from a birthday party

TEXTURES AND SENSATIONS
Air conditioning turned up too high and causing goose bumps, tile floors made slick with puddles from a swimmer, metal bleachers sticking to the backs of one's legs, the sun beating down on the outdoor basketball court, burning muscles in a fitness class, fatigued muscles from a workout in the gym, the patterned bump of a basketball bouncing against one's palm, a paintbrush swishing across a canvas, rolling on a cushioned gymnastics mat, water dripping from a wet swimsuit, water sliding over one's skin, the tightness of a swimming cap or pinch of goggle straps, slapping a palm against a locker door to shut it, the weight of a water bottle in one's hand, the drag of a backpack on one's shoulder, dropping into a soft chair to wait for one's ride

POSSIBLE SOURCES OF CONFLICT

Competition between students

Rooms being double-booked

An instructor not showing up

Broken or inferior equipment

Parents showing up late to pick up kids

Personal belongings being stolen from a locker

Dissatisfaction with an instructor

Inept referees

Delinquent kids

Sports injuries

Instructors being hired without proper background checks

The facility being sued by a parent

Instructors frustrated by the facility's limitations

Parents who like to gossip and find fault

Instructors favoring certain students

Niche classes being cast aside for more popular ones

Low funding causing layoffs and cutbacks that affect the center's quality and safety

PEOPLE COMMONLY FOUND HERE

Administrators, adults, children, coaches, instructors, other employees (after-school care program staff, janitorial staff, maintenance crews), safety inspectors, parents

RELATED SETTINGS THAT MAY TIE IN WITH THIS ONE

Rural Volume: Gymnasium (114), locker room (120)

Urban Volume: Community center (48), fitness center (66), outdoor pool (218), sporting event stands (240)

SETTING NOTES AND TIPS

There are different kinds of rec centers; some cater mostly to children while others service the entire community. Rec centers offer a variety of services: space for many different kinds of classes, after-school care, athletic fields and facilities, and rental space for parties or gatherings. Because most of these facilities are government-sponsored, the kind and quality of amenities offered will vary depending on the funding. Cleanliness and upkeep will also be different from one center to another.

SETTING DESCRIPTION EXAMPLE

Jeremiah walked as fast as he could through the empty corridor. Noises echoed down the hallway from the gym—bouncing balls, shoe squeaks, and Coach's trigger-happy whistle. Jeremiah swallowed, imagining what he'd have to say when he showed up late. Again. His quick walk turned into a jog.

Techniques and Devices Used: Multisensory descriptions

Resulting Effects: Characterization, foreshadowing, hinting at backstory, tension and conflict

RECORDING STUDIO

SIGHTS

Live Rooms: a room with dim lighting, a small booth for vocals with a mic on a boom stand, a large performance area with musical instruments, isolation booths for recording different instruments, cans (headphones), racks of gear (outboard preamps, compressors, reverb units, delay modules), amps, speakers, instrument stands and cases, sheet music and chord charts, water bottles, a storage room with extra gear (instruments, microphones, monitors, guitar pedals), textured walls, floor rugs, a glass partition separating performers from the sound technicians, cords running from instruments to equipment, cords crossing the floor and plugging into walls, an "on air" or "recording" light to indicate that a session is being recorded, musicians and vocalists warming up, voice-over artists reading scripts

Control Room: rolling chairs, computers, cans, multiple consoles and mixers covered with buttons and knobs, interfaces with mics plugged into them, patch bays and multi-colored patch cables, monitors, speakers, seating areas with leather furniture and lamps, clipboards and pads of paper, pens and pencils, potted plants, gold and platinum albums on the walls, plaques and other awards in a case, magazines on the tables, fast food and takeout food, cups of coffee and soda, drug paraphernalia, alcohol

SOUNDS

Music being played on instruments (guitars, keyboards, pianos, drums), musicians tuning their instruments, vocalists singing or humming, sheet music drifting to the floor, sound technicians cutting in to tell musicians to stop playing or to play something again, people talking in the control room, guests chatting in the seating area, phones ringing, recorded music being played back, applause or happy shouts when a recording goes well, musicians arguing, a click track playing, the frightening clarity of hearing one's voice or instrument by itself without accompaniment, doors opening and closing, a vacuum cleaner

SMELLS

Takeout food (burgers, pizza, Chinese food, etc.), coffee, air fresheners, burning candles, cleaning supplies, pot, tobacco, beer

TASTES

Takeout food, vending machine food (sandwiches, candy bars, chips, power bars), bottled water, coffee, hot tea, alcohol

TEXTURES AND SENSATIONS

Cans snug against one's ears, an instrument in one's grip, a swiveling stool or chair, the metallic grid on a microphone head, the textured walls of a recording booth, smooth plastic guitar picks, drumsticks twirling between one's fingers, the vibration of a stick hitting a drum, strings being strummed, smooth piano keys, buttons sliding up and down on a mixer, cords clicking into slots, tripping over a cord, pressing a guitar pedal, tapping a foot to keep the beat, pressing one's hands against one's cans while singing

POSSIBLE SOURCES OF CONFLICT
Creative differences between musicians
Outsiders influencing members of the band (groupies, spouses, etc.)
Large egos
Jealousy between band members
Shoddy recording equipment that produces a less than desirable result
Drunken or high artists
Band members not showing up or arriving late
An extravagant or ambitious studio manager who disregards the facility's budget
A diva who makes unrealistic demands of studio staff
Studio staff fraternizing with artists
Having to work with talentless artists or those who are new to recording
Double-booking a recording studio or having a session run over into someone else's time slot

PEOPLE COMMONLY FOUND HERE
A manager or agent, a receptionist or office manager, actors or voice-over artists, administrators, cleaning staff, instructors, members of an entourage, musicians, parents of underage artists, people delivering food, producers, songwriters, sound engineers and technicians, vocalists, voice coaches

RELATED SETTINGS THAT MAY TIE IN WITH THIS ONE
Green room (208), limousine (262), performing arts theater (224), rock concert (234)

SETTING NOTES AND TIPS
There are many different kinds of studios. High-end establishments are often used by professionals and celebrities; these are rented by the hour and offer a large supply of quality equipment and instruments. Smaller studios offer recording services as well, but they're less expensive with fewer bells and whistles. The digitalization of the music industry has also made the home studio a practical and efficient option for musicians desiring to record an album or voice-over.

SETTING DESCRIPTION EXAMPLE
John squeezed his eyes shut, two fingers on the slider, tuning out everything but Clarissa's voice coming through his headset—her beautifully thick, textured, and slightly sharp voice. He nudged the bar, handling it like a newborn baby, and her pitch leveled out. He grinned. The chair squeaked as he collapsed into it and he flashed her two thumbs up through the glass partition.

Techniques and Devices Used: Simile
Resulting Effects: Establishing mood

ROCK CONCERT

SIGHTS
Backstage: dressing rooms and a green room, a wardrobe room, roadies moving equipment around, equipment being placed strategically backstage, a pyrotechnic crew setting up special effects, a manager directing traffic, musicians stretching, groupies hanging around the talent, food and drinks set out on tables

The Stage: a stage lit with multi-colored spotlights, lights shining up into the ceiling or out into the crowd, scaffolding, backdrops, huge speakers, amps, microphones on stands, musicians playing instruments in wild outfits, bottles of water near each performer, a message projected onto the wall behind the stage (the band's name, the latest album cover, tour insignia), lasers, dry ice or smoke, pyrotechnics and fireworks, pole dancers, video screens, musicians breaking instruments or throwing souvenirs (guitar picks, drum sticks, etc.) into the crowd

The Audience: people crammed together, fans wearing the band's T-shirt, girls sitting on their boyfriend's shoulders, people body surfing, a mosh pit down front, girls near the stage flashing the artists, people drinking and smoking, fans jumping and screaming, lighters waving in the air, people holding up cell phones to record the show, head banging, fistfights, drunk or high people

Elsewhere: a row of portable toilets (for an outdoor venue), a concession stand (selling bottles of water and soda, candy, gum, beer, wine), merchandise vendors (hawking discs, T-shirts, programs, bandanas, jewelry, caps, posters, key chains, and mugs)

SOUNDS
Insanely loud music, people shouting into each other's ears to be heard, feedback squeals, artists speaking into microphones, guitar or drum solos, stomping feet, applause, fans screaming and yelling, ringing in the ears, fans singing along with the band at the top of their lungs

SMELLS
Marijuana, cigarette smoke, body sprays, sweat, body odor, stale beer, vomit

TASTES
Cigarettes, dry mouth, beer and other alcohol

TEXTURES AND SENSATIONS
Being packed shoulder-to-shoulder with other fans, feeling the bass reverberate within one's chest, the near-deafening sound of very loud music in the ears, shouldering one's way through a crowd, being soaked in sweat, weaving in a drunken path, being extremely thirsty, having a drink spilled on oneself, having one's foot stepped on, being pressed against a railing or the stage by a surging crowd

POSSIBLE SOURCES OF CONFLICT
Losing one's ticket
Not getting to go and having to listen to everyone else talk about how great it was
Getting separated from one's friends

Having one's car broken into in the parking lot

Overspending on merchandise

Having to fight for space during the concert

High fans who act unpredictably

Being trampled in a riot

Being groped in the crowd

Being physically assaulted

Getting backstage passes only to be disappointed when one meets the band

Getting puked on

Being constantly elbowed and jostled

An awful opening act

Being stuck behind a really tall person

One's view being obstructed by people holding up their phones to record the entire concert

Heated differences of opinions among fans (about the band's most talented member, best song, worst album, etc.)

PEOPLE COMMONLY FOUND HERE

Agents, custodial staff, event coordinators, fans, groupies, managers, musicians, personal assistants, roadies, sound and lighting technicians, spectators, vendors

RELATED SETTINGS THAT MAY TIE IN WITH THIS ONE

Rural Volume: Mansion (72)

Urban Volume: Green room (208), hotel room (78), limousine (262), performing arts theater (224), recording studio (232), Vegas stage show (242)

SETTING NOTES AND TIPS

Rock concerts tend to be more raucous and wild than those associated with lighter musical fare. But as with any other setting, concerts can vary based on a number of criteria. Questions that need asking: Is the concert being held inside or outside? How big is the venue? Is it a concert for a current band (playing to a modern, hip audience), or is the show a reunion tour, where the audience will be older? Knowing the answers to questions like these will help in determining the audience demographics for the show and will allow you to describe the scene accurately and in detail.

SETTING DESCRIPTION EXAMPLE

I grabbed the water Val handed me and guzzled it down. The August sun was straight up, the sky cloudless and achingly bright. Considering the body heat being generated by a couple thousand people jam-packed together, the temperature on the field had to be at least 110. My neck burned and mud spattered my legs and sucked at my shoes from the last time the water cannons hosed down the crowd. I could barely feel my feet from them getting crushed through the first two shows, but I totally didn't care. Just two more bands, then Acid Bats would be up. I shook back my sweaty hair and screamed as Zombie Sunrise took the stage.

Techniques and Devices Used: Multisensory descriptions, weather

Resulting Effects: Establishing mood, reinforcing emotion

SKATE PARK

SIGHTS
A large structure consisting of a combination of obstacles and challenges (bowls, quarter pipes, half pipes, walls, banks, fun boxes, pyramids, rails, stairs, benches) that can be rearranged, concrete and wooden construction, a flat deck at the top of some obstacles, a perimeter fence, skateboarders and inline skaters, bikers on BMX bikes, kids on scooters, people standing and watching along the decks, skaters sporting earbuds and various bits of safety gear (elbow pads, knee pads, helmets), long shadows falling into the bowls, graffiti on the walls, plain gray concrete or concrete that has been painted to look like graffiti, lights for night skating, garbage cans, a beginner's area where new skaters can learn and the obstacles are not as challenging, foam pits for falling into when learning a new trick, landscaping plants and sidewalks around the park, painted lines to demarcate the edges of obstacles, a small building containing restrooms and gear rentals, chain link fencing, skaters sitting on obstacles and watching, concessions or vending machines, riders with cuts and scrapes, a skater tending to a bleeding gash before heading back out again, friends filming a run with a cellphone to upload to social media later

SOUNDS
Rolling skateboard wheels, the rhythmic sound of someone going by on rollerblades, boards sliding along rails and clanging when they touch the ground, rattling wheels, the thump and slide of a rider falling, a clattering skateboard, birds chirping, people chatting, exclamations and cheers when someone completes a difficult stunt, the gritty sound of wheels rolling over sand, a *thump-thump* noise when skating over a seam in the concrete, nearby urban sounds (cars passing, dogs barking, doors slamming shut), cell phones ringing, music spilling out of someone's earbuds

SMELLS
Wet concrete, cigarette or pot smoke, sweat, body odor, hot pavement and melting tar, fresh spray paint

TASTES
Gum, candy, cigarettes, water, soda, takeout food

TEXTURES AND SENSATIONS
The bumpy feel of one's wheels rolling over concrete, wheels gliding smoothly over wooden sections or thumping over a seam in the concrete, one's body slamming into the ground, scraping one's skin on the rough concrete, a board sliding over a metal rail or bouncing down a flight of steps, the stomach-dropping sensation of catching air, gripping the board with one's shoes, heat rising off the concrete, jerking sideways to avoid another skater, loose clothing catching on an obstacle, wind whipping through one's hair and pulling at one's clothing, hair sliding into one's face, the tight feel of pads strapped to one's elbow and knee joints, a sweaty helmet, hitching up shorts that are too loose in the waist, adjusting padding that slips, probing painful scrapes or bruises and then taping oneself up for another run

POSSIBLE SOURCES OF CONFLICT

Physical injuries

Peer pressure

Unhealthy competitiveness

Skating without proper safety equipment

Skating when one's common sense is inhibited (while angry or frustrated, while under the influence, in the aftermath of a traumatic event)

Using faulty equipment

Skating in a park that hasn't been maintained

Gang or drug activity at a park

Drug dealers hanging around to befriend impressionable kids

Being stereotyped or treated in a prejudicial fashion

Businesses nearby constantly calling the police or petitioning the city in hopes of closing the park down

Being embarrassed by an overprotective parent

Having a friend far more talented than oneself despite being newer to the sport or simply not caring as much

PEOPLE COMMONLY FOUND HERE

BMX bikers, friends, graffiti artists, inline skaters, skateboarders, skateboarding enthusiasts, teens and tweens

RELATED SETTINGS THAT MAY TIE IN WITH THIS ONE

Park (98), parking lot (102), rec center (230)

SETTING NOTES AND TIPS

Skate parks have been around for decades and exist in many different iterations. Most are outdoor, but in colder climates, indoor parks also exist and offer more services, such as a concession stand, free Wi-Fi, a merchandise store, and areas for kids' parties. While the majority of parks are government funded and built according to a general standard, some arise organically, created by skaters within the community out of whatever materials are at hand. Public parks are open to everyone, free of charge. Privately owned venues may charge a fee for admission. All are open during the day but some also allow for night skating.

SETTING DESCRIPTION EXAMPLE

Kaye sat on the hot deck, her board braced upside-down across her knees. Behind her, three teens cruised the bowls, their skates rumbling like a hive of metallic bees. She didn't have to turn around to see what they were doing. She'd been maneuvering the bowls for months. What she hadn't mastered—hadn't even attempted yet—was the street course. Her eyes followed a skater sliding along a rail and jumping a set of stairs. She thumbed a wheel on her board, trying to still her nervous stomach.

    Techniques and Devices Used: Simile

    Resulting Effects: Characterization, establishing mood

SKI RESORT

SIGHTS

The Lodge: fireplaces, sitting areas with comfortable chairs and couches, dining rooms with tables and chairs, places to order food, condiment stations, vending machines, a kiosk for ski equipment rental, lockers, snow being tracked across the floors, melting snow, restrooms, extraneous clothing (hats, gloves, scarves, goggles) thrown over chairs or being used to reserve tables, lodge décor (wooden ceiling beams, vintage ski equipment and antlered heads on the walls, stone fireplaces), walls made of glass for a stunning view of the slopes, mounted TVs showing sports programming and the weather forecast

The Slopes: snow-covered hills, a large lodge nestled at the base, an outdoor skating rink, racks of skis and poles, rocky or tree-dotted mountains rising all around, ski lifts and gondolas going up the mountain, skiers and snowboarders coming down in sweeping wide curves, people lining up at the lift, a hill employee scanning lift tags, kids skiing in a beginner's area, first-time skiers gathered around an instructor, color-designated signs to indicate a slope's difficulty level, warning signs and orange mesh boundaries to mark dangerous areas, moguls and jumps, snow blowers, brown patches of earth showing through the snow, slopes crisscrossed with ski trails, cross-country trails leading into the trees, falling snow, low clouds, individual lodges leaking smoke trails from their chimneys, members of the ski patrol skiing by in orange vests, fogged-up goggles, decreased peripheral vision due to one's goggles

SOUNDS

The clump of ski boots crossing the protective grating at the lodge, a crackling fire in the hearth, the rustle of someone putting on a ski jacket and zipping it up, a lodge packed with people (the murmur of many voices as skiers tell stories, laugh, talk strategy and equipment, review video footage), the snap of boots locking into bindings, the swish of skis through the snow, a lift's mechanical creaking, the whir of a gondola, the carrying sound of people talking as they head up the mountain on lifts, skiers on ski lift chairs clacking their skis together to shake loose snow clumps, snow plopping to the ground, skiers dropping to the ground and sliding along the snow, the sharp sound of skis hitting and sliding on ice, skiers yelling as they fall, people laughing and calling to friends, kids squealing, boots crunching through snow, snow spraying as someone skids to a stop, a sled bouncing over rough bumps, snowboarders or skiers racing by

SMELLS

Coffee, sweat, wood smoke, wet woolen clothing, hot food, sunscreen, lotion, stale air being breathed through one's ski mask or scarf, cold air, the ozone of snow and ice, hot onion breath trapped in a mask, scented lip balm

TASTES

Lip balm, lodge food (standard fast food restaurant fare), coffee, water, soda, hot chocolate, cider, hot tea

TEXTURES AND SENSATIONS
The confinement of bulky clothing, heavy ski boots, cumbersome skis, clumsiness from thick ski gloves or mittens, the awkwardness of walking in ski boots, slipping on ice and falling, struggling to carry skis and poles, finding one's balance on a snowboard, snow melting in one's boots, being swept up by a ski chair, the heavy feel of one's legs dangling with skis on the end of them, a ski chair's sway, a runny nose, wind-burned cheeks, a headache from the snow's glare, cold fingers and toes, damp socks, sweaty hair under a wool cap, the out-of-control feeling of not being able to stop, picking up speed when one hits a patch of ice, skidding to a stop, cold wind blowing in one's face and making the eyes water, stripping off one's outerwear in the lodge, the cold-to-hot transition of stepping from outside into the warm lodge, chapped lips, dry skin, being sprayed by stinging snow, a half-frozen scarf stiffly rubbing at one's face, the pinch of straps on ski goggles

POSSIBLE SOURCES OF CONFLICT
Beginner skiers on slopes that are too difficult for them
Overcrowded slopes and reckless skiers
A warm snap late in the season that threatens a ski vacation
Physically injuring oneself
Leaving the marked trails and getting lost
A blizzard blowing in
A ski dropping from a lift and landing on someone

PEOPLE COMMONLY FOUND HERE
Lodge employees, maintenance crews, members of the ski patrol, rescue teams, skiers, ski instructors, snowboarders

RELATED SETTINGS THAT MAY TIE IN WITH THIS ONE
Rural Volume: Arctic tundra (198), forest (212), mountains (228)
Urban Volume: Outdoor skating rink (220)

SETTING NOTES AND TIPS
While some ski resorts cater to a wealthy clientele, others are reasonably priced to accommodate both vacationers and local skiers who like to hit the slopes for the day. Location will also play a part in the size, atmosphere, and accommodations for a given resort; skiing in North Carolina is vastly different from skiing in the Rockies. The Alps and Andes are different animals altogether. Look into each geographical area carefully to choose one that fits the character and the story.

SETTING DESCRIPTION EXAMPLE
The ski lift carried Brian up the mountain, giving him a bird's-eye view of the slopes at night. Lights twisted down the slopes, outlining the trails like a dot-to-dot map. Voices occasionally wafted up to him, but they were distant, muted—nothing like skiing here during the day. He listened hard, his breath fogging the air. The only sounds were the creak of his ski chair and the wind sliding though the pines.
Techniques and Devices Used: Contrast, light and shadow, metaphor, multisensory descriptions
Resulting Effects: Establishing mood, reinforcing emotion

SPORTING EVENT STANDS

SIGHTS
Fans wearing team jerseys and ball caps while carrying rain gear and plastic cups of beer, painted faces in the stands, tiered seating littered with popcorn, hard metal benches or plastic seats, concrete or metal steps, people waving foam fingers, pennants and flags flying, fans holding up handmade signs or shaking pom-poms, cameras flashing, crumpled-up candy bags and discarded frilly paper hot dog holders in the trash or sitting on the bench, vendors hawking food, fans waving vendors over, floors wet from spills, people sitting or standing shoulder to shoulder, camaraderie between strangers, people with gear tailored to the event (baseball gloves, football helmets, hockey masks), portable seat cushions, jackets slung over the bench or seat back, umbrellas, half-naked men with numbers painted on their chests, souvenirs, sunglasses left behind, empty beer or pop cans, crushed peanut shells, metal railings, the JumboTron, enormous speakers, mascots interacting with the crowd, men ogling the cheerleaders, a T-shirt gun shooting shirts into the crowd, people jumping to catch a fly ball or high puck, opposing team jerseys clustering in small groups here and there, fights breaking out, shouting matches, money changing hands, TV cameras, signs for sponsors, ad banners, fans doing the wave, marching bands taking the field at halftime, a blimp in the sky overhead

SOUNDS
An announcer on the loudspeaker, screams and shouts, cheers, whistles, catcalls, grumbles and groans, beer cans crumpling, seats creaking, laughing, booing and muttering, people trying to talk over the crowd, music playing over the loudspeaker, a referee's whistle, swearing, the crinkle of food wrappers, the crunch of popcorn and chips, slurping on drinks, team members being interviewed, voice-over ads during time-outs, cell phones going off, a crowd chanting in unison, fireworks exploding, music from marching bands blasting across the arena, the patter of popcorn spilling as someone jumps up and down with excitement, the rustle of pom-poms, horns honking, police or security radios, the rattle of a paper sign being shaken, the crunch of popcorn and peanut shells underfoot, people yelling through plastic megaphones, arguments between fans of opposing teams, drinks splashing, cannons or shots being fired when the home team scores, stamping feet

SMELLS
Popcorn, hot dogs, sweaty bodies, perfume, spilled beer, grease, cinnamon, sugar, condiments (mustard, vinegar for fries, ketchup), the ozone-like smell of cement and metal (especially when it's raining or cold)

TASTES
Water, beer, pop, juice, hot dogs, mini doughnuts, churros, fries, burgers, chocolate bars, ice cream, candy, warm peanuts, pretzels, gravy, grease, corn dogs, onion rings, slush drinks, snow cones, popcorn, cotton candy, nachos, cheese, salsa, jalapeños, an oniony burp

TEXTURES AND SENSATIONS

Hard seats, back pain, strain from sitting or standing, sticky spills under one's shoes, giving someone a high five, a neighbor clutching one's arm in an exciting moment, being splashed with beer, tripping in the narrow aisles, patting someone on the back or shoulder, sitting in gum, accidentally kicking trash or empty bottles, stepping on someone else's foot, greasy popcorn, cold condensation from a beverage, elbow jabs, greasy fingers, swiping at the hands or face with a napkin, wiggling around in the seat when one has to go to the restroom but doesn't want to miss the game, ice cream dripping onto fingers and clothes, faintness from the heat, hovering over one's food and drinks so they don't get jostled, easing past fans in a crowded row

POSSIBLE SOURCES OF CONFLICT

Hometown referees showing bias
Bitter rivalries leading to fights in the stands
Overly vocal parents yelling at coaches and players
Someone streaking across the field
A gambling addiction that puts one's finances in jeopardy
Sitting next to someone who ruins the fun (via constant complaining, volatility, use of loud noisemakers, swearing in front of one's children, bumping and jostling, spitting when they talk)
Being unfairly blamed for an altercation and getting kicked out

PEOPLE COMMONLY FOUND HERE

Athletes, cheerleaders, coaches, fans, reporters, sports doctors, sports scouts, venue employees

RELATED SETTINGS THAT MAY TIE IN WITH THIS ONE

Rural Volume: County fair (158), gymnasium (114), rodeo (182)
Urban Volume: Race track (horses) (228)

SETTING NOTES AND TIPS

Sporting event stands are very similar across the board, though there are some differences. Middle and high school sporting events tend to be smaller, with more of a community feel. Small town events may draw fewer people but often will have the most vocal and emotionally invested fans. And then there are large-venue events hosted in big cities with tens of thousands of attendees, such as the NHL playoffs for hockey, the Super Bowl, NBA (basketball) games, and MLB (baseball) games, to name a few. Though the story will most likely determine the kind of sporting event needed, the mood is up to the author.

SETTING DESCRIPTION EXAMPLE

The first game of the season meant there was not a spare seat to be had. The stadium was a sea of red and white, a showcase of the Stampeder pride. As the football players hit the field with both energetic and nervous strides, a familiar chant began in the stands. Soon thousands of throats added to the din, their song swelling until the stands began to vibrate. At the last note, a cascade of fireworks lit up the dusky sky and everyone erupted into ecstatic cheers.

Techniques and Devices Used: Multisensory descriptions, symbolism
Resulting Effects: Establishing mood

VEGAS STAGE SHOW

SIGHTS
A stage surrounded by tiered seating, a multi-level stage with stairs going up to different platforms, spotlights, glittery and sparkly costumes, scantily clad dancers, singers and musicians, showgirls in glitzy costumes and feathered headdresses, garish colors, flashing lights, male dancers in tuxes and top hats with sequined embellishments, large cast shows such as Cirque du Soleil, single-man shows (escape artists on stages shrouded in fog, magicians with all of the usual props, singers and impressionists, etc.), neon and fluorescent lights playing across the stage, pyrotechnics creating fountains of sparks and other special effects, lights pulsing in time with the music, detailed props and backdrops, ushers showing people to their seats, assistants coming into the audience to choose volunteers, standing ovations and encores

SOUNDS
Guests chatting before the show, people shuffling along rows to find their seats, voices over the intercom announcing start times, live orchestra music, singing, heeled shoes dancing or walking on the stage, sound effects, viewers responding to the show (gasping, laughing, yelling, whistling, clapping), small fireworks going off, animals roaring and vocalizing, the ring of an unmuted cell phone quickly being silenced, audience members whispering to each other, feet scuffing the floor behind one's seat, creaking seats

SMELLS
Ozone from dry ice, smoke from a fire prop used on stage, perfume and cologne, alcohol, scents carrying in from concession stands

TASTES
Concession food and drinks (popcorn, mini doughnuts, sugar-dipped pretzels, beer, highball drinks in plastic cups, water bottles) may be eaten during a show if they're allowed.

TEXTURES AND SENSATIONS
A blinding spotlight forcing one's eyes to a squint, a cushioned seat, one's foot falling asleep, being chilly in a too-cold auditorium, excited anticipation as one waits for the show to begin, a drop in the belly during an acrobat's daring stunt, being moved to tears, a glossy playbill or program, a seat that sags or tilts, an un-cushioned armrest digging into one's forearm, dropping a piece of popcorn down one's cleavage and having to retrieve it, greasy fingertips wiping against a napkin, light-headedness from alcohol, nausea from bright flashing lights and too much to drink

POSSIBLE SOURCES OF CONFLICT
Losing one's tickets
Finding someone sitting in one's seats
Sitting next to someone who reeks of alcohol or cologne
Discovering that an understudy will be performing rather than the star one expected to see
Being in a bad mood due to losing big money in the casino prior to arriving

Being reluctantly chosen and brought on stage as a volunteer

Sitting too close to the stage and being picked on by a comedian

Seeing a substandard performance and feeling that one didn't get one's money's worth

An anticipated performance being canceled due to unforeseen circumstances (the illness or death of a celebrity performer, a terrorist attack, a problem with the venue)

Witnessing something disturbing during a show (an animal attack, an acrobat falling from a great height, someone catching on fire from the pyrotechnics)

Taking one's children to a show and discovering that it isn't appropriate

PEOPLE COMMONLY FOUND HERE

Acrobats, animal handlers, audience members, burlesque stars, choreographers, comedians, dancers, headliners, hypnotists, jugglers, magicians and illusionists, managers, producers, showgirls, singers, sound and lighting technicians, stagehands, ushers, videographers

RELATED SETTINGS THAT MAY TIE IN WITH THIS ONE

Big city street (38), casino (202), green room (208), hotel room (78), limousine (262), performing arts theater (224), taxi (280)

SETTING NOTES AND TIPS

Vegas stage shows are known for being over-the-top with glitz and flash. Many shows rely as much on the lighting, pyrotechnics, musical scores, costuming, acrobatics, and dancing support as they do the main performer, since all of this is necessary for creating a memorable experience.

SETTING DESCRIPTION EXAMPLE

From the moment the giant velvet curtain opened until it closed at the end, I sat, stunned by the incredible acrobatics of the Cirque du Soleil group. The costumes, the juggling, the body manipulation and music all wove together to form a story that drew me deeper into each routine, dance, and pose. My throat tightened at seeing such passion for the love of art. I could only imagine the hours and hours that went into making such beauty and skill appear so effortless. At the end, the cast members rushed onto the stage and I leapt to my feet along with everyone else. The theater thundered with applause so loud I felt it in my chest, and my throat grew raw from cheering and whistling appreciation for such an experience.

    Techniques and Devices Used: Multisensory descriptions

    Resulting Effects: Establishing mood, reinforcing emotion

WATER PARK

SIGHTS
A chain link fence around the perimeter, paved pathways, colored tubes and slides twisting high in the air, staircases with long lines of people, multiple swimming pools, water dripping from the rides, water shooting off the end of a slide as a rider hits the bottom, rust spots marring the joints of rides and staircases, puddles of water everywhere, lifeguard stands, flags flying, wet patrons in swimsuits, a wave pool packed with people and inner tubes, striped umbrellas shading beach chairs, towels and blankets on the grass, a colorful kiddie park with water spraying and spouting, concession stands, picnic tables, lockers, restrooms, kids splashing in the play area, kids running, lifeguards with walkie-talkies and lifesavers, signs pointing people to various areas of the park, water carpets, life jackets, kids with water wings, hair ties floating in the water, garbage cans swarmed by wasps, people stretched out in the sun on beach chairs, lights at the top of the slides signaling when it's okay to go, pickup and drop-off points for inner tubes

SOUNDS
Bodies moving swiftly through tubes and down slides, echoing screams and laughter within the tubes, parents talking while relaxing in the sun, kids crying after running too fast and slipping, kids dripping and splattering water on the family's blanket, staircases that creak with each step, feet slapping the pavement and splashing through puddles, piped-in music, wind whipping the flags around, announcements being made over an intercom, lifeguard whistles, lifeguards yelling through megaphones, cell phones ringing in the sunbathing area, soda slurped through straws, crinkling food wrappers, the fart of mostly-empty ketchup and mustard bottles, restroom doors opening and closing, toilets flushing, the whoosh of water down a slide

SMELLS
Chlorine, sunblock, suntan oil, wet bathing suits and towels, food smells, bubblegum, bug repellent, mildew

TASTES
Chlorinated water, sweat, concession food (hamburgers, fries, hot dogs, pizza, nachos, ice cream bars), bottled water, soda, candy bars

TEXTURES AND SENSATIONS
Pavement burning one's feet, jumping from puddle to puddle to keep the soles of one's feet cool on a hot day, bare feet slapping against concrete, the chafe of a wet bathing suit, a wedgie after riding a huge slide, water in one's eyes, wet hair sticking to one's neck and face, sunburn, the greasy feel of sunblock or suntan oil, warm plastic beach chairs, the sticky closeness of crowds, a plastic or fiberglass railing under one's hand, a trembling in the belly as one reaches the top of the stairs, dizziness as one looks over the top and prepares to go down, water splashing on the skin, the sting of a wet towel being snapped, cold drinks and ice cream, a squishy inner tube, cold air in the restroom that raises goose bumps on one's skin, undulating waves in the wave pool, tangled wet hair, water spraying the face, the burn of water going up one's nose, the crackly feel of waterlogged ears, stomach cramps

POSSIBLE SOURCES OF CONFLICT

A drowning or near drowning

Falling down the stairs

Being unable to swim

Having a fear of heights and not wanting one's friends to know

Dictatorial or inattentive lifeguards

Bullies

Overprotective parents trying to watch a fearless child who doesn't swim well

A punctual child who does not show up at a meeting point by the designated time

Pedophiles

Body image issues

Sunburn

Poorly maintained equipment

Water that isn't properly chlorinated and becomes a breeding ground for germs

Going to the park with friends who have different goals (riding as many rides as possible vs. picking up girls vs. picking fights)

A swimsuit malfunction in the wave pool

PEOPLE COMMONLY FOUND HERE

Kids and teenagers, lifeguards, parents, park employees, sunbathers, tourists on vacation

RELATED SETTINGS THAT MAY TIE IN WITH THIS ONE

Amusement park (188), outdoor pool (218)

SETTING NOTES AND TIPS

Tall staircases, death-defying slides, wave pools, metal equipment in a park full of water, young swimmers with poor bladder control—the possibilities for conflict in a water park run the gamut from mildly embarrassing to life threatening. In real life, these parks are closely monitored and regulated, so their safety and cleanliness must meet certain standards for them to remain operational. But in fiction, anything goes and everything is possible. With the proper foundation building, a water park can be the perfect place for a hero or heroine who is simply in the wrong place at the wrong time.

SETTING DESCRIPTION EXAMPLE

I ran up the steep stairs behind Matt, ignoring how the gritty non-slip strips on the steps cut into my feet. At the top, I took in the view of the park at night, how the lights glittered on every wet surface, making it impossible to tell just how high up we were. The wind gusted, and the platform swayed the tiniest bit. My chest tingled as I imagined the crazy plunge I'd be taking in the dark. I gripped the metal railing and wished the guys ahead would hurry up.

Techniques and Devices Used: Light and shadow, multisensory descriptions

Resulting Effects: Characterization, establishing mood

ZOO

SIGHTS

Meandering sidewalks, a park that's subdivided by habitat or animal classification, trees and shrubbery, bamboo thickets, flitting insects, wooden walkways, concession stands, restrooms, picnic tables and benches, gift shops, vending machines near enclosures filled with animal food, personnel on golf carts, parents pushing strollers, teachers and chaperones corralling classroom groups, children climbing onto fence rails to get a better view, a zoo café, a rental kiosk for strollers and wheelchairs, smudged viewing windows, small buildings and fenced enclosures, well-worn animal paths made from pacing, rocks and caves, trees for climbing, pools and streams filled with fish and waterfowl, animal toys scattered around an enclosure, handlers interacting with the animals or cleaning out their spaces, an outdoor amphitheater for animal shows, posted signs that contain animal information and photos, education centers, a playground, an animal infirmary, a nursery where baby animals are kept, a petting zoo, a reptile house, ATM machines, a first aid station, water fountains, a party area

Animals at the Zoo: tigers, elephants, lions, hippos, rhinos, camels, sloths, gorillas, howler and spider monkeys, chimps, hyenas, pandas, lynxes, porcupines, giraffes, bighorn sheep, antelope, zebras, kangaroos, warthogs, otters, wolves, bears (black, grizzly and polar), sea lions, leopards, alligators, turtles, snakes, flamingos, vultures, peacocks, bats, hawks, falcons, ostriches and emus, scorpions, spiders and insects

SOUNDS

People talking, laughter, children asking questions or whining, babies crying, running feet, leaves crunching, stroller wheels rattling over leaves and twigs, wind in the trees, insects buzzing, birds chirping and calling, the flap of bird wings, animals vocalizing, animals splashing in water, personnel giving informative speeches over a microphone or to small groups, food wrappers crinkling, money jingling in pockets, voices echoing in indoor animal enclosures and stations, doors opening and closing, ambient noise coming from hidden speakers (insects buzzing, birds calling, rain pattering), kids knocking on glass enclosures, parents losing their tempers, viewers *ooh*-ing and *aah*-ing, kids shrieking when an animal comes into view, sprinklers coming on

SMELLS

Manure, wet or oily animal hide, algae smells in water enclosures or manmade ponds, garbage, rain, concession food, mosquito repellent, sunblock, perfumes, body odor, diapers that need to be changed, mud, wildflowers, fresh grass or hay, rotting fruit, the stink of an indoor enclosure (such as the reptile or monkey house)

TASTES

Bottled water, soda, concession stand food, sweat, an accidental spray of mosquito repellent, ice cream, chewing tobacco, gum, mints, food from a restaurant or concession (hamburgers, pizza, hot dogs, chicken nuggets, fries, popcorn, cotton candy, snow cones, popcorn, ice cream, chips, etc.)

TEXTURES AND SENSATIONS

Uneven wooden walkways, cracked sidewalks, fallen leaves underfoot, heat rising from the asphalt, the sun beating down, a cool breeze, drizzling rain, sweaty clothes sticking to the skin, noses pressed against plastic or glass enclosures, the frigid air of the penguin house, soda bottles dripping condensation, fence boards beneath one's fingers, gritty bird seed in one's palm, soft or coarse fur at the petting zoo, the tickle of snouts as animals eat from one's hand, ice cream dripping on one's arm, a camera strap pulling at one's neck, a heavy backpack, scratchy sunburn, the weight of a tired child in one's arms

POSSIBLE SOURCES OF CONFLICT

Animals escaping their enclosures
Diseases spreading among the animals or from animals to people
Picketers and protestors
Cruel or inhumane handlers
Bureaucratic administrators who know nothing about animal care
Inner conflict over wanting to see the animals and not wanting them to be caged
The death of a beloved animal

PEOPLE COMMONLY FOUND HERE

Animal handlers, carpenters, concession workers, families, janitors, maintenance workers, students and teachers on a field trip, veterinarians

RELATED SETTINGS THAT MAY TIE IN WITH THIS ONE

Circus (204)

SETTING NOTES AND TIPS

Zoos are a hot-topic issue for many people. While they provide the opportunity for many (especially children) to see animals they wouldn't otherwise get to see, some people are conflicted about the morality of the zoo model. Should animals be kept in cages for humanity's viewing pleasure? Is it humane regardless of the level of treatment and care? Human beings are complicated; some will question the ethics and morality of situations, places, and possibilities that may not bother others at all. Including a setting that creates a moral dilemma for your hero is a great way to bring conflict and depth to your story.

SETTING DESCRIPTION EXAMPLE

I stood at the glass, stretching up on my toes so I could find a spot not smudged by kids' fingers. To see a lion up close at last! I scanned the fallen logs, the grassy hill, under the bower of a poplar tree, searching for the king of the jungle. Finally I found him walking along a dirt path that spanned the fence line. As the great creature paced back and forth, over and over, my excitement faded and my heart began to hurt. It didn't belong here, caged by wire and fed rations of meat. It needed a place without barriers or borders. It deserved a life free of people. I pulled back from the glass and someone claimed the space, gasping in awe of its massive body and silky mane. I decided I'd had enough of the zoo and headed for the exit.

Techniques and Devices Used: Multisensory descriptions
Resulting Effects: Reinforcing emotion

Transportation

AIRPLANE

SIGHT

Narrow carpeted aisles, a first class section (roomier reclining seats, special blankets and pillows, media centers, menus and beverages served in glassware by attentive flight members), a curtain divider, economy class seating, white overhead compartments, armrests with consoles for sound volume and radio channels, seat belts, porthole windows with shutters, air and light controls overhead along with a call button for the flight attendants, people blocking the aisle as they shove bags into overhead compartments, an emergency exit mid plane (opening instructions, door release handle, red or yellow hazard stripes to draw attention), fold down trays, tattered in-flight magazines, a safety instructions manual tucked in a backseat slot, a small television in the seat back (with either touch screen or armrest controls), a barf bag, travelers (typing on laptops, reading, listening to music or playing games on handheld devices, bouncing babies on their laps, eating, adjusting cheap foam pillows), a drink cart (loaded with plastic cups, coffee, pop, water, tea, single serving alcoholic beverages, wrapped cookie or pretzel snacks), an aisle that lights up in case of emergencies, seat-as-flotation devices, oxygen masks that drop down if cabin pressure is compromised, a galley area for food and beverage preparations, several tiny restrooms (a toilet, mirror, stainless steel sink, smoke alarm, paper and soap dispensers), a locked doorway to the pilot's cockpit, an air marshal pretending to be a passenger

SOUNDS

The roar of engines firing up and accelerating during takeoff, the steady sound of the engines during the flight, items jiggling on a beverage cart, the snap-click of overhead compartments shutting, people talking, laughing and snoring, babies crying as parents try to soothe them, the creak of a seat as people readjust, zippers being manipulated on purses or bags, rustling food wrappers, the clunk of a tray locking into position, the rustle of newspapers and magazines, crisp book pages turning, people typing, flight attendants giving instructions or waiting on passengers, the hiss of air conditioning, coughing, throat clearing, a shudder or clatter during air turbulence as luggage jitters in overhead bins, suction toilets flushing, the click of a restroom door shutting, galley bins snapping shut, a loud passenger complaining, bell dings when seat belts can be removed, the captain's voice over the loudspeaker

SMELLS

A seatmate with too much cologne, food smells, fresh coffee, canned air, minty gum, bad breath, beer, a whiff of hand sanitizer, sweat or body odor, musty fabric (if the plane is older), hair products, smelly feet if someone takes their shoes off, diapers that need changing if one is sitting near a baby or toddler, sour vomit if someone has used their airsickness bag

TASTES

Water, coffee, pop, juice, tea, sugar, alcoholic drinks (wine, beer, spirits), plane food or food bought in the airport (sandwiches, chocolate bars, chips, granola bars, bagels, muffins, wraps, cookies), cough drops, mouthwash, mints, gum, a sour or bitter taste from dry mouth

TEXTURES AND SENSATIONS

Armrests that dig into flesh, nudging a seatmate when adjusting or reaching for something, bumping one's head on the low storage compartment as one gets up to enter the aisle, seats that have a lot of give or bounce, cramped and swollen feet inside hot shoes, kinks in the neck, the puffiness of a pillow, leaning against a hard wall as one waits for the restroom, bumps against the back as a kid behind one's row kicks the seat, the pinch of a tight seat belt, jabbing a finger against armrest control buttons, the papery feel of book pages, balling up a napkin, pulling off the wrapper of complimentary cookies, sipping at hot coffee and feeling steam against one's mouth, patting lips with a napkin, brushing crumbs off one's shirt front, lifting or lowering the shade on the window, the comforting weight of an airplane blanket as one tries to sleep

POSSIBLE SOURCES OF CONFLICT

Mechanical trouble

Airsickness

A rude or inappropriate seatmate

Drunk passengers

Medical distress (appendix pain or a heart attack) during a flight

Realizing one has lost something of importance (money, credit cards, a passport)

PEOPLE COMMONLY FOUND HERE

A captain and crew, air marshal, flight attendants, passengers

RELATED SETTINGS THAT MAY TIE IN WITH THIS ONE

Airport (252), hotel room (78), taxi (280)

SETTING NOTES AND TIPS

Airplanes vary depending on size, age and condition. Smaller planes (especially ones built for short trips) may only have little or no service for the flight. Movement and storage may be restricted on small planes due to space, and have only economy class seating. Also, if you are naming a particular airline in your novel, take care to research cabin crew dress and service style to ensure accurate description.

SETTING DESCRIPTION EXAMPLE

As I adjusted my miniscule pillow, I glanced sidelong at the passenger next to me in the window seat. Sweat glistened on his pale face and his hands gripped the armrests so hard I was surprised finger bones didn't bust through. His breath was choppy like he'd run a marathon, not just eaten what was possibly the worst meal in the history of the world. Great. I ditched the pillow and switched on the TV, giving up the idea of sleep. Hopefully we didn't hit air turbulence. Something told me this guy was a hurler, and I didn't trust that he'd be able to make it to the restroom in time.

    Techniques and Devices Used: Hyperbole, multisensory descriptions

    Resulting Effects: Characterization, foreshadowing, tension and conflict

AIRPORT

SIGHTS
Automated glass doors entrances, a long open area leading to multiple airline check-in counters (featuring a luggage scale, monitor, ticket printouts, luggage tags and stickers, airline employees, passengers holding tickets and passports, and conveyer belts for checked luggage), snake-like queues filled with passengers carting luggage, e-ticket terminals, security personnel, airport staff, gates for different airlines (complete with company colors, uniformed staff, logos and monitors displaying information for each), signs from the ceiling directing passengers to different areas of the airport, baggage drop-off areas, restrooms, information desks, a baggage claim section, car rental kiosks, large digital monitors displaying flight departures and arrival times, tables with forms to be filled out (bag tags and pens, baggage forms, customs forms), instructions for carrying on luggage, janitorial employees pushing cleaning trolleys, vending machines, a security area (queued lines, uniformed agents with latex gloves, passengers removing their shoes, a conveyer belt and scanner, bins for pocket contents and purses, laptops sitting in their own bins, body scanners, handheld metal detectors), gate terminal areas with glass windows overlooking the tarmac (planes loading and unloading, luggage trains, ground crew), mass seating at each gate, electrical outlets where phones and laptops are being charged, wide halls with passengers pulling luggage, motorized carts to help disabled or limited-mobility passengers get around, kiosks selling merchandise, restaurants and small airport bars, smoking rooms, rentable Wi-Fi workstations with plug-ins and media hookups, desks at each gate (with personnel checking tickets, assigning seats, and calling missing passengers)

SOUNDS
Automated doors opening and closing, passenger names being called over the intercom, flight arrivals being announced, departure and delay announcements, luggage wheels rolling across the floor, parents telling their kids to keep up, attendants calling for the next customer in line, zippers opening and closing, soft luggage (duffels and backpacks) thumping against the ground, boots and high heels clicking against the floor, the ruffle of papers, e-tickets spitting out of a dispenser, stamps on paperwork, quiet conversation, waiting passengers (making phone calls, clearing their throats, shifting, and making small talk to others in line), the crackle of a security officer's radio, conversations overheard in foreign languages

SMELLS
Coffee, hair products, cologne, perfume, mints or mouthwash, paper, metal, cleaning products, baked goods or hot food from the food court, sweat, bad breath, plastic, rubber

TASTES
Coffee, water, mints, gum, vending machine snacks, easy baked goods (bagels, muffins, wraps, cookies), food bought from a vendor

TEXTURES AND SENSATIONS
Sitting on a hard suitcase during a long wait in line, bumping into other people, a luggage wheel running over one's foot, the rough fabric of the strap that forms a queue, shifting a bag from

one shoulder to the other to relieve pressure, slick boarding passes that have just been printed, a compact passport book, rolling the neck and shoulders to ward off stiffness, craning the neck to read directional signs, tugging a zipper on an overstuffed bag, the firm skim of a security agent's hand over one's body during a routine in-person check, squirming in an uncomfortable seat at one's gate, the heat of coffee in one's hand, resting a foot on one's luggage, travel fatigue setting in as one waits for the last leg of a trip to begin

POSSIBLE SOURCES OF CONFLICT
Misreading the flight's departure time and arriving late
Getting lost in a large airport
Theft
Realizing one has lost something of importance (money, credit cards, a passport)
Having one's flight canceled or overbooked
Bad weather grounding all flights
Getting caught with something in one's luggage that isn't allowed (drugs, weapons, meat, excessive cash)

PEOPLE COMMONLY FOUND HERE
Administrative workers, delivery people, flight crews and airline support staff, ground and baggage crews, maintenance and janitorial staff, police and onsite paramedics, security personnel, travelers

RELATED SETTINGS THAT MAY TIE IN WITH THIS ONE
Airplane (250), casual dining restaurant (140), cheap motel (46), fast food restaurant (148), hotel room (78), public restroom (112), taxi (280)

SETTING NOTES AND TIPS
Airports vary in size. While many are large and sprawling and require shuttles or trains to get to different terminals, ones located in smaller towns will have minimal amenities; some may not even have proper gate areas. In many parts of the world, passengers go outside the terminal to board the plane using a removable staircase rather than travel through an attached hallway. Security will also be run differently around the world, with the airport adhering to the rules and regulations of that country.

SETTING DESCRIPTION EXAMPLE
I shuffled exactly half a step as the ridiculously long American Airlines queue finally moved. This was the real reason they told you to come hours early for each flight—so you could stand around waiting to check your bag. Over at the Korea Air counter, passengers flew through the line like prunes through an eighty-year-old's digestive system. Maybe it was time to switch carriers for these long-haul flights.

   Techniques and Devices Used: Contrast, simile
   Resulting Effects: Reinforcing emotion

AMBULANCE

SIGHTS

A removable stretcher, two captain's chairs or a padded bench seat (which acts as a secondary bed, if needed) along the wall, cabinets and secure shelving, drawers (loaded with bandages, medications, syringes, IV solutions and administration sets, examination gloves, spare batteries, ice packs, and fluids for wound irrigation), airway supplies, intubation tubes, portable oxygen tanks, diagnostic equipment (a blood pressure cuff, a cardiac monitor, a defibrillator), an intravenous pump, transportation equipment (narrow back boards, c-collars, splinting equipment, straps), electrical outlets, pressure gauges and air vents, a paramedic running tests and administering treatment, white sheets and light blankets for the stretcher, a paramedic kit that includes basic supplies, an advanced paramedic kit with medications and airway equipment, metal stretcher clips to hold the bed in place, swinging metal doors, bright overhead lighting, cables, water bottles, a biohazard waste bin, cleaning supplies, an electronic patient chart, an onboard computer for GPS and communication in the cab area, paramedics in uniform (wearing equipment belts with pouches for scissors and medications, radios and microphones clipped at the shoulder, Kevlar vests, stethoscopes, etc.)

SOUNDS

The hiss of pressurized air, bleeps from a cardiac monitor or IV pump, the engine rumbling, a paramedic's voice (calming the patient, asking questions and discussing treatment, speaking to a doctor over the radio), a dispatcher's voice giving instructions, groaning and crying, a patient's rushed breathing, cabinets and drawers being opened and shut, Velcro tearing loose as a blood pressure cuff is removed, sirens blaring, horns honking and other traffic sounds, items shaking in drawers and cabinets during a bumpy ride, plastic wrappings being torn from bandages and sterile equipment, static crackling over the radio

SMELLS

Antiseptic, blood, urine, feces, vomit, cleaning supplies, char or smoke (if the victim was involved in a fire), sweat, clean sheets, exhaust, cologne or aftershave, a patient's boozy breath

TASTES

Plastic from the oxygen mask, blood

TEXTURES AND SENSATIONS

A padded stretcher cushion, cold metal rails bumping against one's arms, the pressure or rub of straps and buckles holding one's body in place, clothing being cut away, blood trickling from a wound, a compress being held to a gash, dry bandages slowly dampening and turning sodden, local pain associated with the wound that intensifies as an injury is moved or splinted, tape tugging at one's skin, the disorientation that accompanies shock, an out-of-body experience, uncontrollable shivers, a cool antiseptic wipe on one's skin, the pinch of a needle, tubing snaking across one's chest, an oxygen mask lightly pressing against the face, oxygen prongs digging into one's nostrils, gauze being taped in place over a wound, gripping the stretcher's rails or the paramedic's hand for comfort or to brace against the pain, the slow cessation of acute discomfort as analgesia enters one's system

POSSIBLE SOURCES OF CONFLICT

Deep ruts or rocky ground that make the ride bumpy, jostling a patient's stretcher and causing more pain

The ambulance getting stuck or having to be rerouted, putting a critical patient in danger

Defective equipment

An unforeseen allergic reaction to a medication

The vehicle being involved in a car accident on the way to the hospital

Treating a patient with a communicable disease

Conflicts of interest (treating a patient who is a known murderer or child molester, a drunk driver, etc.)

Prejudices that cause one to make personal judgments regarding the care of patients

Being unable to accompany a loved one in the ambulance

The patient's condition rapidly worsening

Dealing with patients who have a phobia of hospitals or doctors

PEOPLE COMMONLY FOUND HERE

Family members accompanying the loved one, paramedics, patients, student paramedics

RELATED SETTINGS THAT MAY TIE IN WITH THIS ONE

Rural Volume: Country road (156), house fire (62)

Urban Volume: Big city street (38), car accident (42), emergency room (58), hospital room (76), small town street (120)

SETTING NOTES AND TIPS

Ambulances come in different models and vary in appearance, but they all carry the necessities for lifesaving treatments. They may be stationed at hospitals, EMS stations, or used in fire halls. Some may have an outer storage compartment containing firefighter bunker gear (a heat-proof suit, helmets, a self-contained breathing apparatus, etc.) for situations where a paramedic may need to assist with a fire-related rescue.

SETTING DESCRIPTION EXAMPLE

Doors slammed shut, and the glare of lights dug at Liam's eyes. Pain pulsed through his body, then intensified as the paramedic placed an oxygen mask against his blistered skin. The second he drew in the cool air, his scorched lungs loosened in shaky relief. The ambulance lurched forward, speeding away from the smoking ruins of his home and his mind raced, considering what came next. The paramedic smiled reassuringly and spoke, but Liam was too scattered to focus on her words, too sickened from the smell of his own burned flesh. Something pricked his arm and cool numbness crept through him, dimming the heat of his pain. Tears spilled. Impossibly, he was alive.

Techniques and Devices Used: Multisensory descriptions

Resulting Effects: Contrast, tension and conflict

CITY BUS

SIGHTS
Folding doors that open to a short set of stairs, a driver in his seat, a narrow aisle dividing the seats into two sections on either side of the bus, a yellow line on the floor at the front of the bus for passengers to stay behind, leather hand loops dangling from the ceiling, handrails, benches or plastic molded seats, smudged glass windows, a storage rack over the seats, posters and advertisements between or above the windows, graffiti applied to the bus's interior with markers or pens (images, gang tags, messages, humorous or ironic statements, declarations of love, racial slurs), slumped passengers (minding their own business by reading, texting, listing to music, playing games on a device), torn seat cushions with foam poking through, litter on the floor (napkins, candy wrappers, bits of paper, snack crumbs), city streets and vehicles flashing past the windows, buttons to open the door, a wire to pull when the bus is nearing one's stop, signs telling passengers to stay back from the door, people standing using handholds, passengers (swaying as the vehicle moves, sitting with shopping bags or backpacks between their feet or on the empty seats beside them), newspapers left on seats, groups of animated teens clustered together, gum stuck to the walls, the seats disfigured by burns, punctures or knife marks

SOUNDS
Coins clattering into a change receptacle on older buses (many modern ones have a ticket-only system), the revving motor as the driver hits the gas at a green light or shifts gears, the squeal of brakes, the whoosh of air brakes, the scrape of a door sliding open, shoes scuffling down the aisle, shopping bags crackling and jackets rustling as passengers get settled in their seats, creaks and squeaks as the metal bus frame bounces along a bumpy road, the voices of passengers chatting, music from a passenger's headphones, a child's loud voice, laughter, swearing, the rattle of a newspaper, zippers on purses or backpacks opening and closing, the rustle of plastic bags, coughing and throat clearing, street noise through open windows, bells chiming a stop, boots thumping down the steps in a hurry

SMELLS
Feet, body odor, perfume, body cologne, hair products, leather, greasy hair, dirt, cold metal, stagnant air, warm plastic, a draft of fresh air coming through a cracked window

TASTES
Gum, mints, coffee, bottled water, leftover lunches brought onto the bus

TEXTURES AND SENSATIONS
Hard seats, the shaking and bumping of the bus slowing down and speeding up, brushing against other passengers, squeezing past someone to get to the door, a cold metal handrail against the skin, clamping tight to a purse or backpack, keeping an arm around a small child or holding his sweaty hand in one's own, pushing on a door with a sleeve or shoulder to avoid touching it with one's fingers, holding bags on one's lap so they don't have to be set on the dirty floor, swaying with the bus's motion, scooting over to make room for a new passenger

POSSIBLE SOURCES OF CONFLICT

Drunk or disorderly passengers

Someone on drugs who begins to hallucinate

Not having bus fare or losing one's pass

Getting on the wrong bus

Being forced off in an unfamiliar neighborhood because it's the last stop of the night

A creepy person who won't stop staring

A bus breakdown or accident

Someone who is carrying a concealed knife or other weapon

A group of people who gang up on another passenger or the driver

PEOPLE COMMON TO THIS SETTING

A bus driver, passengers

RELATED SETTINGS THAT MAY TIE IN WITH THIS ONE

Big city street (38), small town street (120)

SETTING NOTES AND TIPS

The mood of a city bus often starts and ends with the driver. Some are highly social, smiling and asking questions of their passengers and talking about local matters. Other drivers are there to do a job: drive. They keep to themselves and reply to questions only when necessary—often in grunts—and prefer to answer questions by directing passengers to a nearby stack of pamphlets that list bus routes and pickup schedules.

As with so many settings, the people inhabiting it will be there for different reasons. A person may be riding the bus because he doesn't own a car, his vehicle is in the shop, he's had his license revoked, or he's an illegal immigrant without documentation to obtain a license. There could be more sinister reasons, like a terrorist planning to detonate a bomb or an escaped convict hoping to travel with anonymity. Everyone has a story. You don't have to know the intimate details behind every character in your novel, but developing a quick snapshot of why they're in that particular setting will provide insight into who they are and what they can do for you.

SETTING DESCRIPTION EXAMPLE

Anna slid closer to the window as a portly businessman dropped into the seat next to her, making the cushion jump. He yammered nonstop into a cell phone, stealing all the room between them. His onion breath was so toxic it could have been classified as a biological weapon. Good grief. This is what she got for claiming an empty bench instead of choosing a seat next to someone else.

    Techniques and Devices Used: Hyperbole, multisensory descriptions

    Resulting Effects: Characterization, reinforcing emotion

CRUISE SHIP

SIGHTS
Outside: open-air decks surrounded by metal railings, a mini-amphitheater for evening entertainment, swimming pools with slides, rock walls, wave pools, a kids' area with sports activities (ping-pong tables, mini-golf, splash pools, basketball and volleyball courts), an exercise track around the ship's perimeter, stacked emergency rowboats, flags flying overhead, hundreds of beach chairs (with passengers laying out, sleeping, reading, chatting, developing sunburn), teens clumped together or listening to music players, kids (running, swimming, splashing, shrieking), drinks condensing in the heat, water and whitecaps far as the eye can see, smaller ships and sailboats in the distance, seabirds flying overhead

Inside: passengers in swimsuits and flip-flops, sharply dressed ship employees, fancy restaurants and fast-food joints, retail stores, bars and lounges, kiosks selling merchandise and snacks, casinos, game rooms for the kids, multiple elevators and stairwells, hand-sanitizing stations, narrow corridors with cabin doors on either side going around the ship's perimeter, half-empty dishes on trays sitting outside of doors, privacy tags hanging from door handles, small but efficiently spaced rooms with all the amenities, towels on the bed folded into interesting shapes (monkeys, birds, puppies), mints on the pillows, heavy curtains covering the balcony door, a glass door leading to a balcony with a small table and chairs, damp towels and suits draped over the chairs, people on the balcony (drinking, leaning on the railing, reading, watching the horizon), passengers dressed up for formal ballroom dinners

SOUNDS
The quiet whoosh of the ship moving through the water, the wind in one's ears, flags flapping, birds squawking, accented voices of ship employees, automatic doors sliding open, squealing and splashing from the kids' area, running feet, music from the ship's speakers, announcements coming over the speakers, basketballs bouncing, people cheering at the wave pool, ping-pong balls pinging, quiet indoor corridors, muted TV sounds and voices from inside cabins, doors opening and closing, employees singing or whistling as they clean cabins, elevators dinging, eating sounds from restaurants, the flap of flip-flops in the daytime and clack of heels at night, music blaring from clubs and bars, muffled steps on carpeted stairs

SMELLS
Briny sea water, sunscreen, lotion, sweat, hot dogs, pizza, beer, hamburgers, floor cleaner, furniture polish, hand sanitizer, hairspray, soap, rain

TASTES
Sweat, cold water, soda, juice, beer, tropical drinks, ice cream, gum, candy, every possible food one could wish to eat

TEXTURES AND SENSATIONS
The sun's heat on one's shoulders, sweat dampening the skin, the wind whipping one's hair into one's face and sticking it to the neck, a clingy wet swimsuit, the plastic slats of beach chairs

pressing into the skin, scratchy towels, refreshing pool water (salt, not chlorine), heavy sunscreen or suntan lotion on the skin, prickly sunburn, the light-headed sensation of getting too much sun, water splashing from the pool, the gritty feel of sweaty skin in need of a shower, a plastic straw between one's lips, moving from the heat of outdoors to a cool indoor hallway, soft carpeting under one's feet, brass railings, foamy hand sanitizer, a cold shower washing away the sweat and sunscreen film, tight-fitting evening wear, the weight of a coat or shawl over the arm in case the evening gets cold, a soft bed and pillows, a warm breeze drifting into the cabin from an open balcony door

POSSIBLE SOURCES OF CONFLICT

Power outages

Contaminated food or drinking water

Infidelity or breakups

Pirates or terrorism (if one is in high-risk or poorly patrolled international waters)

An outbreak of a highly transmittable disease

A passenger with a medical emergency like a heart attack or stroke

A passenger who dies while onboard

PEOPLE COMMONLY FOUND HERE

A captain and crew, cooks, entertainers, event planners, passengers, security, serving and cleaning staff, store and spa facility attendants, the ship's medical staff

RELATED SETTINGS THAT MAY TIE IN WITH THIS ONE

Rural Volume: Beach (202), ocean (230), tropical island (240)

Urban Volume: Bar (138), casino (202), casual dining restaurant (140), fast food restaurant (148), ice cream parlor (150), movie theater (212), outdoor pool (218)

SETTING NOTES AND TIPS

Cruise ships are a dream come true for most, but it isn't the ideal vacation for some. There are many reasons why a cruise might be stressful for a character: if she's an introvert, she's a new mom who doesn't want to leave her kids with a controlling in-law, or she has a fear of crowds, enclosed spaces, or drowning. When researching different settings, always look past the obvious and consider how it can be tweaked to give it a new twist or make things difficult for the character.

SETTING DESCRIPTION EXAMPLE

From the top deck, the ocean's surface glistened like shards of a broken mirror, catching the moon's glow and hurling it back in its face. The wind, salted with rain, breathed something fierce, tangling my hair and pushing me off-balance. I hung on to the metal railing, refusing to budge, and threw Bradley's crumpled goodbye letter into the waves.

Techniques and Devices Used: Personification, simile, weather

Resulting Effects: Establishing mood, hinting at backstory, reinforcing emotion

FISHING BOAT

SIGHTS
Sunlight reflecting on the water, darting fish below the surface, seagulls spiraling overhead, sea lions sunning on rocks in the harbor, a boat mast rising from the deck, radio antennas, a winch and wire coils, a sturdy railing, crates piled up, hooks and grapples hanging on the cabin wall, ladders and nets, coils of hose for cleaning fish and washing down the decks, an anchor held ready, a bar of floodlights, life vests in a tub, barrels of fuel lashed in place, raincoats and waterproof fishing gear hanging from hooks, narrow walkways, welded loops for fishing poles to slide into, a small barbeque, watertight doors to the inside, stackable or foldable chairs, a giant fish cooler with a hatch, cramped crew quarters, storage cubbies in every nook and cranny, a small galley kitchen (coolers or a fridge, economical counter space, fruit and vegetables held in nets for storage, knives and other cutlery, paper towels, a trash bin, a well-used cutting board, a small table, a sink, cupboards with locks, a marine stove), a closet-like bathroom (toilet, sink, a porthole for ventilation), an engine room (generators, tools, spare parts, refrigeration motors, the boat's engine, coolant, wires, pressure gauges, a fire extinguisher), the wheelhouse or pilot house (holding a captain's chair, gauges, rudder sticks or a wheel, a computer, sealed windows, fish finding equipment and radar, a speed gauge, a depth gauge, sonar, throttles, a call whistle, the intercom system, a coffee pot, maps and charts, a marine radio, switches for search lights, safety bars, storage cupboards), sleeping quarters (bunks, blankets, a light, a small storage closet, hooks)

SOUNDS
The engine firing up, waves slapping against the hull, the captain speaking over the intercom, boots squeaking on wet decks, the slap of fish being poured out of a net, the high-pitched whine of the winch drawing up a net, a lightweight storage bin sliding across the deck in bad weather, the creak of taut rope, the sputter of water as the propeller starts up, rain slashing at the boat, the rapid click of a reel quickly letting out line or the patterned click of a measured line release, metal pinging against metal as tools are tossed into a box, the hoot of an excited fisherman over the size of a catch, thunder booming, a seagull's cry, the splash of fish jumping out of the water, the blast of air as a whale briefly surfaces, food being cooked in the galley, silverware scraping over plates, men shifting in their bunks, the sound of footsteps walking overhead

SMELLS
Fish guts, brine, gasoline fumes, motor oil and grease, sweat, body odor, cooking odors (hamburgers, barbecued chicken, fish in herbs and butter), coffee, beer

TASTES
Briny sea water, pan-fried fish and seafood, hot biscuits with butter, stew, grilled chicken, steak, hamburgers, salad, hot dogs, stir fry vegetables, potatoes, corn, porridge, omelets, water, pop, beer, coffee, alcoholic spirits (rum, whisky, etc.), hot chocolate, chocolate bars, chips, popcorn

TEXTURES AND SENSATIONS
Thick rubbery pants and raincoats, slippery fish, wet spray going down one's collar, rain or hail pelting into one's face, the heat of sunburn, coiled rope sliding through calloused hands, pain

at being tossed about in a storm, being slammed against railings or barrels, throwing handfuls of slimy chum overboard, the accidental prick of a fish hook, smooth fishing line, the patter of water dripping onto one's legs and feet when pulling a fish off a single line, a cool plunge into the water to escape the heat, water droplets dripping off one's hair and running down the face, a hot mug in one's hands after a rain-soaked shift

POSSIBLE SOURCES OF CONFLICT
Mechanical breakdowns
Overfishing leading to poor catches
An illness sweeping through the crew
A malfunctioning refrigeration unit causing one's catch to spoil
Pirates (mostly in unpatrolled waters)
Stormy weather
Navigation equipment shorting out
Discovering a body floating in the water (alive or dead)
Bringing in a catch and finding something odd or disturbing in the net
Coming across debris from a shipwreck and needing to search for survivors
Having a crew member pass away while the boat is out to sea

PEOPLE COMMONLY FOUND HERE
A captain, coastguard officers, fishermen, the skipper

RELATED SETTINGS THAT MAY TIE IN WITH THIS ONE
Rural Volume: Beach (202), lighthouse (170), ocean (230), tropical island (240)
Urban Volume: Marina (264)

SETTING NOTES AND TIPS
While fishing boats will have basic similarities, the specialized equipment (such as the processing areas and refrigeration units) will vary depending on the type of catch and size of the boat. Commercial boats are bigger and will have more resources than a small, private fishing boat. The crew size will also fluctuate depending on the size of the operation.

SETTING DESCRIPTION EXAMPLE
Hasan checked the radar one more time and then flicked off the lights. He stepped out of the pilothouse and crossed to the railing, taking a deep draw of the salt air. The quiet was almost absolute, save for the soft chug of the engine far below decks. The sea was in a rare calm, a perfect mirror of the full moon swimming along its surface. Just the right backdrop for a man's long thoughts.
Techniques and Devices Used: Metaphor
Resulting Effects: Establishing mood

LIMOUSINE

SIGHTS
Wrap-around leather couches, an ice chest with complimentary water bottles, LED track lighting creating a neon glow at the ceiling or floor height, controls for a sound system, a tinted privacy divider between the passengers and cab, a sun roof, excited partygoers, a bottle of spirits being passed around or added to cans of pop, a dimmer switch for lights, empty bottles or beer cans on ledges, polished tinted windows, shiny silver door handles, a mini wet bar with glasses and cup holders, a TV and DVD player, USB connections, chrome detailing, a mirrored ceiling around the sunroof, fiber optics backlighting the stereo display, a driver assisting passengers into and out of the limo, each passenger's face bathed in light, couples making out, occupants doing drugs

SOUNDS
Loud music, laughter, partygoers (shouting over the music, standing up to look out the sunroof, watching a movie on the TV, drinking), horns honking outside, static on the radio when switching channels, the whir of an automatic window opening and closing, the driver receiving directions from the passengers, the click of a door shutting, ice cubes clinking against a drink glass, the rush of traffic outside, the steady movement of the wheels over the pavement

SMELLS
Alcohol, sweat, too much perfume or aftershave trapped in a small space, leather, air conditioning

TASTES
Alcohol, water, pop or mix, snacks brought into the limo

TEXTURES AND SENSATIONS
Smooth leather seats, cold ice cubes, bumping against one another in the limo, a sudden wetness as one spills a drink, the jerk and sway of the limousine turning corners or stopping at intersections, feeling the vibration of bass through the seat, standing up through the sun roof to feel the cool night air rush against one's face

POSSIBLE SOURCES OF CONFLICT
People drinking too much and needing to pull over
Traffic snarls that delays busy passengers
A breakdown or flat tire
Speeding and being pulled over by the police
Someone getting carsick and flooding the backseat with a sour smell
Not having cash to tip the driver
Having a passenger that is a well-known criminal or has ties to important people within the mob
Driving the limo and witnessing one's passengers engage in a highly illegal activity

PEOPLE COMMONLY FOUND HERE
A limo driver, passengers (teens on prom night, visiting dignitaries, celebrities, a wedding couple)

RELATED SETTINGS THAT MAY TIE IN WITH THIS ONE

Rural Volume: Mansion (72), prom (128), wedding reception (192)

Urban Volume: Black-tie event (196), casino (202), green room (208), hotel room (78), penthouse suite (104), performing arts theater (224)

SETTING NOTES AND TIPS

While limousines often do carry glassware for passengers to use while drinking, most avoid using them because of sanitary reasons. Limousines also come in all shapes and sizes, including large SUV and Hummer versions.

Vehicles in their various forms have one overarching purpose: to take people from one place to another. As such, they're great for honing in on the theme of transformation. In the story, the character may move from Point A to Point B, but we all know that not all journeys are physical ones. Even a short trip can offer an opportunity for inner thought and reflection about one's character, recent decisions, and future goals. In a setting like this, think about the parallels you might make between your character's starting and ending points and her own inner path of self-fulfillment and where it needs to go.

SETTING DESCRIPTION EXAMPLE

I climbed into the limo after Denise and slid down the leather seat to the end, trying not to gape. A stocked mini bar and two TV sets sat across from me and green track lighting ringed the walls, casting my pale dress in a soft emerald glow. Denise fiddled with a knob on the sound system and music blasted, sending base notes thrumming up through the cushioned seats. Even better, the lights pulsed in time with the beat, turning the interior into our own private disco ball party. Wow. Never in a million years had I imagined my ride to prom would be anything like this. Laura and Stephen were going to fall down and die of supreme envy when we pulled into the parking lot.

Techniques and Devices Used: Hyperbole, light and shadow, multisensory descriptions

Resulting Effects: Establishing mood, reinforcing emotion

MARINA

SIGHTS
A waterway that leads to a larger body of water, concrete sidewalks that run alongside the waterway, piers and narrow wooden docks stretching out into the water, various-sized boats lined up along the sidewalks and piers, nylon ropes tying watercraft to pier cleats, gentle waves, giant rocks along the water's edge, wooden pilings wrapped in rubber bumpers, barnacles on the pilings at the waterline, metal ladders hanging off the docks and extending into the water, plastic storage bins, water hoses and spigots, garbage cans, receptacles for depositing oil and grease, life preservers, fire extinguishers, fishing paraphernalia, people in beach wear prepping their boats for sailing or returning them to dock (carrying supplies aboard, rinsing the decks, waxing), sun sparkling on the water, gleaming chrome and silver bits, fish jumping past the surface and then disappearing, bare masts reaching into the sky, boats mirrored in the still water, birds flying, restaurants and shops at the marina's entrance, slipways for unloading boats on trailers, a fuel dock

SOUNDS
Chains rattling against masts in the wind, water slapping the hulls and pylons, water pouring from boats into the bay, the creak of ropes as they loosen and pull taut, hulls gently bumping against pylons, the sounds of mechanical tools (ratchets, drills, buffers) as people work on their boats, flags snapping in the wind, music playing from the boats and nearby shops, the growl of engines starting up, boats motoring past on their way to water, people calling to one another and chatting excitedly, laughter, the slap of flip-flops on boat decks and docks, the squeak of rubber-soled boat shoes, wind rustling the tree branches or palm fronds, bells jingling, the bellow of boat horns, water splashing from hoses, the call of water birds, the buzz of insects

SMELLS
An open water smell (salt water or fresh), motor oil, fish, wax, sweat, beer, sunscreen, wet clothing, food from nearby restaurants

TASTES
Salt water, sweat, beverages (water, soda, beer), groceries that will be eaten aboard the boat (junk food, chips, fruit, sandwiches, snack foods, takeout food from a restaurant)

TEXTURES AND SENSATIONS
Wind pulling at clothing and tangling one's hair, the prickle of sunburn, one's skin feeling taut from windburn, splintery wooden pylons, rough nylon ropes, the smooth feel of chrome and fiberglass, soft towels, the sway of the boat beneath one's feet, the hot metal ladder under one's fingers, heat from the sun beating down, spray from the water, biting insects, wet clothing chafing the skin, heavy sodden shoes, sweat trickling over one's skin, cool fingertips from a pop can's condensation, the slippery feel of a fish one caught while on the boat, a sore back from lugging coolers and supplies on and off the boat

POSSIBLE SOURCES OF CONFLICT

Being attacked and having to fight in tight quarters along the docks

Suffering a near-drowning

Discovering that one's boat has been vandalized or sabotaged

Finding a corpse floating in the water

Having one's boat impounded

Being at odds with marina owners who are petty enough to make one's life difficult

Spotting a dangerous creature in the water, like a shark or saltwater crocodile

Slipping on one's boat and hitting one's head

Prepping for a fun day at sea and discovering something that cancels one's trip (a leak in the boat, an empty gas tank, an alarming noise coming from the engine)

PEOPLE COMMONLY FOUND HERE

Boat brokers, boat owners and their families, guests preparing to sail, marina owners and workers, mechanics, skippers

RELATED SETTINGS THAT MAY TIE IN WITH THIS ONE

Rural Volume: Beach (202), lake (220), ocean (230), tropical island (240)

Urban Volume: Fishing boat (260), parking lot (102), yacht (286)

SETTING NOTES AND TIPS

A marina is the obvious choice for someone with a boat but no place to store it or for someone who wants to house a boat near the water. Another option for boat-owners is a dry dock, where boats are stored inland and owners are responsible for transporting them to the water. Yacht clubs are exclusive marinas for yacht owners. Boaters may also keep their boats at home and carry them to and from the water on trailers pulled behind their cars. Still others may store their boats at a private dock or a friend's waterfront property.

Marinas are typically calm, peaceful places where people go to relax and spend their leisure time. But many things could happen at a marina to cause tension for your characters. Arguments on the docks, drunken altercations, a drowning, vandalism, sabotage, theft—the possibilities are virtually endless. Don't make the mistake of believing that a sinister setting is required for nefarious dealings. Conflict that occurs in a seemingly happy place can be the most surprising and satisfying for readers.

SETTING DESCRIPTION EXAMPLE

Boats clogged the marina, their hypodermic masts puncturing the leaden sky. Chains clanked and ropes creaked as the vessels rocked back and forth, but the wind was hot and dry, bringing no comfort.

Techniques and Devices Used: Metaphor, multisensory descriptions, weather

Resulting Effects: Establishing mood

MILITARY HELICOPTER

SIGHTS
Two bucket seats for the pilots, windows all around, digital displays, a dashboard with many readouts and indicators, a compass, knobs and controls on the ceiling above the pilot's seat, pilots wearing helmets and headsets that allow them to speak to one another, a pair of gloves on the seat, two joysticks that are used to fly the helicopter, pedals on the floor, seat belts in each seat, stacked cargo held down by rope or netting, coolers and bins of supplies, fire extinguishers, first aid kits, binoculars, side doors that slide open and closed, guns mounted by the doors, troops sitting in seats, wounded soldiers lying on stretchers while a medic assesses and triages, gunners manning weapons at the side doors

SOUNDS
An escalating whine as the engine starts up, the choppy sound of blades spinning through the air, missiles being launched, a machine gun rattling off bullets, pilots speaking into headsets, the tinny sound of a voice coming over the speakers, the jingle of metal bits banging around during flight, heavy boots scuffing on metal floors, ammunition shells hitting the floor, seat belts snapping into place, side doors sliding open and shut

SMELLS
Fuel, sweat, metal, blood, gun oil, antiseptic wipes

TASTES
Some settings have no specific tastes associated with them beyond what the character might bring into the scene (chewing gum, mints, lipstick, cigarettes, etc.). For scenes like these, where specific tastes are sparse, it would be best to stick to descriptors from the other four senses.

TEXTURES AND SENSATIONS
The helicopter's tilt and sway, a dropping sensation in the stomach, seat belt straps jolting against the shoulders, sweating inside one's uniform, grabbing onto a seat or netting handhold when the helicopter takes a sudden turn, minute vibrations or movements in the joysticks and pedals, a hard metal seat, bumping into the soldier in the next seat, wind whipping through open windows and doors, sand and grit scraping exposed skin, trying to maintain balance while standing in a moving helicopter

POSSIBLE SOURCES OF CONFLICT
Being shot down
Falling out of the helicopter
Cargo shifting and falling out or hurting someone
Internal conflict over one's mission
Damage to the helicopter affecting its ability to fly
Being forced to turn back before one can complete a rescue
Missing loved ones back home and trying not to let it affect one's job

Fearing for one's life
A pilot that is ill or flying injured
Second guessing piloting decisions when things go wrong
Having to rely on people who are incapable or untrustworthy
Running out of supplies or ammunition
Having to forcibly land in hostile territory
Having a concussion that leads to airsickness

PEOPLE COMMONLY FOUND HERE
Gunners, mechanics, medics, pilots, troops, wounded soldiers

RELATED SETTINGS THAT MAY TIE IN WITH THIS ONE
Rural Volume: Arctic tundra (198), desert (210), forest (212), mountains (228), tropical island (240)
Urban Volume: Airplane (250), airport (252), military base (88), tank (278)

SETTING NOTES AND TIPS
Helicopters are incredibly versatile vehicles that can be used for a myriad of purposes, including troop transport, carrying supplies into the field, providing medical support, and engaging in combat. The helicopter's contents will vary depending upon its usage. These vehicles have also evolved tremendously through the years, so keep this in mind when choosing and describing helicopters from different time periods.

The military genre has become well established over the years. Thoughts of military helicopters in stories bring to mind images of *Platoon*, *Blackhawk Down*, and *Apocalypse Now*. But despite the success of those stories, it's always good to think beyond the first images that spring to mind to figure out how the setting can be shown in a different way. What if the scene took place in a snowstorm over the arctic, rather than the typical desert or ocean? What if the mission happened in the inky blackness of night instead of bright daylight? An unusual scenario can bring about new conflicts, fears, and images that can add a unique slant or twist to your story.

SETTING DESCRIPTION EXAMPLE
The chopper lifted off the ground, and despite pain from gashes and broken bones, each one of us sagged against the metal frame and grinned. We'd made it. Lights flashed on the control board and the pilot yelled something, but his words were lost in a series of percussive blasts. The helicopter rocked and then dropped, taking my heart with it. I slid sideways, metal rivets digging into the bruised flesh of my thigh. I caught a strap and quickly looped my arm around it to stay in place. The helicopter evened out, and we cut south to get out of range. As we turned, I glanced down at the gout of black smoke rising from the crater that was the hill we'd been standing on. A piece of this world had just been erased—and all of us almost along with it.
Techniques and Devices Used: Multisensory descriptions
Resulting Effects: Reinforcing emotion, tension and conflict

OLD PICK-UP TRUCK

SIGHTS
A cracked or pitted windshield, a dusty dashboard, broken window cranks, muddy floor mats, a missing radio knob, a cassette player, air conditioning or heat that doesn't always work, dusty vents, trash on the floor (hamburger wrappers, soda cups, coffee takeout cups, chocolate bar wrappers, doughnuts boxes), a squashed tissue box on the dash, folded and torn maps, a glove box that won't open or lock, worn or ripped patches in the seats with padding showing through, a metal coffee thermos, a backseat covered with debris (tools, gear, junk, newspapers), wedge-shaped mini windows by the side mirrors that tilt to open, a memento hanging from the rearview mirror that says something about the owner (a garter belt, a rosary or religious emblem, a tree-shaped air freshener, baby shoes, dog tags), a missing hood ornament, dirty running boards, rust spots on the frame, a rust ring or patch over the gas tank cover, scratches and scuffs, rusted wheel wells, bald or mismatched tires, an uneven bumper, a sliding back window, a gun rack, a loose tailgate, various items in the truck bed (road salt, sandbags, ropes, hay bales, tools, a load of wood or lumber), a broken tail light, a rusty muffler sputtering dark gray smoke, a crooked or snapped-off radio antenna, ash trays filled with cigarette butts or crumpled gum wrappers, a cigarette lighter, spills and stains on the seats, mud scuffs on the interior door, a missing mud flap

SOUNDS
A rumbling or sputtering engine, a tinny rattle caused from a loose heat shield, grinding gears, squeaking brakes, backfires, a scraping whine as the starter tries to catch, a chugging or hiccupping motor, the sound of a standard gear dropping heavily into place, the squeak of the clutch being engaged, creaky springs in the seats, items in the trunk sliding around or jumping as the truck hits a rut, the rattle of empty containers being displaced as the truck hits a sharp corner, country or rock music playing, the driver humming or singing, the slurp of a drink through a straw, smacking the dash in hopes of getting the truck to run, swearing, the squeaky rub of the window as it's cranked down or up, doors slamming shut, the hood creaking open, rattling noises from loose knobs or handles, wind rushing in through the open windows

SMELLS
Exhaust, oil and grease, old food, dust, rust, dirt, crumbling foam padding, smelly feet, old spills (soured milk, pop, coffee), hot leather and vinyl, cigarettes, air fresheners, sweat, body odor

TASTES
Cold coffee, water, gum, cigarettes, takeout food, gas station food (beef jerky, chocolate bars, chips, a hot dog, peanuts), pop, energy drinks or energy shots

TEXTURES AND SENSATIONS
Swiping the windshield with a hand in an effort to clear the fog, a rough and cracked dash, exerting pressure to turn the window crank, tepid air blowing from the broken air conditioner, trash crumpling under one's feet, carefully holding a beverage cup between one's thighs because there is no cup holder, the smooth knob of the stick shift, a bouncing seat, the resistance of the

emergency break, spinning the radio or volume knob, shouldering the door to get it to open from the inside, pulling the door handle hard to shut the door all the way, the jerk of motion as the truck starts, a jarring ride over washboard roads, gravel and rocks crunching under the tires, pressing hard on soft brakes, the ridges of the steering wheel under one's hands, tapping the steering wheel to the beat of a song, feeling the truck's vibration as it idles, hot sun on one's arms, a breeze from the window, hanging an arm out of the open window, adjusting a mirror, hitting the horn with the flat of one's hand, dust in the throat from the air outside, sweating heavily thanks to a broken air conditioner, sweaty legs sticking to the vinyl seats

POSSIBLE SOURCES OF CONFLICT

Being embarrassed by the way one's truck sounds or smells
Being denied access to certain places, like a gated community, because of the vehicle one drives
Arriving windblown and sweaty when one wants to make a good impression
Pieces falling off the truck and causing an accident
A passenger falling out of the truck bed
Needing to make a long trip and doubting the truck's reliability
Being crammed into the cab with too many passengers over the course of a long trip
Having to drive slowly and carefully when one is in a hurry

PEOPLE COMMONLY FOUND HERE

A cash-poor teen or person down on his luck, construction workers, farmers, hitchhikers, one's friends

RELATED SETTINGS THAT MAY TIE IN WITH THIS ONE

Rural Volume: Country road (156), farm (160), farmer's market (162), garage (54), landfill (168), orchard (174), quarry (178), ranch (180), rodeo (182)
Urban Volume: Bar (138), convenience store (162), gas station (70), mechanic's shop (86), small town street (120), truck stop (284)

SETTING NOTES AND TIPS

People spend so much time in their vehicles that they become an extension of their personalities. The kind of car a person drives, its general condition, how plain or upgraded it is, the contents and decorative flourishes—all of these things reveal something about the character. As with any setting, make your character's vehicle do double duty: it should serve as a location for events to happen, but it can also reveal a great deal about who your character is.

SETTING DESCRIPTION EXAMPLE

Cool air as good as any air conditioner poured through the windows and sent my pine tree air freshener into a tornado spin. Potholes along the dirt road jarred my teeth and seriously messed up my rendition of "Ring of Fire," but I refused to let that ruin my good mood. Besides, the springy patched seat softened the blows. I grinned and turned up the radio. This truck would probably outlive me.

Techniques and Devices Used: Multisensory descriptions
Resulting Effects: Reinforcing emotion

POLICE CAR

SIGHTS

Front Seat: steering and dashboard equipment, a mounted or hand-held radar for gauging the speed of oncoming cars, a dash camera, a portable microphone that can be placed in a pocket, a laptop mounted in the passenger seat, a LoJack system, buttons to engage the sirens and lights, an organizer containing record-keeping supplies (file folders, forms, pens, notepads, a clipboard), a rifle or shotgun locked into place, cold weather clothing in the winter (jacket, hat, gloves), a communications radio, extra handcuffs or zip ties, neon traffic vests and gloves, a PA system, a beverage in the cup holder

Backseat: a stark and bare interior, hard plastic seats with little leg room, seat belts, impact-resistant windows, door handles that don't work from the inside, bars on the windows, a clear Plexiglas or metal mesh divider between the front and backseats, hard floors (most prisoner transport models have no carpeting)

SOUNDS

The radio crackling to life, sirens wailing, the officer's voice amplified through the PA system, the officer talking in the front seat, a suspect (shifting position on the back plastic seat, nervously tapping the floor or the back of the driver's seat with a foot, yelling, crying, vomiting, mumbling, tapping or banging on the window or the divider between seats), traffic noises outside the car, people walking by, external voices, the beeping of a radar gun, fingers tapping on the laptop as records are retrieved, the car's acceleration and deceleration

SMELLS

Coffee, fast food that was recently picked up and eaten in the car, odors from suspects and detainees (sweat, urine, body odor, vomit, alcohol, cigarette or pot smoke), old fabric (if the vehicle has fabric seats, as some models do), pepper spray

TASTES

Some settings have no specific tastes associated with them beyond what the character might bring into the scene (alcohol, mouthwash, chewing gum, etc.). For scenes like these, where specific tastes are sparse, it would be best to stick to descriptors from the other four senses.

TEXTURES AND SENSATIONS

The crisp cloth of a police uniform, an adrenaline rush kicking in as the sirens blare and the cruiser takes off, a hard plastic backseat, feet sliding on the uncarpeted floor, being cramped in the back of the cruiser, having to duck in order to get into the car, metal handcuffs or zip ties binding one's wrists and causing painful twinges, claustrophobia, sitting awkwardly with one's hands bound behind one's back, sliding across the plastic seat at high speeds, vainly trying to force the door open by bashing against it, nausea, carsickness, adrenaline or drugs in one's system that make one feel jittery or numb

POSSIBLE SOURCES OF CONFLICT

Suspects trying to spit through the mesh divider at an officer
Inebriated suspects whose actions are unpredictable
Abusive officers
The arrest of an innocent suspect
Being arrested and having no one to call for help
Being prone to carsickness and vomiting in the backseat
A large person having to ride in a small backseat
An officer being falsely accused of mistreating a suspect
Misconduct by an officer that is caught on tape
An ethical disagreement between partners
Budget cuts that mean faulty equipment and poorly maintained vehicles
A suspect that suffers a seizure or passes out while in the backseat

PEOPLE COMMONLY FOUND HERE

Criminals, friends and family members doing a sanctioned ride-along, police officers and training officers, suspects

RELATED SETTINGS THAT MAY TIE IN WITH THIS ONE

Rural Volume: Country road (156), house fire (62), house party (64)
Urban Volume: Big city street (38), car accident (42), courtroom (54), parade (222), police station (106), prison cell (108), small town street (120)

SETTING NOTES AND TIPS

People will react very differently to being cuffed and put in the back of a police car, and their responses can reveal a lot to readers. Perhaps the suspect is having a full-blown panic attack that seems over-the-top for his situation. Maybe the suspect is icily calm, showing no emotion whatsoever. What might the reader infer from a happy character, one who won't stop talking, or someone who lies down and goes to sleep on the hard plastic seat? Desperate situations are great for revealing a person's true colors. Make sure that your character reacts according to who he truly is.

SETTING DESCRIPTION EXAMPLE

Janelle's knees shook, making a constant rubbing noise against the reinforced seat divider. The seat was hard and cold, and she had to lean sideways to keep from sitting on her hands. Of course this meant that every time the officer turned a corner, the window grate slammed into her like a baseball bat smacking a piñata. Sadistic creep. The metal cuffs crimped the skin at her wrists and the odd angle sent jolts of pain up to her shoulders. The cop tried to talk to her, but she wasn't that stupid. She could almost hear Dad in her ear, telling her to keep her yap shut until a lawyer showed up. She'd seen him hauled off enough to know how it went, although being the one arrested was a lot different than watching someone else be taken in.

Techniques and Devices Used: Multisensory descriptions, simile
Resulting Effects: Characterization, hinting at backstory, reinforcing emotion, tension and conflict

SUBMARINE

SIGHTS
Portholes and ladders leading down into the boat, narrow corridors with stairs and handrails going up or down, walls covered in paraphernalia (handholds, hoses and wiring, valves, pipes, gauges, switches, buttons, indicators lights, electronic readouts, boxes, fire extinguishers, flotation devices, clipboards, phones, signage), the control room (many consoles covered in buttons and readouts, the pilot and co-pilot), the sonar room with sonar men tracking contacts on consoles filled with bright green traces, the radio room filled with equipment for decrypting and encrypting transmissions, the torpedo room (torpedoes, missiles, overflow berthing, machinist mates doing maintenance or running checks), a missile compartment, a reactor compartment, the engine room (engines, generators, distillers, pumps), the maneuvering room, a medical area (narrow beds, diagnostic and monitoring equipment, IV drips, painkillers and common medicines, a defibrillator, other medical equipment), separate galleys for the officers and crew (containing metal trays, coffee machines, beverage dispensers, a buffet-style line for the crew to get their food, cafeteria-style seating, mounted TVs), bathrooms (heads) for the officers and the crew, small showers, crew bunks (bunks stacked atop one another, blankets and pillows, bunks with curtains that can be drawn around them, small lockers for uniforms, a bin for personal items, individual lights for the bunks, an earphone jack with headphones), private officer staterooms for the captain and executive officer, a small workout and recreational area (off duty crew members playing cards or board games, soldiers in coveralls and soft-soled shoes, on duty crew members cleaning)

SOUNDS
Orders being called and repeated, intercom broadcasts, klaxons and alarms, beeps, sonar pings, crew members talking and laughing, TV noises from the dining area, footsteps on metal ladder rungs and hallways, the clicking of buttons and levers, machinery noises (humming, knocking, rattling, roaring) that vary in different parts of the boat, keyboard clicks, chairs squeaking, clipboards and pens clacking against metal surfaces, Morse code beeps from the radio room, whale and porpoise song, dishes and silverware clinking in the galley

SMELLS
Body odor, sweat, flatulence, oil, machinery, diesel, hydraulic fluid, amine from the carbon dioxide removal system, food cooking in the galley

TASTES
Cafeteria-style foods cooked in the galley in large quantities, chewing gum, water, coffee

TEXTURES AND SENSATIONS
Eyes adjusting to a different type of lighting after coming onboard, shoulders and knees bumping into things in tight quarters, squeezing past other crew members, metal ladders and surfaces, sleeping in a small bunk with a curtain pulled around it, quick and infrequent showers, grungy coveralls that have been worn a number of days in a row, eye strain from staring at a screen

for long periods of time, sitting shoulder-to-shoulder with fellow crew members, leaning as a submarine dives or rises, being thrown off-balance when the boat is rolling and tossing on the surface, claustrophobia, a cap pulled low over one's forehead, a hot cup of coffee in one's hand, the disorienting feeling of not knowing whether it's night or day

POSSIBLE SOURCES OF CONFLICT

A lack of privacy and little personal space
Not being able to see the sun or the sky
Difficulty sleeping in a cramped space surrounded by people
Getting a poor review when seeking a promotion
Equipment malfunctions on the boat
Running out of food or supplies
A crew member dying while the boat is at sea
Falling desperately ill on a mission
A contagious illness that spreads throughout the crew
Having to report for duty and leave loved ones at a difficult time (during an illness, following a serious accident, close to a pregnant spouse's due date)
Worrying over a partner's faithfulness while one is on duty
Friction between crewmembers

PEOPLE COMMONLY FOUND HERE

Officers, crewmembers

RELATED SETTINGS THAT MAY TIE IN WITH THIS ONE

Rural Volume: Beach (202), ocean (230)
Urban Volume: Military base (88)

SETTING NOTES AND TIPS

A submerged submarine is a close, small community where everyone is, literally, in the same boat. As such, the details that would be incredibly obvious to an outsider—such as tight quarters and certain pungent smells—may not be noticed by the crew member who is living it day in and day out. Particulars like these can be fascinating to the author, but when one is writing from the point of view of a specific character, it's important to maintain the proper perspective and only share the details that the character would notice.

SETTING DESCRIPTION EXAMPLE

Johnson squeezed the bridge of his nose, but the nagging headache stuck behind his left eye. He rolled his neck and sat up straighter, gaze darting from his green-tinged screen to the clock on the wall. Forty minutes, and he was off. With the radar bugging out as it had been, his double shift had been brutal. He knocked back the last of his tepid coffee and ran through his itinerary: grub first, then a quick workout, followed by an even quicker shower. Then, lights out.

Techniques and Devices Used: Multisensory descriptions
Resulting Effects: Passage of time, tension and conflict

SUBWAY TRAIN

SIGHT
Bench seats, smudged glass windows that throw back reflections, folding or sliding doors, leather hand loops dangling from the ceiling, vertical poles that extend from the floor to the ceiling, handrails, air vents, posters and advertisements on the walls, public service notices, graffiti, passengers doing their best to avoid making eye contact, friends chatting, texting or watching a video on a phone together, duct tape sealing rips in the seats, commuters holding bags, briefcases, or young children in their laps, litter and pea gravel on the floor, narrow doors between cars, bright lights that occasionally flicker or skip before coming back on, dark tunnels, subway stations with people on platforms flashing past the windows, security call boxes, buttons to open the door, signs to stay back from the door, speakers, a digital display that shows which stop is coming up next, a map of the subway system and it's stops on the wall, an eclectic mix of strangers (business professionals in suits, pink-haired teenagers with piercings and tattoos, mothers pushing strollers, vagrants sleeping on the benches, older men or women with grocery car dollies)

SOUNDS
The whoosh of air brakes, a door scraping open, voices over the speakers announcing stops, creaks and squeaks as the metal tube shimmies at high speed, snaps of electricity from outside, squeaks of rubbing metal during turns, passengers chatting, music drifting from headphones, laughter, swearing, the rattle of a newspaper, pages in a book being turned, the rustle of plastic bags, the creak of fabric and leather as people shift position, the noise from a busy platform drifting in as the doors open

SMELLS
Feet, body odor, perfume, body cologne, hair products, leather, greasy hair, dirt, cold metal, stagnant air, warm plastic, urine

TASTES
Some settings have no specific tastes associated with them beyond what the character might bring into the scene (chewing gum, mints, lipstick, cigarettes, etc.). For scenes like these, where specific tastes are sparse, it would be best to stick to descriptors from the other four senses.

TEXTURES AND SENSATIONS
Hard seats, the vibration of the train causing shakes and bumps, trying to make oneself small to avoid touching other people, squeezing past someone to get out the door, gripping a cold metal handrail, clamping tightly to a purse or backpack, keeping children close so they don't bother other passengers, pushing on a door with a sleeve or shoulder so one doesn't have to touch it, feeling watched but resisting the urge to look up for fear of making eye contact

POSSIBLE SOURCES OF CONFLICT
Riding the subway at times of the day when few people are around
Witnessing someone being harassed and knowing that if one gets involved, it will not end well

A group that comes on the train with the intent of shaking down the passengers

A scuffle between passengers that escalates when someone draws a weapon

Being stared at by someone that makes one feel unsafe

Being followed onto the train by someone one does not know

A medical emergency unfolding while between stations

A breakdown that strands passengers in a dangerous neighborhood

A train derailing

A showdown between a suspect and a security guard that endangers passengers

PEOPLE COMMONLY FOUND HERE
Passengers, security guards, subway workers

RELATED SETTINGS THAT MAY TIE IN WITH THIS ONE
Big city street (38), subway tunnel (276), train station (282)

SETTING NOTES AND TIPS
Not only have movies turned subway trains into an iconic setting by placing innocent passengers in a high-speed box where anything can happen, we have had plenty of horrific real-life events which have taken place in this enclosed space. Acts of terrorism have targeted subway trains because of the high casualty numbers and the ability to destroy a means of transportation for so many people. Taking out a subway system (either literally or simply through widespread fear) can effectively shut down a city.

That being said, while subways have typically been viewed as grungy and dangerous places, this is no longer always the case. As with any setting, where the train system is located and how well it is maintained will be determining factors in its physical appearance. New York City's subway system used to be fairly shady, but a dedicated push by the city's mayor to clean it up and make it safe has changed it drastically. If you're writing about an existing system, make sure to research it effectively to be sure you've got the right details. If your system is coming straight out of your imagination, then, of course, the sky's the limit.

SETTING DESCRIPTION EXAMPLE
The train stopped at the platform, its overheated brakes whistling like fireworks about to blow. I stepped on, wondering what I might see at this hour—a college kid with serious bed-head, making his way home barefoot in a classic walk of shame? A homeless guy catching a nap on the bench? I hoped it was that woman wearing the pirate hat who preached about the end of days. She was my favorite morning traveler, because she claimed to have a spaceship in her backyard. Man, I loved the city.

    Techniques and Devices Used: Multisensory descriptions, simile

    Resulting Effects: Establishing mood

SUBWAY TUNNEL

SIGHTS
Bars of blue-tinged light spaced out along the track, darkness, concrete walls, graffiti, a narrow ledge along one or both walls, pipes running horizontally along the walls, motion sensors, track lines (including the live third track), the lit end of the tunnel appearing larger as one's train approaches a station, train headlights glinting along the metal tracks, debris near the tracks (paper bags, napkins, crushed plastic cups, straws, etc.), colored signal lights (red, yellow, and green), special items for employees to use (a phone, a fire extinguisher, an alarm box), a fork in the track that leads into another tunnel, evidence of squatters in open areas (blankets, newspapers, flattened cardboard boxes, trash, old clothing), the distant lights of an approaching train, the blur of a train speeding by, rats, roaches, trash blowing in the wake of a passing train, puddles of water, fluttering moths, abandoned train stops no longer in use

SOUNDS
The rattle and roar of a passing train, brakes screeching as a high-speed train hits a sharp corner, water dripping, the hum of live tracks, rats squeaking and scrabbling over concrete, the distant sound of a voice on a loudspeaker at a nearby station, blown trash scraping along the ground, shuffling footsteps, echoes, the blare of a subway horn, differing levels of noise depending on the speed of a train passing by, whistling or howling wind, footsteps sinking into loose gravel, the echoing voices of work crews and security guards in the area

SMELLS
Dust, urine, cold concrete, stagnant water, rats, mildew, earth

TASTES
Some settings have no specific tastes associated with them beyond what the character might bring into the scene (chewing gum, mints, lipstick, cigarettes, etc.). For scenes like these, where specific tastes are sparse, it would be best to stick to descriptors from the other four senses.

TEXTURES AND SENSATIONS
Being buffeted by the wind from a passing train, cold concrete under one's hand, rough concrete catching on clothing as one slides along the wall, grit and sand scraping one's skin when a train goes by, debris crunching under one's shoes, being blinded by the light of an oncoming train, a rat skittering over one's foot, a moth fluttering around one's head, cold air wafting out of a nearby tunnel opening, trash blowing into one's legs when a train passes, flattening oneself against the wall to avoid a speeding train, water dripping onto one's head, damp jeans or shoes from walking in puddles, scrapes and scratches from slips or jumps over walls and ledges

POSSIBLE SOURCES OF CONFLICT
Getting hit by an oncoming train
Falling onto the live third track
Running into dangerous people, such as drug users, gangs, or territorial squatters

Getting lost and not being able to find one's way out

Claustrophobia

Fear of the dark

A broken ledge that forces one to walk near the track

Being forced to enter the tunnels as a way of escaping danger

Being discovered by subway crews and security people and being chased

Falling and twisting an ankle far from help

One's pant leg getting caught between rails when the track switches

Finding a dead body

Being in the tunnel when a train is approaching and being unable to climb out

Becoming incapacitated (breaking a leg, being knocked unconscious) on the tracks

PEOPLE COMMONLY FOUND HERE

Homeless people, subway work crews

RELATED SETTINGS THAT MAY TIE IN WITH THIS ONE

Sewers (118), subway train (274)

SETTING NOTES AND TIPS

While subway tunnels are off-limits to the public, people can get into them if they're determined enough. There are also many abandoned tunnels where squatters and homeless folk live. Entire communities exist under the street where the narrow tunnels often open up into larger spaces or lead to old stations no longer in use. Either way, the darkness and isolation of the subway system can add a mysterious and creepy element to one's story.

SETTING DESCRIPTION EXAMPLE

Martin's footsteps echoed in the damp air and a steady breeze blew through his work shirt, chilling his skin. Something squeaked, and his flashlight beam scoured the gravel between the tracks, glancing off a crumpled McDonald's bag, a couple of dirty needles, and a flattened soda can before finding the rat. It stared at him, nose twitching, before skittering off into the dark. Martin blew out his breath. At least it wasn't a zombie.

    Techniques and Devices Used: Light and shadow, multisensory descriptions

    Resulting Effects: Establishing mood, foreshadowing

TANK

SIGHTS

Exterior: armored metal painted to blend with its surroundings (green, brown, tan, gray, or a combination of colors), front headlights, rear convoy lights, a registration plate, cannon and guns, various hatches (the driver's hatch, gunner's hatch, etc.), antennae, storage boxes (to hold food, ammunition, first aid supplies, and tools), sights that are used for looking out of a closed tank, small windshield wipers for each sight, hooks attached to the sides, multiple wheels running along a continuous track, rear tow hooks, caked mud, dirt and dust plastering the frame, grass stuck in the treads, camouflaging materials (netting, moss, cloth) covering the tank's body, soldiers standing in the turret, tracks kicking up clouds of dust and dirt, smoke screens from smoke grenades, fiery blasts emitting from cannons as they shoot, dust flying off the exterior when a cannon is fired

Interior: seats that are positioned under each hatch and surrounded by instruments, a throttle, a brake pedal, digital displays, binocular-type sights, hand wheels for raising or turning equipment on the exterior, switches for toggling between weaponry, firing mechanisms, a control and monitoring unit, power supply equipment, additional storage units, ammunition (armament rounds, machine gun rounds, etc.), external vent controls, firing guards to protect the crew from recoiling guns within the tank, personnel in full gear wearing headsets

SOUNDS

The clank and squeak of a tank's treads, the hum of machinery, the rattling of various metal bits, whining hydraulics, rounds dropping to the metal floor, orders being called within the tank, the *clack-clack-clack* of the machine gun firing, muffled exterior sounds as heard through headphones, voices clearly coming through one's headphones

SMELLS

Grease, sweat, smoke, fuel, hot metal

TASTES

Some settings have no specific tastes associated with them beyond what the character might bring into the scene (chewing gum, mints, candy, etc.). For scenes like these, where specific tastes are sparse, it would be best to stick to descriptors from the other four senses.

TEXTURES AND SENSATIONS

Being in a small space surrounded by lights and instrumentation, the sway of a tank on the move, eyes pressed to a periscope, dust on one's hands, headphones enclosing one's ears, a heavy uniform, smooth buttons and triggers, hand grips on levers, a reclining driver's seat, nervous sensations (tension in the gut, constriction in the throat) as one prepares to fire a weapon, being jostled as the tank moves over uneven ground, cranking a hand wheel, the heft of ammunition rounds, the warmth of an empty munition casing brushing one's leg, metal storage bins, struggling with a too-tight locking mechanism, squinting to see through a narrow sight, brushing against another soldier, squeezing into or out of a hatch, fresh air on one's face from an open hatch

POSSIBLE SOURCES OF CONFLICT

Hostile enemies

Friendly fire

Crewmembers who are incapacitated in some way (by sleep deprivation, substance abuse, sickness or injury, mental instability, etc.)

A disruption in communication that cuts a tank crew off from the chain of command

Malfunctioning hardware or software

Running out of gas

Running out of supplies needed to complete one's mission

Claustrophobia

Homesickness

Panic attacks

Instruments or boxes falling and causing injury

Being given an order that one is hesitant to follow

PEOPLE COMMONLY FOUND HERE

Commanders, drivers, gunners, loaders, mechanics

RELATED SETTINGS THAT MAY TIE IN WITH THIS ONE

Rural Volume: Desert (210), forest (212), pasture (176)

Urban Volume: Military base (88), military helicopter (266)

SETTING NOTES AND TIPS

Tanks have evolved dramatically over time. Speed, weight, size, shock absorbency, noise levels, armor, internal instrumentation—all of these have been streamlined and updated, making a ride in today's tank much different than the experience one would have had in the 1940s. To maintain consistency and believability, it's important to know which kind of tank you want in your story and be intimately acquainted with its characteristics.

SETTING DESCRIPTION EXAMPLE

Welcome silence filled the gunner's ears—no rumbling treads, no hydraulic whine from a shifting turret. Even the back-and-forth in his headset had gone dead, replaced by the bloated quiet of waiting. Comforted by the smell of metal and oil, he focused on the night-vision view out of his sight, scanning the green-tinted landscape for enemies.

Techniques and Devices Used: Multisensory descriptions

Resulting Effects: Establishing mood, passage of time

TAXI

SIGHTS
Well-worn seats, stained or dirty floor mats, trash on the floor (candy and gum wrappers, receipts, crumpled napkins), a semi-crushed tissue box above the backseat, a prominently displayed driver's license, smudged windows, a digital meter, signs regarding passenger conduct and legal disclaimers, a cell phone and radio, a beverage (water, coffee, soda) in the driver's cup holder, a pen hanging from the dashboard on a string, an air freshener hanging from the rearview mirror, dirt and sand on the floor, a cracked or pitted windshield, a clipboard with paper tossed on the dashboard, a credit card machine, an envelope full of receipts and tips, a sign stating that tips are appreciated, a magazine or newspaper on the front passenger seat, takeout containers of food, an umbrella, passengers grabbing onto handles in the backseat

SOUNDS
Local music on the radio, discussions on a cell phone or radio between the driver and dispatcher, squeaky springs in the seats, seats sliding forward or backward as passengers adjust them to make room, traffic noises, the vehicle rattling over potholes and speed bumps, humming, small talk, the click of a seat belt, blips or clicks on the meter, the driver hitting the horn, the purr or rumble of the motor, backfires, grinding gears, squealing brakes, the driver tapping the steering wheel as he drives, coughing and throat clearing, animated conversation between passengers, questions being fired off to the driver, the crinkle of bills, the creak of a door opening, the slam of a trunk, the driver calling out to friends as he drives, the driver pointing out landmarks and sharing trivia along the way, wind rushing through a half-opened window

SMELLS
Old carpet and upholstery, dirt, dust, the cabbie's lunch breath, the lingering odors of coffee and food eaten in the car, cologne or perfume, sweat, air fresheners trying to mask other odors

TASTES
Some settings have no specific tastes associated with them beyond what the character might bring into the scene (chewing gum, mints, lipstick, cigarettes, etc.). For scenes like these, where specific tastes are sparse, it would be best to stick to descriptors from the other four senses.

TEXTURES AND SENSATIONS
A bouncy seat, a secure seat belt pulled over the lap, gripping a handle, metallic coins and wrinkled paper bills, sliding across a leather seat, a cracked leather seat pinching one's skin, warm and stale air, the blast of an air conditioner, air from an open window rushing over one's skin, sitting awkwardly to accommodate a cab full of passengers, carsickness from traversing hills and turns, sweat trickling down one's back, holding oneself steady against a sharp turn, grabbing the front seat for balance, keeping a tight hold on one's purse or bottle of water, holding one's coffee cup carefully so the liquid doesn't slosh out

POSSIBLE SOURCES OF CONFLICT
An unexpectedly high fare
Trying to communicate with a driver that one can't understand
Motion sickness
A taxi driver who takes the long way to get to one's destination
A new cabbie who doesn't know his way around town
An aggressive driver with road rage issues
A passive and incredibly slow driver
Getting into a car accident
Reaching the destination and not having enough money
Splitting a fare with friends but somehow getting stuck with the bill anyway
Being crammed in with too many passengers

PEOPLE COMMONLY FOUND HERE
Drivers, passengers

RELATED SETTINGS THAT MAY TIE IN WITH THIS ONE
Rural Volume: House party (64)
Urban Volume: Airport (252), bar (138), big city street (38), casino (202), cheap motel (46), hotel room (78), nightclub (216), small town street (120), train station (282)

SETTING NOTES AND TIPS
Taxis are fairly standard, wherever they may be found. Drivers make money by transporting as many passengers as possible, so cleanliness is sometimes not a priority. Because fares are short in duration rather than long, aesthetics aren't a concern, either; cosmetic issues like torn seats, smudged windows, chipped paint, and rusted roofs are common. Drivers tend to want to get to their destinations quickly so they can move on to the next fare; as a result, they may drive fast and aggressively. Characters looking for a more glamorous and leisurely ride might be better off renting a limousine or working with a car service.

SETTING DESCRIPTION EXAMPLE
As I settled into the spongy seat and pulled the creaky door shut, I caught a whiff of Kung Pao chicken. Great. A driver with a lust for Sichuan cuisine. I barked out the address and then sat back to wait. Something nudged my shoe—a discarded takeout container dripping vomit-yellow sauce. I pulled out a tissue and scraped the stickiness away. *And there goes the tip, buddy.* The driver smiled at me in the mirror and then popped one of those complimentary "Thank You" candies that comes with takeout, which I supposed was wonderful for him. I pulled my scarf up over my nose and tried not to breathe.
Techniques and Devices Used: Multisensory descriptions
Resulting Effects: Establishing mood, reinforcing emotion, tension and conflict

TRAIN STATION

SIGHTS
A concrete area with a covered awning, paving spotted with old gum, two sets of train tracks going in opposite directions and separated by a fence, gravel between the tracks, a yellow paint line at the edge of the platform to indicate where passengers should not stand, bicycles in bike racks, stairs and an elevator leading to an overhead walkway that passengers use to get to the opposite track, newspaper racks, garbage cans, benches, ticket machines, people sitting or sleeping on benches, signage (no skateboarding, etc.), water fountains, train schedules and routes posted on the wall, a rack of paper schedules, digital signs announcing the arrival time for the next train, a clock, mechanical and electrical rooms, restrooms, vending machines, debris on the ground (straw wrappers, crumpled paper, bottle caps, cigarette butts), birds pecking for crumbs, passengers pulling suitcases, rusty tracks, puddles, a train pulling into the station, people gathering their things and queueing up, passengers greeting or saying goodbye to loved ones, kids running around, passengers eating takeout food while they wait

SOUNDS
Traffic, birds, footsteps, buses and taxis idling outside the station, people talking, elevators dinging, suitcases rattling, announcements being made over an intercom, wind whistling through the walkway, newspapers rustling, people talking on phones, muffled music from a headset, beeping from the ticket machine, tickets clicking out, water dripping from the roof, train doors sliding open, a train rumbling and clacking by, brakes squeaking as a train slows down, the blast of a horn, shoes scraping on steps as people board the train, a slow lurch that picks up speed as a train departs, parents yelling at kids to stay away from the tracks, rain thrumming on the roof, cans clattering out of a vending machine, the rustle of candy wrappers

SMELLS
Rain, fresh air, takeout food, newsprint, dust and gravel

TASTES
A lunch hastily eaten on a bench, vending machine food, soda, water, to-go coffees

TEXTURES AND SENSATIONS
The thump of suitcase wheels over cracks in the concrete, a heavy bag digging into one's shoulder, a burn in the calves from climbing the stairs, a hard metal bench, wind blowing through the station, smudgy newsprint, scratchy and tired eyes, a ticket and receipt clutched in one's hand, lukewarm water from the fountain, rifling through a paper schedule, sliding around metal coins in one's pocket while debating vending machine choices, choosing a cold drink that kisses one's palm with cold, gripping a toddler's hand, the wind from a passing train blowing one's hair back, the prickle of tears at having to leave a loved one, a clinging embrace, passing from warm outdoor air to the air-conditioned cool of a train car

POSSIBLE SOURCES OF CONFLICT

Falling or being pushed onto the tracks
One's luggage being stolen
A broken ticket machine
Missing one's train
Discovering that one's train has been delayed or canceled
Trying to manage rambunctious children around the tracks
Stepping in gum
Unsavory characters that make one feel unsafe
Being handicapped and having to use a station that lacks the proper amenities
People disregarding the safety signs (riding skateboards or bikes on the platform, running, etc.)
Having to lug a broken suitcase
Being hungry yet having no cash for the vending machine
Unhappiness over the trip one is taking
Needing to use the restroom before the long ride but not having time before the train comes

PEOPLE COMMONLY FOUND HERE

Commuters, loved ones dropping people off or waiting for a train to arrive, maintenance staff, passengers, security personnel

RELATED SETTINGS THAT MAY TIE IN WITH THIS ONE

Airplane (250), airport (252), big city street (38), cheap motel (46), city bus (256), hotel room (78), subway tunnel (276), taxi (280)

SETTING NOTES AND TIPS

Trains have come a long way over the years and are still an important method of transportation for people, both for crossing long distances, and to bring large groups in and out of densely populated areas where they live or work. For many, taking a high speed commuter train is just like hoping onto a bus, only the comfort and amenities make the trip either a relaxing one or a productive chance to get some extra work done. Because of this, stations for large commuter trains can be impressive structures and have a lot of people around, especially in the morning and at night. Not all stations are grand and beautiful, however; some are little more than an outside platform and ticket machine. But regardless of their size or the distance the trains travel in a typical run, they serve a strong purpose: allowing people the freedom to get around when traveling by other means is not convenient or economical.

SETTING DESCRIPTION EXAMPLE

I dropped onto the bench. My messenger bag slid off my shoulder and teetered on the edge of the seat. After a sixteen-hour day, my eyelids felt like broken window blinds, rising and falling unevenly. I shook myself upright and glanced around. Two men—one sitting on the far bench, the other leaning against the ticket machine. Neither looked homicidal, but I pulled my bag into my lap anyway. Man, I just wanted to get home.

    Techniques and Devices Used: Simile
    Resulting Effects: Establishing mood, tension and conflict

TRUCK STOP

SIGHTS
A sizable parking lot filled with big vehicles (semitrailers, motor homes, buses, cars pulling trailers or campers, moving trucks), flags flying on rooftops, a convenience store that also sells trucker merchandise (small electronics such as coffee makers and TV/DVD players, portable heaters, videos, audio books, music, road maps, CBs, satellite radio receivers, laundry detergent), a sit-down diner, fast food restaurants, restrooms, shower facilities, a laundromat, an arcade, truck and car washes, a motel nearby, neon signs and bright lights, tall interstate signs indicating the restaurants and services that are provided at a given exit, lines of trucks at the fuel islands, truckers crossing the parking lot, truck lights reflecting off wet asphalt, pavement stained with grease and oil, puddles, drivers walking their dogs on small green spaces, big rigs with the hoods up, trucks lit up with running lights at night, vehicles passing by on the nearby highway or interstate, truckers congregating outside to have a smoke, drivers exiting restaurants with take-home bags and plastic cups, debris in the parking lot (cigarette butts, candy wrappers, crushed soda cans, blown leaves)

SOUNDS
The rumble of big engines (idling, accelerating, decelerating), the rattle and stutter of a truck engine starting up, squealing brakes, truck doors slamming shut, horns blaring, wheels crunching over gravel and small stones, nearby interstate or highway traffic, truckers calling out to one another, chains clanking, exterior storage cubbies being open or shut, the scrape of shoes on concrete, flags flapping in the breeze, the sound of bells or chimes as store doors scrape open, the clatter of pump nozzles sliding into tanks, gas pumps clicking off, the buzz of parking lot lights, music playing over an intercom system or from nearby trucks, beeps and alarms from an arcade machine

SMELLS
Exhaust, gasoline, grease and oil, wet pavement, hot food, fresh air, cigarette smoke

TASTES
Fast food fare, food from a sit-down restaurant, convenience store wares, cigarettes, gum, exhaust

TEXTURES AND SENSATIONS
The shudder of a big rig rolling to a stop, being cramped and tired after a long haul, clambering awkwardly out of a cab, walking on stiff legs, aching joints, a cool breeze on the face, gusts of wind from the interstate pulling at one's clothes, hard concrete under one's feet, stretching out in a restaurant booth, a belly full of warm food, a soft mattress in a sleeping berth, a cold gas pump, stretching to clean the windshield with a long-handled squeegee, limp clothes and lank hair, a warm shower, hot engines, exhaust scratching one's throat and nose, wiping one's hands on a hanky or paper towel after checking the engine, eye strain and fatigue

POSSIBLE SOURCES OF CONFLICT

Someone breaking into one's rig
Drug deals in the parking lot
Being propositioned
Being caught in a compromising position in one's truck
Being far from home and discovering that one's credit card has been canceled
Getting plowed by a runaway car or truck on the nearby interstate
Loneliness
Feeling punchy from a lack of sleep
Experiencing health problems from one's job (headaches, backaches, eye strain, joint pain)
Weight gain from eating too much fast food
Trucks going too fast in the parking lot
Deep potholes that damage one's wheels
Other truckers acting unpredictably
Having one's rig sabotaged by a driver with a competing trucking company
Frustration from working long hours for little pay
Needing to rest for the night but finding truck stops either shut down or full to capacity

PEOPLE COMMONLY FOUND HERE

Prostitutes, truck stop personnel (gas attendants, waiting staff, cooks, management), truckers

RELATED SETTINGS THAT MAY TIE IN WITH THIS ONE

Convenience store (162), diner (146), fast food restaurant (148), laundromat (82), parking lot (102)

SETTING NOTES AND TIPS

Truck stops are different from rest areas in that the latter caters more to cars while the former specifically targets trucks and big rigs. Truck stops can be found along most major interstates and some highways; rural stops tend to be smaller with fewer amenities while those close to major cities have more to offer. Some truck stops are seedier than others, providing additional services such as prostitution and the sale of drugs. This stigma, which used to be considered the norm, is now the exception to the rule. The majority of these places are precisely what they should be: safe havens providing legitimate services for patrons who spend most of their time on the road.

SETTING DESCRIPTION EXAMPLE

I leaned against the bricks, breathing the rain-scented air and taking careful sips of my decaf. Buzzers dinged from the arcade on the other side of the wall, and the intercom announced that *Blade Runner* would be starting in the movie room in ten minutes. Another time, I might've gone to see it; anything was better than sitting in an empty hotel room flipping through channels on the TV. But tonight I was missing the kids something fierce, and it was easier to think of them out here in the fresh air.

Techniques and Devices Used: Multisensory descriptions
Resulting Effects: Establishing mood, reinforcing emotion

YACHT

SIGHTS
Multiple decks, ropes, flags flying at the top of the boat, a main salon (couches and sofas, throw pillows, windows all around with thick curtains, a television, carpeting, a bar and stools), a galley (sink, fridge, freezer, oven, counter space, cabinetry), a dining salon area (table and chairs, dishes, flower arrangements, napkins), a bridge (leather seating, a steering wheel, joysticks, throttles, cup holders, screens, buttons, keypads, knobs, maps, navigational equipment and tools, communications equipment), staircases between floors, multiple cabins below decks (beds and pillows, televisions, mirrors, personal items and furnishings to make the boat more homey), covered decks on various levels with seating, a wet bar and hot tub, cabins for the crew (bunks and pillows, storage, bathrooms, a washer and dryer), an engine room, a gym, a movie theater, masts and rigging (on a sailing yacht), crew dressed in uniform (as they take care of the boat, report to the captain, prepare meals, and attend to guests), first aid kits and flotation devices clipped in place, fire extinguishers on all levels, recreational vehicles (wave runners, inner tubes, kayaks) stored at the back on a platform, a ground-level deck with lounge chairs

SOUNDS
Engine sounds (idling, accelerations, decelerations), the hull slicing through the water, waves crashing against the hull, seabirds crying out as they fly overhead, music playing, people talking and laughing, kids yelling, bare feet slapping against the deck, the splash of kids jumping into the ocean, the mechanical sounds of toilets flushing, metallic anchors being dropped, wind filling one's ears, water pouring into a sink, soda and beer cans cracking open, beverages being poured into glasses, ice cubes clinking against a glass, the crew talking quietly to each other and to the guests, the snap of flags outside, wind rustling curtains and clothing, kitchen noises from the galley, silverware scraping over dishes, water dripping from a wet suit onto the deck, a wave runner engine growling as guests take it out and jump through the waves

SMELLS
Ocean air, wet towels, food cooking, leather, wood polish, coffee, beer and other beverages, clean linens, cleaning products

TASTES
Fresh fish and seafood, soda, water, lemonade, coffee and tea, alcoholic beverages, salt on the skin

TEXTURES AND SENSATIONS
The wind whipping one's hair, ocean spray, wooden decking underfoot, thick carpeting, soft couches, cushioned deck chairs, delicate stemware, glasses wet with condensation, a wooden or stainless steel banister under one's palm, thick coverlets, silky sheets, a cool drink in the throat, sunglasses sliding down one's nose, sunburn, sweat gathering on the skin, water from a wet bikini string dripping down one's back, diving into the salty ocean, salt water stinging one's eyes, a cool shower washing away the sweat and salt that coats one's skin

POSSIBLE SOURCES OF CONFLICT

Falling or being pushed overboard

The mutiny of a rogue crew

Sabotage by a jealous associate or family member

The boat breaking down far from home

Losing one's way and wandering into hostile territory

Running into pirates

Drama among guests or crew members

Unsupervised children playing in dangerous places

Food poisoning or disease that puts one's guests in jeopardy

The sudden death or disappearance of anyone who knows how to drive the boat

A shark attack

The air conditioning quitting while out at sea

Running out of something crucial (food items, medication, drinking water)

PEOPLE COMMONLY FOUND HERE

A chef, captains, deckhands, family members, groups chartering the yacht, guests, mates, stewards and stewardesses, yacht owners

RELATED SETTINGS THAT MAY TIE IN WITH THIS ONE

Rural Volume: Beach (202), beach party (150), ocean (230), tropical island (240)

Urban Volume: Black-tie event (196), limousine (262), marina (264)

SETTING NOTES AND TIPS

Yachts come in a variety of lengths; though definitions vary, it's generally accepted that small yachts begin around 25 feet, mega yachts are in excess of 164 feet long, and super yachts fall somewhere in the middle. Smaller yachts can be driven by the owner, while larger boats often employ a crew, and the size of the boat will determine the onboard amenities and their level of luxuriousness, including swimming pools, elevators, helicopter pads and more.

SETTING DESCRIPTION EXAMPLE

The water was black and warm, like swimming in a tub of ink. Mother would freak out if she knew I'd gone out so far at night, but it wasn't like I could get lost; the distant yacht was lit up like a gigantic parade float, and I bet you could hear its music for miles. Of course, it wasn't the dark or me getting lost that Mother was really worried about. Two muscular arms slipped around my waist while a pair of lips brushed the back of my neck, making me shiver in the tepid water. I grinned and turned to greet Duke.

Techniques and Devices Used: Light and shadow, multisensory descriptions, simile

Resulting Effects: Characterization, establishing mood

APPENDIX A: EMOTIONAL VALUE TOOL

Strong settings will have special meaning to your protagonist and possibly other characters. This emotional value is something writers build into the setting through personalization or mood. To craft an emotionally charged scene, fill in the shapes in the tool below to seed your scene with emotional triggers (people, setting details that serve as symbols, etc.) that can amplify your character's feelings, remind her of the past, and show her options for the future—all of which will nudge her toward a specific decision, choice, or action.

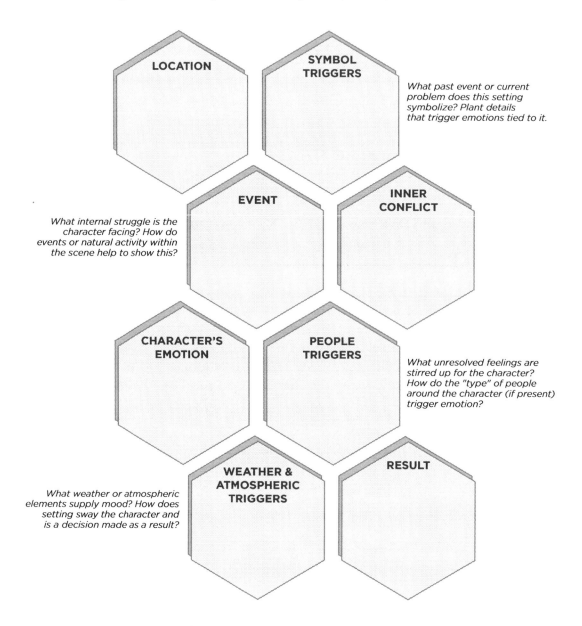

LOCATION

SYMBOL TRIGGERS

What past event or current problem does this setting symbolize? Plant details that trigger emotions tied to it.

EVENT

INNER CONFLICT

What internal struggle is the character facing? How do events or natural activity within the scene help to show this?

CHARACTER'S EMOTION

PEOPLE TRIGGERS

What unresolved feelings are stirred up for the character? How do the "type" of people around the character (if present) trigger emotion?

WEATHER & ATMOSPHERIC TRIGGERS

RESULT

What weather or atmospheric elements supply mood? How does setting sway the character and is a decision made as a result?

A printable version of this checklist is available at www.writershelpingwriters.net/writing-tools.

APPENDIX A: EMOTIONAL VALUE TOOL

Example

LOCATION

The kitchen of Mary's childhood home, a place she has not visited for years

SYMBOL TRIGGERS

A cross on the wall, the same table placemats from her childhood, the wooden chair she was forced to sit in for hours at a time

What past event or current problem does this setting symbolize? Plant details that trigger emotions tied to it.

EVENT

Dinner in silence acts as a reminder of how she was punished repeatedly as a child if she spoke during a meal, even to ask for water

INNER CONFLICT

Wanting to confront her father about his physical abuse but the weight of his religious zealotry & her poor self-worth bears down on her

What internal struggle is the character facing? How do events or natural activity within the scene help to show this?

CHARACTER'S EMOTION

Mary feels a mix of guilt, anger, vulnerability, hatred, and shame

PEOPLE TRIGGERS

Her father (the focal point for her anger) represents the abuse she suffered as a child that affects her to this day

What unresolved feelings are stirred up for the character? How do the "type" of people around the character (if present) trigger emotion?

What weather or atmospheric elements supply mood? How does setting sway the character and is a decision made as a result?

WEATHER & ATMOSPHERIC TRIGGERS

A bright kitchen light shines down on her, making her feel exposed (sinful & unworthy)

RESULT

Mary breaks the silence she feels pressured to keep and confronts father about his abuse and the evil he did in God's name

A printable version of this checklist is available at www.writershelpingwriters.net/writing-tools.

APPENDIX B: SETTING CHECKLIST

Location: _____   Scene or Chapter: _____

Why is this setting the best choice for the action about to unfold?

_____

_____

_____

What I want to achieve through setting description: (Check all that apply)
- ❑ To create conflict or tension
- ❑ To foreshadow a coming event
- ❑ To encourage an emotion-driven action or choice
- ❑ To remind a character of their past (good or bad)
- ❑ To poke at an old wound
- ❑ To challenge the protagonist to face his or her fears
- ❑ To recreate a wounding event so the protagonist can navigate it successfully & let go of past pain
- ❑ To actively deliver important backstory
- ❑ To characterize one or more characters
- ❑ To display symbolism or motifs that reinforce a deeper message or meaning
- ❑ To convey a specific mood
- ❑ To help steer the plot
- ❑ To test through obstacles and setbacks
- ❑ To give the setting an emotional value & deploy emotional triggers

Setting details that will symbolize past events, heighten emotion, or reinforce a message:

_____

_____

_____

Ways my POV character will interact with this setting:

_____

_____

_____

A printable version of this checklist is available at www.writershelpingwriters.net/writing-tools.

THE RURAL SETTING THESAURUS: A WRITER'S GUIDE TO PERSONAL AND NATURAL PLACES

I f you have enjoyed this setting thesaurus book, we have good news for you: there is a second volume in this series. *The Rural Setting Thesaurus* has over 100 additional settings and more how-to help on using figurative language to create vivid imagery and symbolic meaning, as well as lessons on how the setting can steer the plot, provide conflict through story-specific challenges, and influence emotions through mood.

Add deeper authenticity to your writing by bringing fiction and the real world together through common personal and natural places. Here are the locations included in *The Rural Setting Thesaurus*:

Abandoned Mine	County Fair	Hunting Cabin
Ancient Ruins	Creek	Kitchen
Archery Range	Custodial Supply Closet	Lake
Arctic Tundra	Desert	Landfill
Attic	Dorm Room	Lighthouse
Backyard	Elementary School Classroom	Living Room
Badlands	Farm	Locker Room
Barn	Farmer's Market	Man Cave
Basement	Flower Garden	Mansion
Bathroom	Forest	Marsh
Beach	Garage	Mausoleum
Beach Party	Graveyard	Meadow
Birthday Party	Greenhouse	Moors
Block Party	Grotto	Motor Home
Boarding School	Group Foster Home	Mountains
Bomb Shelter	Gymnasium	Nursery
Campsite	Halloween Party	Ocean
Canyon	High School Cafeteria	Orchard
Cave	High School Hallway	Outhouse
Chicken Coop	Hiking Trail	Pasture
Child's Bedroom	Hot Springs	Patio Deck
Church	House Fire	Playground
Country Road	House Party	Pond

Preschool

Principal's Office

Prom

Quarry

Rainforest

Ranch

River

Rodeo

Root Cellar

Salvage Yard

School Bus

Science Lab

Secret Passageway

Slaughterhouse

Summer Camp

Swamp

Taxidermist

Teacher's Lounge

Teenager's Bedroom

Tool Shed

Trailer Park

Tree House

Tropical Island

Underground Storm Shelter

University Lecture Hall

University Quad

Vegetable Patch

Wake

Waterfall

Wedding Reception

Wine Cellar

Winery

Workshop

RECOMMENDED READING

As writing coaches, we come across many great books on all aspects of writing craft. If you are looking to boost your knowledge, we suggest starting with these.

How to Make a Living as a Writer provides everything you need to know to turn your writing dreams into an income-producing reality, by someone who's done it for 25 years. (James Scott Bell)

Structuring Your Novel tackles the question, *Why do some stories work and others don't?* The answer is *structure*. In this award-winning guide, you will discover the universal underpinnings that guarantee powerful plot and character arcs. (K.M. Weiland)

Shoot Your Novel: Cinematic Techniques to Supercharge Your Writing is an essential writing craft guide that will teach you the art of "show don't tell" using time-tested cinematic technique. By utilizing film technique and adapting the various camera shots into your fiction, your writing will undergo a stunning transformation from "telling" to "showing." (C. S. Lakin)

Writing Plots With Drama, Depth and Heart (Nail Your Novel 3) helps you diagnose your story's strengths and weaknesses, find where your plot ideas are hiding, and keep readers riveted. (Roz Morris)

Writing 21st Century Fiction: High Impact Techniques for Exceptional Storytelling encourages writers to add greater depth to their characters and stories, enthralling readers. (Donald Maass)

Writing Screenplays That Sell, New Twentieth Anniversary Edition teaches all writers to think deeply about their characters' motivations, story structure and the art of selling. (Michael Hauge)

And if you are not familiar with the other bestselling books in our Writers Helping Writers® descriptive thesaurus series, please feel free to check them out:

The Emotion Thesaurus: A Writer's Guide to Character Expression is a writer's best friend when it comes to conveying your character's emotions to readers. Armed with a list of the body language, thoughts, and visceral sensations for 75 core emotions, you'll never struggle with the "how do I show this feeling?" problem again.

The Positive Trait Thesaurus: A Writer's Guide to Character Attributes is one half of the character-building puzzle to help you create layered and complex characters that transcend all others. With an arsenal of positive traits and their defining characteristics, you will be able to create authentic, rich characters that fascinate.

The Negative Trait Thesaurus: A Writer's Guide to Character Flaws looks at your character's dark side and the realistic flaws that hold him or her back while complicating your plot. Believable characters have both positive and negative qualities, and understanding their disagreeable aspects means also knowing what motivates them.

The Rural Setting Thesaurus: A Writer's Guide to Personal and Natural Places partners with this urban setting book and provides 100 more settings to explore, as well as offering more elevated description techniques to add emotion, create conflict, and enhance each story on multiple levels for a one-of-a-kind reading experience.

JOIN US AT WRITERS HELPING WRITERS

If you enjoyed this resource, we hope you'll visit us at our home site, Writers Helping Writers. There, you'll find the other bestselling books in this series, articles on the craft of writing to improve your skills, and many posts on publishing and marketing to assist you in navigating your career path. You can also find us on Facebook and Twitter (@angelaackerman and @beccapuglisi).

To stay up to date on forthcoming books, discover helpful writing resources, and access practical writing tips, sign up for our newsletter. And if you wish to look into a truly unique resource for your toolkit, stop by our other site, One Stop For Writers—a unique library that houses descriptive and story-planning material all in one place. Along with innovative tools built to elevate your writing, all of our complete thesauruses (including those in book form) can be found here.

Finally, we also greatly appreciate your honest reviews and referrals, which help other writers make better buying decisions regarding resource books.

Thanks so much, and happy writing!

Becca & Angela

www.writershelpingwriters.net
www.onestopforwriters.com
www.facebook.com/DescriptiveThesaurusCollection

47794426R00172

Made in the USA
San Bernardino, CA
08 April 2017